Moral Philosophy

Second Edition

Moral Philosophy
Text and Readings

Andrew G. Oldenquist

The Ohio State University

Waveland Press, Inc.
Prospect Heights, Illinois

For Riek

For information about this book, write or call:

Waveland Press, Inc.
P.O. Box 400
Prospect Heights, Illinois 60070
(312) 634-0081

Contents

PART TWO READINGS IN MORAL PHILOSOPHY

Preface

This volume provides, under one cover, a textbook and an anthology, each designed for a first course in moral philosophy. The textbook, Part One, takes up a series of topics which either are of basic importance to ethical theory or have been found by the author to be interesting and controversial to students, or are both of these. The nine chapters can be read independently of one another; and while some of them contain references to other chapters, they should be thought of more as a menu than as a cumulatively developing textbook. Chapters 4 through 6—"Universalizing," "Morality and Self-interest," and "Ethical Relativism"—come closest to constituting a sequence.

Each chapter tries to be an informative introduction to the topics named in its title. Nevertheless, my own interests and opinions get expressed, especially in the latter parts of "Rules and Consequences," "Universalizing," "Morality and Self-interest," "Ethical Relativism," and "Religion and Morality." Where my views appear they are offered quite openly as hypotheses and suggestions after the problems have been laid out, and I think there is little danger of their masquerading as received doctrine. In any event, I think I can rely on instructors to tell students where their textbook author is being "objective" and where he has gone mad.

In the anthology, Part Two, I have tried to follow a policy of not making deletions within chapters or articles. The main exceptions to this policy are the Kohlberg and Wilson selections. I also have deleted two chapters from the first book of the Nicomachean Ethics that are not very relevant to the main narrative, and some of the subsections of the Hare chapters. A reader will seldom find a selection broken up by ellipsis points.

Writers who are not professional philosophers are seldom represented on ethical subjects other than casuistry. In the anthology I offer two such "nonprofessionals": the psychologist Lawrence Kohlberg, whose "stages of moral development" greatly influenced the field of moral education; and the sociobiologist Edward O. Wilson, whose dis-

ix

cussion of hypotheses about the evolution of altruism should, in my opinion, be read by every moral philosopher. In the textbook I offer a third: the novelist/philosopher Ayn Rand (whose actual writings I could not reprint). Most moral philosophers discuss and attempt to refute ethical egoism but rarely, if at all, come up with a genuine ethical egoist to discuss. Ayn Rand is, I think, the best representative of ethical egoism, and in Chapter 5 ethical egoism is discussed and appraised in the light of her theory.

Some of the selections—for example, those from Hume, Butler, Kant, Toulmin, Hare, and Wilson—are explained and discussed at length in the textbook; several are discussed less extensively; and Searle, Foot, and Kohlberg are not discussed. Anthologized authors who get more than passing mention in the textbook (with some inaccuracy I include Rand in this category) are mentioned in the table of contents and are introduced in boldface type where discussion of their work begins in the textbook. Short bibliographies are appended to the biographical sketches of the anthologized authors, and there is an index to the textbook at the end of the book.

The author and the publisher are grateful for the assistance of those who made professional reviews of the manuscript. These reviewers, to whom we give thanks, were Theodore M. Benditt, University of Southern California; Ronald L. Burnside, Sinclair Community College; Leslie P. Francis, University of Utah; John Kearney, Saint Joseph's College (Philadelphia); Anthony J. Lisska, Denison University; Paul Seman, Sinclair Community College; and Arnulf Zweig, University of Oregon. The author is grateful to Kenneth Long, Ohio State University, for excellent and good-humored indexing.

Moral Philosophy

PART ONE

Problems in
Moral Philosophy

Chapter 1

Agent Morality and Action Morality

We are all familiar with claims like "What he did was wrong but he meant well." People who say this are making a distinction between judging what a person does and judging the person who does it. *Action morality* is concerned with judging what people *do*, hence with the rightness and wrongness of actions and with obligation, but it is not concerned with praise and blame, moral guilt, or punishment. *Agent morality* is concerned with judging persons and therefore involves praise, blame, motives, intention, and perhaps punishment. This chapter will postpone questions about the morality of actions; the problem we shall encounter here concerns the nature and adequacy of our criteria for judging people.

Moral arguments can become interminable if the participants fail to distinguish carefully between judging an action and judging the motive of the person who does it. Suppose that a woman gives money to a hospital for orphaned children for the sole purpose of reducing her income tax and seeing a statue of herself erected at the entrance. Many of us would believe that such an action is a right action—for it is right to help less fortunate people—but that the woman deserves no praise. It only causes confusion if one argues that the action is wrong because the motive is selfish and shallow, for a person who argues that the action is right very likely means that it is right when considered apart from the motive behind it. On the other hand if an incompetent architect, who honestly thinks he is a good architect, designs a hospital for orphaned children on his own time at his own expense, and the day after it is occupied it crashes to the ground, many of us would

2

believe that what he did was wrong—for it is wrong to do harm—but that nevertheless he should not be blamed for it. We must distinguish between (a) people who mean well, but do harm that no reasonable person could anticipate and (b) people who mean well, but do harm because they are stupid and do not know they are stupid. I think we are less inclined to praise the people in situation (b) than we are to excuse and pity them, even though there is nothing whatever wrong with their motives.

An important reason for this difference is that we praise and blame people not only because they *deserve* it but also to *encourage or discourage certain types of behavior,* and we certainly would not want to encourage behavior of type (b). This latter use of praise and blame seems designed to ensure the morality of actions without attempting to assign to persons what they deserve. We can illustrate these different uses of praise and blame if we contrast morally condemning a man who has betrayed a friend with blaming or punishing disobedient dogs and small children. The former is concerned with moral guilt, looks only to the offense that is in the past, and presupposes that the person is a responsible, free agent. The latter carries no accusation of moral guilt, does not presuppose a responsible, free agent, and aims only at directing behavior in the future. Agent morality, as the evaluation of persons or their character, is concerned with praise and blame only in the former, moral sense.

Many people believe that moral judgments of persons and their character depend only on states of mind such as good or ill will, "meaning well," and conscientiousness. They say, for example, "You can't blame her; she tried to do what she thought was right." The basis of this belief may, in part, be the New Testament view that anyone can be a morally good person if only he has a good heart, quite regardless of other things more dependent on fortune such as intelligence and what one actually succeeds in doing. A belief of this sort possibly explains one of my own grammar school experiences, in which I was given two different grades in each subject, one for accomplishment and one for "effort." Something of the ethical theory held implicitly by the school officials would be revealed if we could know whether the grade for effort was meant to be a serious evaluation of the students' worth or merely a device to make them work harder and, if the former, to which of these grades they attached greater importance for the evaluation of a student.

But let us push further the idea that the morality of persons depends entirely on "meaning well" or the intention and effort to do what one thinks is right. Is it possible that someone might live the life of a Hitler and yet be a completely praiseworthy person? We must answer yes, *if* we believe that moral praiseworthiness depends *entirely* on "good will" or "meaning well," and not at all on what one actually does because then all we need suppose is that such a person honestly tries to do what he thinks is right. This is an extreme case, since I am not supposing that he means one thing but, through incompetence or bad luck, does what is monstrous; instead I am supposing that what he means to do is monstrous (such as exterminating whole races of people), but he nevertheless *thinks* that this is the right thing to do. This sort of case arises on a lesser scale whenever people do what we believe is wrong, not because of blundering but because they have moral opinions that differ from ours. According to the criterion we are considering, such people are morally praiseworthy because they "mean well."

We can now list three kinds of cases in which people are inclined to excuse someone, going from the least controversial to the most controversial.

1. He "means well" but by bad luck unintentionally kills someone: the death is an unforeseeable consequence of what he does.
2. He "means well" but unintentionally kills someone from stupidity or incompetence (but not from carelessness).
3. He intentionally kills someone but honestly thinks he was right in doing so: we think it is wrong but he thinks it is right.

Few of us would blame person (1), but what of person (3)? Should we say he "means well" only if he tries to do what is *actually right*? Or does he mean well whenever he tries to do what *he thinks* is right? Those who are inclined to excuse person (3) very likely will retort, "Actually right *according to whom*? Do you mean we should excuse him only if he tries to do what *we* think is right? We each have our own opinions and he is as sincere as us, so how can you blame him?" The idea behind this is probably a form of ethical relativism (see Chapter 6), perhaps the version which says that everyone ought to do what he thinks is right (and therefore should not be blamed when he tries to do it).

So I think there are two motives behind the inclination to let praise and blame depend only on subjective factors such as meaning well. The first is the New Testament view that human goodness depends only on the state of one's soul—on "what is in one's heart"—on the grounds that only this is wholly within the power of the weakest, most humble person and hence not dependent on things like intelligence, success, or money. The second motive is skepticism about the very idea of an objective rightness and wrongness of the things people try to do.

Yet few of us rest easy with making moral censure depend only on self-admitted bad motives or weak will; most of us think we should censure or punish someone (for example, Hitler) if what he does is *bad enough*, regardless of his sincerity or conscientiousness. The roots of this feeling may lie in the outlook of ancient Greek philosophers such as Aristotle.

Aristotle suggests a general conception of what is required to be a morally good person that is fundamentally different from our ordinary commonsense conceptions of moral worth and from the conceptions of most philosophers writing in the Christian era. The following three remarks point out some views of Aristotle that suggest that he does not, as seriously as we do, take "meaning well" to be the criterion of moral praiseworthiness. First, in his discussion of moral virtue Aristotle says little about intention and will power: it is by correct habituation, not by will power, that the virtuous man is able to resist temptation and do the right thing. If a man is truly virtuous he will take pleasure in doing the right thing; and if he does not find virtuous actions pleasant, but instead must exert will power, his habit (and hence his virtue) is imperfect. For example, in our moral tradition we are expected to admire the moral character of Saint Anthony, an early Christian who went alone to meditate in the Egyptian desert. There he had visions in which he was tempted by voluptuous women and luxury, but after an agonizing, nearly superhuman effort of will he was able to resist his temptations. Now whether or not it is virtuous to resist such desires is beside the point here. Aristotle would reason that in any case Saint Anthony was not a virtuous man since he found virtuous actions difficult and unpleasant, thus revealing that he had not been trained to find virtue pleasant and vice disagreeable.

Second, one can be said to have a virtuous habit only if one *succeeds*, more often than not, at doing virtuous actions; it is not enough merely to have the right motive and to try. According to Aristotle such a person is not a morally good man because, although he tries to do the right thing, he fails more often than he succeeds.

Third, *we* are inclined to distinguish between those qualities for which we *admire* a person, such as intelligence, courage, grace, good sense, and those qualities for which we deem him *morally praiseworthy*, such as good intentions and conscientiousness. We might also admire a horse for the first set of qualities, and with much the same attitude. However, since these admirable qualities are not absolutely within our power, we are inclined, more or less, to reserve moral praise for what *is* in our power, but this seems to include only "meaning well" and conscientiousness. For Aristotle, however, the concept of a good person is not different in kind from that of a good horse, and it is not certain that he would see very much of a distinction between admirable and morally praiseworthy qualities. For example, suppose you own a race horse named Dufuss. Dufuss has short, stubby legs and a limp. He loses all of his races but nevertheless he means well and always tries very hard. Is Dufuss a good race horse? Certainly not, because he *functions poorly* as a race horse and the function of a race horse is to run in horse races. For Aristotle anything that is good, including a human being, performs well the function peculiar to the kind of thing it is, and if it is bad, it performs that function poorly. If we take literally the expression "a fine specimen of a man," we come closer to understanding Aristotle's conception of a morally good person and how this conception differs from that of most philosophers writing in the Christian era.

Moral philosophers differ regarding the emphasis they place on the morality of persons and the morality of actions. John Stuart Mill, for instance, is not much interested in agent morality (though he does not deny the standard criteria for judging persons) and very much interested in action morality. Immanuel Kant is interested in both, and Aristotle appears to be more concerned with agent morality. Kant is concerned with explaining how individual actions may possess moral worth in the sense that they make the person who does them morally praiseworthy. He tells us that only actions done with a good will possess moral worth; that a good will chooses right actions *for the sake of duty* (and not merely actions that happen to be *in accord with* duty); and that an action done for the sake of duty is done from a unique motive that Kant calls "respect" for the moral law. Aristotle, on the other hand, is not concerned to discover particular praiseworthy motives; instead he investigates what it is that makes a person *on the whole* a good or virtuous person. For Aristotle, not particular actions or motives, but states of character or dispositions from which one habitually does certain kinds of actions (courageous actions, temperate actions, and so on) are what constitute the possession of moral virtues.

Present-day concern over rational criteria for praising and blaming people can affect public attitudes toward both morality and criminal law. Should we base our judgment and treatment of people mainly on criteria of excellence and success, as Aristotle does, or should motives and intentions be more important? Should we *never* judge persons in terms of what they "deserve"? What should determine how we punish murderers, rapists, and heroin dealers? Obviously, the extent to which people think that criminal punishment depends on what criminals deserve and, in turn, the extent to which desert depends on motives and intentions, can deeply affect how our society deals with crime. This theme is pursued further in Chapter 7.

Chapter 2

Reason and Feeling

What kind of things are goodness and rightness? Is rightness as much an objective fact about an action as its time and place and therefore something you can discover by means of *reason*? Or is it instead a matter of people's *feelings* toward actions that in themselves are morally neutral? That is, is your judgment "It's immoral!" no more than a verbal expression of your feelings or attitude toward the act? Crudely oversimplified, the issue I have raised is whether the immorality is "out there" in the act, waiting to be discovered by our perception and reason, or whether it is "in us" in the sense that there exist only our aversions and likings, which we evince by saying things like "It's immoral!" It should be obvious that our answers to these questions have implications for what we think the words "right," "good," and "wrong" *mean*.

David Hume's purpose is to demolish the theory that immorality is something reason discovers "out there" in the action itself or in its objective relations to other things, and he offers two arguments that he thinks are conclusive. Hume's first argument begins with the observation that moral judgments can supply us with motives or incentives to action, but the mere facts or truths that reason can discover cannot by themselves motivate us. Therefore, it follows that moral judgments are not merely discoveries of reason. The basis for this claim is found earlier in the *Treatise*, where Hume says, "Reason is, and ought only to be the slave of the passions, and can never pretend to any other office than to serve and obey them." This is not irrationalism on Hume's part. It is instead the claim that reason cannot by itself create goals or ends, that it is one thing to *know* that something exists or has a certain nature, another thing to *desire* or *approve* it. In other words, an *exclusively* rational being would never seek or do anything, since it would not desire anything. Reason can discover the existence and attainability of things that are possible goals, and that become actual goals only if we respond to them with desire or aversion, approval or disapproval.

Second, Hume examines what he thinks are all the possible operations of reason, and shows that what each discovers cannot constitute the morality of an action. Reason can discover truths that are "relations of ideas," such as "triangles have angles equal to 180 degrees" and in general logical and mathematical truths; and it can discover "matters of fact"—causal knowledge either that something exists or of the means sufficient to attain it. But none of these kinds of discovery is what *constitutes* an objective rightness in actions: They are never more than dispassionate assertions that an action is of such and such a nature, that its relations are so and so, or that it has such and such effects. In what has become a famous passage, Hume makes this point in a much more general way when he says that no statement about what *ought* to be can ever be a logical deduction solely from statements about what *is* (page 190). It also follows from this general claim that *errors* of reasoning, whether they are what mislead you into doing an action, or instead are produced in others who view your action, cannot be what wrongness consists in; these errors must be seen for what they are, Hume says: simply mistakes, which are quite different from moral faults.

Hume's positive view is that since the morality of an action is not discerned by reason, it must be by means of a kind of perception, which he calls a "moral sense." But it is important to see that for Hume the moral sense is a peculiar capacity to *feel,* thus locating the origin of rightness and wrongness in yourself; it is not a special faculty of external perception or "sixth sense."

We must, however, take a harder look at what Hume says about reason and morals in order to see what his view amounts to. There is considerable evidence in Hume's *Treatise* that he would accept all of the following four claims.

1. The discoveries of reason cannot, by themselves, motivate us to do anything.
2. The rightness of an action is not a discovery of reason.
3. Moral claims are not knowledge claims; they are neither true nor false.
4. Reason plays important subsidiary roles in moral deliberation by discovering possible objects of moral approval, the means to attain them, and the consistency or inconsistency of moral claims with one another.

Hume's main purpose in the passage reprinted from the *Treatise* is to prove that (2) is true; and he offers (1) as a reason—he thinks that if statement (1) is true, then statement (2) must be true. This is the first of Hume's two arguments described at the beginning of this section.

Let us give the name "moral intellectualist" to the person who claims that reason can discover a special quality or relation called "rightness." Now it might be objected that the above argument against the position of the moral intellectualist is not a good one. One might claim, for example, that reason can discern an objective quality in actions called "rightness," while some other principle, perhaps even a moral sense, produces the feeling of approval necessary to motivate us to act in accord with it. Thus this counterargument maintains that Hume himself confuses what makes us respond to rightness with what discerns it. It is the moral intellectualist's second line of defense since it admits that reason alone cannot create approval of an action, but nevertheless maintains that reason alone discovers rightness.

But Hume anticipates this reply to his argument in the passage in Section I where he says, "It is one thing to know virtue, and another to conform the will to it" (page 187). His point is that if this view, which assigns knowing rightness and feeling approval to separate faculties, were true, it would be possible to apprehend an objective rightness and yet be totally indifferent to it; and his argument is that it is simply impossible to acknowledge that an action is right without at the same time expressing or feeling approval of it. Hence any theory, such as this one, which admits that this is even barely possible, must be false. So even if we claim, as I suggested above, that reason discerns an objective rightness, that a moral sense makes us approve it, and that all humans have this moral sense, Hume still has a point because we then would have to admit the bare possibility that some person might reason quite well but be born with a defective moral sense, and thus acknowledge that an action is right and yet not feel any approval of it. The burden is on the moral intellectualist to rule out this possibility a priori (page 188), and Hume believes that this cannot be done.

Hume's second argument is a *direct* defense of statement (2), "The rightness of an action is not a discovery of reason." The moral intellectualist, we remember, believes that reason can discover an objective moral quality or relation called "rightness." Hume demands that the moral intellectualist produce and point out to him this peculiar moral fact or relation. But when Hume describes the kinds of answers he would be willing to consider, it is quite possible that he is begging the question. Hume produces what he believes is an exhaustive list of basic kinds of relations, such as resemblance, contrariety, degree in quality, and so on, and then demands that the moral relation be found on this list. The relation "rightness," of course, is not on Hume's list, and thus the moral intellectualist's position is ruled out from the start. We, if we are moral intellectualists, are asserting that this special, objective relation is called "rightness" and that it is discovered by reason in certain kinds of situations, of which we can cite instances (for example, murders). Hume himself cannot give any more information about his own classification of the different relations reason can discern: he can point to a resemblance or degree in quality, name it "resemblance" or "degree in quality," and give examples, and that is all. The moral intellectualist can say exactly as much about his special relation called "rightness."

Statement (3) is "Moral claims are not knowledge claims; they are neither true nor false." Of the four claims that were listed above, this is perhaps the most startling. Yet some things Hume says indicate that he believes it is true. For example, when speaking of the moral sense: "We do not infer a character to be virtuous, because it pleases: But in feeling that it pleases after such a particular manner, we in effect feel that it is virtuous" (page 191). Two things need to be said about this statement. First, Hume seems to reassure us that he does not commit the mistake he accuses others of, namely, deducing a moral or "ought" claim from a purely factual claim about what "is." In other words, if Hume meant that we can *deduce* "X is virtuous (or a duty)" from "X pleases in a particular manner," then he would have contradicted what he said earlier about not deducing an "ought" from an "is." Second, Hume appears to be trying to tell us that to judge something virtuous is *identical* with feeling in a certain way. Therefore, to make a moral judgment is not to assert anything that can be true or false, for feelings or "passions," as he says in Section I, are "original facts, complete in themselves," and not capable of being either true or false.

Alfred Jules Ayer also would accept the four statements listed above. But Ayer's main concern is to prove that statement (3) is true. While Hume primarily investigated how we *apprehend* that an action is right (or wrong), Ayer directly questions the *status* of moral judgments. Thus Ayer's "emotive theory" maintains that moral judgments are expressions of feeling, just as shouts and groans are expressions of feeling, and hence are neither true nor false. They are not assertions *that* one has a feeling of approval or disapproval—they are not assertions at all. For example, consider the difference between "It hurts" and "Ouch!" The former makes a true or false *assertion* about a feeling; the latter does not, it *expresses* a feeling. According to Ayer, we can neither prove nor disprove moral claims, since the notions of proof and disproof apply only to what can be true or false.

It should be said that Ayer's chief aim, in this passage from *Language, Truth and Logic*, is not to devise a complete ethical theory, but to complete his program of discovering which types of statement are, and which types are not, cognitively meaningful in the sense that possible observations could show them to be true or false. In the past twenty-five years the emotive theory of value has been made considerably more sophisticated and hence more plausible. Its main tenet, that purely moral claims fundamentally *do not describe anything at all*, but instead "express attitudes," "commend," or "command," remains unchanged. But newer versions of the emotive theory now maintain that expressions of moral attitudes can be justified or unjustified, reasonable or unreasonable, and be either supported or unsupported by reasons. The best example of these newer theories is that of Richard Hare (see Chapter 4).

There is at least one significant difference between the ethical theories of Hume and Ayer. Hume, unlike Ayer, goes out of his way to show that moral approvals, though they are feelings, are not capricious: Hume's moral sense is a nearly universal human tendency to feel approval and disapproval upon viewing certain kinds of actions. Hume believes that the same sentiments are aroused, by similar actions, in the majority of human beings, thus giving to morals, despite the absence of objective "moral qualities," a kind of objectivity not found in Ayer's theory. Indeed, Hume might have been willing to argue that on his theory moral sentiments are even more universal, since basic feelings such as sympathy, contempt, and so on, are more democratically distributed than is reasoning ability. Like Kant, Hume claims that the foundation of morality lies in yourself: it is to be found in human nature, not in the objective relations of external things. But Kant, of course, locates it in our rationality, Hume in the emotional or appetitive part of our nature.

Hume and Ayer have constructed theories about the meaning of moral sentences and the nature of moral beliefs. This probably is as good a place as any to classify theories according to the stands they take on these matters. Most ethical theories fall under one of the following three headings.

1. *Definism* (also called *naturalism*): There are basic moral principles that are true by definition. For example, if a definist claims "The good is pleasure," it is because he thinks the words "good" and "pleasure" mean the same thing or, in other words, that goodness is the same thing as pleasure.

2. *Intuitionism:* There are basic moral principles that can be known to be true, but they are not true by definition. If an intuitionist claims "The good is pleasure," he believes that whatever contains goodness also contains pleasure, but that pleasure and goodness nevertheless are different things.

3. *Noncognitivism* (including emotivism): Basic moral principles are neither true nor false. There is no moral knowledge because the words "good" and "right" do not name anything. If a noncognitivist claims "The good is pleasure," he believes that what he is doing is *expressing* some kind of favorable attitude or feeling toward pleasure, but he is not *asserting* anything.

Definists and intuitionists agree, contrary to noncognitivists, that moral truth and moral knowledge do exist, though they disagree about their nature and origin. People who believe that there can be straightforward scientific answers to ethical problems usually are definists;

they probably have assumed that "bad" and "wrong" mean something like "conflict producing" or "unsatisfying" and they naturally conclude that the most appropriate people to locate and eliminate what is "conflict producing," and so forth, are the behavioral and natural scientists. However, intuitionists, such as George Edward Moore, claim that ethics is not reducible to science and therefore that it is *autonomous;* they argue that it always is an ethical claim—not a scientific one or a definition—to say that what is conflict producing (or whatever) is bad.

It is worth noting that the label "intuitionism" is misleading; but it is the term that is used and I cannot think of a better one. "Intuitionism" seems to imply some special faculty or capacity for "intuiting" moral truths, and it is associated with the view of Moore that we can intuit or apprehend a unique moral property called goodness. But I am using the label for almost any theory that maintains both of the following: (1) some moral principles can be known to be true, and (2) these moral principles are not reducible to or strictly deducible from purely factual claims, that is, from claims that do not contain any moral words.

Intuitionists and noncognitivists agree, contrary to definists, that ethics is autonomous, that is, it cannot be reduced to science. For example, Moore (an intuitionist) argues that all definitions of the word "good" are false and commit what he calls the *naturalistic fallacy.* Hume, Ayer, and Hare, who are noncognitivists, agree. In fact Ayer borrows Moore's arguments in order to show that moral judgments are incapable of being scientifically tested for truth or falsity.

The three types of theories I have listed are examples of *theoretical* or *analytical* ethics rather than *normative* ethics. Theoretical ethics tries to understand the nature of moral phenomena much as scientists try to understand the nature of rocks or human brains; it includes investigating moral language as well as how people think, reason, and feel about morality. The three theories give competing accounts of what the words "good" and "right" *mean or refer to* (if they refer to anything), and hence competing accounts of what it is for something to be good or right. However, these different theories need not imply anything about what things *are* good or bad, or right or wrong. For example, from the standpoint of *any* of the three theories one could accept John Stuart Mill's principle of utility ("the highest good is the greatest happiness of the greatest number of people") together with nearly everything else Mill says in *Utilitarianism.* Definists would claim that the expression "the highest good" means the same thing as "the greatest happiness of the greatest number of people." Intuitionists (again, if they were utilitarians) would claim that a rational person can come to know that the principle of utility is an objective truth about the world, even though it is not true by definition. And noncognitivists or emotivists would claim that their basic moral attitude, on which the rest of their moral attitudes depend, is the principle of utility.

Why should you bother with theoretical ethics if whatever theory you accept makes no difference for your norms, that is, to your actual moral beliefs? There are two answers to this question. First, it is not obvious exactly what the relation is between theoretical and normative ethics, or even what the boundary is between them. I am inclined to think that the *kind of meaning* we think moral words have is normatively irrelevant. However, theoretical ethics is concerned with more than questions of meaning. It deals with many distinctions and points of logic that are important for sound, clearheaded reasoning about normative issues.

Second, anyone who is interested in *nothing but* concrete moral issues very likely will become weary of theoretical ethics and will come to think it is "irrelevant." Theoretical ethics seeks to *understand* that corner of the world called morality, and to engage in theoretical ethics therefore requires intellectual curiosity about this aspect of human thought and behavior. Many people are too fast and loose with the words "irrelevant," and "impractical," for what any person says is impractical or irrelevant *depends on his present interests,* and one aim of education, including ethics courses, is to expand a person's interests. If you were an oyster, or if you were interested in absolutely nothing besides your sex life, money, and a few football teams, most of the world would be irrelevant to you. If one of your deep, long-range interests is *understanding* some aspect of the world, then what serves that interest is, for you, "practical" and "relevant." The aim of a liberal education is to open up a person's interests so that more of the world is "relevant" to him. In addition to its normative concern with appraising moral opinions and principles, philosophical ethics seeks to figure out morality, to find out what it is and what makes it tick, and the indispensable key to getting into this activity is intellectual curiosity.

Chapter 3

Rules and Consequences

There has long been a controversy about the right way to justify particular actions: *Do we appeal to principles or rules, for example "Thou shalt not lie," or do we appeal instead to the consequences or results of the action, such as "It didn't do any harm"?* Since the two methods sometimes give conflicting answers, we cannot simply say that we appeal to both. Kant and Mill appear to give straightforward and opposed answers to this question. Kant argues that consequences are never relevant to the morality of an individual action whereas Mill maintains that actions are right if and only if their consequences have *utility,* that is, tend to maximize the general happiness. Another example of a stand on the rules versus consequences issue is the recent movement within Christian ethics called "situation ethics," which says that we should not be bound by principles but should ask only whether the *results* in a particular case are expressive of Christian love.

The crucial difference is between those who say that *the nature of an action* makes it right or wrong, whatever the consequences, and those who say that the nature of an act doesn't matter so long as it produces good (or harm, as the case may be). The former are called *formalists* or *deontologists,* and their morality consists of rules or principles saying that certain kinds of acts are right (or wrong). The latter are called *teleologists* or *utilitarians.* The Ten Commandments are a deontological code. Some deontologists, for example uncompromising pacifists, claim that nothing can outweigh a rule like "Thou shalt not kill." Kant made the same claim about "Thou shalt not lie." Other deontologists claim that since a single act can fall under a number of rules (for example, "Don't lie" *and* "Save lives"), we must weigh them together to see what is right. On this view rightness is determined by *all* the rules that apply to the act and each rule states your obligation only *presumptively* or *prima facie;* that is, "Don't lie" always determines what you should do unless other applicable rules combine to outweigh it.

One more version of formalism is this: Since no finite set of rules can absolutely guarantee the moral character of *every* act (together with its circumstances) that falls under it, rules are dispensed with. Philosophers who hold this view simply examine all the relevant aspects of some particular act (and about each of those aspects a prima facie rule *could* be formulated), note how these various aspects combine, and then apprehend the morality of the action. Such philosophers are called *act deontologists.*

A great many professional philosophers, and other people as well, are utilitarians (teleologists), and there are different names for the different versions of utilitarianism they support. To begin with, utilitarian theories differ as to which kinds of consequences are good. *Hedonistic utilitarian* theories maintain that only happiness, measured (usually) by pleasure and the absence of pain, is good. A hedonistic theory is *egoistic* if it claims that for each person only his own happiness is ultimately good. One which claims that the total happiness of all persons is good (or the highest good) is *universalistic.* Thus John Stuart Mill is a *universalistic hedonistic utilitarian.* A utilitarian theory that maintains that other kinds of consequences besides pleasure can be good is *agathistic.* G. E. Moore is an agathistic utilitarian, for he claims that "right" means "productive of good consequences" and thinks that several things besides pleasure are good. Shortly we shall consider an important distinction between *act utilitarianism* and *rule utilitarianism.*

The way to test utilitarian theories, which appeal exclusively to consequences, and formalist theories, which ignore consequences, is the same as the main way we test *any theory:* Can you deduce something unacceptable from it? For if a theory logically implies something that you are convinced is false, then you cannot accept the theory. We most often proceed, in both ethics and science, by saying, "Well, *if* your theory is true then it follows that so-and-so; but so-and-so is very doubtful (or false); therefore your theory is very doubtful (or false)."

For example, from a strict formalist system it appears to follow that one is not permitted to lie even to a would-be murderer who asks the whereabouts of his intended victim. Yet it plainly seems to be our duty to mislead the would-be murderer if we can, on the grounds that doing so would have good consequences. As we have seen, some formalist theories (but not that of Kant) attempt to escape this difficulty by applying more than one rule to a single action; in the above case these would be the rules "One ought to tell the truth" and "One ought to save lives." But if we cannot follow the one rule without violating the other, we need a criterion for determining *which* rule we should follow. Teleologists would argue that at some point we would have to appeal to consequences in order to adjudicate between the rules.

The main objection made against formalists is that they are *bound* to leave out morally relevant considerations, for no matter how many rules they apply to some particular action, that unique act will have effects or consequences that are distinct from the action itself; and these consequences, when they are harmful or beneficial to people, are bound to be relevant to whether we should perform the act.

Formalists raise analogous arguments in the attempt to show that teleological theories have unacceptable implications. They argue that teleologists are *bound* to leave out morally relevant considerations, for no matter how extensive and complete the consequences that are considered, the action itself has a nature, distinct from its effects or consequences; and the nature of the act itself, describable in a moral rule, often will be relevant to whether we should perform the action. Examples abound of actions that appear to produce, on the whole, more good than harm but that, almost everyone agrees, are plainly wrong: Should one sometimes punish an innocent person if doing so sets a beneficial example for others that outweighs the harm done? (But see Chapter 4 for more on this.) What if you were forced to choose between killing your spouse or parent and killing two total strangers? The latter action apparently would cause *twice as much harm* to humanity as the former, yet few of us think the right course is that obvious. Finally, it is reasonable to believe that sometimes exterminating a hated racial or religious minority will result in an increase in the total amount of happiness in the world. This is even more plausible if we consider the happiness of future generations, and if we imagine that the minority group already is very unhappy and that the extermination would delight the majority. *If* utilitarianism does indeed "justify" actions like this one, which we have no doubt are wrong actions, then utilitarianism cannot be an acceptable theory.

It should be no surprise that the recent history of ethics contains many attempts, some much more persuasive than others, to rebut these classic objections to both formalism and utilitarianism.

Stephen Toulmin retains the distinction between justification by rules and justification by consequences, but he combines them in a new form that he believes allows a plausible and acceptable role for each. Toulmin begins by arguing that the social function or purpose of an ethics is to reconcile conflicts of interest and prevent avoidable suffering. This, he says, is *why* a society has an ethics at all. This social function of ethics is served on two distinct levels of moral reason-giving: (1) a formalist (deontological) code of *rules* or practices that are authoritative and are learned by rote and (2) a utilitarian (teleological) appeal to *consequences* that reduce avoidable suffering and justify the rules.

Static, tribal societies rely mainly on rigid, formalist codes of duties and taboos. But at some stage in its development a society will recognize and accept the estimation of consequences, both to resolve conflicts of rules and to adopt or reject rules themselves if circumstances render them either necessary or no longer beneficial to the society as a whole. Possibly Toulmin would accept the transition from Old Testament to New Testament ethics (in particular Christ's criticism of the Pharisees) as an example of this evolutionary process.

Yet the "more advanced" society cannot abandon the use of rules or established practices: It appeals to both rules and consequences, but in distinct contexts. We test the *rightness of individual actions* (particular lies, thefts, and so on) by means of rules alone, and we test the *goodness or badness of rules or social practices* themselves by appealing to beneficial and harmful consequences. The question "Is this particular action right?" is answered by appealing to whatever acceptable rule applies to the action, while the question "Ought there to be a rule prohibiting everyone from lying?" is answered by determining whether or not the general adoption of this rule would benefit or harm the society.

Toulmin's theory is an example of *rule utilitarianism*, which is distinguished from *act utilitarianism* (Mill's theory, as commonly interpreted) as follows:

> *Act Utilitarianism:* An action is the right action to do if and only if it produces as much or more good than would any alternative action available to the agent at the time.
>
> *Rule Utilitarianism:* An action is the right action to do if and only if it is commanded by a good rule and a good rule is one whose general acceptance better benefits the society as a whole than would its general rejection.

Toulmin sums up the criticisms of formalism and utilitarianism mentioned earlier when he says that while unqualified formalism reduces morality to mere authority, the unrestricted appeal to consequences reduces morality to mere expediency. His theory aims to avoid both these criticisms by maintaining that we test individual actions by rules and test rules themselves by consequences. However, he qualifies the former test by saying that we may appeal directly to consequences to justify an individual action when either (1) the moral rules that apply to it conflict (for example, life-saving lies); or (2) no established rule clearly applies to the action; or (3) we use a particular act, for example, a certain promise, as a *test case* in order to challenge the justification of the whole practice of promise keeping.

It is important to see that whereas the *general acceptance* of "Don't steal" and "Don't break promises" may benefit society, some of the particular acts required by these rules do not benefit society (or anyone for that matter). Toulmin says that we should follow the rules anyway, and this reveals the deontological aspect of his theory. A theory is not truly deontological unless its rules have *authority of their own;* they cannot merely be rules of thumb (as Mill usually conceived of moral rules), that is, rough and dispensable guides to actions that are likely (but not certain) to have beneficial consequences.

Toulmin's reason why it is illegitimate to appeal to consequences when you ask "Should I keep this promise?" seems to be this: Your obligation to keep the promise depends merely on the fact that you *did* promise, and in that act of promising you tacitly accepted the practice in your society of keeping promises; it does not depend on any calculations you might make about how much good keeping the promise would cause. To consider consequences would be inconsistent with the authority you conceded to the institution of promise keeping by *using* the institution in making the promise in the first place. For Toulmin moral rules are somewhat like laws, where we play both judge and legislator on the appropriate occasions. The judge can decide that a particular action violated a law, but he cannot set aside or change the law; in his role of judging particular actions the law itself is final. The legislator, while she can pass good laws and repeal bad ones by appealing to the probable future consequences of having or not having a given law, has no authority to decide whether a particular action violated a law.

Toulmin's reasons for the authority of moral rules might appear to be rather weak. But a stronger basis for the authority of rules or generalizations exists and is discussed in Chapter 4.

However, we must take a closer look at the distinction between justifying an action by rules and justifying an action by consequences. How, for instance, do we come to make the distinction between an action and its consequences? Consider an example of what happens when a person "does something." Harry opens his mouth, words are spoken that are then understood by Max, Max as a result believes what is false, does something he otherwise would not have done, and thus Max's life is saved, and then Max ... (and so on). All these elements, including countless unstated ones, comprise a series, some of them causally connected, extending indefinitely into the future, and set in motion by Harry.

Let us call the elements of such series "action/consequence components," or components for short, and we can illustrate a series as follows:

Harry sees other car	Nerve message to foot	Foot presses brake	Car stops	Accident avoided	Mafia chief in other car saved
C_1	C_2	C_3	C_4 ...	C_5	C_6 ...... C_n

The series is not completely temporal because some components are simultaneous; some but not all components are causally connected; and it is not at all clear where the series begins, where it ends, or even what to include in it (for example, nerve messages and brain processes). Now if a series is constructed such that it includes everything that "goes on" when Harry performs an action, which components should we include in the description of *his action* and which components should we include in the description of the *consequences of his action?* What seems clear is that there are *many ways* of dividing the series into action and consequences:

1. Harry trod on the brake / with the consequence that the car stopped.
2. Harry stopped the car / with the consequence that an accident was avoided.
3. Harry avoided the accident / with the consequence that the Mafia chief was saved.
4. Harry saved the life of the Mafia chief / with the consequence that X, Y, Z.

What should we now think of deontological theories that claim that only the nature of the act is relevant to what is right and that consequences are irrelevant, and what should we think of teleological theories that claim the opposite? It appears that actions can be so redescribed that what one person legitimately calls a *consequence* of stepping on the brake, another person can legitimately call *what was done.* When someone does something it is to a considerable extent a matter of choice how we divide what takes place into "action" and "consequences of the action." Let us suppose you believe that the fact that a lie saved a life morally justifies it. If you are a teleologist you can say that the act is right *because of its consequences,* that is, a life was saved; if you are a formalist you can say that the act was right *because of its nature,* that is, it was a life-saving lie. Formalists can enlarge their description of the action to include whatever they think is morally relevant; teleologists can contract or simplify their description of the action itself so as to exclude whatever they think is morally relevant.

Given all this, is it sensible to think that the component "saving a life" is morally any more important if it is classified as an action instead of a consequence (or vice versa)? What I am suggesting is that if we are free to classify action/consequence components as either constituents of an act or as consequences of a simpler version of the act, and that whichever we do does not affect the moral importance of the component, then we are free to appeal to rules or consequences as we please. If this is true there is ground for doubting that there is an important difference between formalist moral reasoning, which judges actions by rules or principles, and teleological moral reasoning, which judges actions by their consequences.

In practical affairs people sometimes are criticized for being "unprincipled," "interested only in expediency," and "letting the end justify the means." These are ways of expressing what often are legitimate criticisms. When they are, it is because we think someone acts wrongly or inconsistently, usually out of self-interest. But it is not obvious that principles (which characterize actions) are intrinsically superior to ends (which are the consequences of actions), for what you think is the nub of a moral controversy usually can be cast in the form of either an end or a principle without affecting its importance. *Sometimes* the end does justify the means. Whether or not you think it does depends on the relative moral importance you assign to the principle and to the end you wish to achieve; that is to say, it depends on *the nature of the features or components that concern you* and not on how these features get classified within an act/consequence series. Deciding such matters calls for hard moral thinking, not shallow slogans like "the end justifies (or doesn't justify) the means."

There are, however, limitations on our ability to formulate morally significant components as either actions or consequences. Philosophers concerned with *action theory* have argued persuasively that some actions are *basic actions.* These are simple bodily movements like moving one's finger or foot and cannot, it appears, be consequences of still simpler acts. At the very least, not everything a person does is done by means of (or results from) something else he does, for then we would have to describe an infinite series of actions to explain the movement of a finger. There of course are occurrences that are causally necessary for the basic action of moving one's finger, such as brain processes and nerve messages, but these are not human *actions,* basic or otherwise.

At the other end of the series, some of what transpires can reasonably be described only as consequences and not as something a person *does,* especially when it is remote, unknown, and unintended. Thus a more comprehensive diagram of an action/consequence series should look like this:

Nerve message sent to foot	Harry pushes on brake	The car stops (or: Harry stops car)	Mafia chief saved (or: Harry saves Mafia chief)	Mafia chief survives to have grandchild named Harry	
C1	C2	C3	C4	C5	Cn
Physiological process, not an action	Basic action	Describable either as actions or as consequences of actions		Irreducible consequence	

If a basic action is morally relevant this fact can be expressed only by means of a moral rule. If an irreducible consequence is morally relevant we can express this only by appeal to a consequence or end to be attained. In between these extremes, however, it appears as though deontologists and teleologists (if they agree morally) merely say the same thing in different terminology.

Chapter 4

Universalizing

When someone argues that a certain action of yours is wrong, he will very often ask the rhetorical question, "What if everybody acted like that?" (for example, "What if nobody voted?"). The question is rhetorical because it is assumed that the results would be terrible if everybody acted like that, and the implication intended is that what you did was wrong. Sometimes one asks the rhetorical question when his only intention is to warn that you would be harmed if everybody acted the way you act. In this case it is difficult to imagine how he would cope with the reply, "But everybody *doesn't* act this way." On other occasions the question "What if everybody acted like that?" is used to imply a more formidable type of argument, which consists of two parts. First, it is clearly implied that it would be *wrong* if everybody acted like that because the consequences of everybody's acting like that would be harmful. Second, it is implied that if it is wrong for everybody to act like that, then it is wrong for anybody (including you) to act like that.

Arguments of this kind are called *generalization arguments*. Suppose I doubt that I ought to vote in national elections and point out that my not voting does no harm at all. After all, the chance that the national election will be decided by my one vote probably is less than the chance that I will be struck by lightning or eaten by a lion on the way to the polls. Nor is it plausible to claim my not voting will cause others not to vote, since my neighbors are hardly likely to watch me all day or very much care what I do. And if we add that it is cold and wet on election day, it seems hard to deny that, on utilitarian grounds, my staying home is better than my going out to vote, for it slightly increases my welfare and does no harm to others.

Yet I must admit that if *no one* voted, great harm very likely would result. Perhaps the democracy would collapse and the military would take over. Now what is interesting about this situation is that *each person's* not voting may do no harm at all, and yet *everyone's* not voting would do great harm. This may appear puzzling since we might expect that if fifty million people doing (or forgoing) some act would cause great harm, then *each* of them must do a little harm, the great harm resulting from adding up all the little harms. Yet this isn't always true. We must distinguish the *individual consequences* of everyone's doing it, that is, the consequences that each individual causes, from the *collective consequences* of everyone's doing it, that is, the joint effect of all of us doing it. Regarding many kinds of actions, each act may actually produce more overall benefit than harm (because the benefit to oneself counts too), while the collective effect of all these individually beneficial acts may be more harmful than beneficial. Not taking the trouble to vote, not paying a tax, using more than your share in a drought or gas shortage, and walking on a public lawn all can be examples. Each person's act of course has some describable effect, but what is very doubtful is that that effect, all by itself, constitutes *any* degree of harm. The question "What if everybody did that?" often is meant to imply that while the individual consequences may be good (or at least harmless), the collective consequences would be harmful.

Now how do we get from my admission that it is wrong that *nobody* vote (because harmful) to the conclusion that it is wrong for *me* not to vote (which, we concede, is not harmful)? Well, how can it be right for me to do something if it is not right for everybody to do the same thing? If I may do it and others may not, must I not have a reason? If my action is not significantly different from the kind of action that would be wrong if everybody did it, that is, if I cannot, in good faith, point out a reason why my action is a special case, then of course it also would be wrong for me to do it. Thus the question "What if everybody acted like that?" can be used to test *particular actions* by appealing to the harm or benefit resulting from the *general practice* of doing the same kind of action.

This argument clearly is an appeal to impartiality or fairness as well as a utilitarian appeal to consequences. It implies that you may do only what everybody, in the same circumstances, may do.

The Golden Rule and the "reciprocity rule" of Confucius, "What you do not want done to yourself, do not do to others," are both appeals to this same general principle. That this principle of impartiality is a principle of valid *reasoning*, and not a concrete moral principle, can be seen if we take a closer look at that version of it called the Golden Rule. In Matt. 7:12 Christ said, "Therefore all things whatsoever ye would that men should do to you, do ye even so to them." In what way does this rule tell us the moral thing to do? Presumably as follows. If I wonder how I should treat other people, I can find out by seeing how I "would have" other people treat me. But *how* would I have other people treat me? The Golden Rule does not say. It is of no help to suppose it to mean that we should satisfy others' desires since we all want our own desires satisfied. Interpreted this way, the Golden Rule would require us to satisfy the immoral desires of others as well as the moral ones. It would require us to help others commit suicide or rob banks. If it is to make good sense, the Golden Rule must concern what is right and proper for us to do to others and for others to do to us, and not simply what we desire. It must mean something like this: With regard to all things whatsoever, if it is right for you to act in such-and-such a way toward others, then, if your situations are not different, it is right for others to act in the same way toward you. In other words the Golden Rule, in saying that you may do to others only what they may do to you, does *not* say *what* you may do to others or *what* others may do to you, as do concrete rules like the Ten Commandments; it merely admonishes you to judge similar cases similarly, whether they concern you or others. For example, it says that *if* it is right for you to prevent your neighbor from voting or from applying for a job, then it is right for your neighbor to prevent you from voting or applying for a job, provided only that there is no *relevant* difference (regarding these activities) between you and your neighbor. But the Golden Rule, by itself, does not say that you and your neighbor may vote, nor does it say that you and your neighbor may not vote. Therefore, it appears to be a principle of good reasoning in morals, and not a substantive principle such as "Thou shalt not kill."

This principle, which says that if you may do a certain kind of act then others may do it too, is called the *universalization principle*. Many philosophers, including Kant, claim that it is inconsistent to violate the universalization principle, and recent philosophers such as Richard Hare claim that it shows moral judgments to be different, in their logic, from nonmoral judgments. We must try to see why.

Suppose we see a yellow chair before us. Could there be another chair that was like it in every respect except its color? It seems so. A complication arises when we remember that there must be a cause of the chair's being yellow, a cause absent from the non-yellow chair. So let us rephrase our question: Can the property yellow be the only difference that you *notice* between them? The answer is clearly yes.

Now suppose you thought that one chair was a good one and the other was not. Could *this* be the only difference you notice between them? That is, could they appear to you exactly alike in all respects except that one is a good chair and the other is not? Now the answer is clearly no. So the cases are different: "yellow" is not like "good." Goodness, unlike colors or shapes, cannot be the *only* difference we notice between two things.

This fact is called the *supervenient* or *consequential* character of moral and evaluative terms. If we apprehend that something is good (or right) and that something else is not, we must have apprehended some other difference between them, a difference that accounts for the moral difference. This other, nonevaluative difference must be our basis or *reason* for claiming that one is good and the other is not good. Thus supervenience tells us that we necessarily have reasons for moral differences between things, these reasons being other differences between those things. The contrast with nonsupervenient features such as yellow is obvious and important. Someone can sensibly say, "I just see it is yellow," and not need a further reason. But it seems to be a misuse of the word "good" to say "I just perceive it is good" and not have a reason.

The fact that we call things good only because of nonmoral features we observe (or believe they have) is some evidence, though not conclusive evidence, that goodness is not a *property* of things, for if it were a property it would seem that it could, like yellow, be the only difference between two things that we happen to notice. Of course, if goodness were *identical* with, say, pleasure, then it would be understandable how goodness is a property *and also* clear how two things that differed regarding goodness also would differ regarding pleasantness. For in this case there would be one difference with two names: "good" and "pleasant." But this is the definist alternative and it is rejected by most philosophers (see Chapter 2).

Universalizability (U) *is a logical consequence of supervenience* (S). If you think the chair is a good one, and you think some other chair is exactly like it in all nonevaluative respects, you must admit that the other one is good too. Otherwise you would be claiming that two things could differ only as regards goodness. So too in moral cases: If you think I have the right to vote, you have to admit that anyone has the right to vote who is like me in whatever ways you think relevant to voting.

Two things or situations probably never are *exactly* alike, but many differences are irrelevant to the evaluations and moral judgments we make. So we ignore these when applying the S and U principles: If Diana and Mary differ *only* in height, then S requires us to either admit that height is relevant to our moral judgment of them, or, if we think height is irrelevant, to judge them as though they were exactly similar. S says, regarding actions:

S: Two actions cannot differ only regarding rightness.

It implies U, which says

U: If an action is right, then any action exactly like it in all nonmoral, morally relevant ways is also right.

It is important to see that only *singular* moral judgments must be universalized, that is, judgments about individual things or persons such as "*George* doesn't have the right to vote." Judgments about *kinds* are already universal, for example "*Men* do not have the right to vote" or "*Black men* do not have the right to vote." If someone claims that being male or black is relevant, we may morally reject his position, but his claim, by itself, does not violate the *U* principle.

I should mention here one other possible qualification. It may be that egoistic moral judgments, such as "I ought always to look out for myself first," need not be universalized in certain ways. This is discussed in Chapter 5.

U and *S* are *formal* or procedural principles, and they cannot tell anyone which differences are relevant differences. The *U* principle by itself can never tell you whether an action is right or wrong. It is a conditional claim that says *if* something is right (or good), *then* anything similar in all the ways you think are relevant is also right (or good). Our opinion that something *is* right or good is contained in our *substantive* or concrete moral principles, such as the Ten Commandments or the principle, mentioned earlier, that it is wrong that everyone do what would cause great harm or misery.

Nevertheless, even in the absence of moral principles, *U* is an important and cogent tool in moral argument, since it can force people to acknowledge the need for reasons and also reveal what they think are relevant differences between actions. I shall first give a simple example of this "principle-less" use of *U* and then outline the more elaborate arguments that Immanuel Kant and Richard Hare build upon it.

Suppose someone thinks he can morally defend racial discrimination laws. Let us assume he sincerely wishes to be rational and will not merely ignore our arguments, revile us, or threaten to beat us up. He says "I think blacks should not be allowed to vote, go to school with white children, or hold certain kinds of jobs. My moral position may be *different* from yours and based on different traditions, but you can never prove it is *worse* than yours. I have my moral feelings about the matter and you have yours, and that is the end of it." Notice that he has said that we cannot win an argument with him; therefore he must argue, admit the demands of logic, and allow us to question him.

"What," we ask first, "is the ground for claiming that a white person has some right a black person lacks?" For the *U* principle requires that he have in mind a difference he thinks is relevant, on pain of judging similar cases dissimilarly. "Is this difference mere color, or is it some other difference of which you think color is a clue?" Now he *could* say "just the color," but he would not and no one ever does. He would invite the question, "What has mere skin color, and indeed this particular color from among many, got to do with rights?" He would have to admit that if, in a flash, all light skins turned dark and all dark skins light, that he properly would lose certain rights. If a racist said, "Yes, it's just the color," it might be impossible to refute him; but he does not, as a matter of fact, think this, and knows he would be judged mad or an idiot if he did.

He claims it is other differences with which color is correlated: "They have no sense, think of sex all the time, steal, and keep their yards dirty." Now we have reasons. For the moment lay aside the point, important as it is, that his reasons are demonstrably inaccurate; for his position can be made unacceptable to him by another route. Equally important is that he now offers reasons for disenfranchisement *which have nothing to do with color.* He must, presumably, devise and accept some test for determining who "has no sense" and "thinks of sex all the time," and now his own principles would require that whites and blacks who fail the test lose the right to vote. Were this his view he would not have a *racial* policy but instead an aristocratic, ascetic, and eccentric one. Anyone who starts out to defend racial laws would be very unlikely to be satisfied by colorblind (and fairly administered) voting tests of the sort described.

He faces a dilemma: he must base his voting (or whatever) discrimination either on mere color, or on harsh tests which the U principle requires him to apply regardless of color. He can accept neither and there is no other alternative—mere color is either relevant or it is not. It would not avoid the dilemma to claim that discrimination by color is an infallible guide to who has the real defects, and not only because the claim is demonstrably false but also because the *real reason* given for denying voting rights is "having no sense," and so on, and this must be universally applied regardless of color since he admits that color alone cannot bestow or remove a right to vote.

The lesson of the example is that you need not always fling an opposing principle at someone whose moral position you reject. Doing so might merely require you to defend it, and possibly lead to a stalemate. It is often enough to carefully demand reasons, and more reasons for the differentiation of apparently similar cases, and then his argument may collapse into alternatives that he himself is unable to accept. There are many policies people espouse that cannot be defended, even by means of their own principles, when subjected to a probing and accurate demand to universalize in terms of the differences and similarities they believe are relevant. When the response you get is ridicule, invective or anger, it is a fairly good sign that you have touched a sore spot: a prejudice, assumption, or passion that they are not able to acknowledge or live with when it is exposed to the clear light of day.

Kant maintains that the foundation of morality is the Categorical Imperative: "Act only according to that maxim by which you can at the same time will that it should become a universal law." What this means, first, is that if you allow yourself to do a certain kind of action, you must, because you are a rational being, allow everybody to do that kind of action. Kant says that the fundamental way in which rationality expresses itself is in what he calls "law-like" or consistent judging. It is inconsistent of you to permit yourself to do what you do not permit others to do. By a *maxim* or "subjective principle of volition" Kant means your more or less complete specification of the *kind* of action you propose to allow yourself to do: "When in financial trouble, *I* will borrow money and falsely promise to repay it." By a *universal law* Kant means a rule permitting everyone to do the same thing: "*Everyone* may, when in financial trouble, borrow money and falsely promise to repay it."

The Categorical Imperative says in effect that if a rational or consistent being wills (or permits himself to accept) the maxim, he must also will the universal law; and moreover, that if he *cannot* will both the maxim and the corresponding universal law, the maxim then describes an immoral action. Kant describes two ways in which it can turn out to be impossible to will that one's maxim should become a universal law. First, the universal law itself may be *impossible* in the sense that it is self-defeating. For example, a law or rule allowing everyone to make false promises would have the effect that nobody would believe promises and hence nobody would seriously make them. Second, the universal law may be such that, while it could exist, to *will* that the universal law exist is to will the very opposite of what you willed in your maxim. Kant calls this situation a *contradiction in will*. For example, when you will, in your maxim, that you may spare yourself the trouble of helping others in distress, you will something you desire; and when you will (as you must, as a rational being) that consequently everyone may spare himself the trouble of helping others in distress, you at the same time will what you do not desire. And this clash of will or desire, which your reason forces on you, marks the maxim as an immoral one.

Kant clearly appeals to the principle that what you allow yourself to do, you must allow everybody to do. Does he also appeal to consequences? Critics of Kant have said yes in spite of the fact that Kant says consequences are irrelevant to the rightness or wrongness of an action. The criticism is that Kant implicitly must appeal to the consequences *of a general practice* (for example, "everybody's being allowed to make false promises") in order to show that a universal law allowing that practice is impossible; and that he implicitly must appeal to the expected effects of an *individual action* described by a maxim and *also* to the effects of having the corresponding universal law, in order to show that there can be a contradiction in will, as in the example above about not helping other people in distress. There is also a more general way of making the same criticism. The Categorical Imperative can be a test of the rightness of actions only because in applying it we appeal to *both* of the following facts about *what I propose to do* (my maxim) and about *what I allow everyone to do* (a universal law): (1) they *can* differ as regards the goodness or desirability of their consequences (for these consequences may be good individually and bad collectively); and (2) they *cannot* differ as regards rightness, or in other words, what is right (or wrong) for everyone to do is right (or wrong) for me to do.

It must not be forgotten, however, that one of Kant's aims was to show that the effects of *your individual action* are irrelevant to whether or not it is a morally right action, and the above criticism of Kant does not even claim that he is wrong about this. It purports to show only that the effects of something else, namely, the universal law allowing the general practice of actions like yours, are relevant to the morality of your action. But while the effects of the general practice are admittedly relevant, they are not, by themselves, the test of right and wrong. Generalization arguments as well as rule utilitarianism (see Chapter 3) make the effects of a general practice the test of right and wrong. Kant differs in saying that the mark of a wrong action is the clash or "contradiction" in will; it is the fact that pure reason requires you to will what you want (the maxim) and what you don't want (the general practice) at the same time.

Richard Hare constructs a Golden Rule type argument that, like Kant's, does not need to appeal to any substantive moral principles. He attempts to prove that if a person applies with care two truths about the kind of *meaning* moral sentences have, he will be able to logically deduce that certain courses of action are ones he cannot morally accept. So our first job is to understand his claims about the meaning of moral sentences.

Hare maintains that when you make a moral judgment, for example, "Mary ought to pay me five dollars," your judgment is *universalizable* and *prescriptive*. We know already what it means to say that a judgment is universalizable: If you accept that judgment, you must also accept that *anyone* in circumstances just like Mary's ought to pay five dollars to anyone in circumstances just like yours. It is implied that if you and Mary came to be in each other's shoes (so to speak), you must concede that you ought to pay Mary five dollars.

Hare probes into *why* moral judgments are universalizable, and he concludes that it is because they have *descriptive meaning*. Descriptive meaning is the kind of meaning ordinary nonmoral, descriptive terms like "red," "dangerous," "rich," and so on, have: they name a quality or property, and this allows us to say that if a thing is red, then anything else exactly similar in the respect picked out by the word "red" is also red. All this means is that descriptive judgments like "X is red" are trivially and obviously universalizable; we contradict ourselves if we say that the box is red and also say that another box, exactly similar to it, is not red.

This claim, however, trivial as it is, allows us to conclude that "ought" judgments are just as obviously universalizable *if "ought," just like "red," also has descriptive meaning*. Having descriptive meaning, Hare says, is what guarantees universalizability. What then is the descriptive meaning of "ought"? It is whatever you have in mind in virtue of which you make a particular "ought" judgment. For example, if you say "Mary ought to pay me five dollars" and you think so because she took a five-dollar book of yours, then the descriptive meaning of "ought" is "someone (with Mary's characteristics) taking a five-dollar book of mine." In other words the descriptive meaning of "ought" is highly ambiguous—it is the descriptive content of your *reasons* for the "ought" judgment, whatever they happen to be. *Anything* (logically) can be the descriptive meaning, and it varies from person to person, judgment to judgment, and time to time. This is true of all general moral words such as "ought," "right," "wrong," "good," and "evil," Hare implies.

When you claim something is good or right, people often say, "What's good (or right) about it?" or "What do you mean by good here?" and your answer gives the descriptive meaning of "good" on this occasion of your use of the word. Hare contrasts general moral words with what he calls "secondarily evaluative words," such as "courage" and "honesty," which have relatively fixed (and obvious) descriptive meanings.

Prescriptivity is the second component of the meaning of "ought." When you say "Mary ought to pay me five dollars" you implicitly *prescribe, will,* or *want* that she pay you five dollars. Hare expresses the implied prescription as "Let Mary pay me five dollars." This is the emotive or noncognitivist element of the meaning of moral words, and it ensures that moral judgments do not *just describe things*: they also are *acts of valuing things*. Prescriptivity is Hare's version of the more general noncognitivist view that an essential function of any genuine moral judgment is to express or manifest a favorable or unfavorable attitude toward something; that is, it is to act out (but with words) one's being *for* or *against* something. Kant's position is close to Hare's when he says that you must *will* that your maxim become a universal law, for to *will* a universal claim seems to mean something like to *prescribe* "Let it be so."

Given all of this, Hare's strategy in a moral argument is, first, to make you go from "I should do it to him" to "He should do it to me," in the hypothetical case in which your roles and situations are reversed. But, next, you must *prescribe* or will that he do it to you, and you might not be able to do so if you are very averse to its being done to you. For we cannot will what, all things considered, we are against happening. This amounts to saying that you can, without inconsistency, accept the judgment that you ought to hang Mary *only if* you are able to prescribe or will that Mary hang you in a hypothetical situation in which your characteristics and situations are reversed.

I shall first give an oversimplified outline of the logical moves Hare says we must make if we are to be consistent:

    1. I have an aversion to Mary's hanging me.

∴ 2. I cannot accept the prescription "Let Mary hang me."

∴ 3. I cannot accept that Mary ought to hang me.

∴ 4. I cannot accept that I ought to hang Mary.

Each step follows logically from the preceding one, Hare argues, and thus shows the *logical basis* of the belief that if, all things considered, you do not *want* someone to do a certain thing to you, then you cannot claim that you *ought* to do that thing to him.

Let us reformulate the same argument, this time adding some details and qualifications. The aim will be to show A that she cannot accept that she ought to do X to B *because* (as often is the case) she has an overriding aversion to B's doing the same thing to her.

1. If A accepts that she ought to do X to B, then A must accept that in a hypothetical situation where all the relevant circumstances of A and B are reversed, B ought to do X to A.

2. If A accepts that in the hypothetical situation B ought to do X to A, then A must accept that in the hypothetical situation she accepts the singular prescription "Let B do X to A."

3. If A accepts that in the hypothetical situation she accepts the singular prescription "Let B do X to A," then A cannot have an overriding aversion to B's doing X to A.

4. A has an overriding aversion to B's doing X to A.

∴ 5. A cannot accept that she ought to do X to B.

There is one kind of situation in which Hare admits that his argument will be ineffective. Suppose X is something no normal person would want done to her, like being put in a concentration camp; but A is so convinced people like B belong in concentration camps that if she herself discovered she was a person like B she would not have an overriding aversion to being sent to one. Such a person is the *fanatic* Hare discusses and she cannot be made to agree to (5).

Chapter 5

Morality and Self-interest

Probably the most important ethical problem of all concerns the relation between personal happiness and morality. There are actually many related problems here, but we can conveniently group them into three main types:

1. Can morality as most people understand it, that is, fairness, honesty, and not hurting other people, ever truly require you to give up your own chance for happiness? Put positively, does the moral life lead to happiness, does it always pay? If morality and personal happiness *are* compatible, then much apparent evidence to the contrary must be explained away (think of Job in the Bible); and if they are not, then each of us appears to confront the question, "Why should I be moral?"

2. Suppose morality of the above sort did not pay. You might then deny that there is a satisfactory answer to your question, "Why should I be moral?" You might instead build your conception of value and morals around what furthers and protects your own happiness. That is, making your own happiness your highest value, you might believe that you ought always to do only what best enhances or protects your own happiness. This view is called *ethical egoism*. Is ethical egoism true? Can it be refuted?

3. Is it even *possible* for people knowingly and intentionally to act contrary to their own interest or happiness? The theory that people necessarily act from self-interest is called *psychological egoism*. It currently is a fairly popular view; indeed, whereas a hundred years ago most young people would be embarrassed to discover that some motive they thought was a moral one was really selfish, today many people are embarrassed, or at least surprised, at the idea that a motive of theirs

might *not* be selfish but instead moral or altruistic. Thus we must ask if psychological egoism is true.

Most thinkers have believed that morality and the value people put on their own happiness are *independent* of each other. That is to say, what you should do from morality and what you should do from self-interest have different bases and origins; they are ultimately distinct sources of value and obligation. And this certainly *seems* to be the case, if only because morality says things like "Thou shalt not kill, lie, or steal" and not just "Be happy!" But at the same time most of these thinkers concede that it is difficult if not impossible to show that following morality is fully rational and reasonable, all things considered, unless it is ultimately in *harmony* with the pursuit of one's own happiness. This is the position taken by Plato and Butler.

Plato has best described our initial problem, which goes: "If morality and what furthers my happiness are different, they will clash; and if they clash, how can it be rational of me to follow morality?" In the first book of *The Republic* Thrasymachus, followed by Glaucon and Adeimantus, eloquently present the view that Socrates (Plato's spokesman) ultimately tries to refute: Justice (that is, morality) does not pay as well as injustice and therefore the rational person will be unjust. Thrasymachus argues that justice does not benefit the citizens who are just, because justice is merely any set of rules that strong rulers make in order to benefit themselves. Glaucon and Adeimantus present the more formidable argument, one that seems less to distort the meaning of "justice" than does that of Thrasymachus: They argue that no sensible person really values justice or thinks it pays; people value only the *appearance* of justice. Anyone, they claim, wants others to be just and himself only to *appear* just. This they try to prove by the story of the ring of Gyges: With a ring to make one invisible no reasonable person would be just because he could continue to reap the benefits of seeming just together with the benefits of being unjust. So they demand that Socrates prove that justice *itself* is necessary for happiness, just as health is. For no one thinks it is enough for happiness to be *thought* healthy; one must *be* healthy.

This is what Plato tries to prove in the rest of *The Republic,* that justice is as necessary for happiness as is health. His argument is that justice is a harmony of the parts of the soul, and injustice a disharmony that prevents rational and effective action. But this solution is only hinted at in our selection, the main purpose of which is to present the problem in as challenging and honest a way as possible.

Joseph Butler offers a Christian solution to the problem, but with an interesting twist. Morality, he says, consists of principles independent of self-interest; one ought not to kill, lie, or steal because it is *wrong* to do so, not just because they are poor ways to achieve our happiness. Yet he also thinks that they *are* poor ways to pursue happiness and that benevolence and love of others is a better way. This last point about the relation between benevolence and self-interest is the subject of our Butler selection, and we shall discuss it shortly.

But let us first see his overall scheme. Butler, unlike Plato, never argues that morality is as intimately related to our happiness as is health. He tries to prove that being moral and achieving happiness *usually* coincide, but when they do not, as when morality requires self-sacrifice or when wicked people prosper, then God will even the score in the next world. That is the traditional Christian position, because Christian ethics has not worked out, and perhaps has not even tried to work out, the internal and *necessary* connection between doing right and achieving happiness, which Plato and other ancient Greeks defended. But now Butler makes a novel move and thereby takes a step toward *ethical egoism,* a doctrine we shall examine in the latter part of this chapter. He says (p. 178) that though morality is indeed the pursuit of what is right and good as such, "Yet, that when we sit down in a cool hour, we can neither justify to ourselves this or any other pursuit, till we are convinced that it will be for our happiness or at least not contrary to it." He doesn't say we *will not* act morally when it thwarts happiness; he says we cannot *justify* doing so. What does this mean? It seems to mean that while morality consists in principles independent of self-interest, nonetheless self-interest has veto authority over morality. All the more reason why he needs divine rewards and punishments in the next world, for only this seems to ensure that the veto need never be used!

While Butler's answer to the question "Does morality *always* pay?" is the routine Christian one, his answer to the different question *"Are altruistic motives ever in one's own interest?"* is more interesting. What Butler says should be compared with what seems to be the very different and opposed answer that the ethical egoist Ayn Rand gives to this question (which will be discussed shortly).

The question arises as follows. What we do from self-interest is usually thought to be directed toward our own good or happiness, while what we do out of benevolence or altruism is thought to be for the good of others. Are these two types of motives opposed? Are people who devote their lives to helping others moral heroes, whose only reward is their virtue? If so, you might well ask: "Virtue being the bittersweet reward that it is, why be an altruist, when I can be happy instead?" One of Butler's main points in Sermon XI is that this way of looking at things is nonsense. He says that one totally misunderstands, and perhaps insults, many United Nations workers, jungle doctors, social workers, or fighters for civil rights, when one assumes that they are leading lives of "self-sacrifice," for the good of others instead of for their own good. Butler would remind us that, on the contrary, these people are doing what interests them, what they like doing, and he would find it hard to imagine that anything could be more in accord with self-interest than a life spent doing what one most liked doing.

Nevertheless, Butler says, self-love (or self-interest) is distinct from benevolence; this is because it is distinct from *every* "particular affection" or interest, whether they be benevolent ones like love, friendship, and sympathy, or nonbenevolent ones like hate, anger, and love of money. Self-love is distinct from all of these because it does not seek a particular object at all. Self-love is not itself a kind of desire or interest, it instead is a kind of *judgment*: it is a principle of *ordering* particular interests according to whether we believe them to contribute to our happiness.

Beginning with this insight into the nature of self-love Butler attempts to refute *psychological egoism,* that is, the famous doctrine that absolutely everything any person does is done only for the sake of self-love. In short, this is the view that all human actions are ultimately "selfish." (We must remember that this doctrine is distinct from *ethical egoism,* the theory that one *ought* to act only from self-interest.)

A plausible-sounding form of psychological egoism is this: Particular activities or objects of interest—such as playing tennis or making money—are never sought for their own sakes, but *only as a means* to satisfying self-love with the pleasure or enjoyment they produce. Butler argues that if this were true, self-love would be self-defeating. For example, suppose you maintain that what holds your interest is not playing tennis itself but, rather, the pleasure that playing tennis gives you. How, then, can tennis *give* you pleasure if you have no interest in it? It makes sense to say, "Playing tennis bores me and I only play to impress the boss." In this case tennis is only a means to the satisfaction of another particular interest. However, it hardly makes sense to say, "Tennis itself bores me and I only play for the sake of the pleasure it gives me." You cannot intelligibly separate activities you simply enjoy from the enjoyment gotten from them and let the former be a means to the latter.

This is the first step in his refutation of psychological egoism. He shows that we must have *direct interests* in particular things that are distinct from our happiness, for otherwise we could not get enjoyment from particular things and therefore could not be happy. His second step is to claim that sometimes these distinct, particular interests are *stronger* than self-love: we can knowingly act on them even when self-love says no. Angry outbursts, drug addiction, cigarette smoking, guilty self-punishment, some sexual acts—these all are things people sometimes do while knowing full well that they are incompatible with their rational self-interest. They are all possible cases of what the ancient Greek philosophers called being "enslaved by a passion." Psychological egoists think that you cannot be *enslaved* by a passion; you can at most be *deceived* by it in the sense that at the time you act on it you think it benefits you. How you answer the following question will reveal whether you accept Butler's argument or instead are persuaded by psychological egoism: Consider a heroin addict whose heavy habit has cost him his job, reduced him to petty theft, and is ruining his health and his marriage, and who now has the needle poised over his vein. In order to go ahead with it, *must* he believe that what he is about to do is in his own best interest, on the whole and in the long run? If not, then a person knowingly *can* act contrary to self-interest and psychological egoism is false.

Turning to a related aspect of moral psychology, Butler says that if you treat an activity as the object of a direct and independent interest, you are more likely to enjoy it than if you think of it as only a means to enjoyment. Butler admits that this sounds paradoxical; indeed, philosophers have often noticed this kind of situation and have named it the *hedonistic* (or pleasure-seeking) *paradox*. He explains the hedonistic paradox in terms of his previous point about the *abstract* nature of self-love: We can enjoy only what is concrete, and therefore none of us can be happy unless we have, *in addition to self-love*, particular interests in particular things. Moreover, particular interests thought of merely as means to enjoyment would also be self-defeating, for if our *real* interest is only the abstract goal happiness, no interest remains for the particular object. This is the point of the hedonistic paradox, which is often expressed by saying that you have a better chance to be happy by not thinking about it and instead immersing yourself in activities that interest you.

Which particular interests make a person happy? If we could be sure that there were no hidden undesirable consequences, then what most interested you or whatever you most enjoyed doing would best make you happy, whether this was benevolence and altruism, which aim at the happiness of other people, or business, which aims at money, or whatever. Benevolent interests bear exactly the same relations to self-love as do interest in tennis and all particular interests: They are always *distinct* from self-love, and sometimes they are *compatible* with it and sometimes they are not. The mistake Butler attacks is the belief that the very nature of benevolence and altruism make them *naturally opposed* to self-love. What causes the mistake, of course, is thinking of "my happiness" (which self-love aims at) and "other people's happiness" (which benevolence aims at) as though the *very wording of them* made them mutually exclusive. *Other people's happiness* doesn't exclude *my happiness, it is merely distinct from it, just as is every other particular object of interest such as money, food, or tennis playing.*

Nevertheless, any particular interest can fail to satisfy self-love if it happens to be harmful, unsuitable, or irrational, such as blind passion, foolish whims, or interests driven by pathological guilt feelings. Butler says that the so-called selfish interests and violent emotions—love of money and leisure, as well as hatred, uncontrolled sexual desire, and anger—are even more likely to clash with self-interest than are the so-called unselfish ones, such as love, friendship, and benevolence. Thus both guilt-ridden altruists who forgo what they really want out of life in order to care for a relative, and selfish people and misers, often do the same thing: they satisfy particular interests that are not in accord with self-love.

It follows that the obvious guide to *which* particular interests are in accord with self-love lies in the distinction between intelligent and unintelligent interests, not in the distinction between benevolent and nonbenevolent interests. Intelligence can rank (and hence may redirect) interests by consulting what accords with your temperament and abilities, and by calculating as far as possible the consequences, both short and long range, of ways of acting. It is on these considerations that Aristotle, Butler, Mill, and other philosophers base the traditional claim that benevolence and the other virtuous interests are, more often than not, the most intelligent interests.

In **John Stuart Mill's** system it is possible that on certain occasions the good, which is the general happiness, and one's own happiness might make incompatible demands. But Mill agrees with Butler that, *in general,* there is no natural conflict between desiring the good of others and intelligent self-interest, and that both aims, more often than not, find expression in the same actions. Mill adds, however, that although there is a natural connection between intelligent self-interest and actions that further the general happiness, this connection requires awakening and stimulation. Hence he takes the proper end of education to be the redirecting of people's interests so that in the future people will get their greatest satisfactions from furthering the general happiness or, at least, will not find any satisfaction in doing what hinders it.

Immanuel Kant appears to separate all interests (and hence all motives) into two groups: inclinations, most of which are selfish and some of which are benevolent, and a unique motive called "respect" for the moral law. He believes that there is no sure way to distinguish benevolent inclinations from subtly selfish inclinations. Unlike Aristotle, Kant believes that morality and interest in one's own happiness are totally different concerns, and he tries to establish this in the following way: He first restricts questions about morality to questions about what is our duty or obligation, and then argues that we cannot possibly be morally obligated to do (or not do) either (1) what is impossible for us to do, or (2) what we necessarily or automatically try to do. For example, it makes no sense even to suggest that a cat is morally obligated to act rationally; nor does it make sense to say that God is obligated to act rationally, for the cat cannot do so and God does so anyway. Human beings can be obligated to act rationally since they, unlike cats and God, are neither exclusively irrational nor exclusively rational. However, a human being no more can be morally obligated to seek his own happiness than God can be obligated to act rationally, or a cat can be obligated to hunt mice, since each does these things in any case. Consider ordinary expressions such as "Smith is *obliged* to repay his debts," and "Jones is *bound* by her obligations not to do so-and-so." What is suggested by expressions like these is that no one can be *bound* by an obligation to seek his own happiness, because for obligation to arise there must be at least a possible conflict between what is required and what one desires or automatically tries to do. Kant believes that the very idea of obligation involves the notion of *constraint,* where what constrains is the moral law and what is constrained is inclination, aimed either at particular objects or one's own happiness. Hence Kant maintains that consideration of how an action affects one's own happiness is totally irrelevant to the determination of what is one's duty. That is to say, moral and self-interested motives always are different, although he agrees that they often coincidentally result in similar actions.

Now we must change pace and carefully examine *ethical egoism,* a theory that most philosophers argue is false. I shall do so by presenting the theory of the best known contemporary ethical egoist: the novelist/philosopher Ayn Rand.[1]

Ayn Rand maintains that morality consists in what she calls "rational selfishness." The source of all value, she says, is a person's own life, and morality is the pursuit of what protects and augments the quality of one's life; in other words, it is the pursuit of *one's own* happiness. But it is what *actually* increases your happiness that is right and moral, not just anything you *think* will make you happy. What actually makes a person happy does not depend merely on personal preferences; it also must be suitable to the *nature of man* and this includes, among other things, being a rational being. For these reasons she calls her highest value "*rational* selfishness."

Rand rejects utilitarianism because it claims that morality consists in furthering the *general* happiness. What is wrong with utilitarianism, and Christian ethics as well, is that they determine the morality of an action by the needs of some *beneficiary* of the action. These theories

---

[1] Ayn Rand was born in St. Petersburg (now Leningrad), Russia in 1905, educated at the University of Leningrad, and came to the United States in 1926. She has written several highly successful novels including *The Fountainhead* (1943) and *Atlas Shrugged* (1957). In addition to being works of fiction, these novels are vehicles for her philosophical views: a political philosophy of "pure" capitalism and an ethics of rational egoism, to which she gives the name "objectivism." Her nonfiction works include *For the New Intellectual* (1961), *The Virtue of Selfishness* (1961), and *The New Left: The Anti-Industrial Revolution* (1971).

A good anthology of articles both for and against egoism is David Gauthier's *Morality and Rational Self-Interest,* Prentice-Hall (1970); Gauthier's own essay in this anthology is especially recommended.

assume that *altruism,* that is, benefiting others such as the poor, the unfortunate, or other people in general, is the primary concern of morality. In other words they assume that other people have a *claim on you* to satisfy their needs and interests, quite independently of what they deserve or what they offer in exchange. Nearly all past ethical theories, she says, preach altruism as the essence of morality; that is their great error, an error which has both personal and political consequences that are harmful and degrading.

Altruism, as she defines it, is *self-sacrifice.* Since Rand claims that your own happiness is your *highest* value and that all duties and other values derive from it, it follows that anything you sacrifice your own happiness for is a lesser value or a nonvalue. Therefore she defines altruism and self-sacrifice as "trading a greater value for a lesser," clearly an irrational kind of behavior. Altruism, Rand thinks, is a kind of swindle; it is preached by both Christian ethics and socialist ethics in order to get you to give up your money, property, freedom, or other things that you want for your own good, in return for either nothing or something inferior. She says:

> Observe what this beneficiary-criterion of morality does to a man's life. The first thing he learns is that morality is his enemy: he has nothing to gain from it, he can only lose; ... the grey, debilitating pall of an incomprehensible duty is all that he can expect. He may hope that others might occasionally sacrifice themselves for his benefit, as he grudgingly sacrifices himself for theirs, but he knows that the relationship will bring mutual resentment, not pleasure— and that, morally, their pursuit of values will be like an exchange of unwanted, unchosen, Christmas presents, which neither is morally permitted to buy for himself. Apart from such times as he manages to perform some act of self-sacrifice, he possesses no moral significance. . . .[2]

That Rand defends an ethics of "selfishness" rather than "self-interest" can be a source of confusion. Butler and Mill, like most people, criticize selfishness as crude, offensive, or inconsiderate self-interested behavior; but we also should remember that we readily say, of a person who is self-effacing and always puts himself last, "He should be more selfish." Thus when Rand praises selfishness, and Butler condemns it as wrong and contrary to self-interest, we must be careful not to become confused about words. "Selfish" is usually a term of criticism, applied to grabby children, thoughtless and greedy adults, and so on. Yet on reflection we know that "rational selfishness" and rational self-interest"

[2] Ayn Rand, *The Virtue of Selfishness,* The New American Library and *The Objectivist Newsletter,* Inc., 1961, p. viii.

refer to exactly the same behavior, that is, behavior that aims at one's own good and intelligently seeks (when they are available) the advantages of cooperation, friendship, and mutual assistance. The only difference is that the word "selfish" tends to conjure up negative feelings. Ayn Rand combats this connotation. She knows that people who accept her views will be called selfish, however much their rational pursuit of happiness leads them to friendship, love, and cooperation, and so she appropriates the term "selfish" and attempts to turn it into a term of praise.

Because of Rand's terminology she and Butler appear to differ more than they in fact do. They agree that psychological egoism is mistaken and that irrational self-interest is wrong. They agree that an action cannot be justified if its consequences are contrary to one's own happiness, and they even agree that actions aimed at the benefit of other people are often a means to or constitutive of one's own happiness. But they disagree in two important ways, one moral and the other psychological. First, Butler, like most philosophers, believes that the principles of morality are independent, that is, not derivable from the value you put on your own happiness; and Rand denies this. Second, Rand, while claiming it often pays to help friends and loved ones, appears to doubt that many rational people are able to get genuine satisfaction from helping strangers or the poor. She thinks that very often people do these things only because they have been made to feel guilty about seeking their own happiness, and hence she considers many kinds of sympathetic and helping behavior to be self-sacrificial which, I suspect, most rational people would not consider to be so at all.

One might think that egoism, however rational, would lead one to be crafty: to steal, cheat, and betray, whenever it was in one's interest and when one expected not to be caught. We should remember the arguments of Glaucon and Adeimantus for why a rational person would want merely to *appear* just. Yet she argues that this is not an implication of her position. The general problem she faces is this: Just as traditional moralists have argued that ordinary morality, contrary to superficial appearances, leads one to happiness, Rand argues that ethical egoism, contrary to superficial appearances, leads one to most of ordinary morality. These are two sides of the same problem: Rand *begins* with rational egoism, and is anxious to show that it (in general) requires honesty, etcetera; nonegoists like Plato and Butler *begin* with the virtues justice, honesty, and so on, and are anxious to show that they lead to happiness. When it is argued that two rational egoists, when their important interests conflict, will resort to violence or cheating, Rand replies that there are no conflicts of interest among rational egoists. She maintains that it is immoral to be a parasite and live off the labor of others, or (usually) to lie, steal, or kill. Lying and deceit, for example, are condemned by Rand as cases of "faking reality": speaking or acting as though what is, isn't; and doing this, she says, is irrational. A difficulty with this last argument is that it is not at all obvious why it is irrational to deceive *others* when it is in one's interest to do so, however much it might be irrational to deceive *oneself*. "Faking" is a pejorative word, but what is wrong with faking if rational calculation shows that it benefits me? In general, it is obviously just as difficult (or easy, as the case may be) for an ethical egoist to reconcile rational self-interest with not deceiving, robbing, or hurting people, as it was for nonegoists to reconcile the morality of not deceiving, robbing, or hurting people with rational self-interest.

I do not mean to say that theories of ethics, egoistic as well as nonegoistic, all aim to justify the same kinds of actions. If this were so, they would be of no normative significance. Rand would not bother with her theory if she thought it justified, albeit from different premises, the same actions that "altruistic" theories justified; and of course it does not. Nevertheless Rand, like nearly all philosophers, desires to show that her theory does not have practical implications that are morally repellent or outrageous to reasonable, reflective people. A few of the more obvious practical consequences she claims for her theory are these: Rationality, self-esteem, and pride are highly important virtues; humility is not a virtue at all. Assistance should be given to strangers only in emergencies, and when the risk to yourself is not great.[3] You ought not to value the needs of strangers as equal to those of your friends and loved ones. If your wife is sick, it is morally proper and rational to spend your fortune to save her, even if that money could be used to save the lives of fifty strangers. Human beings are basically *traders* of values, in personal relations as well as in their commercial and political relations with other people; friends trade you their continued presence and friendship when you help them, but strangers or enemies have nothing of comparable value to offer in trade for your help.

To better understand whether or not some repellent and outrageous consequences *also* follow from her theory, we must explore another crucial feature of her version of ethical egoism. Accepting the universalization principle (see Chapter 4) she maintains that if her egoism is justified, so is yours and mine; this means that she is a *universal ethical egoist*. If her own happiness is *her* highest value, then an analogous claim can be made about *every* human being. She says:

> The basic *social* principle of the Objectivist ethics is that just as life is an end in itself, so every living human being is an end in himself, not the means to the ends or the welfare of others—and, therefore, that man must live for his own sake, neither sacrificing himself to others nor sacrificing others to himself. To live for his

---

3 See "The Ethics of Emergencies," in Rand, *The Virtue of Selfishness*.

own sake means that *the achievement of his own happiness is man's highest moral purpose.*[4]

If, like Kant, she says that people are ends in themselves and that no one is a mere means to the welfare of others, it is easier to understand her moral condemnation of lying, stealing, violence, and other ways of using people for one's own ends.

But is her position consistent? If my highest value is my own happiness and achieving it happens to require killing, ruining, or deceiving you, how can I also claim that I ought never to use you as a means to my own ends or welfare? Suppose that you and another ethical egoist are in a one-man lifeboat, accompanied, of course, by the usual circling sharks. Because your highest *value* is your own life and happiness, you claim, "I should throw him to the sharks and be the lone survivor." But that would be to use him as a means. One wants to ask Ayn Rand, "Is your own life of greater value than that of another, or is it not? If it *is,* why not use another as a means? And if it is *not,* how can you claim to be an ethical egoist?" Shortly, I shall suggest a reply she can make to this objection.

Some philosophers have claimed that ethical egoism *must* be universalized if it is to be an ethics at all, and that when it is, it is inconsistent. This is a formidable argument that must now be examined. If *everyone* ought to do whatever is necessary to protect his own life and happiness, must you not claim, in the lifeboat case, both

1. I ought to throw him to the sharks and be the lone survivor.

and

2. He ought to throw me to the sharks and be the lone survivor.

But (1) and (2) are inconsistent; they imply that you ought and ought not to be the lone survivor.

Here are three ways in which an ethical egoist may attempt to avoid the contradiction.

1. He may say that he ought to *try* to throw Harry to the sharks and that Harry ought to *try* to throw him to the sharks, but deny that either ought to succeed. These two claims are not contradictory; in fact, it is now possible that both do what they ought to do, namely, try to throw the other to the sharks. The egoist's position now seems like the attitude we have toward football teams. We may believe that Ohio State ought to try to defeat Michigan and Michigan ought to try to defeat Ohio State. Yet if someone asks "But who ought to win?" we answer either "No one *ought* to win" or "The best team ought to win." And that is the problem: the egoist, when asked "But *who* ought to escape the

---

[4] "The Objectivist Ethics," in Rand, *The Virtue of Selfishness,* p. 27.

sharks and live?" must answer similarly and this seems hard to reconcile with his belief that *his highest value is his own happiness.* How could he believe that and not believe that he should be the one to escape the sharks? And if he says "May the best man survive," he is no longer an egoist, for now his highest value is competence or toughness, whether it be he or Harry who possesses it. He could still *want* to be happy more than he wants Harry to be happy, but he could not believe that he *ought* to be.

2. A more interesting defense consists in denying a certain crucial inference. Ordinarily when we believe things like *"Mary should return the money"* or *"I ought to rescue that child,"* we also believe "The money should be returned" and "The child ought to be rescued." We make the inference from "So-and-so ought to do X" to "X ought to be done (by at least somebody)." When we remove the reference to a particular individual, we show that we mean the obligation impersonally. All of our moral beliefs are like this, with the exception, however, of when we are espousing ethical relativism and noncontradictory forms of ethical egoism.

It is easy to show how denying this inference avoids the inconsistency. Consider the following:

1. I *ought to be* saved and Harry *be thrown* to the sharks.

and

2. Harry *ought to be* saved and I *be thrown* to the sharks.

Given that only one can be saved, (1) and (2) are contradictory, and if this is what universal ethical egoism implies, then universal ethical egoism is contradictory. But

3. I *ought to save* myself and *throw* Harry to the sharks.

and

4. Harry *ought to save* himself and *throw* me to the sharks.

are not contradictory *unless* they are taken to imply the impersonal judgments (1) and (2). So egoism can escape the contradiction by denying the inference we usually make from "ought to do" to "ought to be." Of course, it still will be impossible for *both* Harry and I to do what we ought, but even this difficulty can be avoided by revising (3) and (4) so that they are about *trying:*

5. I ought to try to save myself and throw Harry to the sharks.

and

6. Harry ought to try to save himself and throw me to the sharks.

If the egoist does reject this sort of inference, for example, from "I ought to seek (that is, try to get) my own happiness first" to "My happiness should come first," then it looks as though he is adopting a version of ethical relativism. For when he says "I should try to be the survivor" and "Harry should try to be the survivor," but rejects the question "But which of you *ought to be* the survivor?" he seems to mean that it is *right for him* to do what is necessary for himself to survive and *right for Harry* to do what is necessary for Harry to survive.

We can put the same point another way. When someone claims that world peace is his highest value he means it objectively and impersonally in the sense that there should be world peace: he claims that world peace should exist and that what produces it should be done if it is possible. But when the egoist claims that his highest value is his own happiness and moreover that the same is true of other people, he must mean something quite different if he is to be consistent. We must take him to mean that his own happiness is *his* highest value, Harry's happiness is *Harry's* highest value, but that neither is *the* highest value: neither *ought* to exist, nothing is *the* highest value. The reference to *who* is doing the valuing cannot be eliminated and in just this sense moral and value judgments become irreducibly biographical.

There is some evidence that Ayn Rand accepts this form of ethical relativism (though she certainly rejects other forms of relativism), and if she does she escapes the charge of inconsistency mentioned earlier. She says that each person ought to seek his own happiness as his highest value, but she expresses contempt for the person who says "I ought to be happy." The latter claim implies, she says, that a person thinks that he is due more or owed more, in the nature of things, than are other people, and that this is an irrational thing to think.

3. We must remember that the argument against the ethical egoist, if sound, is a devastating one. It is that he is inconsistent if he does *not* universalize his egoistic judgments and also that he is inconsistent if he *does* universalize them; and that therefore egoism is inconsistent. We have considered his defense against the charge that he is inconsistent if he universalizes and concluded that he need not be inconsistent if he accepts a certain form of ethical relativism. Now, how can he defend himself against the other horn of the dilemma, namely that he is inconsistent if he does not universalize?

To save time I shall assume that you have read Chapter 4 on universalizability. If I say that I ought to save the blond child first I must admit that I also ought to save other blond children first (that is, ahead of nonblonds). If I don't, and also don't have a reason for distinguishing this blond child from other blond children, then I am guilty of judging similar cases dissimilarly. What if I claim that I ought to save *my* child first? The first thing to notice is that there are several ways in which my judgment can be universalized:

1. Everyone ought to save my child first.
2. I ought to save everyone's children first.
3. Everyone ought to save his own children first.

Now the question is not whether I *can* universalize the judgment but whether I *must* do so, on pain of judging similar cases dissimilarly.

Focusing on (3) above, must the egoist concede that Freda ought to save her own child first? Suppose that Freda and I each have a child in danger of drowning; must I admit that these cases are similar in all morally relevant respects? Here is a difference: the one child is mine and the other is not! Now we must make some careful distinctions. They are not always easy to see but are nevertheless important ones. First of all, the expression "my child," unlike "blond child," does not name any repeatable feature in addition to that of being a child. The words "my," "mine," "me," and "I" are called *egocentric particulars.* They are used to refer to oneself but they give *no information* about oneself, unlike descriptive words such as "blond," "wise," and so on. When I say I should save *my* child first I don't mean she should be saved because she is a child, or because she is a child of someone (which is also true of Freda's child). Rather, I mean I should do so just because she is *mine.* There *isn't any feature* in virtue of which I believe I ought to save my child and which might also be a feature of Freda's child; and this is because it isn't in virtue of repeatable features at all that I value my child. Thus it would seem that egoistic judgments I refuse to universalize are not inconsistent, just because I do not value my child or my happiness on the basis of any property that is also shared by Freda's child or Freda's happiness.

Second, it still might be claimed that the egoist's judgment is *arbitrary,* that is, he has no reason for saving his child first that would not also be a reason why Freda should save her own child first. The answer depends on whether or not "It's mine" can be a reason for a moral judgment. In a sense it is not a reason, for it appeals to no repeatable feature. Yet in a sense it is, for we all know what we mean when we call something "mine" and we can tell the difference between "mine" and "thine." At bottom, the ethical egoist seems to be saying, "I value things not because they have certain properties or consequences, but because they benefit a certain *particular* entity. It doesn't matter how similar this entity is to others; what is relevant is that it is numerically distinct from them and that it is *me.*" Such a basis for valuing things hardly seems arbitrary, but it also seems very different from the usual basis for morally distinguishing things.

Is ethical egoism a genuine system of morality or is it merely a way of dressing up in moral language the egoist's resolution to act out of self-interest no matter what? This can be seriously asked because the egoist's "oughts" are not like the "oughts" of other moralists, however much those other moralists might differ from one another. The egoist's "oughts" are not impersonal; they do not imply that anything ought to be the case; it is impossible for everyone to do the things egoism says they should do (though it is possible for them to try), and the egoist's "oughts" are not always determined by the repeatable features of things. Nonetheless, it does not strictly follow from these oddities that it is a mistake to call egoism a system of morality.

Chapter 6

Ethical Relativism

"Ethical relativism" is a label for a collection of views. It is, at its vaguest, the claim that moral values are "relative" and that there are no "moral absolutes." It involves claims that are both very popular and very unclear, so we must sort out several kinds of ethical relativism and then carefully examine each. The word "relative" is itself a relative term, which means that it will not make any sense to say simply that moral values are *relative*. They must be relative *to something* for a doctrine to be a version of ethical relativism. That is, moral values must be claimed to depend on or be a function of something else. Thus strictly speaking, if you think that there is *anything at all* on which right and wrong depend, you could be called an ethical relativist. Yet we shall see when we discuss view (1), below, that this includes too much, for what people who call themselves ethical relativists almost invariably *mean* is that *right and wrong are relative to opinion,* that is, relative to the moral beliefs or opinions of either groups or individuals. The views we shall discuss are the following.

1. An action that is right in one place or society may be wrong in another place or society.
2. Whatever a culture or society thinks is right *is* right, for that culture or society.
3. Whatever a person thinks is right *is* right, *for him.*
4. Everyone ought to do what he thinks is right.

Two other views are sometimes confused with ethical relativism and they have been excluded from the list. The first might be called "moral nihilism." A moral nihilist believes that nothing is right or wrong, that everything is permitted, and perhaps that the words "right" and "wrong" mean nothing at all.

The second is ethical skepticism. It is closely related to ethical relativism and a word should be said about it. The pure ethical skeptic is someone who believes that there are objective moral truths that are independent of people's opinions, but also believes that no one can know what they are. When someone says "Who is to say what is right and wrong?" he might be either a skeptic or a relativist: a relativist if he means to deny there is an impersonal, objective right and wrong, a skeptic if he merely means that no one can prove what is right and wrong. The difference is important. The skeptic *denies that anyone can know or prove* objective and impersonal moral truths; the relativist (and the noncognitivist too) *denies that there is such a thing as* an objective and impersonal moral truth. To take an analogy: No one knows or possibly ever can know how many snowflakes landed on the earth in the year 34,495 B.C. Yet, given a definition of a snowflake, isn't it obvious that some definite number of snowflakes did land? If I say "N snowflakes landed in 34,495 B.C.," N being any number from 0 on, what I say is quite objectively either true or false, and its truth or falsity is not relative to or dependent on the opinions of anyone. So skepticism need not imply relativism, unless, of course, what one is skeptical about is whether there is such a thing as objective, impersonal moral truth.

1. "An act that is right in one place or society may be wrong in another place or society." If this were not true, an intelligent morality would be impossible. For example, washing one's car every day would be morally disapproved in arid parts of the world where water is needed for more essential purposes, but would be considered permissible in Columbus, Ohio. If the action is only superficially specified as "washing one's car every day," it appears as if people in Columbus who permit it, and people in the desert who forbid it, are disagreeing. But the disagreement may be only apparent: It is reasonable to suppose that these people would agree that the circumstances were *different* in each situation, and also would agree about the nature of the circumstances in each situation. Moreover, each would agree that the act was morally permissible in the one place but not in the other. Thus in the case I have imagined there is disagreement about neither *facts* nor *values; and yet the morality of washing one's car every day is "relative" in the sense that it is relative to circumstances.* This seems to be an innocent and uncontroversial variety of relativism. What creates a mistaken appearance of moral disagreement often is an insufficient or overly simple description of actions or their circumstances. Descriptions of actions that are adequate for mere identification or other everyday purposes very often are too superficial when our purpose is moral evaluation.

In the preceding example different beliefs about the effects of the actions accounted for our different moral judgments, and these beliefs happened to be true ones. We have a slightly different case when one party has false or incredible beliefs about the effects of an action. For instance, among some peoples it is still believed that the proper thing to do, on certain occasions, is to eat other people; but we, presumably, do not share this opinion. Consider, however, exactly what it is that many cannibals believe. They believe that on certain ritual occasions it is right to eat parts of the body of an enemy tribesman fallen in battle, because doing so gives them the magical and other powers of the fallen enemy and also may prevent his spirit from tormenting them. Now we share their belief that it is all right to kill enemies in war. Suppose, moreover, that you firmly believed that the rest of these beliefs were *wholly* true and that you also shared the cannibal's moral commitment to achieve maximum prowess in battle in order to insure the survival of his family and tribe. Given these conditions, would you still morally disapprove of cannibalism? If not, you and the cannibal do not disagree about values on this point but only about the facts, and if you got the cannibal to agree with you about the facts, he very likely would come to share your moral opinion. The point is not that there are no purely moral disagreements but rather that moral disagreements between persons in vastly different cultures may well be only apparent, since so many differing factual beliefs about the natures of the actions are involved.

The claim that what is right in one place may be wrong in another is accepted by nearly everyone because we believe that whether an action is right *depends on the facts*—that is, the situation, circumstances, and (usually) the consequences, and these can differ from place to place. Advocates of an objective, nonrelative morality accept it because the nonmoral facts on which rightness depends are themselves objective and *do not depend on opinion*.

So far we have described moral differences (for example, the water case), which disappear when the facts are known about each situation, and moral disagreements (such as the cannibal case), which very likely *would* disappear if both sides were to agree about the facts of the case. It is far from obvious that *all* moral disagreements are reducible in this way to factual differences and disagreements. *An ultimate moral disagreement is a disagreement that would remain even if both sides agreed completely about the nature, circumstances, and consequences of the action in question.* Are there any ultimate moral disagreements? I think there almost surely are, but proving so is very difficult since two people who disagree about the morality of an action seldom even appear to agree about all aspects of its nature, circumstances, and consequences. The contradictory of the claim that there are ultimate moral disagreements I shall call *the unanimity thesis*. The unanimity thesis is the claim that if people agreed about and understood all nonmoral matters they would agree about all matters of morality. It says that moral agreement among rational people is always possible because nonmoral, factual agreement is always possible.

2. Distinct from (1) is *cultural ethical relativism*: "Whatever a culture or society thinks is right *is* right, for that culture or society." This is a classic form of ethical relativism because values are claimed to be relative to feelings or opinions, and not relative merely to circumstances or consequences.

We need to distinguish cultural ethical relativism from the anthropological doctrine called *cultural relativism,* and this can be done simply, as follows:

> *Cultural Relativism:* What is *believed* right in one culture may be believed wrong in another culture.
> *Cultural Ethical Relativism:* What is right in one culture may be wrong in another culture.

Cultural anthropologists (for example, Clyde Kluckhohn, Melvile Herskovits, and Ruth Benedict) have claimed that their field work proves cultural relativism, and then they have gone on to interpret cultural relativism as either equivalent to or as evidence for cultural ethical relativism. This inference from cultural relativism to cultural ethical relativism seems obvious to them, I think, because they implicitly deny that there is any intelligible difference between *being right* and being *believed right.* Yet this is just the point over which relativists and nonrelativists disagree. It begs the question to *assume* that "is right" is no different from "is believed right" and then infer cultural ethical relativism from cultural relativism.

Think of the missionaries who went to Asia with the aim of teaching the people Christian morality. These missionaries would have to *accept* cultural relativism, for if they did not think Asian cultures had different moralities they wouldn't think the Asians required moral re-education. But they would have to *deny* cultural ethical relativism, because if they thought that the Asians' morality was as true, for Asians, as Christian morality was for Christians, they could not justify trying to change the moral beliefs of another culture.

The missionary (and many other people) believe that there are objective moral truths, truths which are not relative to *opinion,* and cultural ethical relativists deny this. Whoever is correct, cultural relativism is no evidence whatever for cultural ethical relativism; to think so is to beg the question by identifying "believes right" with "is right."

Someone who believes that there are moral truths which are not relative to opinion is sometimes called a *moral absolutist.* The label "moral absolutism" is misleading because it means, for some people, the dogmatic view that moral principles apply without exceptions; that is, a moral absolutist often is thought of as someone who thinks it is always wrong to lie, kill, and so on, regardless of the situation, circumstances, or consequences. But we plainly do not have to believe *this* in order to deny cultural ethical relativism. As we saw earlier, it is hard to imagine someone denying that moral beliefs were relative to, that is, dependent on, *anything*. To deny cultural ethical relativism we need only deny that right and wrong are relative to opinion, and we may at the same time assert, if we think it correct, that right and wrong are dependent on circumstances and the consequences of actions and not just on simple moral principles.

Is cultural relativism true? On a superficial level it is plainly true: Some cultures morally condemn polygamy or cannibalism, others do not. Yet the doctrine usually is taken to imply deep disagreement between cultures: incompatible and perhaps irreconcilable basic moral outlooks. And this might not be true, as we saw when we discussed version (1) of ethical relativism. People in different cultures confront different environments and different problems and, moreover, they sometimes have nonmoral beliefs about the world that contradict our own. If it were true that everybody in the world would agree about morality if they agreed about the facts, that is, if the unanimity thesis were true, then cultural relativism would be only superficially true. This is because cross-cultural moral disagreements would not be *ultimate* moral disagreements—since nonmoral agreement would eliminate them.

Is cultural ethical relativism true? This question is easier to answer, but first a short digression on method is in order. The question asks for *your own* reasoned opinion, which for each of you is all that is relevant. It does not ask whether you think that somebody or other, or most people, can accept cultural ethical relativism; it asks whether *you* can. And you can accept cultural ethical relativism only if you find the theory to be coherent *and you can accept its logical consequences.* What, then, are the logical consequences?

First, what is it for a culture to believe that something, say, abortion or the legal punishment of homosexuality, is morally right? Presumably some percentage of people in the culture, such as 50 percent or 90 percent, must believe it is right. If we suppose that a majority will do, then abortion *is* morally right, in your culture, if the majority thinks it is. It follows at once that, within your culture, the majority is always morally correct and the minority always morally mistaken, since the theory says that whatever your culture says is right *is* right, for your culture. This, I think, is a consequence that neither you nor I can accept, for the upshot is that you need not deliberate or reason about the rightness or wrongness of abortion, capital punishment, or anything. You need only to have a poll taken, the result of which will conclusively determine the truth or falsity of your own moral views on these matters. What seems clear is that while we might agree that what our culture believes right another culture may believe wrong (cultural relativism), we are not willing to let our cultures set the *standard* for right and wrong; we do not believe that majorities are lucky, inspired by God, or for *any* reason unable to be mistaken about morality,

The coherence of cultural ethical relativism also is in doubt, for how are we to determine what constitutes a culture? Anthropologists who studied island societies or New Guinean tribes had little difficulty determining cultural boundaries. But what is our culture? Are its boundaries determined by European descent, Christianity, noncommunism, or America? And why stop there? Can being a Roman Catholic, a black person, a Mississippian, or a youth under thirty define one's culture? The cultural standard now becomes meaningless, for anyone can simply locate that majority, however delimited, that already morally agrees with him, call it "his culture," and thereby "prove" his moral beliefs to be true.

3. Individual relativism: "Whatever a person thinks is right *is* right for him." It is probably from this point of view that someone who wanted to be a relativist would criticize cultural ethical relativism: "His *culture* may think it is wrong, but it's right *for him*." Now, the first thing to notice is that the *"for him"* is crucial and the source of whatever appeal this form of ethical relativism is likely to have. Without the "for him" it becomes "Whatever a person thinks is right *is* right," which is plainly unacceptable because it implies that contradictory moral beliefs are both true. What, then, does "right for him" mean, if it doesn't mean "right"?

Compare it with "true for him." Some people have claimed that whatever a person thinks is true *is* true, *for him*. On this view, if I think the world is flat and you think the world is round, then it is true (for me) that the world is flat and at the same time true (for you) that the world is round. Now what does *this* mean? Does it mean that the world is both flat and round at the same time? And that "thinking makes it so"—that we each have a power of mind over matter and can make the world flat or round, to suit our beliefs? We clearly must mean something else by "true for me." Let me suggest that if it means anything at all to say that a belief is true for me, it means that it is my *opinion*, or that I think or *believe* (perhaps with great conviction) that it is true. If this is so—if "true for him" means the same as "he thinks it's true"—the claim that we are now considering means "whatever a person thinks (or believes) is true is something that he thinks (or believes) is true"; but this is trivial and something no one ever would care to deny.

If the analogy between "true for me" and "right for me" holds, then to say "whatever I think is right *is* right, *for me*" means that if I think something is right, then I think, believe, or am convinced that it is right. And this again is completely trivial and not worth saying. It is hard to see what else we could mean by "right for me." It looks as though it must mean either "it is right" or "I believe it is right," both of which are unacceptable.

All of us sometimes change our minds about what we think is right and realize that some of our earlier moral opinions were based on incomplete knowledge or insufficient sensitivity to a situation, or that they were inconsistent with one another. In these cases we do not conclude that we have traded one correct moral opinion for another; we say that our earlier opinions were mistaken or unjustified. It makes a difference to us what moral views we accept or keep, and this implies that we all are aware of a difference between acceptable and unacceptable moral opinions: we try, difficult as it may be, to keep justified opinions and eliminate unjustified ones. However, this seems to be incompatible with any theory, such as the one we are considering here, which implies that *any* moral opinion of ours is as acceptable as any other.

The above argument against the "right for me" doctrine is persuasive, but unfortunately it begs the question. Just as some anthropologists, in their argument for cultural ethical relativism, simply *assumed* that "right" means no more than "believes right," the argument against individual relativism simply *assumes* that "right" is distinct from "believes right." What I mean is this: It is easy to show that if "right for me" means "believes right," individual relativism is trivial and if "right for me" means "right," individual relativism is absurd. But showing this seems to *assume* that "right" contrasts with "believes right" in a way that implies that what one *believes* is objectively true or false. In other words, the argument about what "right for me" means already assumes that "right" contrasts with "believes right" in the same way that "true" contrasts with "believes true," and hence that a person might believe action X is right when X is in fact wrong. Yet I think that it is just this kind of claim that ethical relativists are anxious to deny. They are unhappy interpreting "right for me" as "believes right" when "believes right" is thought of as contrasting with "right" in the way described above.

Ethical relativism, *as relativists usually present it*, does indeed have some totally unacceptable implications, implications that seem to be the opposite of what an ethical relativist is trying to say. For one thing, it implies that moral beliefs are objectively true or false, that they are scientifically testable propositions. According to cultural ethical relativism I can test my moral beliefs for truth or falsity by polling my culture. According to individual ethical relativism, all my moral beliefs will be true (for me) and never in disagreement with yours (which are true for you).

Merely pointing out these implications, however, fails to be sufficiently sensitive to what the relativist is trying to do with the notions of "for him" and "for them." I want to suggest that the "right for me and wrong for you" advocate is not out to establish a method of verifying or testing moral beliefs. He does not wish to claim that moral truth can be scientifically established as a function of the opinions of either groups or individuals. *He wishes to claim that there isn't any moral truth, there is just moral opinion.* The expression "right for him" expresses his rejection of the usual notion that moral opinions divide into true ones and false ones. He resists the assimilation of "right for him" to either "right" or "believes right" for the same kind of reason: he admits that people have moral beliefs but he rejects whatever appears to imply that moral beliefs are true or false propositions.

If this is so, then he is not really a relativist but a kind of noncognitivist (see the last part of Chapter 2). What he really wants is a theory that says that a moral belief is a favorable or unfavorable attitude of some kind and a moral judgment is an expression of such an attitude. On this theory the "right/believes right" distinction can be made to disappear: A person's judging that something is right or good is his *act* of approving, expressing support, holding dear, recommending, or prescribing something; it is his *valuing* something. In all probability ethical relativism is a view expressed by people who really want to be "emotivists" or "noncognitivists" of some sort, but who do not know how to escape the objectivist implications of the "right/believes right" dichotomy. If one offers them any reasonably clear version of noncognitivism they will, with relief, adopt it and abandon these forms of ethical relativism.

Given this, to claim that an action is "right for Georgia" and "wrong for Harry" is an understandable way of putting the matter. It implies neither that all sincere moral judgments are true nor that minorities (in a given culture) are always mistaken. It is a way, though a somewhat awkward way, of saying that Georgia approves of the action and that Harry disapproves, and has the virtue of not implying that in addition to the fact that Georgia approves, and the fact that Harry disapproves, there is yet another fact which is the rightness or wrongness of what is disapproved.

On this interpretation the controversy now is fairly clear: Is noncognitivism true? Is it correct to claim that moral beliefs and judgments are neither true nor false but, somewhat like loves and hates, are attitudes and expressions of attitudes? If a relativist moves to this position, he must defend it, and nothing in the relativist's usual defense and description of his position is evidence for the truth of noncognitivism. On the other hand, if a relativist rejects the noncognitivist interpretation, his theory implies unacceptable and silly tests for the truth of moral beliefs.

4. "Everyone ought to do what he thinks is right." This is asserted sometimes as an implication of (3) and sometimes independently. View (4) is a claim many people think is obviously true. Yet, consider

the actions of Rudolf Hess, the Nazi commandant of Auschwitz concentration camp, who claimed at Nuremberg that he did what at the time he believed was right and his duty. It is worth noting that General Eisenhower, knowing that Hess believed he did right in killing the Jews in Auschwitz, refused to salute only Hess from among the Nazi defendants he interviewed in 1945.

People in general have mixed feelings about this kind of case. We all believe that people ought to do the right thing, but we distinguish this idea from what is *believed* to be right only when we disagree with a moral view someone is about to act on. Once there is a disagreement I think many people are inclined to say both that Hess shouldn't have done so-and-so, and that everyone ought to do what he *thinks* is right, without worrying much about the consistency of saying both of these things. It is easy enough to make such claims look inconsistent. To take a different example, suppose that a black man says that every person ought to do what he believes is right, and suppose further that there exists a white deputy sheriff who believes that it is right for him to shoot black men who go out with white girls. It follows that the black man *must*, on pain of logical inconsistency, agree that the deputy sheriff ought to shoot black men who go out with white girls. He cannot escape the logic of arguments like the following:

1. If the sheriff believes that it is right for him to perform a certain action, then he ought to perform that action.
2. The sheriff believes that it is right for him to shoot me.
∴ 3. The sheriff ought to shoot me.

If the black man also believes that sheriffs ought not to shoot black men who go out with white girls, he contradicts himself.

But he will reformulate his views in the attempt to avoid the contradiction, and it is here that ethical relativism can again enter the picture. What would he be likely to say, as an intelligent nonphilosopher, when confronted with the apparent inconsistency of saying both that the sheriff ought not to shoot him and that the sheriff ought to do what he thinks is right? Very likely what, by now, is familiar: "It is right for him but it is wrong for me, that is to say, the sheriff ought to do it, from his point of view, but he ought not, from my point of view."

We can be brief with the familiar alternatives. If, by "from his point of view," he merely means that *the sheriff thinks* he ought to shoot him, the view is trivial, and if he means that the sheriff *really* ought to shoot him, he makes a racist claim inconsistent (we assume) with what he really believes.

Yet, there again may be another alternative. If you are at all sympathetic to the view, "Everybody ought to do what he thinks is right," notice that while you may be tempted to accept "The sheriff ought to shoot you," you are not at all tempted to accept "You ought to be shot." This is because the latter is an impersonal claim that makes no reference to an individual whose belief about the matter might somehow be relevant. As we saw in Chapter 5, we are usually willing to rephrase moral claims impersonally: If I think I *ought to pay* my debt, I agree that my debt *ought to be paid;* if we think the judge ought to imprison the burglar, we also think the burglar ought to be imprisoned; and so on. We go from "A ought to do so-and-so" to "so-and-so ought to be done."

Now if the black man claims that the sheriff ought to shoot him (because the sheriff thinks he ought), but denies that he ought to be shot, we can take the black man to mean that this obligation exists *only relatively;* and consequently that when he says that it is right for the sheriff to shoot him, he means that the sheriff ought to do it in a sense that does not imply that it ought to be done. Notice that people hold this view, if at all, only for opinions with which they disagree. For if the sheriff thinks he should shoot the fleeing murder suspect, and the black man agrees, he will claim both that the sheriff ought to shoot the fleeing murder suspect and that the fleeing murder suspect ought to be shot.

Now I suspect that this interpretation of ethical relativism most clearly makes sense if one adopts *noncognitivism,* the view discussed in Chapter 2; it may *only* make sense if one is a noncognitivist, but about this I am not sure. In Chapter 5 this distinction between "he ought to do it" and "it ought to be done" is raised as part of a suggestion that *relativizing* ethical egoism is a possible defense against the charge of inconsistency.

In summary, I am inclined to think that ethical relativism, at best, is an awkward and misleading stand-in for emotivism or noncognitivism. Yet there remains an important problem regarding the *attitude toward morality* that an ethical relativist may adopt, once he abandons the naïve forms of cultural and individual ethical relativism. He may say, "It is right *for the sheriff* that he do it and it is wrong *for me* that he do it; but it isn't *really* right or wrong for either of us; therefore my opinion isn't any better (more justified, closer to the truth) than the sheriff's." What disturbs him is his belief that if his moral opinion lacks any objective status, if it merely is a personal attitude, then his personal attitude cannot be superior to the sheriff's personal attitude; it is just one more attitude, on all fours with that of the sheriff. In other words he rejects an objective morality but at the same time believes that morality cannot be the serious and genuine thing it ought to be unless there is an objective morality.

One way to attempt an answer to this problem would be to defend the view that moral beliefs are not just attitudes but propositions, some of which can be rationally defended as more probably true than others.

But if noncognitivism is true—and this is what someone who begins as an ethical relativist is likely to come to believe—then I am not certain that a completely satisfactory answer can be found. Two relevant considerations, however, are the following.

First, many of the steps we take to show the acceptability or unacceptability of a moral belief are independent of whether moral beliefs are attitudes or propositions. We know that some moral beliefs are based on misinformation or distortion, some are confused and incoherent, and some are inconsistent either in themselves or with other things the person believes. These kinds of criticisms, often combined with universalization arguments, can show most moral disputes to be rationally resolvable (whether or not they are actually resolved). In our example, the black man may claim that his belief is "just an attitude" and that the sheriff's belief is "just an attitude." Yet this cannot prevent him from demonstrating, quite objectively, that the sheriff's moral belief is *ignorant,* that is, dependent on beliefs about racial traits, the genetics of interracial mating, and so on, which are simply false; nor is his ethical theory relevant to the truth of the hypothesis that what produces the sheriff's belief and behavior are fears, hostilities, and habits that no informed and rational person would admit to be morally relevant. Where theory becomes relevant is when we have ultimate moral disagreements—that is, disagreements (assuming there are such) that logic and facts cannot resolve. These moral beliefs, given noncognitivism, might properly be called "mere attitudes."

Second, a peculiar kind of confusion may partly account for views like the following: "Well, I guess she's as right as I am, for she believes what she believes and I believe what I believe." In analytical discussions, though not when one is personally engrossed in a problem, a person can be tempted to "step out of himself" and play third party, as though he were a neutral observer with no moral opinion about the matter. And then he may view his own moral belief (about which he actually feels deeply and has no doubts) and the sheriff's moral belief merely as two conflicting attitudes. He may, in this abstracted mood, view himself and the sheriff much as a haughty, "value-free" anthropologist might sit on a hill and watch two tribes slug it out. Imagining himself in the shoes of a third party who has no moral opinion about the matter is as much a mistake as imagining himself in the shoes of the sheriff who has an opposite moral opinion. *He* is neither of those persons and he does not, when he isn't forgetting who he is, think for one minute that the sheriff is as right as he or that the one opinion is no better than the other. What I am trying to emphasize is the difference between thinking of moral beliefs, including your own, as just a collection of dull biographical facts, and realizing that *your own* moral beliefs, like your loves and aversions, are unique in that they are what *you* accept and want to live by.

Chapter 7

Punishment:
Utility and Retribution

On what grounds, if any, are we sometimes justified in punishing people for what they do? That people *do* intentionally punish or penalize others is indisputable, for example, we spank and deny privileges to children; we fine, imprison, or execute people convicted of crimes; and we censure, suspend, fire, excommunicate, demote, or expel officials, police officers, executives, students, soldiers, and so on.

It is almost always done for a reason that is intended to *justify* it. Moreover, however much we may want someone punished, we never say merely, "I *want* her fired" (or killed, and so on) when we aim to justify it. Almost all reasons for punishment belong to one or another of two famous theories of punishment: *utilitarianism,* exemplified when we say of the sentenced criminal, "Let him be an example for others," and *retribution,* exemplified when we say, "She had it coming to her." We must examine each to see if it can provide rational and coherent reasons for punishing people.

Utilitarianism starts from the premise that all punishing is doing harm to someone, together with the principle that no one ever deserves to be harmed. The logical conclusion is that punishment is never justified for any behavior *unless* it also does good—to the punished person or to others—that outweighs the harm it does. When we propose to spank, censure, or execute somebody, the utilitarian's crucial question is always, "What good will it do?" If it does none, or none that outweighs the pain or loss to the punished person, but merely expresses our desire for revenge, "justice," or retribution, then the punishment is unjustified and immoral. For example, to a utilitarian, God is immoral if He ever sends people to hell because infinitely long suffering in hell is not outweighed by any good this produces, and in any case more good or happiness would be produced by sending everyone to heaven.

There are three kinds of good or utility that punishment can produce.

1. *Prevention:* Jailing people for stealing cars prevents them from stealing cars, at least while they are in jail. The good produced is the safety and continued possession of our cars.
2. *Rehabilitation:* Spanking children or fining lawbreakers may increase the likelihood that they will behave better in the future. Jailing people gives officials the opportunity to reform them and teach them a trade as an alternative to crime.
3. *Deterrence:* Jailing, fining, or executing people for specific kinds of acts makes other people afraid to do those kinds of acts and therefore has the beneficial effect that the harmful acts are done less frequently.

A good example to examine is capital punishment for murder. What good does it do? First, there is no doubt that it *prevents* the murderer from murdering again. Second, it is equally plain that it does not rehabilitate. Finally, does it *deter?* Of course. But the important question is this: Is execution a *better* deterrent than some otherwise acceptable alternative such as a life sentence? On the answer to this question utilitarians rest their case. If they think that execution is a better deterrent than life sentences, they will conclude that capital punishment is the more justified of these two alternatives, otherwise not. For the utilitarian the answer lies in carefully analyzing and comparing the murder rates in capital punishment states and in abolition states, in order to determine which of these punishments makes us safer. Prevention is less important because records show that few people sentenced to prison for murder commit murder again in prison and very few paroled murderers commit murder again.

The retributivist's basic principles are that no one should be punished at all unless he deserves to be punished and that no one should be given a greater punishment than he deserves. Whether a person deserves punishment depends only on what he did and his state of mind when he did it (some say, only on his state of mind, including how he conceived of what he did). Retributivists deny that a person should be punished just because punishing him will produce some benefit in the future. They look only to the past to justify punishment, whereas utilitarians look only to the future. For this reason retributivists dismiss the question "What good will it do?" as irrelevant to what a person deserves.

The retributivist's claim that a person's punishment must fit his offense is the basis for one famous objection to utilitarianism. For a utilitarian, if a punishment has superior utility it is justified; what the person is thought to *deserve* plays no role because no one deserves to suffer no matter what he does. Therefore it appears that it need not matter whether a person actually did what he is punished for; it could be enough if most people think he did it and his punishment "sets an example for others." Yet punishing an innocent person always seems to be unjust and unfair.

There is an equally well-known answer to this objection. Mill probably would claim that the *general practice* of punishing innocent people would be generally injurious, on the grounds that it would make people fearful and cynical about our system of criminal justice. In other words he would ask: "What if everybody (with appropriate authority) did that?" The crucial claim is that the general practice of punishing innocent people could lack utility even though each particular act of this sort could, considered by itself, have utility. When a utilitarian makes this kind of response he has changed his theory to what is called "rule utilitarianism" (see Chapter 3). He no longer applies his basic happiness principle to individual acts but instead uses it to justify *rules* such as "One ought not to punish innocent persons."

Yet there is a related and more general problem that each theory has a very difficult time resolving: How can we find satisfactory grounds for determining *how much* a person should be punished? Let us take auto theft as an example. The utilitarian appeals to several factors including (1) how much punishment is needed to keep the auto theft rate at an acceptable level; (2) public revulsion to severe punishment—death by torture, while it would nicely lower the auto theft rate, would lack utility because the public would hate it and perhaps juries would refuse to convict; (3) how much the public hates and fears the crime, which determines what it considers an "acceptable level," for example, we are willing to tolerate more auto theft than murder.

A clear merit of utilitarianism is that the above constitutes a definite, empirical method, complicated though it is, for calculating how severely a person should be punished. The problem is that it seems unjust. Suppose I steal a car to repaint and keep for myself. It seems unjust to determine my punishment by how many other people have been stealing cars lately: I might be given a longer sentence if the theft rate is on the upswing, or a shorter one if the judge or lawmakers notice that the rate has declined. I am not responsible for other people's auto thefts and what I do seems to be no worse just because of what other people do.

The retributivists' problem is this: They do not even have a method for determining punishment. Retributivists wish to give a murderer the punishment he deserves, not the punishment that is most useful in controlling future would-be murderers. What a particular murderer deserves depends on two things: (1) how guilty he is and (2) what degree of punishment is appropriate to that degree of guilt. However, there is no quantifiable method for determining this. One would have to be able, like God, to see into a murderer's mind and determine his degree of guilt and, *in addition,* match that particular degree of guilt with the "proper" degree of punishment. How does one even begin to do this?

Here are two often heard answers. The first is the "eye for an eye" method. Even if it worked for eyes and killings, how would it work for rapists? Should rapists be raped, and what if they would enjoy it? And how would we apply this method to public drunks, propertyless vandals, blackmailers with clean pasts, and spies? More importantly, the "eye for an eye" doctrine completely ignores the intentions and other mental factors that are essential to retributivism. What of the person who carelessly kills or blinds another? It is impossible for the law to set out to "carelessly" kill or blind him, nor does reciprocation ever seem just for that majority of crimes that are not fully premeditated.

The other popular suggestion is that the victim should determine the offender's punishment. One objection is that punishments wouldn't be predictable; another is that it would be to a criminal's advantage to choose "forgiving" types of victims. More important, punishments would be unreflective and overly severe. Many victims of even minor crimes are enraged at their victimization and would want to see their assailant shot, beaten to death, or imprisoned, in cases where impartial, reflective observers, including judges and juries, would mete out much lighter penalties. Think of the people who believe that they are justified in shooting trespassers.

What usually happens is that the retributivist who attempts to defend a certain degree of punishment finds himself appealing to utilitarian considerations, such as the frequency of the crime or the degree to which other people fear and hate it. Yet these seem to be irrelevant to what a person deserves.

A common criticism of retributivism is that no one ever deserves to suffer and that retribution is nothing more than revenge. Of course, what the utilitarian calls "revenge" the retributivist calls "justice" and merely *calling* it revenge is not to refute it. The beginning of an argument is the point, mentioned above, that there seems to be no rational method for determining how much punishment a person deserves (as distinct from how much would be useful).

There is, however, something that the "mere revenge" objection usually overlooks. If you are convinced that no one ever deserves retribution or "has it coming to him," are you equally convinced that no one ever deserves happiness or deserves a certain benefit, grade, or reward? If the notion of "deserving something" makes sense at all, and some people deserve good things, why isn't it also true that some people deserve bad things? Most of us do believe that heroes, athletes, and students should get their medals, prizes, and good grades *if and only if they deserve them* and that it would be unjust to withhold earned benefits simply because doing so would make the world on the whole a little happier. If it is true that sometimes people ought to get something, either a good or an evil, because they deserve it and not just because their getting it has utility, then it is false that utilitarianism is the sole basis for what we ought to do. It should be mentioned that this argument, whether or not it is a strong one, applies equally to rule utilitarianism and act utilitarianism, for if it is true that sometimes an individual *deserves* a benefit, then it will be false that he should get it *only because* his getting it has utility, and also false that he should get it *only because* the general practice of benefiting people who do what he did has utility.

Chapter 8

Religion and Morality

Millions of people say or imply that there cannot be morality without religion. Given how much people differ from one another, we must admit that a great many claims about the relation between religion and morality may, psychologically speaking, be true of some people. More important, however, are claims implying that religion is in some sense *necessary for anyone* to have a morality. We shall consider five such claims and try to show that each of them, with the possible exception of the last, is either false, very doubtful, or does not really give religion an essential role in morality:

1. The very meaning of the word "wrong" is "disapproved by God."
2. God is the only reliable source of moral knowledge.
3. Divine sanctions are necessary for almost anyone to act morally.
4. God, as the idea of an ideal observer, is the standard of morality.
5. God's authority is the only alternative to ethical relativism.

1. *Theological definitions of moral words:* If someone claims that "right" and "wrong" mean "whatever God approves and disapproves" and that otherwise these words have no meaning, he is proposing what in Chapter 2 I called a *definist ethical theory.* We must remember that this is a claim about *what words mean,* distinct from other (perhaps more appealing) views such as "Only God can tell us what is right and wrong" or "God sets the standard of right and wrong." People who say that the word "right" *means* "what God approves" usually either say it only for rhetorical effect or have no clear distinction in mind between definitions and moral principles. Yet we have to consider the position.

We must be careful to distinguish the claim that "approved by God" is *a* meaning of the word "right" from the claim that it is *the* one and only correct meaning of the word. If atheists accepted the latter claim they would have to admit that they could not even *believe* that anything is right or wrong, on the grounds that they do not believe there is a God to approve or disapprove anything. Yet atheists naturally do not admit that "approved by God" is the one and only correct meaning of "right," and there does not seem to be any way to prove that they should admit this. The very most that atheists are likely to admit is that they and the religious moralists give different meanings to the words "right" and "wrong," and perhaps even that the religious definition is the more commonly used and accepted one. This concession would still allow atheists to have a morality. It would not even imply that atheists and religious moralists disagreed morally, for they might believe the very same actions to be right and wrong, though for different ultimate reasons. Further, it would not have been shown that the atheists' sense of right and wrong is an incorrect or inferior one, but only that they do not mean "approved by God" by the word "right."

However, an atheist need not concede even this much. First, there isn't any good evidence that "right" and "wrong" are definable at all, and moreover there is considerable evidence that atheists and religious people mean the same thing by "right" and "wrong." For example, they may agree about what actions are right and wrong, and feel remorse, guilt, and satisfaction on similar occasions. The word "meaning" often is used very loosely when talking about right and wrong, and there is nothing necessarily bad about this. We often say "What do you mean by 'right'?" when we merely want to know what things you think *are* right. But if " 'right' means 'approved by God' " is offered as a strict definition, then it has to be defended as a *linguistic* claim. And how can this definition be defended except by appealing to usage, including the usage of atheists?

Arguments about what moral words mean tend to become very difficult and confusing, partly because what "meaning" is is perplexing and controversial, and partly because people who offer religious definitions of "right" and "wrong" really want to make different kinds of claims, claims that are not just about words. Let us then get on to these other claims.

2. *God as the only reliable information source:* Suppose someone says that the only way a person can know for sure that anything is right or wrong is to learn it from God. People have conflicting moral opinions, and the only way to prove which of these opinions are true and which are false is to consult the word of God. The basis for this is simply that because God knows everything, He knows what is right and wrong.

How would you come to know God's word? Either because God speaks directly to you ("voices," mystical experiences), or from a conscience implanted by God, or from revealed scripture. The mystical experiences view will not support the claim that religion is necessary for morality because very few people even claim to hear God directly, and so morality would be inaccessible to most of us. Neither will the conscience view, for three main reasons: First, people disagree about what the "voice of conscience" says. Even if we said that only the true, uncorrupted voice of conscience comes from God, we would be left without a way to distinguish true from corrupted promptings of conscience. Second, atheists appear to have consciences too. To deny this seems to require the question-begging assumption that God implants consciences only in religious people. Third, if I ask you to consult your conscience, I don't expect you to listen for a little voice, distinct from yourself, as though it were a radio buried in your head. I would mean that you should consult your moral principles and earnestly try to figure out how they apply in some particular case. In fact, with the exception of mystics who claim to hear God directly, asking people what their conscience says seems to be the same as asking them what their moral beliefs are; and it is also, I think, asking them to pay attention to the morality of a situation when you suspect that they might not. So there appears to be nothing about conscience that can be shown to depend on religion, unless we can first show that moral beliefs themselves depend on religion.

This leaves us with revealed scripture. The obvious problems are: (1) Books which are claimed to be the revealed word of God disagree about some matters of morality, so how are we to determine which is the word of God and which is not? The New Testament, the Old Testament, the Koran, the Book of Mormon, or yet some other book? (2) These books not only are silent on many current moral issues, for example, oral contraception and the use of atomic bombs, they also are subject to furious and apparently endless controversy regarding their correct interpretation.

I would like to suggest a more basic criticism. What, long ago, made people first come to think that certain ethical writings were the revealed word of God? My suggestion is that such decisions are made partly on moral grounds: We first discover that a book agrees with what we already believe are our deepest and noblest moral opinions and then, since we also believe that God is good, we conclude that what the book says is the moral viewpoint of God. If this is so, people did not learn what was moral from holy books—they decided that the books were holy in large part because the books said what people already thought was moral.

Consider the matter in another way. The documents that became part of the New Testament were authenticated, by various Church councils in the early Christian centuries, in large part on the basis of their imputed history, their style, the language they were written in, and so on. Imagine a document to be exactly like one that was judged authentic, with one exception: It taught that you should always look out only for yourself and that you should kill your neighbor if he gets in your way. There is no chance that this document would be thought a correct account of the teachings of Christ (and hence of God) and incorporated within the New Testament. If at first attributed to an apostle, the attribution would be denied or the author would be denied to be a true apostle. The Church Fathers would reject it as a genuine part of the Bible because it said what they already knew to be immoral.

I have been offering the suggestion that morality does not literally come from God but that, instead, people attribute to God whatever they already believe is true morality. If this is so, then it is not true that revealed scripture is the origin of our knowledge of right and wrong.

However, other points can be made on the side of religion. There is no doubt that religion, when spread by conversion or military conquest, brought moral change, and where established, was the chief agency of formal moral education. Where Islam, Christianity, and Buddhism went, moral practices changed, very often for the better, such as in greater care for the poor and sick and the elimination of human sacrifice, and sometimes for the worse, as in the case of burning witches and slaughtering nonbelievers. We should not forget that the clergy, of whatever religion, are the only professional group in the world who see moral education, advice, and reform as an integral and important part of their professional duties.

3. *Divine sanctions:* A *sanction* is a threat or an enticement designed to make a person willing to do (or to forbear doing) what he otherwise might not be willing to do (or forbear doing). A criminal penalty for auto theft that is written into the law is a sanction. It does not say what is right or wrong; it merely states what is likely to happen to you if you steal a car, but in so doing it supplies a prudential motive or reason for not stealing cars. Lawmakers presumably create the sanction because they think auto theft is wrong and harmful, but the existence and effectiveness of the sanction does not depend on anyone thinking that auto theft is wrong.

John Stuart Mill argues that the sanctions available to utilitarianism are of two kinds, *external sanctions,* which are the law and social disapproval, and an *internal sanction,* which is one's conscience. He apparently thinks of conscience as a source of satisfaction when you do what is right and of discomfort when you do what is wrong. We all know that regret, remorse, and "pangs of conscience" are genuine phenomena. But a difficulty Mill doesn't mention arises if you treat conscience *merely* as a sanction. If bad conscience is merely a source of discomfort, why shouldn't a person suffering from this malady find it best simply to treat it, for example, with psychiatry, drugs, or by repeating the act until one gets used to it and one's conscience is numbed? For example, if lying made your nose grow, even when you thought there was nothing wrong with lying, the rational solution would be to find an appropriate drug to counteract this effect. The point is that bad conscience is not *just* a pain or inconvenience, but involves and arises from your own *belief* that you did what was wrong. For this reason clever countermeasures cannot eliminate it, as they can eliminate or circumvent criminal sanctions, without first eliminating or altering the moral belief that lies behind it. Because bad conscience is inseparable from your moral beliefs, it is not a sanction in the sense in which we defined it above.

Divine sanctions are the punishment of hell or purgatory and the reward of heaven. Perhaps it is better to say that divine sanctions are the *promise* of these, and not heaven and hell themselves, for no one ever reports back that he has been in either. Is morality dependent on religion in the sense that very few people would be moral if they did not fear hell or desire heaven? The answer is pretty obviously no, because probably more than half the people in the world do not believe in an afterlife, and I am aware of no evidence that they are less moral than people who do. There are several kinds of reasons why people act morally, when they do, in addition to divine sanctions. There are other external sanctions such as law and social disapproval; there is social conditioning including education; people often reason out moral conclusions and then are moved by the force of that reasoning; and, finally, there is some evidence (see Chapter 9) that people are genetically disposed to engage in certain kinds of behavior of which we morally approve.

4. *God as the idea of an ideal observer:* Nearly everyone agrees that moral beliefs based on false information, logical mistakes, or confusion are unacceptable. Whatever other grounds we may have for criticism, it cannot be denied that when we criticize a moral claim on *these* grounds our criticism is *objective* in the sense that a provable mistake is involved and not just a different value or principle. Moral judgments that are not ignorant, illogical, or confused are more likely to be ones we ultimately will accept, and this suggests the hypothesis that if all people agreed about the facts, made no logical errors, and were not confused or crazy, they would agree about all matters of morality. This hypothesis will be recognized as a form of the unanimity thesis, and while it can be doubted, in any case it is plain that moral disagreement would be greatly diminished if the above conditions were met.

If we assume the truth of this hypothesis, we are easily led to a second hypothesis: A moral belief is true or acceptable if it is one a fully informed, logical, and clear-thinking observer would make. We can call such an observer an *ideal observer,* and theories that maintain that correct moral judgments are those an ideal observer would make are called ideal observer theories. Yet, no human being is an ideal observer. God (if He exists) would be one, for God by definition is omniscient, rational, and so on. If the ideal observer theory is true, then the idea of a correct moral judgment is dependent on the *idea* of an ideal observer, which it is not unreasonable to call God; but it is not dependent on the *existence* of an ideal observer.

It is irrelevant whether or not an ideal observer exists because the theory does not propose the ideal observer as someone you might consult; it does not, as does (2), maintain that an ideal observer or God is a source of moral information. Instead, the theory aims to show *how there can be such a thing* as a true or false moral opinion, contrary to the view many people hold that there are just moral opinions and no such thing as moral truth: A true moral opinion *is* one that an ideal observer *would* make *if* he existed. Yet the theory partly answers another question: Which moral opinions are true? For the theory implies that the more informed, logical, and clear-headed you are, the more likely you are to be morally correct.

5. *God's authority as the only alternative to ethical relativism:* What would happen if a person ceased to believe that morality is grounded in the will of God? Is it merely that she would lose a reliable method of confirmation and would no longer be sure which of her moral beliefs were true? Many religious people claim that the consequence would be much worse than this. What they claim is that nothing would really be either right or wrong, that, as Dostoevsky's character Ivan Karamazov put it, "If there is no God then anything is possible." Religious people sometimes express this by saying that if there were no God, then all there would be are lots of people with different moral opinions, and no one of these opinions would be "any better" or any closer to objective truth than any other opinion.

Of course, this way of putting the matter begs the question, for not only might there be objective moral truth without God, there might also be a rational procedure for determining what it is. More important, however, I want to suggest that what many people lost when they abandoned belief in God as the basis of morality is *not truth but authority.* What I mean is that if a person thinks of moral principles as objective *truths* (or falsehoods), then these principles are fair game for anyone to attempt to discover, and the most one would lose without God would be a degree of certainty. Although people might err when interpreting Holy Scripture, they would be more likely to err if they had to do all of their own moral truth seeking. This kind of loss does not begin to explain the tendency of people to think that nothing is really right or wrong if morality does not derive from God.

As a matter of history, morality has been externalized and objectified by being vested in authority: in the authority of one's God, one's nation, and so on. It is possible that one important reason for the durability of these doctrines is that they enable people to pass the responsibility for their moral beliefs and for the consequences of conscientiously acting on them to God, or to the Church, the State, or even to What Everybody Thinks. These entities, or those who speak for them, have accepted this responsibility and the power that goes with it.

When I say that many people accept God's authority in matters of morals, I do not mean that they accept him as an authority in the sense in which I accept Roger Tory Peterson as an authority about birds, that is, as someone who can be relied upon to utter truths about birds. I mean that many people accept God's authority in the way in which children often accept their parents' authority regarding what they are permitted and not permitted to do. If such moralists are asked the relatively abstract question, "Is what God forbids wrong?" they may reply yes and go on to say it is true that what God forbids is wrong. However, this response might involve a merely honorific use of the word "true." These moralists may mean only that they accept God's commands about how they should behave.

That is why this position is also different from (1), which says that "A is immoral" means "A is disapproved by God." On the present view moral claims are neither true by definition nor true as a matter of fact. They are not truths at all but commands issuing from an authority, and such moralists certainly need not accept or argue for linguistic claims about what moral words mean; unlike the definists they are not interested in words.

When moral skeptics and relativists ask rhetorically, "Who is to say what is right and wrong?" what they may mean is, "Who can replace God as the authority that grounds morality?" Philosophers, attempting to substitute objective knowledge for authority, might answer, "Whoever it is who knows." But skeptics and relativists may not be looking for a person who knows something; they reveal this by ritually questioning, ad infinitum, every further reason that a person who claims to know offers, regardless of whether or not they personally agree with the reasons offered. They may be looking for a being *whose saying so suffices*; if so, they are interested in his nature and status, not in his knowledge.

This position regarding the dependence of an "objective" morality on God's authority is difficult to appraise. Some people, whether or not they are atheists, believe that there are moral truths that are as "objective" as geological truths and, in principle, as knowable. For them, God's authority is not needed. Others deny that there is moral knowledge—they are emotivists or noncognitivists who believe that moral judgments are neither true nor false but are individual acts of expressing approval or disapproval; and it can be argued that there is a degree of skepticism and/or relativism implicit in this view. Now suppose that noncognitivism is correct, which is quite possible. It is plausible to suppose that if we also believed God existed and issued moral commands to us, then we would have and accept a morality by comparison with which secular noncognitivism would not be considered a morality at all. This indeed may be how many religious people view all secular morality, and it may sometimes be what lies behind the claim that there cannot be morality without religion. For God's authority and the interpersonal standards it implies would be superior to the competing *human* authorities implied by some versions of noncognitivism: with the latter come intractable moral conflicts on basic issues and the sense that we cannot confute our moral opponents with *either* truth *or* divine authority.

Chapter 9

Reasons and Causes

If a typical American had been brought up from infancy in a small village in India instead of in America he or she undoubtedly would have been a Hindu instead of a Christian or Jew. We can surmise that some of his or her moral beliefs also would have been different. Hypotheses like this seem to lead to the following claim: Moral opinions are *produced or caused* by social and religious conditioning. This claim is most plausible if we take it to mean only that *most* people brought up in such-and-such an environment will have certain predictable moral opinions, for we know that moral eccentricity, rebellion, and reform occur and often are very difficult to explain in terms of what we know of an individual's environment. People sometimes make more specific causal claims such as "Harry's traumatic childhood experiences *made him* believe that sex is evil" or "Mary believes that national health insurance is morally wrong *because* her father is a rich physician and her own ambition is to be a rich physician."

Now it is fairly clear that these causal claims are made in order to criticize or dismiss Harry's and Mary's moral beliefs. The criticism lies in the fact that the causes obviously do not justify the moral beliefs: They provide no *reason* why anyone, including Mary, should think that national health insurance is wrong. When we offer causes in criticism of a moral belief, we commit what is called the *genetic fallacy. The fallacy lies in assuming that a belief is false, unjustified, or unsupported by good reasons, because it has a certain causal origin (or genesis).* Even if our causal account of Mary's belief is true, there still can be good reasons for her position on national health insurance, and in fact Mary herself may offer these reasons.

There can be both *reasons for* and *causes of* Mary's moral belief that are quite distinct from one another. In fact, if we accept the hypo-thesis we began with, *every* moral belief that exists had a causal origin sufficient to produce it, but only *some* moral beliefs are supported or supportable by reasons that we think are rational and informed. Mary's moral belief may be one of these even if it is true that what *makes* her hold the belief is her desire to be a rich physician. This is why the genetic fallacy is a fallacy.

Reasons for and causes of beliefs *are about different things.* The cause accounts for a certain biographical fact about Mary—"Mary's believing X is wrong." The reason aims to *justify* what Mary believes —"X is wrong," which is a moral claim, not a biographical claim about Mary. Whatever the cause of her having the belief, the reasons she gives for it could be good reasons, other reasons for her claim could be good ones too, and her claim could be a justified one.

Our claim that Mary's financial ambitions caused her to morally condemn national health insurance is not a criticism of Mary's *moral belief* but a criticism of *Mary,* for we imply that the reason she gives (assuming she gives a reason) is "not the real reason" why she con-demns it. The "real reason" is her desire to be rich, and this is neither admirable nor relevant as a basis for her moral position. Suppose that Mary says her reason is that national health insurance is inefficient as well as unjust to physicians, and suppose further that she is sincere— she really thinks that is why it is wrong. We might still claim that the "real reason" (by which we mean, of course, "the cause") why she thinks it is wrong is her desire for wealth. If so, we mean that Mary is rationalizing. *To rationalize is to give reasons in justification of one's belief or behavior when the real cause of the belief or behavior is some-thing entirely different.* Sometimes there is the suggestion that ration-alizers are deceiving themselves (whatever this means) or that the real cause is fear or self-interest.

To commit the genetic fallacy often is to accuse someone of ra-tionalizing, especially when the causes adduced are the person's de-sires, fears, or pet ideas; we say things like "She only thinks it's wrong because she's afraid of so-and-so." Nevertheless, we can claim that someone is rationalizing without our committing the genetic fallacy.

An example should make this clear. President Richard Nixon, shortly before he resigned, claimed it would be wrong for him to hand over the famous Watergate tape recordings, for the reasons that execu-tive privilege and the constitutional separation of powers must be preserved. Now one might argue that he lied—he did not really think handing over the tapes was wrong; he merely feared it would result in impeachment. But suppose he sincerely thought it was wrong; we can still claim that "the real reason" (that is, the cause) for his moral belief was his fear of impeachment. In other words, we can claim that he was rationalizing. *If* we went on to claim that *therefore* he should hand over the tapes, we would be guilty of the genetic fallacy. But we can claim that he is rationalizing whether or not we think the reasons he gave are good reasons: We might agree that Nixon ought not to turn over the tapes, for the reasons he gave, and still think that what made Nixon think he should keep the tapes is nothing but his fears. There is yet another possibility: Maybe Nixon was neither lying nor rationalizing. In this case we would mean that Nixon believed the act would be wrong *because of* the reasons he gave, and this implies that he would still have thought that it was wrong even if he did not fear impeachment.

If our reasons can be good ones, whatever the causes, why should we care what causes our moral beliefs? For one thing, our intellectual self-respect seems to require that we believe that the reasons we think are justifying reasons are *also* what make us hold the beliefs they justify. I think this is probably true of all reason giving, whether it be reasons in support of actions, of moral beliefs, or of nonmoral beliefs. For example, if a man believes flying saucers are real, he hopes he believes it because of the evidence he offers; he would be disturbed if he learned that a drug or hypnotic suggestion made him believe it and that he would believe it whether or not he had his evidence. If a woman believes that abortion is immoral, she thinks she believes it *because of* the principles and factual beliefs she offers as reasons: She not only thinks that these principles are why abortion *is* immoral, she also thinks that these principles are a necessary part of why *she believes* abortion is immoral. And if she came to think that something else, like a drug or her father's shouting, is what made her believe it and that her principles were irrelevant to her believing it, she would feel that she was irrational.

Sometimes we rationalize and sometimes we do not. When we do, we lack a certain kind of self-knowledge, in the sense that we do not know what makes us hold our moral belief (and consequently do not know what kind of change would make us abandon it). The rationalizer thinks he believes X because of the reasons he gives, but he does not; he would believe X in any case and therefore the reasons are ornaments, produced or acquired after the fact.

Occasionally people say, "I think national health insurance is wrong because I was brought up to believe that way" or "Society has conditioned me to think that heroin using is immoral." They are guessing at causes of their own moral beliefs. Their attitude is hard to understand, for if they do not think there are reasons why these things are wrong, why *do* they think they are wrong? And if they *do* have reasons, why do they give mere causes?

Imagine saying this: "Harry over there hypnotized me and said that when he snapped his fingers, I would wake up and believe my shoes cost $50. He snapped his fingers, I woke up, and that's why I believe my shoes cost $50." The silliness of this involves more than just an affront to intellectual self-respect. You might say that because of the hypnosis you believed for awhile that your shoes cost $50, or that someone else now believes it, but it is almost impossible to imagine your saying this about *your own present belief* and meaning it.

You may, before the hypnotic suggestion is revealed to you, imagine remembering paying $50 for the shoes. This is a good example of a rationalization (though without the usual implication of a self-serving interest). When you learn what happened and see the supposed memory of paying $50 as a rationalization, *your knowledge liberates you* from the belief that your shoes cost $50. In general, we are simply unable to continue believing what we come to see we have no good reason to believe and good reasons for disbelieving. I am inclined to think that this shows that people are more rational regarding their beliefs than they often fancy themselves to be.

It seems equally difficult to understand people who say they think that national health insurance, heroin use, or abortion, is immoral because "I was conditioned to believe it," "brought up that way," or "brainwashed." Nobody ever would offer these causes as *reasons* why they believe abortion is wrong, for everybody knows that they are completely irrelevant to the right or wrong of abortion.

Ultimate moral beliefs might be exceptions to the points I have been making about reasons and causes. By definition, ultimate moral beliefs do not have reasons, but since, as with all beliefs, something must produce them, we assume that they have causes. If ultimate moral beliefs are neither supported by reasons nor perceived to be self-evidently true, then the *only* account we can give of them is a causal one. Noncognitivists would have to agree to this conclusion. But definists and intuitionists, while admitting that an ultimate belief lacks reasons, would still claim that it is more rational to accept it than to reject it, the intuitionist because it can simply be known to be true, and the definist because it can be known to be true by definition.

If we reject intuitionism and definism it will make sense to say, for example, "I think happiness is good, benevolence is (in general) good, and killing is (in general) wrong, simply because I am caused to think so." We may not know what the causes are beyond the fact that they lie in our genetic make-up together with our environment. It is important to remind ourselves, however, that few moral beliefs are ultimate ones and that most moral disagreements are not over ultimate principles. No one should think that his moral opinion of national health insurance, heroin use, or even abortion, is an ultimate moral belief in this sense.

Yet we must be cautious because our definition of an ultimate moral belief is simply that it is a belief unsupported by reasons. It seems to follow that *any* moral belief for which a person lacks reasons is an ultimate belief of that person. Sometimes people say, about highly specific and (to us) minor matters such as imbibing stimulants or some detail of sexual behavior, "I accept your arguments and rationally I see that there is nothing wrong with it, but I still *feel* (or think) that it is wrong." Given our definition, these may have to count as ultimate beliefs, in explanation of which we can supply only causes that we know to be irrelevant as reasons. Yet we often are ashamed of such beliefs unless they are very basic, general, and deeply felt ones, and often the knowledge that reasons we can accept are lacking eventually liberates us from them.

Just as it makes little sense to say "I believe abortion is immoral because I was brainwashed," it also makes little sense to say "I believe abortion is wrong because I want to believe it (or because I think I'll be happier believing it)." The reason is basically the same: You cannot believe something unless you think you have good reason to believe it, and this means that you cannot become self-conscious about your rationalizations and continue to hold the beliefs they purported to support. Again, ultimate moral beliefs may be exceptions. You and I know full well that *wanting* to believe something and thinking it will make us happy to believe something are absolutely irrelevant to whether or not the belief is true or justified or based on good reasons. Our wants and desires are just as irrelevant as reasons as are hypnotic suggestions and "brainwashing."

Again, consider an example. Suppose I offer you a million dollars for doing one very simple thing: All you have to do is believe the world is flat or believe that dancing is wicked (assuming you don't already believe these things). You have to believe it, not just say it. You cannot do it, of course, because you do not believe that my giving you a million dollars has anything to do with the shape of the earth or the morality of dancing. Sometimes people say that a person can believe what he wants to believe about morality or even that he can choose what moral principles to believe. But this cannot be true if taken literally. To believe something is to think it is true, justified, or supported by the best reasons, and the suggestion that you can *choose* your beliefs amounts to suggesting that you think you are able, by a mere act of will, to make some belief true, justified, or supported by the best reasons.

Yet there is a grain of truth in the claim that people sometimes believe what they want to believe, for as we have seen people can rationalize. It is possible, barely, that your desire for my million dollars could be what makes you believe that the world is flat or that dancing is wicked. But it does not seem possible that *you* could know this; you would have to think you had good reasons. You can know, of course, that some of your beliefs are rationalizations, but it is very doubtful that you could know *which* these were. This is somewhat analogous to the fact that, whereas I know that some of my present beliefs are false (since I am not God), I certainly cannot know *which* of my present beliefs are false.

So far we have discussed the irrelevance of causes to moral justification as well as some of the ways in which reasons and causes can be confused. There is, however, a positive and constructive side to the scientific investigation of the causes of moral beliefs. Let us turn our attention to causal explanations of morality, with the full realization that we are *not* now concerned with reasons and justification or with substitutes for them. Once scientists begin to inquire into the causes of people's moral beliefs, questions of ultimate origins become paramount. It is more intriguing the farther back such causes are traced, both because this gives us a sense that we are getting to the bottom of things and because it suggests the possibility of discovering cross-cultural moral attitudes which, unlike the products of particular cultures, are common to human nature.

Edward O. Wilson, in the book from which our selections are drawn, attempts to proclaim and organize the relatively new science of sociobiology. Sociobiology is a synthesis of evolutionary biology, genetics, and population biology that aims to bridge the gap between biological and cultural explanations of human behavior and attitudes. Wilson argues that some basic moral beliefs (and behavior) very likely are the product of natural selection or, in other words, that they are genetically determined or "innate" rather than "acquired." In particular, he defends the hypothesis that human beings, as a result of natural selection, are genetically determined to be *altruistic* in the sense of being disposed to help other people even when they do not think it is to their long-run advantage. Moreover, he maintains that we are not just disposed to *act* altruistically but also disposed to *approve* of it and to incorporate it within our morality.

Before we continue, something must be said about the potentially confusing notions of *innate* and *acquired*. People usually mean by an "acquired" trait one that is *neither inherited nor inheritable,* like learning English (rather than French). "Innate" traits are said to be in our genes, like brown eyes and sexual urges, and are inherited and inheritable. Many people think in terms of a rigid "innate/acquired" dichotomy, where what is acquired is learned and changeable and what is innate is "instinctive" and something we can do nothing to change.

What is wrong with the "innate/acquired" dichotomy is that *nothing* is wholly innate or "from nature" and nothing is wholly acquired or "from nurture": Behavior as well as bodily structures are always jointly affected by both genes and environment. This means that similar genes may have different behavioral effects in different cultures, just as in similar environments different genes may produce different effects. Behavior tends to get called *acquired* when the environmental causes are more interesting and more under our control than are the genetic causes. Behavior tends to get called *innate* when it is fairly similar in different environments, environments whose differences happen to interest us more than their similarities. The capacity of a gene to show a similar effect in different environments is called its *degree of penetrance* (though no gene will have the same effect in *all* environments, for we can always devise an environment in which the gene's effect will not appear).

A relatively clear though limited use of the notions of "innate" and "acquired" is this: When we ask if a pattern of behavior or a kind of moral belief is innate or "from nature," we are not asking if its causes include evolved genetic ones. The causes always include evolved genetic ones. We ask instead either of two different questions: (1) are people with a certain kind of moral belief genetically different from otherwise similar people without it? or (2) are the genetic causes of sufficient penetrance that the moral belief, or ones very similar to it, are shared by nearly all of humanity? These questions are important ones and to the second one, at least, Wilson and the biologists he discusses offer an answer.

It would seem that a kind of behavior, like anything else, can evolve only if it increases the organism's fitness, that is, makes it better able to produce offspring and therefore pass on the genes that determine the behavior. The primary obstacle to the evolution of altruistic attitudes and behavior is that altruism appears to benefit others rather than the altruist and therefore does not increase his fitness.

An example will show this. Birds of some flocking species give alarm cries when they see an approaching predator. This enables the flock to take cover sooner than it might otherwise, but it also appears to increase the likelihood that the predator will notice and catch the bird who gave the alarm cry. Flocks whose members regularly give alarm signals will have greater fitness than otherwise similar flocks. But how could this behavior ever evolve in the first place? If every so often gene mutations cause a small number of birds to give alarm cries, they will be more likely than their silent comrades to be eaten before they can reproduce. This means that the alarm-giving birds will be less fit than the silent ones; they will be selected against in evolution, and their alarm cry genes will not spread through the flock. An analogous objection to the genetic basis of human altruism is obvious, for altruism implies taking risks.

W. D. Hamilton's theory of *kin selection*, which Wilson recounts, attempts to overcome this objection by means of the notion of *inclusive fitness*. The notion is quite simple: One way to help pass on your kind of genes is to increase the fitness of your relatives, since they share your genes in proportion to how closely or distantly they are related to you. Inclusive fitness in the alarm-giving-bird case is simply the sum of the alarm giver's fitness (diminished because he attracts hawks) and the effects his behavior has on the fitness of his relatives (increased because he warns them of hawks). The alarm-giving genes spread if the gain to the relatives (or, more accurately, to the proportions of his genes his various relatives carry) outweighs the loss to the alarm giver. Hamilton summarizes his view this way:

> ... for a hereditary tendency to perform an action of this kind to evolve the benefit to a sib must average at least twice the loss to the individual, the benefit to a half-sib must be at least four times the loss, to a cousin eight times and so on. To express the matter more vividly, in the world of our model organisms, whose behavior is determined strictly by genotype, we expect to find that no one is prepared to sacrifice his life for any single person but that everyone will sacrifice it when he can thereby save more than two brothers, or four half-brothers, or eight first cousins. . . .[1]

Reciprocal altruism is a complementary, not a competing, theory of the evolution of altruism. The theory assumes that some of our early ancestors became genetically predisposed to help other altruists more readily than they helped nonaltruists, in other words, to be nicer to nice guys than to bad guys. If you and I are both genetically disposed to help helpers, and I help you, my act enhances my individual fitness because it enables you to identify me as a suitable person to be helped when the occasion arises. The small but certain risk required by my altruistic act of rescue is outweighed by the great though uncertain gain of future rescue.

In propounding his theory of reciprocal altruism Robert Trivers[2] plausibly assumes that a population that gives mutual aid will have greater fitness, that is, reproduce more successfully, than a population of egoists who looked out only for themselves. Using a method borrowed from game theory he lays out the alternatives (Figure I.1). For Trivers and Wilson these outcomes rank Darwinian fitness. The claim is that altruists in a world of egoists will be selected against (boxes ii and iii); but altruists who can identify, and be altruistic only toward, each other (box i) will comprise a group that is selectively superior to a group of egoists (box iv).

Kin selection is interesting precisely because it explains how altruism could be "selected for" even when it is genuinely self-sacrificial. Trivers' theory, on the other hand, aims to show that altruistic acts merely appear to be self-sacrificial: Altruism benefits the altruist be-

---

[1] W. D. Hamilton, "The Genetical Evolution of Social Behavior, I," *Journal of Theoretical Biology*, 1964.

[2] Robert Trivers, "The Evolution of Reciprocal Altruism," *Quarterly Review of Biology*, 46 (1971):35–57.

	B is an altruist	B is an egoist
A is an altruist	Box i 2/2	Box ii 4/1
A is an egoist	Box iii 1/4	Box iv 3/3

Figure I.1   Game Theory: Altruists versus Egoists

How *A* fares compared with *B* is shown in each box, 1 being the best outcome, 4 the worst. In each box, *A*'s outcome is the number on the left, *B*'s outcome the number on the right.

cause it identifies him to other altruists as a potential recipient of altruistic acts. His view is analogous to that age-old claim of moral philosophers that virtue, contrary to appearances, is really what best serves one's self-interest. However, the "virtue" with which he is concerned is greatly contracted because his reciprocal altruists are nice only to nice people and therefore run lower overall risks.

The evolution of altruism, if true, appears to have some interesting implications. First, it very likely follows that psychological egoism, the theory that all people act only for the sake of their own good or advantage, is false. If we are genetically disposed to help others spontaneously even when it is to our own disadvantage, then it is most unlikely that we should always *think* that these altruistic acts *are* to our advantage. Second, it would follow that some moral values such as altruism, or to take another kind of example, the prohibition of incest, are not arbitrary or a matter of choice. Moreover, the values common to a group would only partly be determined by culture and environment; this leaves open the possibility that some moral attitudes are "innate" or universal in the sense of being common to all cultures. Thus if some moral attitudes have specific genetic causes, and if these genes do not vary from culture to culture, then it is certainly possible that these moral attitudes will not easily, if at all, be overridden by purely cultural influences.

PART TWO

Readings in Moral Philosophy

Plato (428–348 B.C.)

Plato, born into a distinguished Athenian family, was attracted while still a young man by the remarkable intellect and personality of Socrates. Before Plato's thirtieth year, Socrates was tried and executed in Athens on charges probably resulting from his political incorruptibility. As a result Plato temporarily gave up political ambitions and went to Megara. When he returned to Athens Plato began writing philosophy, mostly dramatic dialogues in which Socrates was given the principal role. About 390 B.C. Plato went to Sicily to influence Dionysius, the ruler of Syracuse, in the first of two attempts to achieve his ideal, propounded at length in The Republic, of combining philosophical wisdom with political power. His attempts at practical politics failed and he returned to Athens to found his school, the Academy, where he gathered together other students of philosophy and attempted to perpetuate Socrates' conversational method of inquiry. Certainly the most famous of Plato's associates in the Academy was Aristotle.

The Republic, Plato's best known dialogue, develops in detail a political utopia along with an underlying theory of knowledge, but the opening sections that are reprinted here present dilemmas for moral philosophy, and only hint at Plato's later answers to them. Some other dialogues of Plato that take up problems of moral philosophy are the Euthyphro, Apology, Crito, Gorgias, Protagoras, and the Laws. The following are among the many worthwhile books containing discussions of Plato's ethics: Outlines of the History of Ethics (1886), Chapter II, by Henry Sidgwick; Lectures on the Republic of Plato (1937) by R. C. Nettleship; Plato: The Man and His Work (1956) by A. E. Taylor; In Defense of Plato (1953) by R. B. Levinson. Alasdair MacIntyre's A Short History of Ethics (1966) contains three chapters on Plato's ethics as well as chapters on several other of our anthologized authors. A good anthology is Plato's Republic (1966), edited by A. Sesonske.

The Republic

Persons of the Dialogue

Socrates, who is the narrator   Cephalus
Glaucon   Thrasymachus
Adeimantus   Cleitophon
Polemarchus

and others who are mute auditors

The scene is laid in the house of Cephalus at the Piraeus; and the whole dialogue is narrated by Socrates the day after it actually took place to Timaeus, Hermocrates, Critias, and a nameless person, who are introduced in the *Timaeus.*

BOOK ONE

I went down yesterday to the Piraeus with Glaucon the son of Ariston, that I might offer up my prayers to the goddess;* and also because I wanted to see in what manner they would celebrate the festival, which was a new thing. I was delighted with the procession of the inhabitants; but that of the Thracians was equally, if not more, beautiful. When we had finished our prayers and viewed the spectacle, we turned in the direction of the city; and at that instant Polemarchus the son of Cephalus chanced to catch sight of us from a distance as we were starting on our way home, and told his servant to run and bid us wait for him. The servant took hold of me by the cloak behind, and said: Polemarchus desires you to wait.

I turned round, and asked him where his master was.

There he is, said the youth, coming after you, if you will only wait.

Certainly we will, said Glaucon; and in a few minutes Polemarchus appeared, and with him Adeimantus, Glaucon's brother, Niceratus the son of Nicias, and several others who had been at the procession.

Translated by B. Jowett, 3d. (1892).
* Bendis, the Thracian Artemis.

Polemarchus said to me: I perceive, Socrates, that you and your companion are already on your way to the city.

You are not far wrong, I said.

But do you see, he rejoined, how many we are?

Of course.

And are you stronger than all these? for if not, you will have to remain where you are.

May there not be the alternative, I said, that we may persuade you to let us go?

But can you persuade us, if we refuse to listen to you? he said.

Certainly not, replied Glaucon.

Then we are not going to listen; of that you may be assured.

Adeimantus added: Has no one told you of the torch-race on horseback in honour of the goddess which will take place in the evening?

With horses! I replied: That is a novelty. Will horsemen carry torches and pass them one to another during the race?

Yes, said Polemarchus, and not only so, but a festival will be celebrated at night, which you certainly ought to see. Let us rise soon after supper and see this festival; there will be a gathering of young men, and we will have a good talk. Stay then, and do not be perverse.

Glaucon said: I suppose, since you insist, that we must.

Very good, I replied.

Accordingly we went with Polemarchus to his house; and there we found his brothers Lysias and Euthydemus, and with them Thrasymachus the Chalcedonian, Charmantides the Paeanian, and Cleitophon the son of Aristonymus. There too was Cephalus the father of Polemarchus, whom I had not seen for a long time, and I thought him very much aged. He was seated on a cushioned chair, and had a garland on his head, for he had been sacrificing in the court; and there were some other chairs in the room arranged in a semicircle, upon which we sat down by him. He saluted me eagerly, and then he said:—

You don't come to see me, Socrates, as often as you ought: If I were still able to go and see you I would not ask you to come to me. But at my age I can hardly get to the city, and therefore you should come oftener to the Piraeus. For let me tell you, that the more the pleasures of the body fade away, the greater to me is the pleasure and charm of conversation. Do not then deny my request, but make our house your resort and keep company with these young men; we are old friends, and you will be quite at home with us.

I replied: There is nothing which for my part I like better, Cephalus, than conversing with aged men; for I regard them as travellers who have gone a journey which I too may have to go, and of whom I ought to enquire, whether the way is smooth and easy, or rugged and difficult. And this is a question which I should like to ask of you who have arrived at that time which the poets call the 'threshold of old age'—Is life harder towards the end, or what report do you give of it?

I will tell you, Socrates, he said, what my own feeling is. Men of my age flock together; we are birds of a feather, as the old proverb says; and at our meetings the tale of my acquaintance commonly is—I cannot eat, I cannot drink; the pleasures of youth and love are fled away: there was a good time once, but now that is gone, and life is no longer life. Some complain of the slights which are put upon them by relations, and they will tell you sadly of how many evils their old age is the cause. But to me, Socrates, these complainers seem to blame that which is not really in fault. For if old age were the cause, I too being old, and every other old man, would have felt as they do. But this is not my own experience, nor that of others whom I have known. How well I remember the aged poet Sophocles, when in answer to the question, How does love suit with age, Sophocles,—are you still the man you were? Peace, he replied; most gladly have I escaped the thing of which you speak; I feel as if I had escaped from a mad and furious master. His words have often occurred to my mind since, and they seem as good to me now as at the time when he uttered them. For certainly old age has a great sense of calm and freedom; when the passions relax their hold, then, as Sophocles says, we are freed from the grasp not of one mad master only, but of many. The truth is, Socrates, that these regrets, and also the complaints about relations, are to be attributed to the same cause, which is not old age, but men's characters and tempers; for he who is of a calm and happy nature will hardly feel the pressure of age, but to him who is of an opposite disposition youth and age are equally a burden.

I listened in admiration, and wanting to draw him out, that he might go on—Yes, Cephalus, I said: but I rather suspect that people in general are not convinced by you when you speak thus; they think that old age sits lightly upon you, not because of your happy disposition, but because you are rich, and wealth is well known to be a great comforter.

You are right, he replied; they are not convinced: and there is something in what they say; not, however, so much as they imagine. I might answer them as Themistocles answered the Seriphian who was abusing him and saying that he was famous, not for his own merits but because he was an Athenian: 'If you had been a native of my country or I of yours, neither of us would have been famous.' And to those who are not rich and are impatient of old age, the same reply may be made; for to the good poor man old age cannot be a light burden, nor can a bad rich man ever have peace with himself.

May I ask, Cephalus, whether your fortune was for the most part inherited or acquired by you?

Acquired! Socrates; do you want to know how much I acquired? In the art of making money I have been midway between my father and grandfather: for my grandfather, whose name I bear, doubled and trebled the value of his patrimony, that which he inherited being much what I possess now; but my father Lysanias reduced the property below what it is at present: and I shall be satisfied if I leave to these my sons not less but a little more than I received.

That was why I asked you the question, I replied, because I see that you are indifferent about money, which is a characteristic rather of those who have inherited their fortunes than of those who have acquired them; the makers of fortunes have a second love of money as a creation of their own, resembling the affection of authors for their own poems, or of parents for their children, besides that natural love of it for the sake of use and profit which is common to them and all men. And hence they are very bad company, for they can talk about nothing but the praises of wealth.

That is true, he said.

Yes, that is very true, but may I ask another question?—What do you consider to be the greatest blessing which you have reaped from your wealth?

One, he said, of which I could not easily expect to convince others. For let me tell you, Socrates, that when a man thinks himself to be near death, fears and cares enter into his mind which he never had before; the tales of a world below and the punishment which is exacted there of deeds done here were once a laughing matter to him, but now he is tormented with the thought that they may be true: either from the weakness of age, or because he is now drawing nearer to that other place, he has a clearer view of these things; suspicions and alarms crowd thickly upon him, and he begins to reflect and consider what wrongs he has done to others. And when he finds that the sum of his transgressions is great he will many a time like a child start up in his sleep for fear, and he is filled with dark forebodings. But to him who is conscious of no sin, sweet hope, as Pindar charmingly says, is the kind nurse of his age:

> 'Hope,' he says, 'cherishes the soul of him who lives in justice and holiness and is the nurse of his age and the companion of his journey;—hope which is mightiest to sway the restless soul of man.

How admirable are his words! And the great blessing of riches, I do not say to every man, but to a good man, is, that he has had no occasion to deceive or to defraud others, either intentionally or unintentionally; and when he departs to the world below he is not in any apprehension about offerings due to the gods or debts which he owes to men. Now to this peace of mind the possession of wealth greatly contributes; and therefore I say, that, setting one thing against another, of the many advantages which wealth has to give, to a man of sense this is in my opinion the greatest.

Well said, Cephalus, I replied; but as concerning justice, what is it? —to speak the truth and to pay your debts—no more than this? And even to this are there not exceptions? Suppose that a friend when in his right mind has deposited arms with me and he asks for them when he is not in his right mind, ought I to give them back to him? No one would say that I ought or that I should be right in doing so, any more than they would say that I ought always to speak the truth to one who is in his condition.

You are quite right, he replied.

But then, I said, speaking the truth and paying your debts is not a correct definition of justice.

Quite correct, Socrates, if Simonides is to be believed, said Polemarchus interposing.

I fear, said Cephalus, that I must go now, for I have to look after the sacrifices, and I hand over the argument to Polemarchus and the company.

Is not Polemarchus your heir? I said.

To be sure, he answered, and went away laughing to the sacrifices.

Tell me then, O thou heir of the argument, what did Simonides say, and according to you truly say, about justice?

He said that the repayment of a debt is just, and in saying so he appears to me to be right.

I should be sorry to doubt the word of such a wise and inspired man, but his meaning, though probably clear to you, is the reverse of clear to me. For he certainly does not mean, as we were just now saying, that I ought to return a deposit of arms or of anything else to one who asks for it when he is not in his right senses; and yet a deposit cannot be denied to be a debt.

True.

Then when the person who asks me is not in his right mind I am by no means to make the return?

Certainly not.

When Simonides said that the repayment of a debt was justice, he did not mean to include that case?

Certainly not; for he thinks that a friend ought always to do good to a friend and never evil.

You mean that the return of a deposit of gold which is to the injury of the receiver, if the two parties are friends, is not the repayment of a debt,—that is what you would imagine him to say?

Yes.

And are enemies also to receive what we owe to them?

To be sure, he said, they are to receive what we owe them, and an enemy, as I take it, owes to an enemy that which is due or proper to him —that is to say, evil.

Simonides, then, after the manner of poets, would seem to have spoken darkly of the nature of justice; for he really meant to say that justice is the giving to each man what is proper to him, and this he termed a debt.

That must have been his meaning, he said.

By heaven! I replied; and if we asked him what due or proper thing is given by medicine, and to whom, what answer do you think that he would make to us?

He would surely reply that medicine gives drugs and meat and drink to human bodies.

And what due or proper thing is given by cookery, and to what?

Seasoning to food.

And what is that which justice gives, and to whom?

If, Socrates, we are to be guided at all by the analogy of the preceding instances, then justice is the art which gives good to friends and evil to enemies.

That is his meaning then?

I think so.

And who is best able to do good to his friends and evil to his enemies in time of sickness?

The physician.

Or when they are on a voyage, amid the perils of the sea?

The pilot.

And in what sort of actions or with a view to what result is the just man most able to do harm to his enemy and good to his friend?

In going to war against the one and in making alliances with the other.

But when a man is well, my dear Polemarchus, there is no need of a physician?

No.

And he who is not on a voyage has not need of a pilot?

No.

Then in time of peace justice will be of no use?

I am very far from thinking so.

You think that justice may be of use in peace as well as in war?

Yes.

Like husbandry for the acquisition of corn?

Yes.

Or like shoemaking for the acquisition of shoes,—that is what you mean?

Yes.

And what similar use or power of acquisition has justice in time of peace?

In contracts, Socrates, justice is of use.

And by contracts you mean partnerships?

Exactly.

But is the just man or the skilful player a more useful and better partner at a game of draughts?

The skilful player.

And in the laying of bricks and stones is the just man a more useful or better partner than the builder?

Quite the reverse.

Then in what sort of partnership is the just man a better partner than the harp-player, as in playing the harp the harp-player is certainly a better partner than the just man?

In a money partnership.

Yes, Polemarchus, but surely not in the use of money; for you do not want a just man to be your counsellor in the purchase or sale of a horse; a man who is knowing about horses would be better for that, would he not?

Certainly.

And when you want to buy a ship, the shipwright or the pilot would be better?

True.

Then what is that joint use of silver or gold in which the just man is to be preferred?

When you want a deposit to be kept safely.

You mean when money is not wanted, but allowed to lie?

Precisely.

That is to say, justice is useful when money is useless?

That is the inference.

And when you want to keep a pruning-hook safe, then justice is useful to the individual and to the state; but when you want to use it, then the art of the vine-dresser?

Clearly.

And when you want to keep a shield or a lyre, and not to use them, you would say that justice is useful; but when you want to use them, then the art of the soldier or of the musician?

Certainly.

And so of all the other things;—justice is useful when they are useless, and useless when they are useful?

That is the inference.

Then justice is not good for much. But let us consider this further point: Is not he who can best strike a blow in a boxing match or in any kind of fighting best able to ward off a blow?

Certainly.

And he who is most skilful in preventing or escaping from a disease is best able to create one?

True.

And he is the best guard of a camp who is best able to steal a march upon the enemy?

Certainly.

Then he who is a good keeper of anything is also a good thief?

That, I suppose, is to be inferred.

Then if the just man is good at keeping money, he is good at stealing it.

That is implied in the argument.

Then after all the just man has turned out to be a thief. And this is a lesson which I suspect you must have learnt out of Homer; for he, speaking of Autolycus, the maternal grandfather of Odysseus, who is a favourite of his, affirms that

He was excellent above all men in theft and perjury.

And so, you and Homer and Simonides are agreed that justice is an art of theft; to be practised however 'for the good of friends and for the harm of enemies,' that was what you were saying?

No, certainly not that, though I do not now know what I did say; but I still stand by the latter words.

Well, there is another question: By friends and enemies do we mean those who are so really, or only in seeming?

Surely, he said, a man may be expected to love those whom he thinks good, and to hate those whom he thinks evil.

Yes, but do not persons often err about good and evil: many who are not good seem to be so, and conversely?

That is true.

Then to them the good will be enemies and the evil will be their friends?

True.

And in that case they will be right in doing good to the evil and evil to the good?

Clearly.

But the good are just and would not do an injustice?

True.

Then according to your argument it is just to injure those who do no wrong?

Nay, Socrates; the doctrine is immoral.

Then I suppose that we ought to do good to the just and harm to the unjust?

I like that better.

But see the consequence:—Many a man who is ignorant of human nature has friends who are bad friends, and in that case he ought to do harm to them; and he has good enemies whom he ought to benefit; but, if so, we shall be saying the very opposite of that which we affirmed to be the meaning of Simonides.

Very true, he said: and I think that we had better correct an error into which we seem to have fallen in the use of the words 'friend' and 'enemy.'

What was the error, Polemarchus? I asked.

We assumed that he is a friend who seems to be or who is thought good.

And how is the error to be corrected?

We should rather say that he is a friend who is, as well as seems, good; and that he who seems only, and is not good, only seems to be and is not a friend; and of an enemy the same may be said.

You would argue that the good are our friends and the bad our enemies?

Yes.

And instead of saying simply as we did at first, that it is just to do good to our friends and harm to our enemies, we should further say: It is just to do good to our friends when they are good and harm to our enemies when they are evil?

Yes, that appears to me to be the truth.

But ought the just to injure any one at all?

Undoubtedly he ought to injure those who are both wicked and his enemies.

When horses are injured, are they improved or deteriorated?

The latter.

Deteriorated, that is to say, in the good qualities of horses, not of dogs?

Yes, of horses.

And dogs are deteriorated in the good qualities of dogs, and not of horses?

Of course.

And will not men who are injured be deteriorated in that which is the proper virtue of man?

Certainly.

And that human virtue is justice?

To be sure.

Then men who are injured are of necessity made unjust?

That is the result.

But can the musician by his art make men unmusical?

Certainly not.

Or the horseman by his art make them bad horsemen?

Impossible.

And can the just by justice make men unjust, or speaking generally, can the good by virtue make them bad?

Assuredly not.

Any more than heat can produce cold?

It cannot.

Or drought moisture?

Clearly not.

Nor can the good harm any one?

Impossible.

And the just is the good?

Certainly.

Then to injure a friend or any one else is not the act of a just man, but of the opposite, who is the unjust?

I think that what you say is quite true, Socrates.

Then if a man says that justice consists in the repayment of debts, and that good is the debt which a man owes to his friends, and evil the debt which he owes to his enemies,—to say this is not wise; for it is not true, if, as has been clearly shown, the injuring of another can be in no case just.

I agree with you, said Polemarchus.

Then you and I are prepared to take up arms against any one who attributes such a saying to Simonides or Bias or Pittacus, or any other wise man or seer?

I am quite ready to do battle at your side, he said.

Shall I tell you whose I believe the saying to be?

Whose?

I believe that Periander or Perdiccas or Xerxes or Ismenias the Theban, or some other rich and mighty man, who had a great opinion of his own power, was the first to say that justice is 'doing good to your friends and harm to your enemies.'

Most true, he said.

Yes, I said; but if this definition of justice also breaks down, what other can be offered?

Several times in the course of the discussion Thrasymachus had made an attempt to get the argument into his own hands, and had been put down by the rest of the company, who wanted to hear the end. But when Polemarchus and I had done speaking and there was a pause, he could no longer hold his peace; and, gathering himself up, he came at us like a wild beast, seeking to devour us. We were quite panic-stricken at the sight of him.

He roared out to the whole company: What folly, Socrates, has taken possession of you all? And why, sillybillies, do you knock under to one another? I say that if you want really to know what justice is, you should not only ask but answer, and you should not seek honour to yourself from the refutation of an opponent, but have your own answer; for there is many a one who can ask and cannot answer. And now I will not have you say that justice is duty or advantage or profit or gain or interest, for this sort of nonsense will not do for me; I must have clearness and accuracy.

I was panic-stricken at his words, and could not look at him without trembling. Indeed I believe that if I had not fixed my eye upon him, I should have been struck dumb: but when I saw his fury rising, I looked at him first, and was therefore able to reply to him.

Thrasymachus, I said, with a quiver, don't be hard upon us. Polemarchus and I may have been guilty of a little mistake in the argument, but I can assure you that the error was not intentional. If we were seeking for a piece of gold, you would not imagine that we were 'knocking under to one another,' and so losing our chance of finding it. And why, when we are seeking for justice, a thing more precious than many pieces of gold, do you say that we are weakly yielding to one another and not doing our utmost to get at the truth? Nay, my good friend, we are most willing and anxious to do so, but the fact is that we cannot. And if so, you people who know all things should pity us and not be angry with us.

How characteristic of Socrates! he replied, with a bitter laugh;— that's your ironical style! Did I not foresee—have I not already told you, that whatever he was asked he would refuse to answer, and try irony or any other shuffle, in order that he might avoid answering?

You are a philosopher, Thrasymachus, I replied, and well know that if you ask a person what numbers make up twelve, taking care to prohibit him whom you ask from answering twice six, or three times four, or six times two, or four times three, 'for this sort of nonsense will not do for me,'—then obviously, if that is your way of putting the question, no one can answer you. But suppose that he were to retort, 'Thrasymachus, what do you mean? If one of these numbers which you interdict be the true answer to the question, am I falsely to say some other number which is not the right one?—is that your meaning?'—How would you answer him?

Just as if the two cases were at all alike! he said.

Why should they not be? I replied; and even if they are not, but only appear to be so to the person who is asked, ought he not to say what he thinks, whether you and I forbid him or not?

I presume then that you are going to make one of the interdicted answers?

I dare say that I may, notwithstanding the danger, if upon reflection I approve of any of them.

But what if I give you an answer about justice other and better, he said, than any of these? What do you deserve to have done to you?

Done to me!—as becomes the ignorant, I must learn from the wise —that is what I deserve to have done to me.

What, and no payment! a pleasant notion!

I will pay when I have the money, I replied.

But you have, Socrates, said Glaucon: and you, Thrasymachus, need be under no anxiety about money, for we will all make a contribution for Socrates.

Yes, he replied, and then Socrates will do as he always does—refuse to answer himself, but take and pull to pieces the answer of some one else.

Why, my good friends, I said, how can any one answer who knows, and says that he knows, just nothing; and who, even if he has some faint notions of his own, is told by a man of authority not to utter them? The natural thing is, that the speaker should be some one like yourself who professes to know and can tell what he knows. Will you then kindly answer, for the edification of the company and of myself?

Glaucon and the rest of the company joined in my request and Thrasymachus, as any one might see, was in reality eager to speak; for he thought that he had an excellent answer, and would distinguish himself. But at first he affected to insist on my answering; at length he consented to begin. Behold, he said, the wisdom of Socrates; he refuses to teach himself, and goes about learning of others, to whom he never even says thank you.

That I learn of others, I replied, is quite true; but that I am ungrateful I wholly deny. Money I have none, and therefore I pay in praise, which is all I have: and how ready I am to praise any one who appears to me to speak well you will very soon find out when you answer; for I expect that you will answer well.

Listen, then, he said; I proclaim that justice is nothing else than the interest of the stronger. And now why do you not praise me? But of course you won't.

Let me first understand you, I replied. Justice, as you say, is the interest of the stronger. What, Thrasymachus, is the meaning of this? You cannot mean to say that because Polydamas, the pancratiast, is stronger than we are, and finds the eating of beef conducive to his bodily strength, that to eat beef is therefore equally for our good who are weaker than he is, and right and just for us?

That's abominable of you, Socrates; you take the words in the sense which is most damaging to the argument.

Not at all, my good sir, I said; I am trying to understand them; and I wish that you would be a little clearer.

Well, he said, have you never heard that forms of government differ; there are tyrannies, and there are democracies and there are aristocracies?

Yes, I know.

And the government is the ruling power in each state?

Certainly.

And the different forms of government makes laws democratical, aristocratical, tyrannical, with a view to their several interests; and these laws, which are made by them for their own interests, are the justice which they deliver to their subjects, and him who transgresses them they punish as a breaker of the law, and unjust. And that is what I mean when I say that in all states there is the same principle of justice, which is the interest of the government; and as the government must be supposed to have power, the only reasonable conclusion is, that everywhere there is one principle of justice, which is the interest of the stronger.

Now I understand you, I said; and whether you are right or not I will try to discover. But let me remark, that in defining justice you have yourself used the word 'interest' which you forbade me to use. It is true, however, that in your definition the words 'of the stronger' are added.

A small addition, you must allow, he said.

Great or small, never mind about that: we must first enquire whether what you are saying is the truth. Now we are both agreed that justice is interest of some sort, but you go on to say 'of the stronger'; about this addition I am not so sure, and must therefore consider further.

Proceed.

I will; and first tell me, Do you admit that it is just for subjects to obey their rulers?

I do.

But are the rulers of states absolutely infallible, or are they sometimes liable to err?

To be sure, he replied, they are liable to err.

Then in making their laws they may sometimes make them rightly, and sometimes not?

True.

When they make them rightly, they make them agreeably to their interest; when they are mistaken, contrary to their interest; you admit that?

Yes.

And the laws which they make must be obeyed by their subjects,— and that is what you call justice?

Doubtless.

Then justice, according to your argument, is not only obedience to the interest of the stronger but the reverse?

What is that you are saying? he asked.

I am only repeating what you are saying, I believe. But let us consider: Have we not admitted that the rulers may be mistaken about their own interest in what they command, and also that to obey them is justice? Has not that been admitted?

Yes.

Then you must also have acknowledged justice not to be for the interest of the stronger, when the rulers unintentionally command things to be done which are to their own injury. For if, as you say, justice is the obedience which the subject renders to their commands, in that case,

O wisest of men, is there any escape from the conclusion that the weaker are commanded to do, not what is for the interest, but what is for the injury of the stronger?

Nothing can be clearer, Socrates, said Polemarchus.

Yes, said Cleitophon, interposing, if you are allowed to be his witness.

But there is no need of any witness, said Polemarchus, for Thrasymachus himself acknowledges that rulers may sometimes command what is not for their own interest, and that for subjects to obey them is justice.

Yes, Polemarchus,—Thrasymachus said that for subjects to do what was commanded by their rulers is just.

Yes, Cleitophon, but he also said that justice is the interest of the stronger, and, while admitting both these propositions, he further acknowledged that the stronger may command the weaker who are his subjects to do what is not for his own interest; whence follows that justice is the injury quite as much as the interest of the stronger.

But, said Cleitophon, he meant by the interest of the stronger what the stronger thought to be his interest,—this was what the weaker had to do; and this was affirmed by him to be justice.

Those were not his words, rejoined Polemarchus.

Never mind, I replied, if he now says that they are, let us accept his statement. Tell me, Thrasymachus, I said, did you mean by justice what the stronger thought to be his interest, whether really so or not?

Certainly not, he said. Do you suppose that I call him who is mistaken the stronger at the time when he is mistaken?

Yes, I said, my impression was that you did so, when you admitted that the ruler was not infallible but might be sometimes mistaken.

You argue like an informer, Socrates. Do you mean, for example, that he who is mistaken about the sick is a physician in that he is mistaken? or that he who errs in arithmetic or grammar is an arithmetician or grammarian at the time when he is making the mistake, in respect of the mistake? True, we say that the physician or arithmetician or grammarian has made a mistake, but this is only a way of speaking; for the fact is that neither the grammarian nor any other person of skill ever makes a mistake in so far as he is what his name implies; they none of them err unless their skill fails them, and then they cease to be skilled artists. No artist or sage or ruler errs at the time when he is what his name implies; though he is commonly said to err, and I adopted the common mode of speaking. But to be perfectly accurate, since you are such a lover of accuracy, we should say that the ruler, in so far as he is the ruler, is unerring, and, being unerring, always commands that which is for his own interest; and the subject is required to execute his commands; and therefore, as I said at first and now repeat, justice is the interest of the stronger.

Indeed, Thrasymachus, and do I really appear to you to argue like an informer?

Certainly, he replied.

And do you suppose that I ask these questions with any design of injuring you in the argument?

Nay, he replied, 'suppose' is not the word—I know it; but you will be found out, and by sheer force of argument you will never prevail.

I shall not make the attempt, my dear man; but to avoid any misunderstanding occurring between us in future, let me ask, in what sense do you speak of a ruler or stronger whose interest, as you were saying, he being the superior, it is just that the inferior should execute—is he a ruler in the popular or in the strict sense of the term?

In the strictest of all senses, he said. And now cheat and play the informer if you can; I ask no quarter at your hands. But you never will be able, never.

And do you imagine, I said, that I am such a madman as to try and cheat, Thrasymachus? I might as well shave a lion.

Why, he said, you made the attempt a minute ago, and you failed.

Enough, I said, of these civilities. It will be better that I should ask you a question: Is the physician, taken in that strict sense of which you are speaking, a healer of the sick or a maker of money? And remember that I am now speaking of the true physician.

A healer of the sick, he replied.

And the pilot—that is to say, the true pilot—is he a captain of sailors or a mere sailor?

A captain of sailors.

The circumstance that he sails in the ship is not to be taken into account; neither is he to be called a sailor; the name pilot by which he is distinguished has nothing to do with sailing, but is significant of his skill and of his authority over the sailors.

Very true, he said.

Now, I said, every art has an interest?

Certainly.

For which the art has to consider and provide?

Yes, that is the aim of art.

And the interest of any art is the perfection of it—this and nothing else?

What do you mean?

I mean what I may illustrate negatively by the example of the body. Suppose you were to ask me whether the body is self-sufficing or has wants, I should reply: Certainly the body has wants; for the body may be ill and require to be cured, and has therefore interests to which the art of medicine ministers; and this is the origin and intention of medicine, as you will acknowledge. Am I not right?

Quite right, he replied.

But is the art of medicine or any other art faulty or deficient in any quality in the same way that the eye may be deficient in sight or the ear fail of hearing, and therefore requires another art to provide for the interests of seeing and hearing—has art in itself, I say, any similar liability to fault or defect, and does every art require another supplementary art to provide for its interests, and that another and another without end? Or have the arts to look only after their own interest? Or have they no need either of themselves or of another?—having no faults or defects, they have no need to correct them, either by the exercise of their own art or of any other; they have only to consider the interest of their subject-matter. For every art remains pure and faultless while remaining true—that is to say, while perfect and unimpaired. Take the words in your precise sense and tell me whether I am not right.

Yes, clearly.

Then medicine does not consider the interest of medicine, but the interest of the body?

True, he said.

Nor does the art of horsemanship consider the interests of the art of horsemanship, but the interests of the horse; neither do any other arts care for themselves, for they have no needs; they care only for that which is the subject of their art?

True, he said.

But surely, Thrasymachus, the arts are the superiors and rulers of their own subjects?

To this he assented with a good deal of reluctance.

Then, I said, no science or art considers or enjoins the interest of the stronger or superior, but only the interest of the subject and weaker?

He made an attempt to contest this proposition also, but finally acquiesced.

Then I continued, no physician, in so far as he is a physician, considers his own good in what he prescribes, but the good of his patient; for the true physician is also a ruler having the human body as a subject, and is not a mere money-maker; that has been admitted?

Yes.

And the pilot likewise, in the strict sense of the term, is a ruler of sailors and not a mere sailor?

That has been admitted.

And such a pilot and ruler will provide and prescribe for the interest of the sailor who is under him, and not for his own or the ruler's interest?

He gave a reluctant 'Yes.'

Then, I said, Thrasymachus, there is no one in any rule who, in so far as he is a ruler, considers or enjoins what is for his own interest, but always what is for the interest of his subject or suitable to his art;

to that he looks, and that alone he considers in everything which he says and does.

When we had got to this point in the argument, and every one saw that the definition of justice had been completely upset, Thrasymachus, instead of replying to me, said: Tell me, Socrates, have you got a nurse?

Why do you ask such a question, I said, when you ought rather to be answering?

Because she leaves you to snivel, and never wipes your nose: she has not even taught you to know the shepherd from the sheep.

What makes you say that? I replied.

Because you fancy that the shepherd or neatherd fattens or tends the sheep or oxen with a view to their own good and not to the good of himself or his master; and you further imagine that the rulers of states, if they are true rulers, never think of their subjects as sheep, and that they are not studying their own advantage day and night. Oh, no; and so entirely astray are you in your ideas about the just and unjust as not even to know that justice and the just are in reality another's good; that is to say, the interest of the ruler and stronger, and the loss of the subject and the servant; and injustice the opposite; for the unjust is lord over the truly simple and just; he is the stronger, and his subjects do what is for his interest, and minister to his happiness, which is very far from being their own. Consider further, most foolish Socrates, that the just is always a loser in comparison with the unjust. First of all, in private contracts: wherever the unjust is the partner of the just you will find that, when the partnership is dissolved, the unjust man has always more and the just less. Secondly, in their dealings with the State: when there is an income tax, the just man will pay more and the unjust less on the same amount of income; and when there is anything to be received the one gains nothing and the other much. Observe also what happens when they take an office; there is the just man neglecting his affairs and perhaps suffering other losses, and getting nothing out of the public, because he is just; moreover he is hated by his friends and acquaintances for refusing to serve them in unlawful ways. But all this is reversed in the case of the unjust man. I am speaking, as before, of injustice on a large scale in which the advantage of the unjust is more apparent; and my meaning will be most clearly seen if we turn to that highest form of injustice in which the criminal is the happiest of men, and the sufferers or those who refuse to do injustice are the most miserable—that is to say tyranny, which by fraud and force takes away the property of others, not little by little but wholesale; comprehending in one, things sacred as well as profane, private and public; for which acts of wrong, if he were detected perpetrating any one of them singly, he would be punished and incur great disgrace—they who do such wrong in particular cases are called robbers of temples, and man-stealers and burglars and swindlers and thieves. But when a man besides taking away the money of the citizens has made slaves of them, then, instead of these names of reproach, he is termed happy and blessed, not only by the citizens but by all who hear of his having achieved the consummation of injustice. For mankind censure injustice, fearing that they may be the victims of it and not because they shrink from committing it. And thus, as I have shown, Socrates, injustice, when on a sufficient scale, has more strength and freedom and mastery than justice; and, as I said at first, justice is the interest of the stronger, whereas injustice is a man's own profit and interest.

Thrasymachus, when he had thus spoken, having, like a bathman, deluged our ears with his words, had a mind to go away. But the company would not let him; they insisted that he should remain and defend his position; and I myself added my own humble request that he would not leave us. Thrasymachus, I said to him, excellent man, how suggestive are your remarks! And are you going to run away before you have fairly taught or learned whether they are true or not? Is the attempt to determine the way of man's life so small a matter in your eyes —to determine how life may be passed by each one of us to the greatest advantage?

And do I differ from you, he said, as to the importance of the enquiry?

You appear rather, I replied, to have no care or thought about us, Thrasymachus—whether we live better or worse from not knowing what you say you know, is to you a matter of indifference. Prithee, friend, do not keep your knowledge to yourself; we are a large party, and any benefit which you confer upon us will be amply rewarded. For my own part I openly declare that I am not convinced, and that I do not believe injustice to be more gainful than justice, even if uncontrolled and allowed to have free play. For, granting that there may be an unjust man who is able to commit injustice either by fraud or force, still this does not convince me of the superior advantage of injustice, and there may be others who are in the same predicament with myself. Perhaps we may be wrong; if so, you in your wisdom should convince us that we are mistaken in preferring justice to injustice.

And how am I to convince you, he said, if you are not already convinced by what I have just said; what more can I do for you? Would you have me put the proof bodily into your souls?

Heaven forbid! I said; I would only ask you to be consistent; or, if you change, change openly and let there be no deception. For I must remark, Thrasymachus, if you will recall what was previously said, that although you began by defining the true physician in an exact sense, you did not observe a like exactness when speaking of the shepherd; you thought that the shepherd as a shepherd tends the sheep not with a view to their own good, but like a mere diner or banqueter with a view to the pleasures of the table; or, again, as a trader for sale in the market, and not as a shepherd. Yet surely the art of the shepherd is concerned only with the good of his subjects; he has only to provide the best for them, since the perfection of the art is already ensured whenever all the requirements of it are satisfied. And that was what I was saying just now about the ruler. I conceived that the art of the ruler, considered as ruler, whether in a state or in private life, could only regard the good of his flock or subjects; whereas you seem to think that the rulers in states, that is to say, the true rulers, like being in authority.

Think! Nay, I am sure of it.

Then why in the case of lesser offices do men never take them willingly without payment, unless under the idea that they govern for the advantage not of themselves but of others? Let me ask you a question: Are not the several arts different, by reason of their each having a separate function? And, my dear illustrious friend, do say what you think, that we may make a little progress.

Yes, that is the difference, he replied.

And each art gives us a particular good and not merely a general one—medicine, for example, gives us health; navigation, safety at sea, and so on?

Yes, he said.

And the art of payment has the special function of giving pay: but we do not confuse this with other arts, any more than the art of the pilot is to be confused with the art of medicine, because the health of the pilot may be improved by a sea voyage. You would not be inclined to say, would you, that navigation is the art of medicine, at least if we are to adopt your exact use of language?

Certainly not.

Or because a man is in good health when he receives pay you would not say that the art of payment is medicine?

I should say not.

Nor would you say that medicine is the art of receiving pay because a man takes fees when he is engaged in healing?

Certainly not.

And we have admitted, I said, that the good of each art is specially confined to the art?

Yes.

Then, if there be any good which all artists have in common, that is to be attributed to something of which they all have the common use?

True, he replied.

And when the artist is benefited by receiving pay the advantage is gained by an additional use of the art of pay, which is not the art professed by him?

He gave a reluctant assent to this.

Then the pay is not derived by the several artists from their respective arts. But the truth is, that while the art of medicine gives health, and the art of the builder builds a house, another art attends them which is the art of pay. The various arts may be doing their own business and benefiting that over which they preside, but would the artist receive any benefit from his art unless he were paid as well?

I suppose not.

But does he therefore confer no benefit when he works for nothing?

Certainly, he confers a benefit.

Then now, Thrasymachus, there is no longer any doubt that neither arts nor governments provide for their own interests; but, as we were before saying, they rule and provide for the interests of their subjects who are the weaker and not the stronger—to their good they attend and not to the good of the superior. And this is the reason, my dear Thrasymachus, why, as I was just now saying, no one is willing to govern; because no one likes to take in hand the reformation of evils which are not his concern without remuneration. For, in the execution of his work, and in giving his orders to another, the true artist does not regard his own interest, but always that of his subjects; and therefore in order that rulers may be willing to rule, they must be paid in one of three modes of payment: money, or honour, or a penalty for refusing.

What do you mean, Socrates? said Glaucon. The first two modes of payment are intelligible enough, but what the penalty is I do not understand, or how a penalty can be a payment.

You mean that you do not understand the nature of this payment which to the best men is the great inducement to rule? Of course you know that ambition and avarice are held to be, as indeed they are, a disgrace?

Very true.

And for this reason, I said, money and honour have no attraction for them; good men do not wish to be openly demanding payment for governing and so to get the name of hirelings, nor by secretly helping themselves out of the public revenues to get the name of thieves. And not being ambitious they do not care about honour. Wherefore necessity must be laid upon them, and they must be induced to serve from the fear of punishment. And this, as I imagine, is the reason why the forwardness to take office, instead of waiting to be compelled, has been deemed dishonourable. Now the worst part of the punishment is that he who refuses to rule is liable to be ruled by one who is worse than himself. And the fear of this, as I conceive, induces the good to take office, not because they would, but because they cannot help—not under the idea that they are going to have any benefit or enjoyment themselves, but as a necessity, and because they are not able to commit the task of ruling to any one who is better than themselves, or indeed as good.

For there is reason to think that if a city were composed entirely of good men, then to avoid office would be as much an object of contention as to obtain office is at present; then we should have plain proof that the true ruler is not meant by nature to regard his own interest, but that of his subjects; and every one who knew this would choose rather to receive a benefit from another than to have the trouble of conferring one. So far am I from agreeing with Thrasymachus that justice is the interest of the stronger. This latter question need not be further discussed at present; but when Thrasymachus says that the life of the unjust is more advantageous than that of the just, his new statement appears to me to be of a far more serious character. Which of us has spoken truly? And which sort of life, Glaucon, do you prefer?

I for my part deem the life of the just to be the more advantageous, he answered.

Did you hear all the advantages of the unjust which Thrasymachus was rehearsing?

Yes, I heard him, he replied, but he has not convinced me.

Then shall we try to find some way of convincing him, if we can, that he is saying what is not true?

Most certainly, he replied.

If, I said, he makes a set speech and we make another recounting all the advantages of being just, and he answers and we rejoin, there must be a numbering and measuring of the goods which are claimed on either side, and in the end we shall want judges to decide; but if we proceed in our enquiry as we lately did, by making admissions to one another, we shall unite the offices of judge and advocate in our own persons.

Very good, he said.

And which method do I understand you to prefer? I said.

That which you propose.

Well, then, Thrasymachus, I said, suppose you begin at the beginning and answer me. You say that perfect injustice is more gainful than perfect justice?

Yes, that is what I say, and I have given you my reasons.

And what is your view about them? Would you call one of them virtue and the other vice?

Certainly.

I suppose that you would call justice virtue and injustice vice?

What a charming notion! So likely too, seeing that I affirm injustice to be profitable and justice not.

What else then would you say?

The opposite, he replied.

And would you call justice vice?

No, I would rather say sublime simplicity.

Then would you call injustice malignity?

No; I would rather say discretion.

And do the unjust appear to you to be wise and good?

Yes, he said: at any rate those of them who are able to be perfectly unjust, and who have the power of subduing states and nations; but perhaps you imagine me to be talking of cutpurses. Even this profession if undetected has advantages, though they are not to be compared with those of which I was just now speaking.

I do not think that I misapprehend your meaning, Thrasymachus, I replied; but still I cannot hear without amazement that you class injustice with wisdom and virtue, and justice with the opposite.

Certainly I do so class them.

Now, I said, you are on more substantial and almost unanswerable ground; for if the injustice which you were maintaining to be profitable had been admitted by you as by others to be vice and deformity, an answer might have been given to you on received principle; but now I perceive that you will call injustice honourable and strong, and to the unjust you will attribute all the qualities which were attributed by us before to the just, seeing that you do not hesitate to rank injustice with wisdom and virtue.

You have guessed most infallibly, he replied.

Then I certainly ought not to shrink from going through with the argument so long as I have reason to think that you, Thrasymachus, are speaking your real mind; for I do believe that you are now in earnest and are not amusing yourself at our expense.

I may be in earnest or not, but what is that to you?—to refute the argument is your business.

Very true, I said; that is what I have to do: But will you be so good as answer yet one more question? Does the just man try to gain any advantage over the just?

Far otherwise; if he did he would not be the simple, amusing creature which he is.

And would he try to go beyond just action?

He would not.

And how would he regard the attempt to gain an advantage over the unjust; would that be considered by him as just or unjust?

He would think it just, and would try to gain the advantage; but he would not be able.

Whether he would or would not be able, I said, is not to the point. My question is only whether the just man, while refusing to have more than another just man, would wish and claim to have more than the unjust?

Yes, he would.

And what of the unjust—does he claim to have more than the just man and to do more than is just?

Of course, he said, for he claims to have more than all men.

And the unjust man will strive and struggle to obtain more than the unjust man or action, in order that he may have more than all?

True.

We may put the matter thus, I said—the just does not desire more than his like but more than his unlike, whereas the unjust desires more than both his like and his unlike?

Nothing, he said, can be better than that statement.

And the unjust is good and wise, and the just is neither?

Good again, he said.

And is not the unjust like the wise and good and the just unlike them?

Of course, he said, he who is of a certain nature, is like those who are of a certain nature; he who is not, not.

Each of them, I said, is such as his like is?

Certainly, he replied.

Very good, Thrasymachus, I said; and now to take the case of the arts: you would admit that one man is a musician and another not a musician?

Yes.

And which is wise and which is foolish?

Clearly the musician is wise, and he who is not a musician is foolish.

And he is good in as far as he is wise, and bad in as far as he is foolish?

Yes.

And you would say the same sort of thing of the physician?

Yes.

And do you think, my excellent friend, that a musician when he adjusts the lyre would desire or claim to exceed or go beyond a musician in the tightening and loosening the strings?

I do not think that he would.

But he would claim to exceed the non-musician?

Of course.

And what would you say of the physician? In prescribing meats and drinks would he wish to go beyond another physician or beyond the practice of medicine?

He would not.

But he would wish to go beyond the non-physician?

Yes.

And about knowledge and ignorance in general; see whether you think that any man who has knowledge ever would wish to have the choice of saying or doing more than another man who has knowledge. Would he not rather say or do the same as his like in the same case?

That, I suppose, can hardly be denied.

And what of the ignorant? would he not desire to have more than either the knowing or the ignorant?

I dare say.

And the knowing is wise?

Yes.

And the wise is good?

True.

Then the wise and good will not desire to gain more than his like, but more than his unlike and opposite?

I suppose so.

Whereas the bad and ignorant will desire to gain more than both?

Yes.

But did we not say, Thrasymachus, that the unjust goes beyond both his like and unlike? Were not these your words?

They were.

And you also said that the just will not go beyond his like but his unlike?

Yes.

Then the just is like the wise and good, and the unjust like the evil and ignorant?

That is the inference.

And each of them is such as his like is?

That was admitted.

Then the just has turned out to be wise and good and the unjust evil and ignorant.

Thrasymachus made all these admissions, not fluently, as I repeat them, but with extreme reluctance; it was a hot summer's day and the perspiration poured from him in torrents; and then I saw what I had never seen before, Thrasymachus blushing. As we were now agreed that justice was virtue and wisdom, and injustice vice and ignorance, I proceeded to another point.

Well, I said, Thrasymachus, that matter is now settled; but were we not also saying that injustice had strength; do you remember?

Yes, I remember, he said, but do not suppose that I approve of what you are saying or have no answer; if however I were to answer, you would be quite certain to accuse me of haranguing; therefore either permit me to have my say out, or if you would rather ask, do so, and I will answer 'Very good,' as they say to story-telling old women, and will nod 'Yes' and 'No.'

Certainly not, I said, if contrary to your real opinion.

Yes, he said, I will, to please you, since you will not let me speak. What else would you have?

Nothing in the world, I said; and if you are so disposed I will ask and you shall answer.

Proceed.

Then I will repeat the question I asked before, in order that our examination of the relative nature of justice and injustice may be carried on regularly. A statement was made that injustice is stronger and more powerful than justice, but now justice, having been identified with wisdom and virtue, is easily shown to be stronger than injustice, if injustice is ignorance; this can no longer be questioned by any one. But I want to view the matter, Thrasymachus, in a different way: You would not deny that a state may be unjust and may be unjustly attempting to enslave other states, or may have already enslaved them, and may be holding many of them in subjection?

True, he replied; and I will add that the best and most perfectly unjust state will be most likely to do so.

I know, I said, that such was your position; but what I would further consider is, whether this power which is possessed by the superior state can exist or be exercised without justice or only with justice.

If you are right in your view, and justice is wisdom, then only with justice; but if I am right, then without justice.

I am delighted, Thrasymachus, to see you not only nodding assent and dissent, but making answers which are quite excellent.

That is out of civility to you, he replied.

You are very kind, I said; and would you have the goodness also to inform me, whether you think that a state, or an army, or a band of robbers and thieves, or any other gang of evil-doers could act at all if they injured one another?

No indeed, he said, they could not.

But if they abstained from injuring one another, then they might act together better?

Yes.

And this is because injustice creates divisions and hatreds and fighting, and justice imparts harmony and friendship; is not that true, Thrasymachus?

I agree, he said, because I do not wish to quarrel with you.

How good of you, I said; but I should like to know also whether injustice, having this tendency to arouse hatred, wherever existing, among slaves or among freemen, will not make them hate one another and set them at variance and render them incapable of common action?

Certainly.

And even if injustice be found in two only, will they not quarrel and fight, and become enemies to one another and to the just?

They will.

And suppose injustice abiding in a single person, would your wisdom say that she loses or that she retains her natural power?

Let us assume that she retains her power.

Yet is not the power which injustice exercises of such a nature that wherever she takes up her abode, whether in a city, in an army, in a family, or in any other body, that body is, to begin with, rendered incapable of united action by reason of sedition and distraction; and does it not become its own enemy and at variance with all that opposes it, and with the just? Is not this the case?

Yes, certainly.

And is not injustice equally fatal when existing in a single person; in the first place rendering him incapable of action because he is not at unity with himself, and in the second place making him an enemy to himself and the just? Is not that true, Thrasymachus?

Yes.

And O my friend, I said, surely the gods are just?

Granted that they are.

But if so, the unjust will be the enemy of the gods, and the just will be their friend?

Feast away in triumph, and take your fill of the argument; I will not oppose you, lest I should displease the company.

Well then, proceed with your answers, and let me have the remainder of my repast. For we have already shown that the just are clearly wiser and better and abler than the unjust, and that the unjust are incapable of common action; nay more, that to speak as we did of men who are evil acting at any time vigorously together, is not strictly true, for if they had been perfectly evil, they would have laid hands upon one another; but it is evident that there must have been some remnant of justice in them, which enable them to combine; if there had not been they would have injured one another as well as their victims; they were but half-villains in their enterprises; for had they been whole villains, and utterly unjust, they would have been utterly incapable of action. That, as I believe, is the truth of the matter, and not what you said at first. But whether the just have a better and happier life than the unjust is a further question which we also proposed to consider. I think that they have, and for the reasons which I have given; but still I should like to examine further, for no light matter is at stake, nothing less than the rule of human life.

Proceed.

I will proceed by asking a question: Would you not say that a horse has some end?

I should.

And the end or use of a horse or of anything would be that which could not be accomplished, or not so well accomplished, by any other thing?

I do not understand, he said.

Let me explain: Can you see, except with the eye?

Certainly not.

Or hear, except with the ear?

No.

These then may be truly said to be the ends of these organs?

They may.

But you can cut off a vine-branch with a dagger or with a chisel, and in many other ways?

Of course.

And yet not so well as with a pruning-hook made for the purpose?

True.

May we not say that this is the end of a pruning-hook?

We may.

Then now I think you will have no difficulty in understanding my meaning when I asked the question whether the end of anything would be that which could not be accomplished, or not so well accomplished, by any other thing?

I understand your meaning, he said, and assent.

And that to which an end is appointed has also an excellence? Need I ask again whether the eye has an end?

It has.

And has not the eye an excellence?

Yes.

And the ear has an end and an excellence also?

True.

And the same is true of all other things; they have each of them an end and a special excellence?

That is so.

Well, and can the eyes fulfil their end if they are wanting in their own proper excellence and have a defect instead?

How can they, he said, if they are blind and cannot see?

You mean to say, if they have lost their proper excellence, which is sight; but I have not arrived at that point yet. I would rather ask the question more generally, and only enquire whether the things which fulfil their ends fulfil them by their own proper excellence, and fail of fulfilling them by their own defect?

Certainly, he replied.

I might say the same of the ears; when deprived of their own proper excellence they cannot fulfil their end?

True.

And the same observation will apply to all other things?

I agree.

Well; and has not the soul an end which nothing else can fulfil? for example, to superintend and command and deliberate and the like. Are not these functions proper to the soul, and can they rightly be assigned to any other?

To no other.

And is not life to be reckoned among the ends of the soul?

Assuredly, he said.

And has not the soul an excellence also?

Yes.

And can she or can she not fulfil her own ends when deprived of that excellence?

She cannot.

Then an evil soul must necessarily be an evil ruler and superintendent, and the good soul a good ruler?

Yes, necessarily.

And we have admitted that justice is the excellence of the soul, and injustice the defect of the soul?

That has been admitted.

Then the just soul and the just man will live well, and the unjust man will live ill?

That is what your argument proves.

And he who lives well is blessed and happy, and he who lives ill the reverse of happy?

Certainly.

Then the just is happy, and the unjust miserable?

So be it.

But happiness and not misery is profitable.

Of course.

Then, my blessed Thrasymachus, injustice can never be more profitable than justice.

Let this, Socrates, he said, be your entertainment at the Bendidea.

For which I am indebted to you, I said, now that you have grown gentle towards me and have left off scolding. Nevertheless, I have not been well entertained; but that was my own fault and not yours. As an epicure snatches a taste of every dish which is successively brought to table, he not having allowed himself time to enjoy the one before, so have I gone from one subject to another without having discovered what I sought at first, the nature of justice. I left that enquiry and turned away to consider whether justice is virtue and wisdom or evil and folly; and when there arose a further question about the comparative advantages of justice and injustice, I could not refrain from passing on to that. And the result of the whole discussion has been that I know nothing at all. For I know not what justice is, and therefore I am not likely to know whether it is or is not a virtue, nor can I say whether the just man is happy or unhappy.

BOOK TWO

With these words I was thinking that I had made an end of the discussion; but the end, in truth, proved to be only a beginning. For

Glaucon, who is always the most pugnacious of men, was dissatisfied at Thrasymachus' retirement; he wanted to have the battle out. So he said to me: Socrates, do you wish really to persuade us, or only to seem to have persuaded us, that to be just is always better than to be unjust?

I should wish really to persuade you, I replied, if I could.

Then you certainly have not succeeded. Let me ask you now:— How would you arrange goods—are there not some which we welcome for their own sakes, and independently of their consequences, as, for example, harmless pleasures and enjoyments, which delight us at the time, although nothing follows from them?

I agree in thinking that there is such a class, I replied.

Is there not also a second class of goods, such as knowledge, sight, health, which are desirable not only in themselves, but also for their results?

Certainly, I said.

And would you not recognize a third class, such as gymnastic, and the care of the sick, and the physician's art; also the various ways of money-making—these do us good but we regard them as disagreeable; and no one would choose them for their own sakes, but only for the sake of some reward or result which flows from them?

There is, I said, this third class also. But why do you ask?

Because I want to know in which of the three classes you would place justice?

In the highest class, I replied,—among those goods which he who would be happy desires both for their own sake and for the sake of their results.

Then the many are of another mind; they think that justice is to be reckoned in the troublesome class, among goods which are to be pursued for the sake of rewards and of reputation, but in themselves are disagreeable and rather to be avoided.

I know, I said, that this is their manner of thinking, and that this was the thesis which Thrasymachus was maintaining just now, when he censured justice and praised injustice. But I am too stupid to be convinced by him.

I wish, he said, that you would hear me as well as him, and then I shall see whether you and I agree. For Thrasymachus seems to me, like a snake, to have been charmed by your voice sooner than he ought to have been; but to my mind the nature of justice and injustice have not yet been made clear. Setting aside their rewards and results, I want to know what they are in themselves, and how they inwardly work in the soul. If you please, then, I will revive the argument of Thrasymachus. And first I will speak of the nature and origin of justice according to the common view of them. Secondly, I will show that all men who practise justice do so against their will, of necessity, but not as a good. And thirdly, I will argue that there is reason in this view, for the life of the unjust is after all better far than the life of the just—if what they say is true, Socrates, since I myself am not of their opinion. But still I acknowledge that I am perplexed when I hear the voices of Thrasymachus and myriads of others dinning in my ears; and, on the other hand, I have never yet heard the superiority of justice to injustice maintained by any one in a satisfactory way. I want to hear justice praised in respect of itself; then I shall be satisfied, and you are the person from whom I think that I am most likely to hear this; and therefore I will praise the unjust life to the utmost of my power, and my manner of speaking will indicate the manner in which I desire to hear you too praising justice and censuring injustice. Will you say whether you approve of my proposals?

Indeed I do; nor can I imagine any theme about which a man of sense would oftener wish to converse.

I am delighted, he replied, to hear you say so, and shall begin by speaking, as I proposed, of the nature and origin of justice.

They say that to do injustice is, by nature, good; to suffer injustice, evil; but that the evil is greater than the good. And so when men have both done and suffered injustice and have had experience of both, not being able to avoid the one and obtain the other, they think that they had better agree among themselves to have neither; hence there arise laws and mutual covenants; and that which is ordained by law is termed by them lawful and just. This they affirm to be the origin and nature of justice;—it is a mean or compromise, between the best of all, which is to do injustice and not be punished, and the worst of all, which is to suffer injustice without the power of retaliation; and justice, being at a middle point between the two, is tolerated not as a good, but as the lesser evil, and honoured by reason of the inability of men to do injustice. For no man who is worthy to be called a man would ever submit to such an agreement if he were able to resist; he would be mad if he did. Such is the received account, Socrates, of the nature and origin of justice.

Now that those who practice justice do so involuntarily and because they have not the power to be unjust will best appear if we imagine something of this kind: having given both to the just and the unjust power to do what they will, let us watch and see whither desire will lead them; then we shall discover in the very act the just and unjust man to be proceeding along the same road, following their interest, which all natures deem to be their good, and are only diverted into the path of justice by the force of law. The liberty which we are supposing may be most completely given to them in the form of such a power as is said to have been possessed by Gyges the ancestor of Croesus the Lydian. According to the tradition, Gyges was a shepherd in the service of the king of Lydia; there was a great storm, and an earthquake made an opening in the earth at the place where he was feeding his flock.

Amazed at the sight, he descended into the opening, where, among other marvels, he beheld a hollow brazen horse, having doors, at which he stooping and looking in saw a dead body of stature, as appeared to him, more than human, and having nothing on but a gold ring; this he took from the finger of the dead and reascended. Now the shepherds met together, according to custom, that they might send their monthly report about the flocks to the king; into their assembly he came having the ring on his finger, and as he was sitting among them he chanced to turn the collet of the ring inside his hand, when instantly he became invisible to the rest of the company and they began to speak of him as if he were no longer present. He was astonished at this, and again touching the ring he turned the collet outwards and reappeared; he made several trials of the ring, and always with the same result—when he turned the collet inwards he became invisible, when outwards he reappeared. Whereupon he contrived to be chosen one of the messengers who were sent to the court; where as soon as he arrived he seduced the queen, and with her help conspired against the king and slew him, and took the kingdom. Suppose now that there were two such magic rings, and the just put on one of them and the unjust the other; no man can be imagined to be of such an iron nature that he would stand fast in justice. No man would keep his hands off what was not his own when he could safely take what he liked out of the market, or go into houses and lie with anyone at his pleasure, or kill or release from prison whom he would, and in all respects be like a God among men. Then the actions of the just would be as the actions of the unjust; they would both come at last to the same point. And this we may truly affirm to be a great proof that a man is just, not willingly or because he thinks that justice is any good to him individually, but of necessity, for wherever any one thinks that he can safely be unjust, there he is unjust. For all men believe in their hearts that injustice is far more profitable to the individual than justice, and he who argues as I have been supposing, will say that they are right. If you could imagine any one obtaining this power of becoming invisible, and never doing any wrong or touching what was another's, he would be thought by the lookers-on to be a most wretched idiot, although they would praise him to one another's faces, and keep up appearances with one another from a fear that they too might suffer injustice. Enough of this.

Now, if we are to form a real judgment of the life of the just and unjust, we must isolate them; there is no other way; and how is the isolation to be effected? I answer: Let the unjust man be entirely unjust, and the just man entirely just; nothing is to be taken away from either of them, and both are to be perfectly furnished for the work of their respective lives. First, let the unjust be like other distinguished masters of craft; like the skilful pilot or physician, who knows intuitively his own powers and keeps within their limits, and who, if he fails at any point, is able to recover himself. So let the unjust make his unjust attempts in the right way, and lie hidden if he means to be great in his injustice (he who is found out is nobody): for the highest reach of injustice is: to be deemed just when you are not. Therefore I say that in the perfectly unjust man we must assume the most perfect injustice; there is to be no deduction, but we must allow him, while doing the most unjust acts, to have acquired the greatest reputation for justice. If he has taken a false step he must be able to recover himself; he must be one who can speak with effect, if any of his deeds come to light, and who can force his way where force is required by his courage and strength, and command of money and friends. And at his side let us place the just man in his nobleness and simplicity, wishing, as Aeschylus says, to be and not to seem good. There must be no seeming, for if he seem to be just he will be honoured and rewarded, and then we shall not know whether he is just for the sake of justice or for the sake of honours and rewards; therefore, let him be clothed in justice only, and have no other covering; and he must be imagined in a state of life the opposite of the former. Let him be the best of men, and let him be thought the worst; then he will have been put to the proof; and we shall see whether he will be affected by the fear of infamy and its consequences. And let him continue thus to the hour of death; being just and seeming to be unjust. When both have reached the uttermost extreme, the one of justice and the other of injustice, let judgment be given which of them is the happier of the two.

Heavens! my dear Glaucon, I said, how energetically you polish them up for the decision, first one and then the other, as if they were two statues.

I do my best, he said. And now that we know what they are like there is no difficulty in tracing out the sort of life which awaits either of them. This I will proceed to describe; but as you may think the description a little too coarse, I ask you to suppose, Socrates, that the words which follow are not mine.—Let me put them into the mouths of the eulogists of injustice: They will tell you that the just man who is thought unjust will be scourged, racked, bound—will have his eyes burnt out; and, at last, after suffering every kind of evil, he will be impaled: Then he will understand that he ought to seem only, and not to be, just; the words of Aeschylus may be more truly spoken of the unjust than of the just. For the unjust is pursuing a reality; he does not live with a view to appearances—he wants to be really unjust and not to seem only:—

'His mind has a soil deep and fertile,
Out of which spring his prudent counsels.'

In the first place, he is thought just, and therefore bears rule in the city; he can marry whom he will, and give in marriage to whom he will;

also he can trade and deal where he likes, and always to his own advantage, because he has no misgivings about injustice; and at every contest, whether in public or private, he gets the better of his antagonists, and gains at their expense, and is rich, and out of his gains he can benefit his friends, and harm his enemies; moreover, he can offer sacrifices, and dedicate gifts to the gods abundantly and magnificently, and can honour the gods or any man whom he wants to honour in a far better style than the just, and therefore he is likely to be dearer than they are to the gods. And thus, Socrates, gods and men are said to unite in making the life of the unjust better than the life of the just.

I was going to say something in answer to Glaucon, when Adeimantus, his brother, interposed: Socrates, he said, you do not suppose that there is nothing more to be urged?

Why, what else is there? I answered.

The strongest point of all has not been even mentioned, he replied.

Well, then, according to the proverb, 'Let brother help brother'—if he fails in any part do you assist him; although I must confess that Glaucon has already said quite enough to lay me in the dust, and take from me the power of helping justice.

Nonsense, he replied. But let me add something more: There is another side to Glaucon's argument about the praise and censure of justice and injustice, which is equally required in order to bring out what I believe to be his meaning. Parents and tutors are always telling their sons and their wards that they are to be just; but why? not for the sake of justice, but for the sake of character and reputation; in the hope of obtaining for him who is reputed just some of those offices, marriages, and the like which Glaucon has enumerated among the advantages accruing to the unjust from the reputation of justice. More, however, is made of appearances by this class of persons than by the others; for they throw in the good opinion of the gods, and will tell you of a shower of benefits which the heavens, as they say, rain upon the pious; and this accords with the testimony of the noble Hesiod and Homer, the first of whom says, that the gods make the oaks of the just—

'To bear acorns at their summit, and bees in the middle;
And the sheep are bowed down with the weight of their fleeces.'

and many other blessings of a like kind are provided for them. And Homer has a very similar strain; for he speaks of one whose fame is—

'As the fame of some blameless king who, like a god,
Maintains justice; to whom the black earth brings forth
Wheat and barley, whose trees are bowed with fruit,
And his sheep never fail to bear, and the sea gives him fish.'

Still grander are the gifts of heaven which Musaeus and his son vouchsafe to the just; they take them down into the world below, where they have the saints lying on couches at a feast, everlastingly drunk, crowned with garlands; their idea seems to be that an immortality of drunkenness is the highest meed of virtue. Some extend their rewards yet further; the posterity, as they say, of the faithful and just shall survive to the third and fourth generation. This is the style in which they praise justice. But about the wicked there is another strain; they bury them in a slough in Hades, and make them carry water in a sieve; also while they are yet living they bring them to infamy, and inflict upon them the punishments which Glaucon described as the portion of the just who are reputed to be unjust; nothing else does their invention supply. Such is their manner of praising the one and censuring the other.

Once more, Socrates, I will ask you to consider another way of speaking about justice and injustice, which is not confined to the poets, but is found in prose writers. The universal voice of mankind is always declaring that justice and virtue are honourable, but grievous and toilsome; and that the pleasures of vice and injustice are easy of attainment, and are only censured by law and opinion. They say also that honesty is for the most part less profitable than dishonesty; and they are quite ready to call wicked men happy, and to honour them both in public and private when they are rich or in any other way influential, while they despise and overlook those who may be weak and poor, even though acknowledging them to be better than the others. But most extraordinary of all is their mode of speaking about virtue and the gods: they say that the gods apportion calamity and misery to many good men, and good and happiness to the wicked. And mendicant prophets go to rich men's doors and persuade them that they have a power committed to them by the gods of making an atonement for a man's own or his ancestor's sins by sacrifices or charms, with rejoicings and feasts; and they promise to harm an enemy, whether just or unjust, at a small cost; with magic arts and incantations binding heaven, as they say, to execute their will. And the poets are the authorities to whom they appeal, now smoothing the path of vice with the words of Hesiod:—

> 'Vice may be had in abundance without trouble; the way is smooth and her dwelling-place is near. But before virtue the gods have set toil,'

and a tedious and uphill road: then citing Homer as a witness that the gods may be influenced by men; for he also says:—

> 'The gods, too, may be turned from their purpose; and men pray to them and avert their wrath by sacrifices and soothing entreaties, and by libations and the odour of fat, when they have sinned and transgressed.'

And they produce a host of books written by Musaeus and Orpheus, who were children of the Moon and the Muses—that is what they say—

according to which they perform their ritual, and persuade not only individuals, but whole cities, that expiations and atonements for sin may be made by sacrifices and amusements which fill a vacant hour, and are equally at the service of the living and the dead; the latter sort they call mysteries, and they redeem us from the pains of hell, but if we neglect them no one knows what awaits us.

He proceeded: And now when the young hear all this said about virtue and vice, and the way in which gods and men regard them, how are their minds likely to be affected, my dear Socrates,—those of them, I mean, who are quickwitted, and, like bees on the wing, light on every flower, and from all that they hear are prone to draw conclusions as to what manner of persons they should be and in what way they should walk if they should make the best of life? Probably the youth will say to himself in the words of Pindar—

'Can I by justice or by crooked ways of deceit ascend a loftier tower which may be a fortress to me all my days?'

For what men say is that, if I am really just and am not also thought just, profit there is none, but the pain and loss on the other hand are unmistakable. But if, though unjust, I acquire the reputation of justice, a heavenly life is promised to me. Since then, as philosophers prove, appearance tyrannizes over truth and is lord of happiness, to appearance I must devote myself. I will describe around me a picture and shadow of virtue to be the vestibule and exterior of my house; behind I will trail the subtle and crafty fox, as Archilochus, greatest of sages, recommends. But I hear some one exclaiming that the concealment of wickedness is often difficult; to which I answer, Nothing great is easy. Nevertheless, the argument indicates this, if we should be happy, to be the path along which we should proceed. With a view to concealment we will establish secret brotherhoods and political clubs. And there are professors of rhetoric who teach the art of persuading courts and assemblies; and so, partly by persuasion and partly by force, I shall make unlawful gains and not be punished. Still I hear a voice saying that the gods cannot be deceived, neither can they be compelled. But what if there are no gods? or, suppose them to have no care of human things— why in either case should we mind about concealment? And even if there are gods, and they do care about us, yet we know of them only from tradition and the genealogies of the poets; and these are the very persons who say that they may be influenced and turned by 'sacrifices and soothing entreaties and by offerings.' Let us be consistent then, and believe both or neither. If the poets speak truly, why then we had better be unjust, and offer of the fruits of injustice; for if we are just, although we may escape the vengeance of heaven, we shall lose the gains of injustice; but, if we are unjust, we shall keep the gains, and by our sinning and praying, and praying and sinning, the gods will be propitiated, and we shall not be punished. 'But there is a world below in which either we or our posterity will suffer for our unjust deeds.' Yes, my friend, will be the reflection, but there are mysteries and atoning deities, and these have great power. That is what mighty cities declare; and the children of the gods, who were their poets and prophets, bear a like testimony.

On what principle, then, shall we any longer choose justice rather than the worst injustice? when, if we only unite the latter with a deceitful regard to appearances, we shall fare to our mind both with gods and men, in life and after death, as the most numerous and the highest authorities tell us. Knowing all this, Socrates, how can a man who has any superiority of mind or person or rank or wealth, be willing to honour justice; or indeed to refrain from laughing when he hears justice praised? And even if there should be some one who is able to disprove the truth of my words, and who is satisfied that justice is best, still he is not angry with the unjust, but is very ready to forgive them, because he also knows that men are not just of their own free will; unless peradventure, there be some one whom the divinity within him may have inspired with a hatred of injustice, or who has attained knowledge of the truth—but no other man. He only blames injustice who, owing to cowardice or age or some weakness, has not the power of being unjust. And this is proved by the fact that when he obtains the power, he immediately becomes unjust as far as he can be.

The cause of all this, Socrates, was indicated by us at the beginning of the argument, when my brother and I told you how astonished we were to find that of all the professing panegyrists of justice—beginning with the ancient heroes of whom any memorial has been preserved to us, and ending with the men of our own time—no one has ever blamed injustice or praised justice except with a view to the glories, honours, and benefits which flow from them. No one has ever adequately described either in verse or prose the true essential nature of either of them abiding in the soul, and invisible to any human or divine eye; or shown that of all the things of a man's soul which he has within him, justice is the greatest good, and injustice the greatest evil. Had this been the universal strain, had you sought to persuade us of this from our youth upwards, we should not have been on the watch to keep one another from doing wrong, but every one would have been his own watchman, because afraid, if he did wrong, of harbouring in himself the greatest of evils. I dare say that Thrasymachus and others would seriously hold the language which I have been merely repeating, and words even stronger than these about justice and injustice, grossly, as I conceive, perverting their true nature. But I speak in this vehement manner, as I must frankly confess to you, because I want to hear from you the opposite side; and I would ask you to show not only the superiority which justice has over injustice, but what effect they have on the possessor of them which makes the one to be a good and the other an evil to him.

And please, as Glaucon requested of you, to exclude reputations; for unless you take away from each of them his true reputation and add on the false, we shall say that you do not praise justice, but the appearance of it; we shall think that you are only exhorting us to keep injustice dark, and that you really agree with Thrasymachus in thinking that justice is another's good and the interest of the stronger, and that injustice is a man's own profit and interest, though injurious to the weaker. Now as you have admitted that justice is one of that highest class of goods which are desired indeed for their results, but in a far greater degree for their own sakes—like sight or hearing or knowledge or health, or any good—I would ask you in your praise of justice to regard one point only: I mean the essential good and evil which justice and injustice work in the possessors of them. Let others praise justice and censure injustice, magnifying the rewards and honours of the one and abusing the other; that is a manner of arguing which, coming from them, I am ready to tolerate, but from you who have spent your whole life in the consideration of this question, unless I hear the contrary from your own lips, I expect something better. And therefore, I say, not only prove to us that justice is better than injustice, but show what they either of them do to the possessor of them, which makes the one to be a good and the other an evil, whether seen or unseen by gods and men.

Aristotle (384–322 B.C.)

Aristotle was born in Stagira, in Thrace. His father was court physician to the king of Macedonia, which may account for Aristotle's great interest in the biological sciences. When he was eighteen, Aristotle went to the Academy in Athens and remained there as Plato's student until the latter's death nearly twenty years later. He then traveled and studied in Asia Minor, returned briefly to Athens, and in 343 B.C. was called back to Macedonia to tutor Alexander, the young son of King Philip who was later to become Alexander the Great. There is no evidence that Alexander's political or philosophical outlook was significantly molded by the three years he spent as Aristotle's student. In 335 B.C. Aristotle returned to Athens and founded his own school, the Lyceum, and for the next twelve years studied and wrote extensively. He is supposed to have written many dialogues of high literary quality, but these have been lost, and the works of Aristotle as we know them are sets of prepared lectures along with notes on lectures taken by his students. In 323 B.C. Alexander the Great died and Athens revolted against Macedonian rule. Endangered because of his earlier association with the great conqueror and afraid that the Athenians would kill him and thus, as he is supposed to have said, "sin twice against philosophy," Aristotle fled to Chalcis, where he died the following year.

Aristotle's *Ethics* and his *Politics* are meant to be the first and second parts of a single work. *Aristotle* (London, 1937) by W. David Ross and *Outlines of the History of Ethics* (1886) by Henry Sidgwick contain sections on Aristotle's ethics. Other books are *Aristotle, The Nicomachean Ethics* (1951) by H. H. Joachim, *Aristotle* (1960) by J. H. Randall, *Greek Ethics* (1967) by P. Huby, and *Aristotle's Ethical Theory* (1968) by W. F. R. Hardie. *Aristotle's Ethics: Issues and Interpretations* (1967), edited by J. J. Walsh and H. L. Shapiro, contains seven critical essays. In *Aristotle: A Collection of Critical Essays* (1967), edited by J. Moravesik, Part IV contains four relatively advanced essays on Aristotle's ethics.

The Nicomachean Ethics

BOOK ONE

Aristotle begins, in a way characteristic of his method, with a general-
ization which, if accepted, will lead to a more exact account of his
subject. It is a generalization which is fundamental to his philosophy
and in his own mind there is no doubt about the truth of it. Yet he is
not at this point asserting its truth. He is content to state a position
which he has found reason to hold. It may be defined in some such
words as these: The good is that at which all things aim. If we are to
understand this, we must form to ourselves a clear notion of what is
meant by an aim or, in more technical language, an 'end.' The first chap-
ter of the Ethics is concerned with making the notion clear.

CHAPTER ONE

It is thought that every activity, artistic or scientific, in fact every deliberate action or pursuit, has for its object the attainment of some good.
We may therefore assent to the view which has been expressed that 'the
good' is 'that at which all things aim.' * Since modes of action involving
the practised hand and the instructed brain are numerous, the number
of their ends is proportionately large. For instance, the end of medical
science is health; of military science, victory; of economic science,
wealth. All skills of that kind which come under a single 'faculty'—a skill
in making bridles or any other part of a horse's gear comes under the
faculty or art of horsemanship, while horsemanship itself and every
branch of military practice comes under the art of war, and in like
manner other arts and techniques are subordinate to yet others—in all
these the ends of the master arts are to be preferred to those of the

---

Translated by J. A. K. Thompson (London: George Allen & Unwin Ltd., 1953).
Reprinted by permission of the publisher.

* It is of course obvious that to a certain extent they do not all aim at the same
thing, for in some cases the end will be an activity, in others the product which goes
beyond the actual activity. In the arts which aim at results of this kind the results
or products are intrinsically superior to the activities.

subordinate skills, for it is the former that provide the motive for pursuing the latter.*

CHAPTER TWO

Now if there is an end which as moral agents we seek for its own sake, and which is the cause of our seeking all the other ends—if we are not to go on choosing one act for the sake of another, thus landing ourselves in an infinite progression with the result that desire will be frustrated and ineffectual—it is clear that this must be the good, that is the absolutely good. May we not then argue from this that a knowledge of the good is a great advantage to us in the conduct of our lives? Are we not more likely to hit the mark if we have a target? If this be true, we must do our best to get at least a rough idea of what the good really is, and which of the sciences, pure or applied, is concerned with the business of achieving it.

Ethics is a branch of politics. That is to say, it is the duty of the statesman to create for the citizen the best possible opportunity of living the good life. It will be seen that the effect of this injunction is not to degrade morality but to moralize politics. The modern view that 'you cannot make men better by act of parliament' would have been repudiated by Aristotle as certainly as by Plato and indeed by ancient philosophers in general.

Now most people would regard the good as the end pursued by that study which has most authority and control over the rest. Need I say that this is the science of politics? It is political science that prescribes what subjects are to be taught in states, which of these the different sections of the population are to learn, and up to what point. We see also that the faculties which obtain most regard come under this science: for example, the art of war, the management of property, the ability to state a case. Since, therefore, politics makes use of the other practical sciences, and lays it down besides what we must do and what we must not do, its end must include theirs. And that end, in politics as well as in ethics, can only be the good for man. For even if the good of the community coincides with that of the individual, the good of the community is clearly a greater and more perfect good both to get and to keep. This is not to deny that the good of the individual is worth while. But what is good for a nation or a city has a higher, a diviner, quality.

---

* It makes no difference if the ends of the activities are the activities themselves or something over and above these, as in the case of the sciences I have mentioned.

Such being the matters we seek to investigate, the investigation may fairly be represented as the study of politics.

The study of politics is not an exact science.

CHAPTER THREE

In studying this subject we must be content if we attain as high a degree of certainty as the matter of it admits. The same accuracy or finish is not to be looked for in all discussions any more than in all the productions of the studio and the workshop. The question of the morally fine and the just—for this is what political science attempts to answer—admits of so much divergence and variation of opinion that it is widely believed that morality is a convention and not part of the nature of things. We find a similar fluctuation of opinion about the character of the good. The reason for this is that quite often good things have hurtful consequences. There are instances of men who have been ruined by their money or killed by their courage. Such being the nature of our subject and such our way of arguing in our discussion of it, we must be satisfied with a rough outline of the truth, and for the same reason we must be content with broad conclusions. Indeed we must preserve this attitude when it comes to a more detailed statement of the views that are held. It is a mark of the educated man and a proof of his culture that in every subject he looks for only so much precision as its nature permits. For example, it is absurd to demand logical demonstrations from a professional speaker; we might as well accept mere probabilities from a mathematician.

Political science is not studied with profit by the young.

Every man is a good judge of what he understands: in special subjects the specialist, over the whole field of knowledge the man of general culture. This is the reason why political science is not a proper study for the young. The young man is not versed in the practical business of life from which politics draws its premises and its data. He is, besides, swayed by his feelings, with the result that he will make no headway and derive no benefit from a study the end of which is not *knowing* but *doing*. It makes no difference whether the immaturity is in age or in character. The defect is not due to lack of years but to living the kind of life which is a succession of unrelated emotional experiences. To one who is like that, knowledge is as unprofitable as it is to the morally unstable. On the other hand for those whose desires and actions have a rational basis a knowledge of these principles of morals must be of great advantage. . . .

This, however, is something of a digression. Let us resume our consideration of what is the end of political science. For want of a better word we call it 'Happiness.' People are agreed on the word but not on its meaning.

CHAPTER FOUR

To resume. Since every activity involving some acquired skill or some moral decision aims at some good, what do we take to be the end of politics—what is the supreme good attainable in our actions? Well, so far as the name goes there is pretty general agreement. 'It is happiness,' say both intellectuals and the unsophisticated, meaning by 'happiness' living well or faring well. But when it comes to saying in what happiness consists, opinions differ, and the account given by the generality of mankind is not at all like that given by the philosophers. The masses take it to be something plain and tangible, like pleasure or money or social standing. Some maintain that it is one of these, some that it is another, and the same man will change his opinion about it more than once. When he has caught an illness he will say that it is health, and when he is hard up he will say that it is money. Conscious that they are out of their depths in such discussions, most people are impressed by anyone who pontificates and says something that is over their heads. Now it would no doubt be a waste of time to examine all these opinions; enough if we consider those which are most in evidence or have something to be said for them. Among these we shall have to discuss the view held by some that, over and above particular goods like those I have just mentioned, there is another which is good in itself and the cause of whatever goodness there is in all these others.

A digression on method.

We must be careful not to overlook the difference that it makes whether we argue *from* or *to* first principles. Plato used very properly to advert to this distinction. Employing a metaphor from the race-course, where the competitors run from the starting-point and back to it again, he would ask whether the appropriate procedure in a particular enquiry was *from* or *to* first principles. Of course we must start from what is known. But that is an ambiguous expression, for things are known in two ways. Some are known 'to us' and some are known absolutely. For members of the Lyceum there can be little doubt that we must start from what is known to us. So the future student of ethics and politics, if he is to study them to advantage, must have been well brought up. For we begin with the *fact*, and if there is sufficient reason for accepting it as such, there will be no need to ascertain also the *why* of the fact. Now a lad with such an upbringing will have no difficulty in grasping the first principles of morals, if he is not in possession of them already. If he has neither of these qualifications, he had better take to heart what Hesiod says:

> That man is best who sees the truth himself;
> Good too is he who hearkens to wise counsel.
>   But who is neither wise himself nor willing
> To ponder wisdom, is not worth a straw.

A man's way of life may afford a clue to his genuine views upon the nature of happiness. It is therefore worth our while to glance at the different types of life.

CHAPTER FIVE

Let us return from this digression. There is a general assumption that the manner of a man's life is a clue to what he on reflection regards as the good—in other words, happiness. Persons of low tastes (always in the majority) hold that it is pleasure. Accordingly they ask for nothing better than the sort of life which consists in having a good time. (I have in mind the three well-known types of life—that just mentioned, that of the man of affairs, that of the philosophic student.) The utter vulgarity of the herd of men comes out in their preference for the sort of existence a cow leads. Their view would hardly get a respectful hearing, were it not that those who occupy great positions sympathize with a monster of sensuality like Sardanapalus. The gentleman, however, and the man of affairs identify the good with honour, which may fairly be described as the end which men pursue in political or public life. Yet honour is surely too superficial a thing to be the good we are seeking. Honour depends more on those who confer than on him who receives it, and we cannot but feel that the good is something personal and almost inseparable from its possessor. Again, why do men seek honour? Surely in order to confirm the favourable opinion they have formed of themselves. It is at all events by intelligent men who know them personally that they seek to be honoured. And for what? For their moral qualities. The inference is clear; public men prefer virtue to honour. It might therefore seem reasonable to suppose that virtue rather than honour is the end pursued in the life of the public servant. But clearly even virtue cannot be quite the end. It is possible, most people think, to possess virtue while you are asleep, to possess it without acting under its influence during any portion of one's life. Besides, the virtuous man may meet with the most atrocious luck or ill-treatment; and nobody, who was not arguing for argument's sake, would maintain that a man with an existence of that sort was 'happy.' The third type of life is the 'contemplative,' and this we shall discuss later.

As for the life of the business man, it does not give him much freedom of action. Besides, wealth obviously is not the good we seek, for the sole purpose it serves is to provide the means of getting something else. So far as that goes, the ends we have already mentioned would have a better title to be considered the good, for they are desired on their own account. But in fact even their claim must be disallowed. We may say that they have furnished the ground for many arguments, and leave the matter at that.

Aristotle now passes to a criticism of the Platonic theory of a 'universal good,' often called the 'idea' or 'form' of the Good. The criticism is too famous, and in parts too acute, to be omitted, but it does not show Aristotle at his best. Plato thought of his forms as 'eternal' in the sense in which God is eternal, that is, as existing out of space and time. This Aristotle either could not or would not understand. It is true of course that Plato represents the forms as coming into some kind of relation with objects of sense, and Aristotle is fully entitled to criticize his account of this relation. But the existence of the forms—if they exist—is not thereby disproved.

CHAPTER SIX

But we can hardly avoid examining the problem raised by the concept of a universal good. One approaches it with reluctance because the theory of 'forms' was brought into philosophy by friends of mine. Yet surely it is the better, or rather the unavoidable, course, above all for philosophers, to defend the truth even at the cost of our most intimate feelings, since, though both are dear, it would be wrong to put friendship before the truth.

Those who introduced the theory of forms did not suppose that there existed forms of *groups* of things in which one of the things is thought of as prior in nature to another. This accounts for their not attempting to construct a form of 'number' as distinct from particular numbers. Now a thing may be called good in three ways: in itself, in some quality it has, in some relation it bears to something else. But the 'essence' of a thing—what it is in itself—is by its very nature prior to any relation it may have, such a relation being an offshoot or 'accident' of it. Therefore there cannot be one form embracing *both* the absolutely *and* the relatively good.

Again, the word 'good' is used in as many senses as the word 'is.' We may describe a person or a thing—God, for instance, or the reasoning faculty—as good in the sense of absolutely good. Or we may speak of things as good when we are thinking of their qualities or special excellences. Or we may use the word in connexion with the quantity of something, when we mean that there is a right amount of it; or in connexion with its relation to something else, as when we say that it is 'useful,' meaning good as means to an end; or in connexion with its occurrence in time, describing it as 'the right moment,' or in connexion with its position in space, as 'a good place to live in.' And so on. Using technical language we may predicate 'good' in the categories of (a) substance, (b) quality, (c) quantity, (d) relation, (e) time, (f) space. Clearly then 'good' is not something that can be said in one and the same sense of everything called 'good.' For then it could not be said in all these *different* senses, but only in one.

Again, things of which there is a single form must be things of which there is a single science. Consequently there should be (if the view we are discussing is right) a single science dealing with *all* good things. But what do we find? An indefinite number of sciences dealing with the goods coming under even one of the heads we have mentioned. Take 'the right moment.' The right moment in war is studied under military science, the right moment in sickness under the science of medicine. Similarly the right quantity in diet is considered by medicine, in bodily exercise by physical training.

Next, what do they mean by 'the thing as it really is'? The question deserves some answer. For in their own terminology 'man as he really is' is just another way of saying 'man.' In this respect, then, there will be no difference between them—they are both 'man.' But, if we are allowed to argue on these lines, we shall find no difference either between the really good and the good, in so far as both are good. Nor will the really good be any more good by being 'eternal.' You might as well say that a white thing which lasts a long time is whiter than one which lasts only a day.*

To the arguments we have been using the objection may present itself that the champions of the forms did not mean their words to apply to *every* good. What they meant (it may be argued) was this. Those things, and those things only, which are pursued and desired on their own account are good. They are good as belonging to one species, while things tending in any way to produce or conserve them, or to check their opposites, are good in a different way, namely as means of achieving them. Clearly then there would be two kinds of 'goods'—things good in themselves and things good as means to these. Let us take them separately. Consider first the things that are good in themselves. Are they called 'good' because they come under a single form? Then what sort of things are the good in themselves? Are they all those things—

---

* On this point it may be thought that the Pythagoreans (followed, it would seem, by Speusippus) have a more probable doctrine; they place unity in their column of 'goods.' But we must leave the discussion of this point to another occasion.

intelligence, for example, or sight or certain pleasures and honours—that are sought entirely on their own merits? For these are things which, even if we pursue them with some remoter object in view, might be classified as things good in themselves. Or is there nothing good in itself except the form of the good? That would leave the class empty of content. If on the other hand things of the kind I have mentioned do form a class of things good in themselves, it will follow that the same notion of good will be as clearly recognizable in them as the same notion of whiteness presents itself to us in snow and in white lead. But when it comes to honour and sagacity and pleasure, the notions we have of them in respect of their goodness are different and distinguishable. Therefore 'good' is not a general term corresponding to a single form. How then does it happen that these different things are all called 'good'? It can hardly be a mere coincidence. Various answers suggest themselves. All goods may derive from a single good, or all may contribute to form a single good. Or perhaps the answer may be expressed in an equation 'As sight is good in the body, so is rationality in the mind.' We could frame a series of such equations. But perhaps it is better to drop the discussion of that point here, since a full examination of it is more suited to another branch of philosophy. And we must follow the same course in dealing with the form of the good. For, even if the good which is predicated of a number of different things exists only in one element common to them all, or has a separate existence of its own, clearly it cannot be realized in action or acquired by man. Yet it is just a good of that kind that is the subject of our present inquiry. The thought may indeed suggest itself that a knowledge of the absolute good may be desirable as a means of attaining to those goods which a man may acquire and realize in practice. Might we not use it as a pattern to guide us in acquiring a better knowledge of the things that are good 'for us' and, so knowing, obtaining them? The argument has a certain plausibility, but it manifestly does not accord with the procedure followed by the sciences. For all these aim at some *particular* good and seek to fill up the gaps in their knowledge of how to attain *it*. They do not think it any business of theirs to learn the nature of the *absolute* good. Now it will take some persuading to make us believe that all the masters of technique do not possess, or even make an effort to possess, this knowledge, if it be so powerful an aid to them as is pretended. And there is another puzzle. What advantage in his art will a weaver or a joiner get from a knowledge of the absolute good? Or how shall a doctor or a general who has had a vision of Very Form become thereby a better doctor or general? As a matter of fact it does not appear that the doctor makes a study even of health in the abstract. What he studies is the health of the human subject or rather of a particular patient. For it is on such a patient that he exercises his skill....

What then is the good? If it is what all men in the last resort aim at,
it must be happiness. And that for two reasons: (1) happiness is every-
thing it needs to be, (2) it has everything it needs to have.

CHAPTER SEVEN

From this digression we may return to the good which is the object of
our search. What is it? The question must be asked because good seems
to vary with the art of pursuit in which it appears. It is one thing in
medicine and another in strategy, and so in the other branches of human skill. We must inquire, then, what is the good which is the end
common to all of them. Shall we say it is that for the sake of which
everything else is done? In medicine this is health, in military science
victory, in architecture a building, and so on—different ends in different
arts; every consciously directed activity has an end for the sake of
which everything that it does is done. This end may be described as
its good. Consequently, if there be some one thing which is the end of
all things consciously done, this will be the doable good; or, if there be
more than one end, then it will be all of these. Thus the ground on
which our argument proceeds is shifted, but the conclusion arrived at
is the same.

I must try, however, to make my meaning clearer.

In our actions we aim at more ends than one—that seems to be certain—but, since we choose some (wealth, for example, or flutes and
tools or instruments generally) as means to something else, it is clear
that not all of them are ends in the full sense of the word, whereas
the good, that is the supreme good, is surely such an end. Assuming
then that there is some one thing which alone is an end beyond which
there are no further ends, we may call *that* the good of which we are
in search. If there be more than one such final end, the good will be
that end which has the highest degree of finality. An object pursued
for its own sake possesses a higher degree of finality than one pursued
with an eye to something else. A corollary to that is that a thing which
is never chosen as a means to some remoter object has a higher degree
of finality than things which are chosen both as ends in themselves and
as means to such ends. We may conclude, then, that something which
is always chosen for its own sake and never for the sake of something
else is without qualification a final end.

Now happiness more than anything else appears to be just such
an end, for we always choose it for its own sake and never for the
sake of some other thing. It is different with honour, pleasure, intelligence and good qualities generally. We choose them indeed for their
own sake in the sense that we should be glad to have them irrespective
of any advantage which might accrue from them. But we also choose

them for the sake of our happiness in the belief that they will be instrumental in promoting that. On the other hand nobody chooses happiness as a means of achieving them or anything else whatsoever than just happiness.

The same conclusion would seem to follow from another consideration. It is a generally accepted view that the final good is self-sufficient. By 'self-sufficient' is meant not what is sufficient for oneself living the life of a solitary but includes parents, wife and children, friends and fellow-citizens in general. For man is a social animal.* A self-sufficient thing, then, we take to be one which on its own footing tends to make life desirable and lacking in nothing. And we regard happiness as such a thing. Add to this that we regard it as the most desirable of all things without having it counted in with some other desirable thing. For, if such an addition were possible, clearly we should regard it as more desirable when even the smallest advantage was added to it. For the result would be an increase in the number of advantages, and the larger sum of advantages is preferable to the smaller.

Happiness then, the end to which all our conscious acts are directed, is found to be something final and self-sufficient.

But we desire a clearer definition of happiness. The way to this may be prepared by a discussion of what is meant by the 'function' of a man.

But no doubt people will say, 'To call happiness the highest good is a truism. We want a more distinct account of what it is.' We might arrive at this if we could grasp what is meant by the 'function' of a human being. If we take a flautist or a sculptor or any craftsman—in fact any class of men at all who have some special job or profession—we find that his special talent and excellence comes out in that job, and this is his function. The same thing will be true of man simply as man—that is of course if 'man' does have a function. But is it likely that joiners and shoemakers have certain functions or specialized activities, while man as such has none but has been left by Nature a functionless being? Seeing that eye and hand and foot and every one of our members has some obvious function, must we not believe that in like manner a human being has a function over and above these particular functions? Then what exactly is it? The mere act of living is not peculiar to man —we find it even in the vegetable kingdom—and what we are looking for is something peculiar to him. We must therefore exclude from our definition the life that manifests itself in mere nurture and growth. A

---

* Of course we must draw the line somewhere. For, if we stretch it to include ancestors and descendants and friends' friends, there will be no end to it. But there will be another opportunity of considering this point.

step higher should come the life that is confined to experiencing sensations. But that we see is shared by horses, cows, and the brute creation as a whole. We are left, then, with a life concerning which we can make two statements. First, it belongs to the rational part of man. Secondly, it finds expression in actions. The rational part may be either active or passive: passive in so far as it follows the dictates of reason, active in so far as it possesses and exercises the power of reasoning. A similar distinction can be drawn within the rational life; that is to say, the reasonable element in it may be active or passive. Let us take it that what we are concerned with here is the reasoning power in action, for it will be generally allowed that when we speak of 'reasoning' we really mean *exercising* our reasoning faculties. (This seems the more correct use of the word.) Now let us assume for the moment the truth of the following propositions. (a) The function of a man is the exercise of his non-corporeal faculties or 'soul' in accordance with, or at least not divorced from, a rational principle. (b) The function of an individual and of a *good* individual in the same class—a harp player, for example, and a good harp player, and so through the classes—is generically the same, except that we must add superiority in accomplishment to the function, the function of the harp player being merely to play on the harp, while the function of the good harp player is to play on it well. (c) The function of man is a certain form of life, namely an activity of the soul exercised in combination with a rational principle or reasonable ground of action. (d) The function of a good man is to exert such activity well. (e) A function is performed well when performed in accordance with the excellence proper to it.—If these assumptions are granted, we conclude that the good for man is 'an activity of soul in accordance with goodness' or (on the supposition that there may be more than one form of goodness) 'in accordance with the best and most complete form of goodness.'

Happiness is more than momentary bliss.

There is another condition of happiness; it cannot be achieved in less than a complete lifetime. One swallow does not make a summer; neither does one fine day. And one day, or indeed any brief period of felicity, does not make a man entirely and perfectly happy.

So far, however, we have merely drawn the outline of happiness; the details must be filled in gradually. In the exact sciences precise conclusions are reached, and reached once for all. In ethics we can only approximate to such conclusions.

It is not pretended that we have given more than an outline of the good. But we must be content with that at this stage, for doubtless the proper way of going to work is to draw an outline and fill in the details afterwards—when the sketch is well done, anybody can finish the picture. In this work Time is believed to put his shoulder to the wheel and even point the way to new discoveries. In fact progress in the arts has usually been made in that fashion, for anybody can fill in the gaps in a formula. But we must not forget what we said before about not looking for the same exactness in all we study or labour at, but only as much as the subject-matter in each case allows, or is appropriate to the particular method followed by the student or workman. For example the carpenter and the geometrician alike try to find the right angle, but they do it in different ways, the carpenter being content with such precision as satisfies the requirements of his job, the geometrician as a student of scientific truth seeking to discover the nature and attributes of the right angle. We ought to follow this procedure in other studies as well, always asking ourselves what degree of accuracy is to be expected in them, in order that we may not unnecessarily complicate the facts by introducing side issues.

Nor must we demand in every subject an account of the cause or reason why it is what it is, for there are cases in which it is quite enough if the fact itself is proved. We shall find that this applies to 'beginnings,' which is our name for first principles; in them the fact *is* the beginning. Some are grasped by a process of induction, some by a kind of perception, some at the end of a period of training or habituation, others in other ways. On every occasion we must seek to arrive at first principles in the way natural to them in the instance that presents itself. We must also make a point of finding good definitions of them, because such definitions are an immense advantage to us as we pursue the subject. The proverb says that 'the half is greater than the whole,' but we may go further and say that the beginning is greater than the whole, for the beginning clears up many obscurities together in the matter we may be investigating.

It follows that our first principle—our definition of happiness—should be tested not only by the rules of logic but also by the application to it of current opinions on the subject.

CHAPTER EIGHT

So we must examine our first principle not only logically, that is as a conclusion from premises, but also in the light of what is currently said about it. For if a thing be true, the evidence will be found in harmony with it; and, if it be false, the evidence is quickly shown to be discordant with it.

But first a note about 'goods.' They have been classified as (a) external, (b) of the soul, (c) of the body. Of these we may express our belief that goods of the soul are the best and are most properly designated as 'good.' Now according to our definition happiness is an expression of the soul in considered actions, and that definition seems to be confirmed by this belief, which is not only an old popular notion but is accepted by philosophers. We are justified, too, in saying that the end consists in certain acts or activities, for this enables us to count it among goods of the soul and not among external goods. We may also claim that our description of the happy man as the man who lives or fares well chimes in with our definition. For happiness has pretty much been stated to be a form of such living or faring well. Again, our definition seems to include the elements detected in the various analyses of happiness—virtue, practical wisdom, speculative wisdom, or a combination of these, or one of them in more or less intimate association with pleasure. All these definitions have their supporters, while still others are for adding material prosperity to the conditions of a happy life. Some of these views are popular convictions of long standing; others are set forth by a distinguished minority. It is reasonable to think that neither the mass of men nor the sages are mistaken altogether, but that on this point or that, or indeed on most points, there is justice in what they say.

Now our definition of happiness as an activity in accordance with virtue is so far in agreement with that of those who say that it *is* virtue, that such an activity *involves* virtue. But of course it makes a great difference whether we think of the highest good as consisting in the *possession* or in the *exercise* of virtue. It is possible for a disposition to goodness to exist in a man without anything coming of it; he might be asleep or in some other way have ceased to exercise his function of a man. But that is not possible with the activity in our definition. For in 'doing well' the happy man will of necessity *do.* Just as at the Olympic Games it is not the best-looking or the strongest men present who are crowned with victory but competitors—the successful competitors—so in the arena of human life the honours and rewards fall to those who show their good qualities in action.

Observe, moreover, that the life of the actively good is inherently pleasant. Pleasure is a psychological experience, and every man finds that pleasant for which he has a liking—'fond of' so-and-so is the expression people use. For example, a horse is a source of pleasure to a man who is fond of horses, a show to a man who is fond of sightseeing. In the same way just actions are a source of pleasure to a man who likes to see justice done, and good actions in general to one who likes goodness. Now the mass of men do not follow any consistent plan in the pursuit of their pleasures, because their pleasures are not inherently pleasurable. But men of more elevated tastes and sentiments find pleasure in things which are in their own nature pleasant, for instance virtuous actions, which are pleasant in themselves and not merely to such men. So their life does not need to have pleasure fastened about it like a necklace, but possesses it as a part of itself. We may go further and assert that he is no good man who does not find pleasure in noble deeds. Nobody would admit that a man is just, unless he takes pleasure in just actions; or liberal, unless he takes pleasure in acts of liberality; and so with the other virtues. Grant this, and you must grant that virtuous actions are a source of pleasure in themselves. And surely they are also both good and noble, and that always in the highest degree, if we are to accept, as accept we must, the judgment of the good man about them, he judging in the way I have described. Thus, happiness is the best, the noblest, the most delightful thing in the world, and in it meet all those qualities which are separately enumerated in the inscription upon the temple at Delos:

> *Justice is loveliest, and health is best,*
> *And sweetest to obtain is heart's desire.*

All these good qualities inhere in the activities of the virtuous soul, and it is these, or the best of them, which we say constitute happiness.

For all that those are clearly right who, as I remarked, maintain the necessity to a happy life of an addition in the form of material goods. It is difficult, if not impossible, to engage in noble enterprises without money to spend on them; many can only be performed through friends, or wealth, or political influence. There are also certain advantages, such as the possession of honoured ancestors or children, or personal beauty, the absence of which takes the bloom from our felicity. For you cannot quite regard a man as happy if he be very ugly to look at, or of humble origin, or alone in the world and childless, or—what is probably worse —with children or friends who have not a single good quality or whose virtues died with them. Well, as I said, happiness seems to require a modicum of external prosperity—thus leading some to identify it with the condition of those who are 'favourites of fortune. . . .'

However, we must guard against misunderstanding. Fortune can supply the happy man with the means, and create for him the conditions, of his happiness; it cannot create his happiness.

CHAPTER NINE

From this springs another problem. Is happiness (a) capable of being acquired by some intellectual process or the formation of a habit or some other method of training, or (b) does it come to us simply by some divine dispensation, or even by the caprice of events? Well, in the first place, if anything is a gift of the gods to men, it is reasonable to suppose that happiness is such a gift, particularly as of all human possessions it is the best.* Yet, even if happiness is not sent by a special providence but is acquired by virtue, or study, or practice, we look on it as one of our greatest blessings. For the crown and end of goodness is surely of all things the best, and the best we may also call divine and blissful. In the second place we look on happiness as something that may be widely spread. For through some process—of study or application of our mental powers—it may fall to any man who does not suffer from some disability or incapacity to achieve excellence. Thirdly, assuming that it is a better thing to reach happiness by these efforts of our own than by a stroke of luck, we may reasonably think that happiness is in fact reached in that way. The productions of nature have an innate tendency in the direction of the best condition of which they are capable, and so have the creations of the craftsman and artist and whatever has an efficient cause of any kind, especially if that cause ranks highest in the scale of excellence. But that the greatest and finest thing of all should be at the mercy of chance is a thought that strikes a very jarring note.

The problem may receive some illumination from our description of happiness as an activity of the soul, all the other good things of life being either necessary adjuncts of happiness or useful in helping it to perform its function in the way that tools are helpful to the workman. The conclusion that happiness depends upon ourselves is in harmony with what I said in the first of these lectures, when I laid it down that the highest good is the end which is sought by political science. What the statesman is most anxious to produce is a certain moral character in his fellow-citizens, namely a disposition to virtue and the performance of virtuous actions. That is why we do not naturally speak of a cow or a horse or other beast as 'happy,' for none of the brute creation can take part in moral activities. For the same reason no child is 'happy' either, for its age precludes it from taking part as yet in such actions; if we choose to call one happy, it is because he gives promise of being so. For, as I have already observed, we cannot have happiness unless we have complete goodness in a complete lifetime. Life is full of chances and changes, and the most prosperous of men may in the evening of his days meet with great misfortunes, like Priam in the stories we read in the epic poets. A man who has encountered such blows of fate and suffered a tragic death is called happy by no one. . . .

Aristotle now produces a new argument designed to show that happiness is the end of life—happiness as he has defined it. He draws a dis-

---

* This, however, is a topic which appears more germane to another branch of study, such as theology.

tinction between things that are praised and things that are regarded as above or beyond praise. The end of life must be something beyond praise; and such is happiness.

CHAPTER TWELVE

Now after settling these questions let us see if we can discover whether happiness is something to be *praised* or something to be *valued*. (One thing is clear, it is not a mere potentiality of good.) By a thing to be praised we evidently mean always something that is commended for a certain quality it has or a certain relation which it bears to something else. Thus we praise the just and the brave and the good and goodness generally on the strength of what they do or produce. In like manner we praise the strong and the swift and so on, on the ground of their possessing certain native gifts and standing in a certain relation to something good and excellent. Another way of apprehending the truth of this is to think of praise addressed to the gods. Praise is relative, and if the gods are praised, it can only be in comparison with us mortals. This shows that to praise them is a manifest absurdity. Since praise is of things capable of being related to other things, it is clear that the supremely good things call not for praise but for something greater and better, as plainly appears in the case of the gods, whom we are content to call 'happy' or 'blessed,' an epithet we apply also to such men as most closely resemble the gods. We see that it is so also with *things* that are good. No one praises happiness as he praises justice—no, we think it something more divine and higher in the scale of values. Hence Eudoxus is held to have made a good point in his plea for awarding the first prize to pleasure when he adduced the following argument. The fact that pleasure (which is one of the things recognized as good) is not praised is evidence that it is superior to the goods that are praised. And this character, he thought, belongs also to God and to the supreme good, which is the standard to which all other goods are referred.

While praise is given to goodness—for goodness is the inspiration to noble actions—panegyrics or encomiums are bestowed on the high deed done, wheher bodily feat or intellectual achievement. We must, however, leave the detailed examination of this subject to those who have made a special study of the encomium, for no doubt it is more in their line than in ours. But so far as we are concerned the arguments that have been adduced must have convinced us that happiness is one of those things that are perfect and beyond praise. We might infer as much from the consideration that it is a first principle, as is proved by the fact that everything we do is done with a view to it, and we regard it as fundamental that the first principle and cause of the things called good should be something above price and divine.

Our definition of happiness compels us to consider the nature of virtue.
But before we can do this we must have some conception of how the
human soul is constituted. It will serve our purpose to take over (for
what it is worth) the current psychology which divides the soul into
'parts.' (Section 18 of the chapter which follows is omitted as unintel-
ligible except to a specialist in Greek mathematics and unimportant
even to him.)

CHAPTER THIRTEEN

Happiness, then, being an activity of the soul in conformity with perfect goodness, it follows that we must examine the nature of goodness.
When we have done this we should be in a better position to investigate the nature of happiness. There is this, too. The genuine statesman
is thought of as a man who has taken peculiar pains to master this
problem, desiring as he does to make his fellow-citizens good men
obedient to the laws.* Now, if the study of moral goodness is a part of
political science, our inquiry into its nature will clearly follow the lines
laid down in our preliminary observations.

   Well, the goodness we have to consider is human goodness. This—
I mean human goodness or (if you prefer to put it that way) human
happiness—was what we set out to find. By human goodness is meant
not fineness of physique but a right condition of the soul, and by happiness a condition of the soul. That being so, it is evident that the
statesman ought to have some inkling of psychology, just as the doctor
who is to specialize in diseases of the eye must have a general knowledge of physiology. Indeed, such a general background is even more
necessary for the statesman in view of the fact that his science is of a
higher order than the doctor's. Now the best kind of doctor takes a
good deal of trouble to acquire a knowledge of the human body as a
whole. Therefore the statesman should also be a psychologist and study
the soul with an eye to his profession. Yet he will do so only as far as
his own problems make it necessary; to go into greater detail on the
subject would hardly be worth the labour spent on it.

   Psychology has been studied elsewhere and some of the doctrines
stated there may be accepted as adequate for our present purpose and
used by us here. The soul is represented as consisting of two parts, a
rational and an irrational.† As regards the irrational part there is one
subdivision of it which appears to be common to all living things, and

---

   * We may point to the lawgivers of Crete and Sparta, and similar historical
characters.
   † Whether the parts are separate like the parts of the body or anything that is
physically divisible, or, like the concave and convex aspects of the arc of a circle,
are distinguishable only by definition and in thought, is here an irrelevant question.

this we may designate as having a 'vegetative' nature, by which I mean that it is the cause of nutrition and growth, since one must assume the existence of some such vital force in all things that assimilate food.* Now the excellence peculiar to this power is evidently common to the whole of animated nature and not confined to man. This view is supported by the admitted fact that the vegetative part of us is particularly active in sleep, when the good and the bad are hardest to distinguish.† Such a phenomenon would be only natural, for sleep is a cessation of that function on the operation of which depends the goodness or badness of the soul.‡ But enough of this, let us say no more about the nutritive part of the soul, since it forms no portion of goodness in the specifically *human* character.

But there would seem to be another constituent of the soul which, while irrational, contains an element of rationality. It may be observed in the types of men we call 'continent' and 'incontinent.' They have a principle—a rational element in their souls—which we commend, because it encourages them to perform the best actions in the right way. But such natures appear at the same time to contain an irrational element in active opposition to the rational. In paralytic cases it often happens that when the patient wills to move his limbs to the right they swing instead to the left. Exactly the same thing may happen to the soul; the impulses of the incontinent man carry him in the opposite direction from that towards which he was aiming. The only difference is that, where the body is concerned, we see the uncontrolled limb, while the erratic impulse we do not see. Yet this should not prevent us from believing that besides the rational an irrational principle exists running opposite and counter to the other.§ Yet, as I said, it is not altogether irrational; at all events it submits to direction in the continent man, and may be assumed to be still more amenable to reason in the 'temperate' and in the brave man, in whose moral make-up there is nothing which is at variance with reason.

We have, then, this clear result. The irrational part of the soul, like the soul itself, consists of two parts. The first of these is the vegetative, which has nothing rational about it at all. The second is that from which spring the appetites and desire in general; and this does in

---

* I include embryos, which share this power with fully developed organisms. That is more reasonable than to assume that the latter can assimilate food in a different way.

† Hence the saying, 'For half their lives no man is happier than another.'

‡ This statement requires some modification, because there are some bodily processes which can reach the centres of consciousness during sleep, thus providing us with the reason why virtuous persons have better dreams than the average man.

§ What forms the difference between them is a question which does not here arise.

a way participate in reason, seeing that it is submissive and obedient to it. . . . That the irrational element in us need not be heedless of the rational is proved by the fact that we find admonition, indeed every form of censure and exhortation, not ineffective. It may be, however, that we ought to speak of the appetitive part of the soul as rational, too. In that event it will rather be the rational part that is divided in two, one division rational in the proper sense of the word and in its nature, the other in the derivative sense in which we speak of a child as 'listening to reason' in the person of its father.

These distinctions within the soul supply us with a classification of the virtues. Some are called 'intellectual,' as wisdom, intelligence, prudence. Others are 'moral,' as liberality and temperance. When we are speaking of a man's *character* we do not describe him as wise or intelligent but as gentle or temperate. Yet we praise a wise man, too, on the ground of his 'disposition' or settled habit of acting wisely. The dispositions so praised are what we mean by 'virtues.'

BOOK TWO

This book is the first of a series (II–V) dealing with the moral virtues. But first we have to ask what moral virtue or goodness is. It is a confirmed disposition to act rightly, the disposition being itself formed by a continuous series of right actions.

CHAPTER ONE

Virtue, then, is of two kinds, intellectual and moral. Of these the intellectual is in the main indebted to teaching for its production and growth, and this calls for time and experience. Moral goodness, on the other hand, is the child of habit, from which it has got its very name, ethics being derived from *ethos*, 'habit,' by a slight alteration in the quantity of the *e*. This is an indication that none of the moral virtues is implanted in us by Nature, since nothing that Nature creates can be taught by habit to change the direction of its development. For instance a stone, the natural tendency of which is to fall down, could never, however often you threw it up in the air, be trained to go in that direction. No more can you train fire to burn downwards. Nothing in fact, if the law of its being is to behave in one way, can be habituated to behave in another. The moral virtues, then, are produced in us neither *by* Nature nor *against* Nature. Nature, indeed, prepares in us the ground for their reception, but their complete formation is the product of habit.

Consider again these powers or faculties with which Nature endows us. We acquire the ability to use them before we do use them. The senses provide us with a good illustration of this truth. We have not acquired the sense of sight from repeated acts of seeing, or the sense of hearing from repeated acts of hearing. It is the other way round. We had these senses before we used them, we did not acquire them as a result of using them. But the moral virtues we do acquire by first exercising them. The same is true of the arts and crafts in general. The craftsman has to learn how to make things, but he learns in the process of making them. So men become builders by building, harp players by playing the harp. By a similar process we become just by performing just actions, temperate by performing temperate actions, brave by performing brave actions. Look at what happens in political societies—it confirms our view. We find legislators seeking to make good men of their fellows by making good behaviour habitual with them. That is the aim of every law-giver, and when he is unable to carry it out effectively, he is a failure; nay, success or failure in this is what makes the difference between a good constitution and a bad.

Again, the creation and the destruction of any virtue are effected by identical causes and identical means; and this may be said, too, of every art. It is as a result of playing the harp that harpers become good or bad in their art. The same is true of builders and all other craftsmen. Men will become good builders as a result of building well, and bad builders as a result of building badly. Otherwise what would be the use of having anyone to teach a trade? Craftsmen would all be born either good or bad. Now this holds also of the virtues. It is in the course of our dealings with our fellow-men that we become just or unjust. It is our behaviour in a crisis and our habitual reactions to danger that make us brave or cowardly, as it may be. So with our desires and passions. Some men are made temperate and gentle, others profligate and passionate, the former by conducting themselves in one way, the latter by conducting themselves in another, in situations in which their feelings are involved. We may sum it all up in the generalization, 'Like activities produce like dispositions.' This makes it our duty to see that our activities have the right character, since the differences of quality in them are repeated in the dispositions that follow in their train. So it is a matter of real importance whether our early education confirms us in one set of habits or another. It would be nearer the truth to say that it makes a very great difference indeed, in fact all the difference in the world.

If, then, everything depends upon the way in which we act, clearly it is incumbent on us to inquire what this way is, never forgetting that we must not look for the precision attainable in the exact sciences.

CHAPTER TWO

Since the branch of philosophy on which we are at present engaged differs from the others in not being a subject of merely intellectual interest—I mean we are not concerned to know what goodness essentially is, but how we are to become good men, for this alone gives the study its practical value—we must apply our minds to the solution of the problems of conduct. For, as I remarked, it is our actions that determine our dispositions.

Now that when we act we should do so according to the right principle, is common ground and I propose to take it as a basis of discussion.* But we must begin with the admission that any theory of conduct must be content with an outline without much precision in details. We noted this when I said at the beginning of our discussion of this part of our subject that the measure of exactness of statement in any field of study must be determined by the nature of the matter studied. Now matters of conduct and considerations of what is to our advantage have no fixity about them any more than matters affecting our health. And if this be true of moral philosophy as a whole, it is still more true that the discussion of particular problems in ethics admits of no exactitude. For they do not fall under any science or professional tradition, but those who are following some line of conduct are forced in every collocation of circumstances to think out for themselves what is suited to these circumstances, just as doctors and navigators have to do in their different *métiers*. We can do no more than give our arguments, inexact as they necessarily are, such support as is available.

After this reminder Aristotle proceeds to lay down a proposition or generalization which is cardinal in his system of ethics. Excess or deficiency in his actions impairs the moral quality of the agent.

Let us begin with the following observation. It is in the nature of moral qualities that they can be destroyed by deficiency on the one hand and excess on the other. We can see this in the instances of bodily health and strength.† Physical strength is destroyed by too much and also by too little exercise. Similarly health is ruined by eating and drinking either too much or too little, while it is produced, increased, and pre-

---

* There will be an opportunity later of considering what is meant by this formula, in particular what is meant by 'the right principle' and how, in its ethical aspect, it is related to the moral virtues.

† If we are to illustrate the material, it must be by concrete images.

served by taking the right quantity of drink and victuals. Well, it is the same with temperance, courage, and the other virtues. The man who shuns and fears everything and can stand up to nothing becomes a coward. The man who is afraid of nothing at all, but marches up to every danger, becomes foolhardy. In the same way the man who indulges in every pleasure without refraining from a single one becomes incontinent. If, on the other hand, a man behaves like the Boor in comedy and turns his back on every pleasure, he will find his sensibilities becoming blunted. So also temperance and courage are destroyed both by excess and deficiency, and they are kept alive by observance of the mean.

Our virtues are employed in the same kinds of action as established them.

Let us go back to our statement that the virtues are produced and fostered as a result, and by the agency, of actions of the same quality as effect their destruction. It is also true that after the virtues have been formed they find expression in actions of that kind. We may see this in a concrete instance—bodily strength. It results from taking plenty of nourishment and going in for hard training, and it is the strong man who is best fitted to cope with such conditions. So with the virtues. It is by refraining from pleasures that we become temperate, and it is when we have become temperate that we are most able to abstain from pleasures. Or take courage. It is by habituating ourselves to make light of alarming situations and to confront them that we become brave, and it is when we have become brave that we shall be most able to face an alarming situation.

There is one way of discovering whether we are in full possession of a virtue or not. We possess it if we feel pleasure in its exercise; indeed, it is just with pleasures and pains that virtue is concerned.

CHAPTER THREE

We may use the pleasure (or pain) that accompanies the exercise of our dispositions as an index of how far they have established themselves. A man is temperate who abstaining from bodily pleasures finds this abstinence pleasant; if he finds it irksome, he is intemperate. Again, it is the man who encounters danger gladly, or at least without painful sensations, who is brave; the man who has these sensations is a coward. In a word, moral virtue has to do with pains and pleasures. There are a number of reasons for believing this. (1) Pleasure has a way of making us do what is disgraceful; pain deters us from doing what is right and fine. Hence the importance—I quote Plato—of having been brought up to find pleasure and pain in the right things. True education is just such a training. (2) The virtues operate with actions and emotions, each of which is accompanied by the pleasure or pain. This is only another way of saying that virtue has to do with pleasures and pains. (3) Pain is used as an instrument of punishment. For in her remedies Nature works by opposites, and pain can be remedial. (4) When any disposition finds its complete expression it is, as we noted, in dealing with just those things by which it is its nature to be made better or worse, and which constitute the sphere of its operations. Now when men become bad it is under the influence of pleasures and pains when they seek the wrong ones among them, or seek them at the wrong time, or in the wrong manner, or in any of the wrong forms which such offences may take; and in seeking the wrong pleasures and pains they shun the right. This has led some thinkers to identify the moral virtues with conditions of the soul in which passion is eliminated or reduced to a minimum. But this is to make too absolute a statement—it needs to be qualified by adding that such a condition must be attained 'in the right manner and at the right time' together with the other modifying circumstances.

So far, then, we have got this result. Moral goodness is a quality disposing us to act in the best way when we are dealing with pleasures and pains, while vice is one which leads us to act in the worst way when we deal with them.

The point may be brought out more clearly by some other considerations. (5) There are three kinds of things that determine our choice in all our actions—the morally fine, the expedient, the pleasant; and three that we shun—the base, the harmful, the painful. Now in his dealings with all of these it is the good man who is most likely to go right, and the bad man who tends to go wrong, and that most notably in the matter of pleasure. The sensation of pleasure is felt by us in common with all animals, accompanying everything we choose, for even the fine and the expedient have a pleasurable effect upon us. (6) The capacity for experiencing pleasure has grown in us from infancy as part of our general development, and human life, being dyed in grain with it, received therefrom a colour hard to scrape off. (7) Pleasure and pain are also the standards by which with greater or less strictness we regulate our considered actions. Since to feel pleasure and pain rightly or wrongly is an important factor in human behaviour, it follows that we are primarily concerned with these sensations. (8) Heraclitus says it is hard to fight against anger, but it is harder still to fight against pleasure. Yet to grapple with the harder has always been the business, as of art, so of goodness, success in a task being proportionate to its difficulty. This gives us another reason for believing that morality and statesmanship must concentrate on pleasures and pains, seeing it is the man who deals rightly with them who will be good, and the man who deals with them wrongly who will be bad.

Here, then, are our conclusions. (*a*) Virtue is concerned with pains and pleasures. (*b*) The actions which produce virtue are identical in character with those which increase it. (*c*) These actions differently performed destroy it. (*d*) The actions which produced it are identical with those in which it finds expression.

Aristotle now meets an obvious objection: How can a man perform (say) just actions unless he is already just?

CHAPTER FOUR

A difficulty, however, may be raised as to what we mean when we say that we must perform just actions if we are to become just, and temperate actions if we are to be temperate. It may be argued that, if I do what is just and temperate, I am just and temperate already, exactly as, if I spell words or play music correctly, I must already be literate or musical. This I take to be a false analogy, even in the arts. It is possible to spell a word right by accident or because somebody tips you the answer. But you will be a scholar only if your spelling is done as a scholar does it, that is thanks to the scholarship in your own mind. Nor will the suggested analogy with the arts bear scrutiny. A work of art is good or bad in itself—let it possess a certain quality, and that is all we ask of it. But virtuous actions are not done in a virtuous—a just or temperate—way merely because *they* have the appropriate quality. The *doer* must be in a certain frame of mind when he does them. Three conditions are involved. (1) The agent must act in full consciousness of what he is doing. (2) He must 'will' his action, and will it for its own sake. (3) The act must proceed from a fixed and unchangeable disposition. Now these requirements, if we except mere knowledge, are not counted among the necessary qualifications of an artist. For the acquisition of virtue, on the other hand, knowledge is of little or no value, but the other requirements are of immense, of sovran, importance, since it is the repeated performance of just and temperate actions that produces virtue. Actions, to be sure, are *called* just and temperate when they are such as a just or temperate man would do. But the doer is just or temperate not because he does such things but when he does them in the way of just and temperate persons. It is therefore quite fair to say that a man becomes just by the performance of just, and temperate by the performance of temperate, actions; nor is there the smallest likelihood of a man's becoming good by any other course of conduct. It is not, however, a popular line to take, most men preferring theory to practice under the impression that arguing about morals proves them to be philosophers, and that in this way they will turn out to be fine characters. Herein they resemble invalids, who listen carefully to all the doctor says but do not carry out a single one of his orders. The bodies of such people will never respond to treatment—nor will the souls of such 'philosophers.'

It is now time to produce a formal definition of virtue. In the Aristotelian system this means stating its genus and differentia—that is to say, the class of things to which it belongs and the point or points which distinguish it from other members of the class.

CHAPTER FIVE

We now come to the formal definition of virtue. Note first, however, that the human soul is conditioned in three ways. It may have (1) feelings, (2) capacities, (3) dispositions; so virtue must be one of these three. By 'feelings' I mean desire, anger, fear, daring, envy, gratification, friendliness, hatred, longing, jealousy, pity and in general all states of mind that are attended by pleasure or pain. By 'capacities' I mean those faculties in virtue of which we may be described as capable of the feelings in question—anger, for instance, or pain, or pity. By 'dispositions' I mean states of mind in virtue of which we are well or ill disposed in respect of the feelings concerned. We have, for instance, a bad disposition where angry feelings are concerned if we are disposed to become excessively or insufficiently angry, and a good disposition in this respect if we consistently feel the due amount of anger, which comes between these extremes. So with the other feelings.

Now, neither the virtues nor the vices are feelings. We are not spoken of as good or bad in respect of our feelings but of our virtues and vices. Neither are we praised or blamed for the way we feel. A man is not praised for being frightened or angry, nor is he blamed just for being angry; it is for being angry in a particular way. But we *are* praised and blamed for our virtues and vices. Again, feeling angry or frightened is something we can't help, but our virtues are in a manner expressions of our will; at any rate there is an element of will in their formation. Finally, we are said to be 'moved' when our feelings are affected, but when it is a question of moral goodness or badness we are not said to be 'moved' but to be 'disposed' in a particular way. A similar line of reasoning will prove that the virtues and vices are not capacities either. We are not spoken of as good or bad, nor are we praised or blamed, merely because we are *capable* of feeling. Again, what capacities we have, we have by nature; but it is not nature that makes us good or bad. . . . So, if the virtues are neither feelings nor capacities, it remains that they must be dispositions. . . .

We have now to state the 'differentia' of virtue. Virtue is a disposition; but how are we to distinguish it from other dispositions? We may say that it is such a disposition as enables the good man to perform his function well. And he performs it well when he avoids the extremes and chooses the mean in actions and feelings.

CHAPTER SIX

It is not, however, enough to give this account of the *genus* of virtue—that it is a disposition; we must describe its *species*. Let us begin, then, with this proposition. Excellence of whatever kind affects that of which it is the excellence in two ways. (1) It produces a good state in it. (2) It enables it to perform its function well. Take eyesight. The goodness of your eye is not only that which makes your eye good, it is also that which makes it function well. Or take the case of a horse. The goodness of a horse makes him a good horse, but it also makes him good at running, carrying a rider, and facing the enemy. Our proposition, then, seems to be true, and it enables us to say that virtue in a man will be the disposition which (a) makes him a good man, (b) enables him to perform his function well. We have already touched on this point, but more light will be thrown upon it if we consider what is the specific nature of virtue.

To make his meaning clearer Aristotle draws an illustration from mathematics. It is Greek mathematics, and the terminology is no longer quite the same as ours; for example, what he calls 'arithmetical proportion' we should rather call 'arithmetical progression.' It may be doubted whether the illustration makes his meaning—which after all is simple —any clearer. Perhaps it only disguises the danger of passing from mathematical to ethical values. Like other Greek thinkers Aristotle cannot always shake himself free from the associations clustering about Greek words, Greek being the only language he knew. Dividing a material object in half instead of in two unequal parts is not, or is not necessarily, moral action. It cannot be said that Aristotle is unaware of this, for he sees that in conduct the too much and the too little and the mean vary for each agent—a thing abhorrent to the mathematician. So his illustration rather hinders than helps him.

In anything continuous and divisible it is possible to take the half, or more than the half, or less than the half. Now these parts may be larger, smaller, and equal either in relation to the thing divided or in relation to us. The equal part may be described as a mean between too much and too little. By the mean of the thing I understand a point equidistant from the extremes; and this is one and the same for everybody. Let me give an illustration. Ten, let us say, is 'many' and two is 'few' of something. We get the mean of the thing if we take six;* that is, six exceeds and is exceeded by an equal number. This is the rule which gives us the arithmetical mean. But such a method will not give us the mean in relation to ourselves. Let ten pounds of food be a large, and two pounds a small, allowance for an athlete. It does not follow that the trainer will prescribe six pounds. That might be a large or it might be a small allowance for the particular athlete who is to get it. It would be little for Milo but a lot for a man who has just begun training.† It is the same in all walks of life. The man who knows his business avoids both too much and too little. It is the mean he seeks and adopts—not the mean of the thing but the relative mean.

Every form, then, of applied knowledge, when it performs its function well, looks to the mean and works to the standard set by that. It is because people feel this that they apply the *cliché*, 'You couldn't add anything to it or take anything from it' to an artistic masterpiece, the implication being that too much and too little alike destroy perfection, while the means preserves it. Now if this be so, and if it be true, as we say, that good craftsmen work to the standard of the mean, then, since goodness like Nature is more exact and of a higher character than any art, it follows that goodness is the quality that hits the mean. By 'goodness' I mean goodness of moral character, since it is moral goodness that deals with feelings and actions, and it is in them that we find excess, deficiency, and a mean. It is possible, for example, to experience fear, boldness, desire, anger, pity, and pleasures and pains generally, too much or too little or to the right amount. If we feel them too much or too little, we are wrong. But to have these feelings at the right times on the right occasions towards the right people for the right motive and in the right way is to have them in the right measure, that is, somewhere between the extremes; and this is what characterizes goodness. The same may be said of the mean and extremes in actions. Now it is in the field of actions and feelings that goodness operates; in them we find excess, deficiency, and, between them, the mean, the first two being wrong, the mean right and praised as such.‡ Goodness, then, is a mean condition in the sense that it aims at and hits the mean.

Consider, too, that it is possible to go wrong in more ways than one. [In Pythagorean terminology evil is a form of the Unlimited, good of the Limited.] But there is only one way of being right. That is why going wrong is easy, and going right difficult; it is easy to miss the bull's-eye and difficult to hit it. Here, then, is another explanation of

---

* $6 - 2 = 10 - 6$.
† What applies to gymnastics applies also to running and wrestling.
‡ Being right or successful and being praised are both indicative of excellence.

why the too much and the too little are connected with evil and the mean with good. As the poet says,

Goodness is one, evil is multiform.

We are now in a position to state our definition of virtue with more precision. Observe that the kind of virtue meant here is moral, not intellectual, and that Aristotle must not be taken as saying that the kind of virtue which he regards as the highest and truest is any sort of mean.

We may now define virtue as a disposition of the soul in which, when it has to choose among actions and feelings, it observes the mean relative to us, this being determined by such a rule or principle as would take shape in the mind of a man of sense or practical wisdom. We call it a mean condition as lying between two forms of badness, one being excess and the other deficiency; and also for this reason, that, whereas badness either falls short of or exceeds the right measure in feelings and actions, virtue discovers the mean and deliberately chooses it. Thus, looked at from the point of view of its essence as embodied in its definition, virtue no doubt is a mean; judged by the standard of what is right and best, it is an extreme.

Aristotle enters a caution. Though we have said that virtue observes the mean in actions and passions, we do not say this of all acts and all feelings. Some are essentially evil and, when these are involved, our rule of applying the mean cannot be brought into operation.

But choice of a mean is not possible in every action or every feeling. The very names of some have an immediate connotation of evil. Such are malice, shamelessness, envy among feelings, and among actions adultery, theft, murder. All these and more like them have a bad name as being evil in themselves; it is not merely the excess or deficiency of them that we censure. In their case, then, it is impossible to act rightly; whatever we do is wrong. Nor do circumstances make any difference in the rightness or wrongness of them. When a man commits adultery there is no point in asking whether it is with the right woman or at the right time or in the right way, for to do anything like that is simply wrong. It would amount to claiming that there is a mean and excess and defect in unjust or cowardly or intemperate actions. If such a thing were possible, we should find ourselves with a mean quantity of excess, a mean of deficiency, an excess of excess and a deficiency of deficiency. But just as in temperance and justice there can be no mean or excess or deficiency, because the mean in a sense *is* an extreme, so there can be no mean or excess or deficiency in those vicious actions—however done, they are wrong. Putting the matter into general language, we may say that there is no mean in the extremes, and no extreme in the mean, to be observed by anybody.

After the definition comes its application to the particular virtues. In these it is always possible to discover a mean—at which the virtue aims —between an excess and a deficiency. Here Aristotle found that a table or diagram of the virtues between their corresponding vices would be useful, and we are to imagine him referring to this in the course of his lectures.

CHAPTER SEVEN

But a generalization of this kind is not enough; we must show that our definition fits particular cases. When we are discussing actions particular statements come nearer the heart of the matter, though general statements cover a wider field. The reason is that human behaviour consists in the performance of particular acts, and our theories must be brought into harmony with them.

You see here a diagram of the virtues. Let us take our particular instances from that.

In the section confined to the feelings inspired by danger you will observe that the mean state is 'courage.' Of those who go to extremes in one direction or the other the man who shows an excess of fearlessness has no name to describe him,* the man who exceeds in confidence or daring is called 'rash' or 'foolhardy,' the man who shows an excess of fear and a deficiency of confidence is called a 'coward.' In the pleasures and pains—though not all pleasures and pains, especially pains— the virtue which observes the mean is 'temperance,' the excess is the vice of 'intemperance.' Persons defective in the power to enjoy pleasures are a somewhat rare class, and so have not had a name assigned to them: suppose we call them ''unimpressionable.' Coming to the giving and acquiring of money, we find that the mean is 'liberality,' the excess 'prodigality,' the deficiency 'meanness.' But here we meet a complication. The prodigal man and the mean man exceed and fall short in opposite ways. The prodigal exceeds in giving and falls short in getting money, whereas the mean man exceeds in getting and falls short in giving it away. Of course this is but a summary account of the matter —a bare outline. But it meets our immediate requirements. Later on these types of character will be more accurately delineated.

But there are other dispositions which declare themselves in the way they deal with money. One is 'lordliness' or 'magnificence,' which

---

* We shall often have to make similar admissions.

differs from liberality in that the lordly man deals in large sums, the liberal man in small. Magnificence is the mean state here, the excess is 'bad taste' or 'vulgarity,' the defect is 'shabbiness.' These are not the same as the excess and defect on either side of liberality. How they differ is a point which will be discussed later. In the matter of honour the mean is 'proper pride,' the excess 'vanity,' the defect 'poor-spiritedness.' And just as liberality differs, as I said, from magnificence in being concerned with small sums of money, so there is a state related to proper pride in the same way, being concerned with small honours, while pride is concerned with great. For it is possible to aspire to small honours in the right way, or to a greater or less extent than is right. The man who has this aspiration to excess is called 'ambitious'; if he does not cherish it enough, he is 'unambitious'; but the man who has it to the right extent—that is, strikes the mean—has no special designation. This is true also of the corresponding dispositions with one exception, that of the ambitious man, which is called 'ambitiousness.' This will explain why each of the extreme characters stakes out a claim in the middle region. Indeed we ourselves call the character between the extremes sometimes 'ambitious' and sometimes 'unambitious.' That is proved by our sometimes praising a man for being ambitious and sometimes for being unambitious. The reason will appear later. In the meantime let us continue our discussion of the remaining virtues and vices, following the method already laid down.

Let us next take anger. Here too we find excess, deficiency, and the mean. Hardly one of the states of mind involved has a special name; but, since we call the man who attains the mean in this sphere 'gentle,' we may call his disposition 'gentleness.' Of the extremes the man who is angry over much may be called 'irascible,' and his vice 'irascibility'; while the man who reacts too feebly to anger may be called 'poor-spirited' and his disposition 'poor-spiritedness.'

Some virtues and vices appear in social intercourse.

There are, in addition to those we have named, three other modes of observing the mean which in some ways resemble and in other ways differ from one another. They are all concerned with what we do and say in social intercourse, but they differ in this respect, that one is concerned with truthfulness in such intercourse, the other two with the agreeable, one of these two with the agreeable in amusement, the other with the agreeable element in every relation of life. About these two, then, we must say a word, in order that we may more fully convince ourselves that in all things the mean is to be commended, while the extremes are neither commendable nor right but reprehensible. I am afraid most of these too are nameless; but, as in the other cases, we must try to coin names for them in the interests of clearness and to make it easy to follow the argument. Well then, as regards veracity, the character who aims at the mean may be called 'truthful' and what he aims at 'truthfulness.' Pretending, when it goes too far, is 'boastfulness' and the man who shows it is a 'boaster' or 'braggart.' If it takes the form of understatement, the pretence is called 'irony' and the man who shows it 'ironical.' In agreeableness in social amusement the man who hits the mean is 'witty' and what characterizes him is 'wittiness.' The excess is 'buffoonery' and the man who exhibits that is a 'buffoon.' The opposite of the buffoon is the 'boor' and his characteristic is 'boorishness.'

In the other sphere of the agreeable—the general business of life —the person who is agreeable in the right way is 'friendly' and his disposition 'friendliness.' The man who makes himself too agreeable, supposing him to have no ulterior object, is 'obsequious', if he has such an object, he is a 'flatterer.' The man who is deficient in this quality and takes every opportunity of making himself disagreeable may be called 'peevish' or 'sulky' or 'surly.'

But it is not only in settled dispositions that a mean may be observed; it may be observed in passing states of emotion.

Even when feelings and emotional states are involved one notes that mean conditions exist. And here also, it would be agreed, we may find one man observing the mean and another going beyond it, for instance, the 'shamefaced' man, who is put out of countenance by anything. Or a man may fall short here of the due mean. Thus any one who is deficient in a sense of shame, or has none at all, is called 'shameless.' The man who avoids both extremes is 'modest,' and him we praise. For, while modesty is not a form of goodness, it is praised; it and the modest man. Then there is 'righteous indignation.' This is felt by any one who strikes the mean between 'envy' and 'malice,' by which last word I mean a pleased feeling at the misfortunes of other people. These are emotions concerned with the pains and pleasures we feel at the fortunes of our neighbours. The man who feels righteous indignation is pained by undeserved good fortune; but the envious man goes beyond that and is pained at anybody's success. The malicious man, on the other hand, is so far from being pained by the misfortunes of another that he is actually tickled by them.

However, a fitting opportunity of discussing these matters will present itself in another place. And after that we shall treat of justice. In that connexion we shall have to distinguish between the various kinds of justice—for the word is used in more senses than one—and show in what way each of them is a mean. . . .

*But after all, proceeds Aristotle, the true determinant of the mean is
not the geometer's rod but the guiding principle in the good man's soul.
The diagram of the virtues and vices, then, is just an arrangement and,
as Aristotle goes on to show, an unimportant one at that.*

CHAPTER EIGHT

Thus there are three dispositions, two of them taking a vicious form
(one in the direction of excess, the other of defect) and one a good
form, namely, the observance of the mean. They are all opposed to one
another, though not all in the same way. The extreme states are opposed both to the mean and one another, and the mean is opposed to
both extremes. For just as the equal is greater compared with the less,
and less compared with the greater, so the mean states (whether in
feelings or actions) are in excess if compared with the deficient, and
deficient if compared with the excessive, states. Thus a brave man appears rash when set beside a coward, and cowardly when set beside a
rash man; a temperate man appears intemperate beside a man of dull
sensibilities, and dull if contrasted with an intemperate man. This is
the reason why each extreme character tries to push the mean nearer
the other. The coward calls the brave man rash, the rash man calls him
a coward. And so in the other cases. But, while all the dispositions are
opposed to one another in this way, the greatest degree of opposition
is that which is found between the two extremes. For they are separated by a greater interval from one another than from the mean, as
the great is more widely removed from the small, and the small from
the great, than either from the equal. It may be added that sometimes
an extreme bears a certain resemblance to a mean. For example, rashness resembles courage, and prodigality resembles liberality. But between the extremes there is always the maximum dissimilarity. Now
opposites are by definition things as far removed as possible from one
another. Hence the farther apart things are, the more opposite they will
be. Sometimes it is the deficiency, in other instances it is the excess,
that is more directly opposed to the mean. Thus cowardice, a deficiency, is more opposed to courage than is rashness, an excess. And it
is not insensibility, the deficiency, that is more opposed to temperance
but intemperance, the excess. This arises from one or other of two
causes. One lies in the nature of the thing itself and may be explained
as follows. When one extreme is nearer to the mean and resembles it
more, it is not that extreme but the other which we tend to oppose to
the mean. For instance, since rashness is held to be nearer and liker to
courage than is cowardice, it is cowardice which we tend to oppose
to courage on the principle that the extremes which are remoter from
the mean strike us as more opposite to it. The other cause lies in ourselves. It is the things to which we are naturally inclined that appear

to us more opposed to the mean. For example, we have a natural inclination to pleasure, which makes us prone to fall into intemperance. Accordingly we tend to describe as opposite to the mean those things towards which we have an instinctive inclination. For this reason intemperance, the excess, is more opposed to temperance than is insensibility to pleasure, the deficiency.

CHAPTER NINE

I have said enough to show that moral excellence is a mean, and I have shown in what sense it is so. It is, namely, a mean between two forms of badness, one of excess and the other of defect, and is so described because it aims at hitting the mean point in feelings and in actions. This makes virtue hard of achievement, because finding the middle point is never easy. It is not everybody, for instance, who can find the centre of a circle—that calls for a geometrician. Thus, too, it is easy to fly into a passion—anybody can do that—but to be angry with the right person and to the right extent and at the right time and with the right object and in the right way—that is not easy, and it is not everyone who can do it. This is equally true of giving or spending money. Hence we infer that to do these things properly is rare, laudable and fine.

Aristotle now suggests some rules for our guidance.

In view of this we shall find it useful when aiming at the mean to observe these rules. (1) *Keep away from that extreme which is the more opposed to the mean.* It is Calypso's advice:

Swing round the ship clear of this surf and surge.

For one of the extremes is always a more dangerous error than the other; and—since it is hard to hit the bull's eye—we must take the next best course and choose the least of the evils. And it will be easiest for us to do this if we follow the rule I have suggested. (2) *Note the errors into which we personally are most liable to fall.* (Each of us has his natural bias in one direction or another.) We shall find out what ours are by noting what gives us pleasure and pain. After that we must drag ourselves in the opposite direction. For our best way of reaching the middle is by giving a wide berth to our darling sin. It is the method used by a carpenter when he is straightening a warped board. (3) *Always be particularly on your guard against pleasure and pleasant things.* When Pleasure is at the bar the jury is not impartial. So it will be best for us if we feel towards her as the Trojan elders felt towards Helen, and regularly apply their words to her. If we are for packing her off, as they were with Helen, we shall be the less likely to go wrong.

To sum up. These are the rules by observation of which we have the best chance of hitting the mean. But of course difficulties spring up, especially when we are confronted with an exceptional case. For example, it is not easy to say precisely what is the right way to be angry and with whom and on what grounds and for how long. In fact we are inconsistent on this point, sometimes praising people who are deficient in the capacity for anger and calling them 'gentle,' sometimes praising the choleric and calling them 'stout fellows.' To be sure we are not hard on a man who goes off the straight path in the direction of too much or too little, if he goes off only a little way. We reserve our censure for the man who swerves widely from the course, because then we are bound to notice it. Yet it is not easy to find a formula by which we may determine how far and up to what point a man may go wrong before he incurs blame. But this difficulty of definition is inherent in every object of perception; such questions of degree are bound up with the circumstances of the individual case, where our only criterion *is* the perception.

So much, then, has become clear. In all our conduct it is the mean state that is to be praised. But one should lean sometimes in the direction of the more, sometimes in that of the less, because that is the readiest way of attaining to goodness and the mean.

BOOK THREE

Aristotle now approaches the question of moral responsibility, so important in modern ethics. It never occurred to him to doubt the freedom of the will, but he is as much alive as any modern thinker to the fact— and the importance of the fact—that our acts are not all voluntary. In the following chapter he distinguishes between the degrees of their voluntariness.

CHAPTER ONE

We have found that moral excellence or virtue has to do with feelings and actions. These may be voluntary or involuntary. It is only to the former that we assign praise or blame, though when the involuntary are concerned we may find ourselves ready to condone and on occasion to pity. It is clearly, then, incumbent on the student of moral philosophy to determine the limits of the voluntary and involuntary. Legislators also find such a definition useful when they are seeking to prescribe appropriate rewards and punishments.

Actions are commonly regarded as involuntary when they are performed (a) under compulsion, (b) as the result of ignorance. An act, it
is thought, is done under compulsion when it originates in some external cause of such a nature that the agent or person subject to the
compulsion contributes nothing to it. Such a situation is created, for
example, when a sea captain is carried out of his course by a contrary
wind or by men who have got him in their power. But the case is not
always so clear. One might have to consider an action performed for
some fine end or through fear of something worse to follow. For example, a tyrant who had a man's parents or children in his power might
order him to do something dishonourable on condition that, if the man
did it, their lives would be spared; otherwise not. In such cases it might
be hard to say whether the actions are voluntary or not. A similar difficulty is created by the jettison of cargo in a storm. When the situation
has no complications you never get a man voluntarily throwing away
his property. But if it is to save the life of himself and his mates, any
sensible person will do it. Such actions partake of both qualities, though
they look more like voluntary than involuntary acts. For at the time
they are performed they are the result of a deliberate choice between
alternatives, and when an action is performed the end or object of that
action is held to be the end it had at the moment of its performance. It
follows that the terms 'voluntary' and 'involuntary' should be used
with reference to the time when the acts were being performed. Now
in the imaginary cases we have stated the acts are voluntary. For the
movement of the limbs instrumental to the action originates in the agent
himself, and when this is so it is in a man's own power to act or not to
act. Such actions therefore are voluntary. But they are so only in the
special circumstances; otherwise of course they would be involuntary.
For nobody would choose to do anything of the sort purely for its own
sake. Occasionally indeed the performance of such actions is held to
do a man credit. This happens when he submits to some disgrace or
pain as the only way of achieving some great or splendid result. But if
his case is just the opposite he is blamed, for it shows a degraded nature to submit to humiliations with only a paltry object in view, or at
any rate not a high one. But there are also cases which are thought to
merit, I will not say praise, but condonation. An example is provided
when a man does something wrong because he is afraid of torture too
severe for flesh and blood to endure. Though surely there are some
things which a man cannot be compelled to do—which he will rather
die than do, however painful the mode of death. Such a deed is matri-
cide; the reasons which 'compelled' Alcmaeon in Euripides' play to kill
his mother carry their absurdity on the face of them. Yet it is not always easy to make up our minds what is our best course in choosing
one of two alternatives—such and such an action instead of such and
such another—or in facing one penalty instead of another. Still harder

is it to stick to our decision when made. For, generally speaking, the consequences we expect in such imbroglios are painful, and what we are forced to do far from honourable. Then we get praised or blamed according as we succumb to the compulsion or resist it.

What class of actions, then, ought we to distinguish as 'compulsory'? It is arguable that the bare description will apply to any case where the cause of the action is found in things external to the agent when he contributes nothing to the result. But it may happen that actions, though, abstractly considered, involuntary, are deliberately chosen at a given time and in given circumstances in preference to a given alternative. In that case, their origin being in the agent, these actions must be pronounced voluntary in the particular circumstances and because they are preferred to their alternatives. In themselves they are involuntary, yet they have more of the voluntary about them, since conduct is a sequence of particular acts, and the particular things done in the circumstances we have supposed are voluntary. But when it comes to saying which of two alternative lines of action should be preferred—then difficulties arise. For the differences in particular cases are many.

If it should be argued that pleasurable and honourable things exercise constraint upon us from without, and therefore actions performed under their influence are compulsory, it may be replied that this would make every action compulsory. For we all have some pleasurable or honourable motive in everything we do. Secondly, people acting under compulsion and against their will find it painful, whereas those whose actions are inspired by the pleasurable and the honourable find that these actions are accompanied by pleasure. In the third place it is absurd to accuse external influences instead of ourselves when we fall an easy prey to such inducements and to lay blame for all dishonourable deeds on the seductions of pleasure, while claiming for ourselves credit for any fine thing we have done. It appears, then, that an action is compulsory only when it is caused by something external to itself which is not influenced by anything contributed by the person under compulsion.

Then there are acts done through ignorance. Any act of this nature is other than voluntary, but it is involuntary only when it causes the doer subsequent pain and regret. For a man who has been led into some action by ignorance and yet has no regrets, while he cannot be said to have been a voluntary agent—he did not know what he was doing—nevertheless cannot be said to have acted involuntarily, since he feels no compunction. We therefore draw a distinction. (a) When a man who has done something as the result of ignorance is sorry for it, we take it that he has acted involuntarily. (b) When such a man is not sorry, the case is different and we shall have to call him a 'non-voluntary' agent. For it is better that he should have a distinctive name in order to mark the distinction. Note, further, that there is evidently a difference between acting *in consequence* of ignorance and acting *in* ignorance. When a man is drunk or in a passion his actions are not supposed to be the result of ignorance but of one or other of these conditions. But, as he does not realize what he is doing, he is acting *in* ignorance. To be sure every bad man is ignorant of what he ought to do and refrain from doing, and it is just this ignorance that makes people unjust and otherwise wicked. But when we use the word 'involuntary' we do not apply it in a case where the agent does not know what is for his own good. For involuntary acts are not the consequence of ignorance when the ignorance is shown in our choice of ends; what does result from such ignorance is a completely vicious condition. No, what I mean is not general ignorance—which is what gives ground for censure—but particular ignorance, ignorance that is to say of the particular circumstances or the particular persons concerned. In such cases there may be room for pity and pardon, because a man who acts in ignorance of such details is an involuntary agent. It will therefore no doubt be well to define the nature and determine the number of these particular circumstances. They are (1) the agent, (2) the act, (3) that which is the object or within the range of the act. Sometimes we must add (4) the instrument (e.g. a tool), (5) the effect or result (e.g. when a man's life is saved), (6) the manner (e.g. gently or roughly). Now nobody in his right mind could be ignorant of *all* these circumstances. Obviously he cannot be ignorant of (1) the agent—how he can fail to know himself? But a man may fail to know (2) what he is doing, as when people say that a remark 'escaped' them or that they did not know they were betraying secrets. (A good instance is that of Aeschylus' supposed revelation of the Mysteries.) Or like the man who was accused of killing another with a catapult, you might say you only wanted to show him how the thing worked. Then (3) you might mistake, say, your son for an enemy, like Merope in the play, or (4) take a naked spear instead of one with the button on, or a lump of rock in mistake for a pumice stone, or (5) you might be the death of a man with a medicine which you hoped would save his life, or (6) hit your antagonist a blow when you only meant to grip his hand, as in 'open' wrestling. Seeing then that there is the possibility of ignorance in any of these special circumstances, one who has acted in ignorance of any one of them is considered to have acted involuntarily, especially if it was the most important of them that he did not know, which by general agreement are (2) the act and (3) the effect of the act.

An involuntary act being one performed under compulsion or as the result of ignorance, a voluntary act would seem to be one of which the origin or efficient cause lies in the agent, he knowing the particular circumstances in which he is acting. I believe it to be an error to say that acts occasioned by anger or desire are involuntary. For in the first place if we maintain this we shall have to give up the view that any of the lower animals, or even children, are capable of voluntary action. In the second place, when we act from desire or anger are none of our actions voluntary? Or are our fine actions voluntary, our ignoble actions involuntary? It is an absurd distinction, since the agent is one and the same person. It is surely paradoxical to describe as 'involuntary' acts inspired by sentiments which we quite properly desire to have. There are some things at which we *ought* to feel angry, and others which we *ought* to desire—health, for instance, and the acquisition of knowledge. Thirdly, people assume that what is involuntary must be painful and what falls in with our own wishes must be pleasant. Fourthly, what difference is there in point of voluntariness between wrong actions which are calculated and wrong actions which are done on impulse? Both are to be avoided; and the further reflection suggests itself, that the irrational emotions are no less typically human than our considered judgment. Whence it follows that actions inspired by anger or desire are equally typical of the human being who performs them. Therefore to classify these actions as 'involuntary' is surely a very strange proceeding.

Aristotle is now led to consider the nature of proairesis, *a word which he uses to express the choice both of ends and of the means to an end. In the medieval Latin versions it was translated by* electio. *We can hardly revive that use of 'election' now, but so long as we keep in mind that* proairesis *always implies an act of deliberate choice, we shall follow his meaning well enough.*

CHAPTER TWO

Having distinguished between voluntary and involuntary actions, we must now examine what is meant by *proairesis* or 'deliberate choice.' It is evidently related to goodness in a specially intimate way, and we may take it as affording a better test of character than is supplied by actions.

Now such choice is clearly a voluntary act. But 'choice' and 'the voluntary' are not interchangeable expressions, the voluntary having a wider connotation. Thus children and animals are as capable of voluntary action as adult men; but they have not the same capacity for deliberate choice. Also things done on the inspiration of the moment, though we may call them voluntary, are not said to be done of deliberate choice. Some identify it with desire, some with passion, others with wish, others with belief or opinion of some kind. But none of these theories carries conviction. Let us consider them one by one.

(1) The brutes do not share with man the power of deliberate

choice, but like him they feel desire and passion. Moreover, the man who lacks self-control feels desire when he acts but does not exercise choice, while the exact opposite is true of the man who is master of his passions. Again, desire may be in conflict with choice, but not one desire with another. Finally, the object of desire presents itself as painful or pleasant, but the object of choice is neither the one nor the other. (2) Still less is choice to be identified with passion. Acts which are the effects of passion are surely the very last that can be called acts of deliberate choice. (3) Nor is choice anything like a wish, though there is a superficial connexion between them. There can be no choice where impossibilities are involved; a man who should declare that he 'chose' something incapable of realization would be considered a half-wit. On the other hand it is just impossibilities for which we do tend to wish—for instance, to live for ever. Again, we may form a wish for some result which could never be achieved by our own efforts—for instance, the success of a particular actor or athlete. Nobody, however, *chooses* things like that but only what he imagines he could accomplish by his own efforts. Again, our wishes are directed more to ends than to means. For example, our *wish* is to be healthy, but what we *choose* are things which will make us healthy. We 'wish'—it is the regular word in this connexion—to be happy, but it would be an incorrect expression to say we 'choose' to be happy. In fine, choice is evidently concerned with things which we regard as attainable. (4) Neither can it be opinion, for it seems possible to entertain an opinion about anything—about things that are eternal and impossible—just as much as about things which we suppose attainable. Besides, we distinguish opinions as true or false, not as good or bad, which is the distinction drawn when we make a choice. Probably, then, no one goes so far as to identify choice with opinion in general. But neither can it be identified with any particular opinion. For it is on our choice of good or evil, not on our opinion about it, that it depends whether we are to be good or bad. Again, when we choose, it is to take or avoid something good or bad. But, when we form an opinion, it is of what a thing is, or for whom it is profitable and in what way, whereas taking or avoiding something is hardly a matter of opinion. Again, when a choice is commended, it is because the right thing or the right course has been chosen rather than for any other reason. But when we praise an opinion, it is on the ground that it has been arrived at in the right way. And when we choose it is those things which we know for certain to be good, but when we form an opinion it is about things which we do not certainly know to be true. Again, it is generally believed that the same people are not equally good at choosing the best actions and forming the best opinions; there are people whose opinions tend to be true but who choose the wrong actions out of sheer devilry. That an act of choice must be preceded or accompanied by an opinion respecting it is true but immaterial. It is not that we are investigating, but whether choice is just a kind of opinion.

Now if none of the definitions we have enumerated is right, what *is* the nature and character of *proairesis*—its genus and differentia? Obviously it belongs to the genus of things voluntary. But not everything that is voluntary is chosen. May we then define it as a voluntary act preceded by deliberation? The qualification is suggested by the fact that you cannot have a choice without reasoning and reflecting. Such previous deliberation seems to be indicated by the very word *proaireton*, which means chosen *before* something else.

Our next step, then, must be to ascertain what we mean by 'deliberation.'

CHAPTER THREE

We must now ask ourselves about 'deliberation.' May anything be matter for deliberation, or are there some things that cannot be deliberated about at all? (I assume that we ought not to apply the expression 'object of deliberation' to something about which a fool or a lunatic might deliberate; it should be applied only to something about which a reasonable person might deliberate.) Surely nobody 'deliberates' about eternal things, such as the stellar system or the incommensurability of the diagonal with the side of a square. Nor is deliberation concerned with things in motion when the motions are regular, whether the cause of this is the necessity of their being, or the law of their growth, or something else—things, I mean, like the solstices or the dawn. Neither do we deliberate about things that do not happen in regular sequences—droughts, for example, or abnormal rainfalls. Nor about things that are the result of luck or accident, like finding a crock of gold. In all these cases the reason why we do not deliberate about them is that nothing we can do affects the issue. No, it is about things which we can influence by our action that we deliberate.* Even here we have to admit exceptions in deliberating about human affairs. Thus you will not find a Spartan deliberating about the best form of constitution for the Scythians. What we find is that particular groups or societies deliberate about matters which can be brought to an issue by their own exertions. Again, deliberation is out of place when the subject of it is some branch of art or science that has been worked out in detail and is complete within its own limits. An instance of this is

---

* These in fact are all we need consider, for nature, necessity, chance *plus* intelligence and human agency may be taken as forming a complete list of the generally admitted causes.

spelling. We have never any doubt how a word should be spelt. It is things where our own agency is effective (though not always to the same extent) which engage our deliberations. Such are the practice of medicine and business methods, to which we may add navigation, though here there is a greater call for deliberation than in the case of gymnastic training, because navigation has not been reduced to such exact rules. These observations may be applied to other forms of skill. Finally, deliberation is more in place when it is applied to the arts than to the sciences, because the arts present us with more grounds for a difference of opinion. Deliberation, then, is concerned with things which, while in general following certain definite lines, have no predictable issues, or the result of which cannot be clearly stated, or in which, when important decisions have to be made, we take others into our counsels, distrusting our own ability to settle the point.

Observe also that we do not deliberate about ends but always about means. A doctor does not deliberate whether or not he will cure his patients, nor an orator whether or not he is to win over his audience, nor a statesman whether or not he is to produce law and order, nor does anyone else deliberate about the end at which he is aiming. No, they set some end before themselves and then proceed to consider how and by what means it can be attained. If it appears that there is a variety of means of doing this, they consider which of these will be the easiest and most effective. If it appears that there is only one way of achieving the result, they go on to consider how it will be achieved thereby, and by what means that in turn is to be realized, until they come at last to the cause which, although it is the last in the order of discovery, is the first in the chain of causes.* If they then discover that they have run into an impossibility—if for example they find that a business they would like to start needs capital and they have not got the means of supplying it—they drop the scheme. But, if the thing seems feasible, they try to push it through. By 'feasible' is to be understood what can be achieved by the efforts of ourselves and our friends, since what we do through them is pretty much what we do ourselves, for the cause of their so acting has its origin in us.

For the craftsman the question sometimes is what tools he is to use, sometimes what use he is to make of them; and in the same way in other activities it is sometimes what means we are to use, sometimes how we are to use whatever means we find to hand.

---

* Anyone deliberating in the manner I have described seems to be engaged in a process of investigation or analysis, like a mathematician studying a geometrical figure—of course not every investigation (mathematical investigation, for instance) is deliberation, but every deliberation is investigation—and what comes last in the analysis comes first in the process as a result of which the subject investigated is brought into being.

To repeat our conclusions. A man is the originating cause of his actions; deliberation has for the sphere of its operation acts which are within his own power of doing them; all that we do is done with an eye to something else. It follows that when we deliberate it is about means and not ends. And in our deliberations we are not concerned with particular facts. When we see a loaf we do not deliberate whether it is a loaf, or whether it has been long enough in the oven; we have only to look at it or taste it to find out that. There must be a limit somewhere to deliberation; otherwise there will be no end to it.

Now the thing we deliberate about and the thing we choose are one and the same. The only difference is that, when a thing is chosen, it is already set apart, inasmuch as it has been already selected as a result of the deliberation. We all stop asking how we are going to act when we have traced the origin of action back to ourselves, that is to the ruling or rational part of ourselves, for that it is which makes deliberate choice. The procedure is exemplified in the prehistoric constitutions which we find depicted in the Homeric poems—the kings merely announced their decisions to the people.

Since, therefore, when we choose, we choose something within our reach which we desire as the result of deliberation, we may describe *proairesis* as 'the deliberate desire of something within our power.' The deliberation comes first, then the selection, lastly the desire of following the result of the deliberation. . . .

We choose the means and wish the end. What then is it that we do when we wish? It is all very well to say that we wish for the good. The question is, Do we wish for what is really good or only what seems good to us?

CHAPTER FOUR

I have said that wishing, as distinguished from choosing, is directed to ends. Now there are two views about it. (1) It is directed to the good. (2) It is directed to what *appears* to be good. But there are objections to both. (1) Those who maintain that the object of wish is the good are bound to argue that what a man wishes is not wished at all when the end he chooses is chosen under a misapprehension. For according to them if a thing is wished, it must be good. But what is to prevent a man from wishing something bad? (2) Those who say that what we wish is the apparent good are bound to maintain that there is no such thing as a 'natural' object of wish, but that every man wishes what appears to him personally to be good. Yet different persons have different, and sometimes contradictory, views of what is good. Clearly this will not do. In the circumstances we may content ourselves with the proposition that in the true and absolute sense we wish for the good, so long as the personal factor does not come in. When it does, each man wishes what seems to him individually to be good. This allows us to believe that what the good man wishes is truly wished, while what the bad man wishes is just anything that happens to attract him.* For in every moral problem the good man's view of the truth corresponds to the truth, and so he forms a correct judgement. Moral beauty and the sources of pleasure manifest themselves in special forms corresponding to each disposition that is capable of feeling them, and the good man shows his superiority above all in his power of seeing the truth in every department of conduct. He is, so to speak, the standard and yardstick of what is fine and pleasant. Most men, it seems only too clear, are led astray by the siren Pleasure. To them she falsely seems a blessing; her they choose as a good, and shun pain as an evil.

The question is now raised whether it is at all times in our power to be good and to do the right. The answer is yes. And it is also in our power at all times to be vicious.

CHAPTER FIVE

Since then it is the end that is the object of our wishing, and the means to the end that is the object of our deliberating and choosing, the actions which deal with means must be done by choice and must be voluntary. Now when the virtues are exercised it is upon means. So virtue also is attainable by our own exertions. And so is vice. For what it lies in our power to do, it lies in our power not to do; when we can say 'no,' we can say 'yes.' If, then, it is in our power to perform an action when it is right, it will be equally in our power to refrain from performing it when it is wrong; and if it lies with us to refrain from doing a thing when that is right, it will also lie with us to do it when that is wrong. But if it is in our power to do the right or the wrong thing, and equally in our power to refrain from doing so; and if doing right or wrong is, as we saw, the same as being good or bad ourselves, we must conclude that it depends upon ourselves whether we are to be virtuous or vicious. The words

> *To sin and suffer—that offends us still:*
> *But who is ever blest against his will?*

must be regarded as a half-truth. It is true that no one is blest against his will, but untrue that wickedness is involuntary. Otherwise we shall

---

* Thus when a regimen is followed you find, if you are in good health, that what is truly wholesome is wholesome to you; but, if you are not well, you will find that other things suit you. You will get the same result if you try the experiment with things that are bitter or sweet or hot or heavy and so on.

have to deny the truth of what we have just been saying and maintain that a man is not the originator of his own actions, of which he might be described as the begetter. But if he demonstrably is so, and we cannot trace our actions to any other springs than those which are found within ourselves, then actions which have such an origin are themselves within our control and are voluntary. In support of this conclusion it seems possible to call in evidence the practice of both private individuals and of legislators. For they inflict pains and penalties for misbehaviour, except in cases where the offender is not held responsible, because he has acted from ignorance or under duress. On the other hand they bestow honours on those who have done some fine action. Their motive in the first case is to stop evil practices, in the second to encourage the well-doer. Now nobody encourages us to do things which it is not in our power to do and which are not voluntary. It does not help at all to be made to believe that there is no such thing as getting hot, or feeling pain or anger, and so on. We shall feel them all the same. We even find that the circumstance that an offence was committed out of ignorance is made a reason for punishment when the offender is held responsible for his ignorance, as is shown, for instance, by the sentence in a case where the accused had been drunk. It may then be doubled on the ground that the offence originated with the offender, since it was open to him to refrain from getting drunk and his drunkenness was responsible for his not knowing what he was doing when he committed the offence. We punish people, too, for breaking the law through ignorance of some point in it which it was their business to know and which they could have known without much trouble. And punishment follows also when the ignorance is thought to have been due to carelessness, it being held that the guilty party need not have shown this ignorance. He should have noticed what he was doing—it was his duty to notice. You may say that very likely he could not help it, he is just that sort of man. But there is an answer to that. Such people have only themselves to blame for having acquired a character like that by their loose living, just as they have only themselves to blame for being unjust, if they make a practice of unjust behaviour, or intemperate, if they spend their time in drinking or other forms of dissipation. It is their persistent activities in certain directions that make them what they are. This is well illustrated by the behaviour of men who are training for some competition or performance: they devote their whole time to the appropriate exercises. The man, then, must be a perfect fool who is unaware that people's characters take their bias from the steady direction of their activities. If a man, well aware of what he is doing, behaves in such a way that he is bound to become unjust, we can only say that he is voluntarily unjust.

Again, while we cannot fairly argue that when a man behaves unjustly he does not wish to be unjust, or that when he plunges into dissipation he has no wish to be dissipated, it is by no means true that he can stop being unjust or dissolute merely by wishing it. You might as well expect a sick man to get better by wishing it. Yet the illness may be voluntary in the sense that it has been caused by loose living and neglecting the doctor's orders. There was a time when he need not have been ill; but once he let himself go, the opportunity was lost. When once you have thrown a stone, it is gone for good and all. Still it lay with yourself to let it lie instead of picking it up and throwing it; the origin of the act was in you. Similarly it was open to the dishonest and dissolute fellow to avoid becoming such a character; so that his original action was voluntary. But once he is hardened in vice the possibility of reforming disappears. Nor is it only vices of character that are voluntary. It is not rare to find bodily defects which are so too. Doubtless nobody blames a man for being born ugly, but we do blame those who lose their looks from want of exercise and neglect of hygiene. We may have the same feeling when a man's physique is weakened or impaired. Thus blindness is not an object of censure but of compassion when it is the result of a congenital defect or an illness or a blow. But if it is the result of alcoholic poisoning of general debauchery, then no one has any sympathy with the blind man. It comes to this. Physical defects which could have been avoided are blamed, but not those which a man cannot help, and for which he is therefore not responsible. But, this granted, we must be held responsible for moral failings which are generally reprobated.

But someone may say, 'We all aim at what appears to us to be good, but over this appearance we have no control. How the end appears is determined by the character of the individual. Now one of two things. Either the individual is in a manner responsible for his moral character or he is not. If he is, he will also be in a manner responsible for the way in which the end—that is the good—appears to him. If he is not, then none of us will be responsible for his own misdeeds. The wrong doer will be acting wrongly because he is ignorant of the true end and thinks that by such wrongdoing he will attain the highest good. That he should aim at the end in this fashion is not a matter of his own choosing. We must be born with an eye for a moral issue which will enable us to form a correct judgement and choose what is truly good. A man who has this natural gift is one of Nature's favourites, and such an endowment is one of the greatest and noblest in the world. It is something that cannot be acquired or learned; and if a man possesses it just as it was when it was bestowed upon him at birth, he will have all the native gifts and graces in their genuine and fullest form.' But if this be a sound argument, how will it be possible to maintain that virtue is more voluntary than vice? To the good and the bad man alike the end presents and establishes itself in the same way, whatever that may be, whether an instinctive process or not; and whatever they do, they do it somehow with reference to the end as they see it. One is driven then to hold one of two positions. Either (*a*) the view one takes of the end—whatever that view may be—is not imposed on us by Nature but is partly due to oneself. Or (*b*) the end is given by Nature but virtue is voluntary, because the virtuous man does voluntarily whatever he has left himself to do in order to attain his end. In either case vice will be just as voluntary as virtue. For the free agency of the bad man is just as important for his conduct as the free agency of the good man for his, even if we agree that it does not appear in the bad man's choice of an end. So if we say that the virtues are voluntary,* then our vices are voluntary too. The cases are identical. . . .

Our dispositions, however, have a different kind of voluntariness from that of our actions. We are masters of an action of ours from start to finish, and it is present to our minds at every stage, so that we know what we are doing. But with dispositions it is otherwise. Their beginning is something we can control, but as they develop step by step the stages of their development elude our observation—it is like the progress of a disease. They are, however, voluntary in the sense that it was originally in our power to exercise them for good or for evil.

Let us now resume our discussion of the virtues, taking them one by one, saying what each is, in what sort of things it finds its expression and in what way. From this method it will transpire how many virtues there are.

---

* As a matter of fact we ourselves in a way contribute something to the causes which produce our moral character, and it is because we have such and such a character that we set before ourselves such and such an end.

Joseph Butler (1692–1752)

Joseph Butler was born in the town of Wantage, in Berkshire, England, of Presbyterian parents. In his early twenties he corresponded with the then well-known philosopher Samuel Clarke, criticizing the latter's a priori arguments for the existence of God. By the time he received his B.A. from Oxford, in 1718, Butler had gone over to the Church of England. Soon after this he was ordained a priest and then appointed Preacher at the Rolls Chapel. In 1738 Butler was made Bishop of Bristol, and in 1750, Bishop of Durham. He never married; he lived a generally quiet and retiring life, but he did serve for a time in the courts of both Queen Caroline and George II.

Butler's present philosophical fame justly rests on his ethical system and penetrating moral psychology, contained primarily in his *Fifteen Sermons Preached at the Rolls Chapel,* which was published in 1726, his last year at the Rolls. But in his own time he was better known for the *Analogy of Religion* (1736), a careful defense of natural religion and Christian revelation. Butler wrote only two other works of note, a *Preface* to the second edition of the *Fifteen Sermons* (1729) and the *Dissertation on Virtue,* published together with the *Analogy of Religion.*

The doctrine of "universal selfishness" that Butler was much concerned to refute can be found in Thomas Hobbes' *Leviathan,* Part I, Chapters XIV and XV. A good book is *Butler's Moral Philosophy* (1952) by Austin Duncan-Jones. Chapter III of *Five Types of Ethical Theory* (1930) by C. D. Broad is devoted to the moral philosophy of Butler. In H. Sidgwick's *Methods of Ethics* (1874), Book I, Chapter 8, and Book IV are relevant. Two other books are *Bishop Butler, Moralist and Divine* (1940) by J. H. Randall and *Butler's Ethics* (1964) by P. Carlsson. Chapter 5 of our text discusses Butler in general and also compares Butler and Ayn Rand on the topic of ethical egoism.

Fifteen Sermons Preached at the Rolls Chapel

SERMON XI **Upon the Love of Our Neighbor**

And if there be any other commandment, it is briefly compre-
hended in this saying, namely, Thou shalt love thy neighbour as
thyself.

ROMANS XIII:9

It is commonly observed that there is a disposition in men to complain of the viciousness and corruption of the age in which they live,
as greater than that of former ones; which is usually followed with this
further observation that mankind has been in that respect much the
same in all times. Now, not to determine whether this last be not contradicted by the accounts of history, thus much can scarce be doubted
—that vice and folly takes different turns, and some particular kinds
of it are more open and avowed in some ages than in others; and I
suppose it may be spoken of as very much the distinction of the present
to profess a contracted spirit and greater regards to self-interest than
appears to have been done formerly. Upon this account it seems worth
while to inquire whether private interest is likely to be promoted in
proportion to the degree in which self-love engrosses us, and prevails
over all other principles, *or whether the contracted affection may not*
possibly be so prevalent as to disappoint itself, and even contradict its
own end, private good.

And since, further, there is generally thought to be some peculiar
kind of contrariety between self-love and the love of our neighbor,
between the pursuit of public and of private good, insomuch that when
you are recommending one of these, you are supposed to be speaking
against the other; and from hence arises a secret prejudice against and
frequently open scorn of all talk of public spirit and real goodwill to
our fellow creatures; it will be necessary to *inquire what respect be-*
nevolence has to self-love, and the pursuit of private interest to the

---

The text is from the edition of J. H. Bernard (1900) but, more often than not,
the shorter paragraphing of the edition of W. E. Gladstone (1896) is used. Some
spelling and punctuation is modernized; an occasional word enclosed in square
brackets is the addition of the editor.

pursuit of public; or whether there be anything of that peculiar inconsistency and contrariety between them, over and above what there is
between self-love and other passions and particular affections, and
their respective pursuits.

These inquiries, it is hoped, may be favorably attended to; for
there shall be all possible concessions made to the favorite passion,
which has so much allowed to it, and whose cause is so universally
pleaded: it shall be treated with the utmost tenderness and concern
for its interests.

In order to do this, as well as to determine the forementioned questions, it will be necessary to *consider the nature, the object, and end
of that self-love, as distinguished from other principles or affections in
the mind and their respective objects.*

Every man has a general desire of his own happiness, and likewise
a variety of particular affections, passions, and appetites to particular
external objects. The former proceeds from or is self-love, and seems
inseparable from all sensible creatures who can reflect upon themselves
and their own interest or happiness, so as to have that interest an object to their minds; what is to be said of the latter is that they proceed
from, or together make up, that particular nature according to which
man is made. The object the former pursues is something internal—our
own happiness, enjoyment, satisfaction, whether we have or have not
a distinct particular perception what it is or wherein it consists; the
objects of the latter are this or that particular external thing which the
affections tend towards, and of which it has always a particular idea or
perception. The principle we call 'self-love' never seeks anything external for the sake of the thing, but only as a means of happiness or
good; particular affections rest in the external things themselves. One
belongs to man as a reasonable creature reflecting upon his own interest or happiness. The other, though quite distinct from reason, are as
much a part of human nature.

That all particular appetites and passions are toward *external
things themselves,* distinct from the *pleasure arising from them,* is
manifested from hence—that there could not be this pleasure were it
not for that prior suitableness between the object and the passion; there
could be no enjoyment or delight from one thing more than another,
from eating food more than from swallowing a stone, if there were not
an affection or appetite to one thing more than another.

Every particular affection, even the love of our neighbor, is as
really our own affection as self-love; and the pleasure arising from its
gratification is as much my own pleasure as the pleasure self-love
would have—from knowing I myself should be happy some time hence
—would be my own pleasure. And if, because every particular affection is a man's own, and the pleasure arising from its gratification his
own pleasure, or pleasure to himself, such particular affection must be
called self-love: according to this way of speaking no creature what-

ever can possibly act but merely from self-love, and every action and every affection whatever is to be resolved up into this one principle. But then this is not the language of mankind; or if it were, we should want words to express the difference between the principle of an action proceeding from cool consideration that it will be to my own advantage, and an action, suppose of revenge or of friendship, by which a man runs upon certain ruin to do evil or good to another. It is manifest the principles of these actions are totally different, and so want different words to be distinguished by; all that they agree in is that they both proceed from and are done to gratify an inclination in a man's self. But the principle or inclination in one case is self-love, in the other, hatred or love of another. There is then a distinction between the cool principle of self-love or general desire of our happiness, as one part of our nature and one principle of action, and the particular affections toward particular external objects, as another part of our nature and another principle of action. How much soever therefore is to be allowed to self-love, yet it cannot be allowed to be the whole of our inward constitution, because, you see, there are other parts or principles which come into it.

Further, private happiness or good is all which self-love can make us desire or be concerned about; in having this consists its gratification: it is an affection to ourselves, a regard to our own interest, happiness, and private good; and in the proportion a man has this, he is interested, or a lover of himself. Let this be kept in mind; because there is commonly, as I shall presently have occasion to observe, another sense put upon these words. On the other hand, particular affections tend toward particular external things; these are their objects; having these is their end—in this consists their gratification, no matter whether it be, or be not, upon the whole, our interest or happiness. An action done from the former of these principles is called an interested action. An action proceeding from any of the latter has its denomination of passionate, ambitious, friendly, revengeful, or any other, from the particular appetite or affection from which it proceeds. Thus self-love as one part of human nature and the several particular principles as the other part are, themselves, their objects and ends, stated and shown.

From hence it will be easy to see how far, and in what ways, each of these can contribute and be subservient to the private good of the individual. Happiness does not consist in self-love. The desire of happiness is no more the thing itself than the desire of riches is the possession or enjoyment of them. People may love themselves with the most entire and unbounded affection, and yet be extremely miserable. Neither can self-love anyway help them out, but by setting them on work to get rid of the causes of their misery, to gain or make use of those objects which are by nature adapted to afford satisfaction. Happiness or satisfaction consists only in the enjoyment of those objects which are by nature suited to our several particular appetites, passions, and affections. So that if self-love wholly engrosses us, and leaves no room for any other principle, there can be absolutely no such thing at all as happiness, or enjoyment of any kind whatever, since happiness consists in the gratification of particular passions, which supposes the having of them. Self-love then does not constitute *this* or *that* to be our interest or good; but, our interest or good being constituted by nature and supposed, self-love only puts us upon obtaining and securing it.

Therefore, if it be possible that self-love may prevail and exert itself in a degree or manner which is not subservient to this end, then it will not follow that our interest will be promoted in proportion to the degree in which that principle engrosses us, and prevails over others. Nay, further, the private and contracted affection, when it is not subservient to this end, private good, may, for anything that appears, have a direct contrary tendency and effect. And if we will consider the matter, we shall see that it often really has. *Disengagement* is absolutely necessary to enjoyment; and a person may have so steady and fixed an eye upon his own interest, whatever he places it in, as may hinder him from *attending* to many gratifications within his reach, which others have their minds free and open to. Overfondness for a child is not generally thought to be for its advantage; and if there be any guess to be made from appearances, surely that character we call selfish is not the most promising for happiness. Such a temper may plainly be, and exert itself in a degree and manner which may give unnecessary and useless solicitude and anxiety, in a degree and manner which may prevent obtaining the means and materials of enjoyment, as well as the making use of them. Immoderate self-love does very ill consult its own interest; and how much soever a paradox it may appear, it is certainly true that even from self-love we should endeavor to get over all inordinate regard to and consideration of ourselves. Every one of our passions and affections has its natural stint and bound, which may easily be exceeded; whereas our enjoyments can possibly be but in a determinate measure and degree. Therefore such excess of the affection, since it cannot procure any enjoyment, must in all cases be useless, but is generally attended with inconveniences, and often is downright pain and misery. This holds as much with regard to self-love as to all other affections. The natural degree of it, so far as it sets us on work to gain and make use of the materials of satisfaction, may be to our real advantage; but beyond or besides this, it is in several respects an inconvenience and disadvantage. Thus it appears that private interest is so far from being likely to be promoted in proportion to the degree in which self-love engrosses us, and prevails over all other principles, that the contracted affection may be so prevalent as to disappoint itself, and even contradict its own end, private good.

'But who, except the most sordidly covetous, ever thought there was any rivalship between the love of greatness, honor, power, or between sensual appetites, and self-love? No, there is a perfect harmony between them. It is by means of these particular appetites and affections that self-love is gratified in enjoyment, happiness, and satisfaction. The competition and rivalship is between self-love and the love of our neighbor, that affection which leads us out of ourselves, makes us regardless of our own interest, and substitute that of another in its stead.' Whether then there be any peculiar competition and contrariety in this case, shall now be considered.

Self-love and interestedness was stated to consist in or be an affection to ourselves, a regard to our own private good; it is therefore distinct from benevolence, which is an affection to the good of our fellow creatures. But that benevolence is distinct from, that is, not the same thing with self-love, is no reason for its being looked upon with any peculiar suspicion; because every principle whatever, by means of which self-love is gratified, is distinct from it; and all things which are distinct from each other are equally so. A man has an affection or aversion to another; that one of these tends to and is gratified by doing good, that the other tends to and is gratified by doing harm, does not in the least alter the respect which either one or the other of these inward feelings has to self-love. We use the word 'property' so as to exclude any other persons having an interest in that of which we say a particular man has the property. And we often use the word 'selfish' so as to exclude in the same manner all regards to the good of others. But the cases are not parallel; for though that exclusion is really part of the idea of property, yet such positive exclusion, or bringing this peculiar disregard to the good of others into the idea of self-love, is in reality adding to the idea, or changing it from what it was before stated to consist in, namely, in an affection to ourselves. This being the whole idea of self-love, it can no otherwise exclude goodwill or love of others than merely by not including it, no otherwise than it excludes love of arts or reputation, or of anything else. Neither, on the other hand, does benevolence, any more than love of arts or of reputation, exclude self-love. Love of our neighbor then has just the same respect to, is no more distant from, self-love than hatred of our neighbor, or than love or hatred of anything else.

Thus the principles from which men rush upon certain ruin for the destruction of an enemy, and for the preservation of a friend, have the same respect to the private affection, and are equally interested or equally disinterested; and it is of no avail whether they are said to be one or the other. Therefore, to those that are shocked to hear virtue spoken of as disinterested, it may be allowed that it is indeed absurd to speak thus of it, unless hatred, several particular instances of vice, and all the common affections and aversions in mankind are acknowledged to be disinterested too. Is there any less inconsistency between the love of inanimate things, or of creatures merely sensitive, and self-love than between self-love and the love of our neighbor? Is desire of and delight in the happiness of another any more a diminution of self-love than desire of and delight in the esteem of another? They are both equally desire of and delight in something external to ourselves: either both or neither are so. The object of self-love is expressed in the term 'self'; and every appetite of sense and every particular affection of the heart are equally interested or disinterested because the objects of them are all equally self or something else. Whatever ridicule therefore the mention of a disinterested principle or action may be supposed to lie open to, must, upon the matter being thus stated, relate to ambition and every appetite and particular affection, as much as to benevolence. And indeed all the ridicule and all the grave perplexity, of which this subject has had its full share, is merely from words. The most intelligible way of speaking of it seems to be this: that self-love and the actions done in consequence of it (for these will presently appear to be the same as to this question) are interested; that particular affections toward external objects, and the actions done in consequence of those affections, are not so. But everyone is at liberty to use words as he pleases. All that is here insisted upon is that ambition, revenge, benevolence, all particular passions whatever, and the actions they produce, are equally interested or disinterested.

Thus it appears that there is no peculiar contrariety between self-love and benevolence, no greater competition between these than between any other particular affections and self-love. This relates to the affections themselves. Let us now see whether there be any peculiar contrariety between the respective courses of life which these affections lead to, whether there be any greater competition between the pursuit of private and of public good than between any other particular pursuits and that of private good.

There seems no other reason to suspect that there is any such peculiar contrariety, but only that the course of action which benevolence leads to has a more direct tendency to promote the good of others than that course of action which love of reputation suppose, or any other particular affection leads to. But that any affection tends to the happiness of another does not hinder its tending to one's own happiness too. That others enjoy the benefit of the air and the light of the sun does not hinder but that these are as much one's private advantage now as they would be if we had the property of them exclusive of all others. So a pursuit which tends to promote the good of another, yet may have as great tendency to promote private interest as a pursuit which does not tend to the good of another at all or which is mischievous to him. All particular affections whatever, resentment, benevolence, love of arts, equally lead to a course of action for their own gratification, that is, the gratification of ourselves; and the gratification of each gives delight; so far then it is manifest they have all the same respect to private interest. Now take into consideration further, concerning these three pursuits, that the end of the first is the harm, of the second, the good of another, of the last, something indifferent; and is there any necessity that these additional considerations should alter the respect which we before saw these three pursuits had to private interest, or render any one of them less conducive to it than any other? Thus one man's affection is to honor as his end, in order to obtain which he thinks no pains too great. Suppose another, with such a singularity of mind as to have the same affection to public good as his end, which he endeavors with the same labor to obtain. In case of success, surely the man of benevolence has as great enjoyment as the man of ambition; they both equally having the end [of] their affections, in the same degree, tended to; but in case of disappointment, the benevolent man has clearly the advantage, since endeavoring to do good, considered as a virtuous pursuit, is gratified by its own consciousness, that is, is in a degree its own reward.

And as to these two, or benevolence and any other particular passions whatever, considered in a further view as forming a general temper which more or less disposes us for enjoyment of all the common blessings of life, distinct from their own gratification: is benevolence less the temper of tranquility and freedom than ambition or covetousness? Does the benevolent man appear less easy with himself, from his love to his neighbor? Does he less relish his being? Is there any peculiar gloom seated on his face? Is his mind less open to entertainment, to any particular gratification? Nothing is more manifest than that being in good humor, which is benevolence while it lasts, is itself the temper of satisfaction and enjoyment.

Suppose then a man sitting down to consider how he might become most easy to himself and attain the greatest pleasure he could—all that which is his real natural happiness. This can only consist in the enjoyment of those objects which are by nature adapted to our several faculties. These particular enjoyments make up the sum total of our happiness; and they are supposed to arise from riches, honors, and the gratification of sensual appetites; be it so, yet none profess themselves so completely happy in these enjoyments but that there is room left in the mind for others if they were presented to them; nay, these, as much as they engage us, are not thought so high but that human nature is capable even of greater.

Now there have been persons in all ages who have professed that they found satisfaction in the exercise of charity, in the love of their neighbor, in endeavoring to promote the happiness of all they had to do with, and in the pursuit of what is just and right and good, as the general bent of their mind and end of their life; and that doing an action of baseness or cruelty would be as great violence to *their* self, as much breaking in upon their nature as any external force. Persons of this character would add, if they might be heard, that they consider themselves as acting in the view of an infinite Being, who is in a much higher sense the object of reverence and of love than all the world besides; and therefore they could have no more enjoyment from a wicked action committed under His eye than the persons to whom they are making their apology could, if all mankind were the spectators of it; and that the satisfaction of approving themselves to His unerring judgment, to Whom they thus refer all their actions, is a more continued settled satisfaction than any this world can afford; as also that they have, no less than others, a mind free and open to all the common innocent gratifications of it, such as they are. And if we go no further, does there appear any absurdity in this? Will any one take it upon him to say that a man cannot find his account in this general course of life as much as in the most unbounded ambition and the excesses of pleasure? Or that such a person has not consulted so well for himself, for the satisfaction and peace of his own mind, as the ambitious or dissolute man? And though the consideration that God Himself will in the end justify their taste, and support their cause, is not formally to be insisted upon here, yet thus much comes in, that all enjoyments whatever are much more clear and unmixed from the assurance that they will end well. Is it certain then that there is nothing in these pretensions to happiness, especially when there are not wanting persons who have supported themselves with satisfactions of this kind in sickness, poverty, disgrace, and in the very pangs of death, whereas it is manifest all other enjoyments fail in these circumstances? This surely looks suspicious of having something in it. Self-love methinks should be alarmed. May she not possibly pass over greater pleasures than those she is so wholly taken up with?

The short of the matter is no more than this: happiness consists in the gratification of certain affections, appetites, passions, with objects which are by nature adapted to them. Self-love may indeed set us on work to gratify these, but happiness or enjoyment has no immediate connection with self-love, but arises from such gratification alone. Love of our neighbor is one of those affections. This, considered as a *virtuous principle,* is gratified by a consciousness of endeavoring to promote the good of others; but considered as a *natural affection,* its gratification consists in the actual accomplishment of this endeavor. Now indulgence or gratification of this affection, whether in that consciousness or this accomplishment, has the same respect to interest as indulgence of any other affection; they equally proceed from or do not proceed from self-love; they equally include or equally exclude this principle. Thus it appears that *benevolence and the pursuit of public good has at least as great respect to self-love and the pursuit of private good as any other particular passions, and their respective pursuits.*

Neither is covetousness, whether as a temper or pursuit, any exception to this. For if by covetousness is meant the desire and pursuit of riches for their own sake, without any regard to, or consideration of, the uses of them, this has as little to do with self-love as benevolence has. But by this word is usually meant, not such madness and total distraction of mind, but immoderate affection to and pursuit of riches as possessions in order to some further end, namely, satisfaction, interest, or good. This therefore is not a particular affection or particular pursuit, but it is the general principle of self-love and the general pursuit of our own interest; for which reason the word 'selfish' is by everyone appropriated to this temper and pursuit. Now, as it is ridiculous to assert that self-love and the love of our neighbor are the same, so neither is it asserted that following these different affections has the same tendency and respect to our own interest. The comparison is not between self-love and the love of our neighbor, between pursuit of our own interest and the interest of others, but between the several particular affections in human nature toward external objects, as one part of the comparison, and the one particular affection to the good of our neighbor, as the other part of it; and it has been shown that all these have the same respect to self-love and private interest.

There is indeed frequently an inconsistency or interfering between self-love or private interest and the several particular appetites, passions, affections, or the pursuits they lead to. But this competition or interfering is merely accidental, and happens much oftener between pride, revenge, sensual gratifications, and private interest, than between private interest and benevolence. For nothing is more common than to see men give themselves up to a passion or an affection to their known prejudice and ruin, and in direct contradiction to manifest and real interest and the loudest calls of self-love; whereas the seeming competitions and interfering between benevolence and private interest relate much more to the materials or means of enjoyment than to enjoyment itself. There is often an interfering in the former, when there is none in the latter. Thus as to riches: so much money as a man gives away, so much less will remain in his possession. Here is a real interfering. But though a man cannot possibly give without lessening his fortune, yet there are multitudes [that] might give without lessening their own enjoyment, because they may have more than they can turn to any real use or advantage to themselves. Thus, the more thought and time anyone employs about the interests and good of others, he must necessarily have less to attend his own; but he may have so ready and large a supply of his own wants, that such thought might be really useless to himself, though of great service and assistance to others.

The general mistake, that there is some greater inconsistency between endeavoring to promote the good of another and self-interest than between self-interest and pursuing anything else, seems, as has already been hinted, to arise from our notions of property; and to be carried on by this property's being supposed to be itself our happiness or good. People are so very much taken up with this one subject that they seem from it to have formed a general way of thinking, which they apply to other things that they have nothing to do with. Hence, in a confused and slight way, it might well be taken for granted that another's having no interest in an affection (that is, his good not being the object of it), renders, as one may speak, the proprietor's interest in it greater; and that if another had an interest in it, this would render his less, or occasion that such affection could not be so friendly to self-love, or conducive to private good, as an affection or pursuit which has not a regard to the good of another.

This, I say, might be taken for granted, whilst it was not attended to that the object of every particular affection is equally something external to ourselves; and whether it be the good of another person, or whether it be any other external thing, makes no alteration with regard to its being one's own affection, and the gratification of it one's own private enjoyment. And so far as it is taken for granted that barely having the means and materials of enjoyment is what constitutes interest and happiness; that our interest or good consists in possessions themselves, in having the property of riches, houses, lands, gardens, not in the enjoyment of them: so far it will even more strongly be taken for granted, in the way already explained, that an affection's conducing to the good of another must even necessarily occasion it to conduce less to private good, if not to be positively detrimental to it. For if property and happiness are one and the same thing, as by increasing the property of another, you lessen your own property, so by promoting the happiness of another, you must lessen your own happiness. But whatever occasioned the mistake, I hope it has been fully proved to be one, as it has been proved that there is no peculiar rivalship or competition between self-love and benevolence; that as there may be a competition between these two, so there may also between any particular affection whatever and self-love; that every particular affection, benevolence among the rest, is subservient to self-love by being the instrument of private enjoyment; and that in one respect benevolence contributes more to private interest, that is, enjoyment or satisfaction, than any other of the particular common affections, as it is in a degree its own gratification.

And to all these things may be added that religion, from whence arises our strongest obligation to benevolence, is so far from disowning the principle of self-love that it often addresses itself to that very principle, and always to the mind in that state when reason presides; and there can no access be had to the understanding but by convincing men that the course of life we would persuade them to is not contrary to their interest. It may be allowed, without any prejudice to the cause of virtue and religion, that our idea of happiness and misery are of all our ideas the nearest and most important to us; that they will, nay, if you please, that they ought to prevail over those of order and beauty and harmony and proportion, if there should ever be, as it is impossible there ever should be, any inconsistency between them; though these last, too, as expressing the fitness of actions, are real as truth itself. Let it be allowed, though virtue or moral rectitude does indeed consist in affection to and pursuit of what is right and good, as such; yet, that when we sit down in a cool hour, we can neither justify to ourselves this or any other pursuit, till we are convinced that it will be for our happiness or at least not contrary to it.

Common reason and humanity will have some influence upon mankind, whatever becomes of speculations; but, so far as the interests of virtue depend upon the theory of it being secured from open scorn, so far its very being in the world depends upon its appearing to have no contrariety to private interest and self-love. The foregoing observations, therefore, it is hoped, may have gained a little ground in favor of the precept before us; the particular explanation of which shall be the subject of the next discourse.

I will conclude at present with observing the peculiar obligation which we are under to virtue and religion, as enforced in the verses following the text, in the Epistle for the day, from our Saviour's coming into the world. 'The night is far spent, the day is at hand; let us therefore cast off the works of darkness, and let us put on the armour of light,' etc. The meaning and force of which exhortation is that Christianity lays us under new obligations to a good life, as by it the will of God is more clearly revealed, and as it affords additional motives to the practice of it, over and above those which arise out of the nature of virtue and vice; I might add, As our Saviour has set us a perfect example of goodness in our own nature. Now love and charity is plainly the thing in which He has placed His religion; in which therefore, as we have any pretense to the name of Christians, we must place ours. He has at once enjoined it upon us by way of command with peculiar force and by His example, as having undertaken the work of our salvation out of pure love and goodwill to mankind. The endeavor to set home this example upon our minds is a very proper employment of this season, which is bringing on the festival of His birth; which as it may teach us many excellent lessons of humility, resignation, and obedience to the will of God, so there is none it recommends with greater authority, force and advantage than this of love and charity; since it was 'for us men and for our salvation' that 'He came down from heaven, and was incarnate, and was made man'; that He might teach us our duty, and more specially that He might enforce the practice of it, reform mankind, and finally bring us to that 'eternal salvation,' of which 'He is the Author to all those that obey Him.'

David Hume (1711–1776)

Born and educated in Edinburgh, David Hume first tried a business career but was unhappy at it. Hume then went to France to study and there, while still in his twenties, wrote his best philosophical work, *A Treatise of Human Nature.* Its main parts are I "Of the Understanding," II "Of the Passions," and III "Of Morals." But Hume was disappointed by the book's reception, feared that its serious style was at fault, and rewrote parts of it, which appeared as *An Enquiry Concerning Human Understanding* (1748) and *An Enquiry Concerning the Principles of Morals* (1751). Though now generally acknowledged to be England's greatest philosopher, he was turned down more than once when he applied for university teaching positions because his ideas were considered offensive to the established religion. He made his livelihood by turns as tutor, librarian, and diplomat. During his lifetime he achieved some fame from his *History of England* (1755) and *Political Discourses* (1752), but his second most important work, *Dialogues Concerning Natural Religion,* was not published until three years after his death. Hume, who never married, spent his life as a scholar. He retained a cheerful disposition, enjoyed the company of famous French and English thinkers of his time, and spent his last years in retirement in Edinburgh.

Hume's moral philosophy is restated, with some changes, in *An Enquiry Concerning the Principles of Morals.* Chapter IV of *Five Types of Ethical Theory* (1930) by C. D. Broad and *Reason and Conduct in Hume's Treatise* (1946) by R. M. Kydd are devoted to Hume's moral philosophy. Part Two, Chapter II, of D. G. C. McNabb's *David Hume: His Theory of Knowledge and Morality* is about reason and feeling in Hume's moral philosophy. Also of interest are the sections on Hume in *The Moral Sense* (1947) by D. D. Raphael and *The Moral Philosophy of David Hume* (1964) by R. D. Broiles.

A Treatise of Human Nature

BOOK III

SECTION I **Moral Distinctions Not Derived from Reason**

There is an inconvenience which attends all abstruse reasoning, that it may silence, without convincing an antagonist, and requires the same intense study to make us sensible of its force, that was at first requisite for its invention. When we leave our closet, and engage in the common affairs of life, its conclusions seem to vanish like the phantoms of the night on the appearance of the morning; and it is difficult for us to retain even that conviction which we had attained with difficulty. This is still more conspicuous in a long chain of reasoning, where we must preserve to the end the evidence of the first propositions, and where we often lose sight of all the most received maxims, either of philosophy or common life. I am not, however, without hopes, that the present system of philosophy will acquire new force as it advances; and that our reasonings concerning *morals* will corroborate whatever has been said concerning the *understanding* and the *passions*. Morality is a subject that interests us above all others: We fancy the peace of society to be at stake in every decision concerning it; and it is evident that this concern must make our speculations appear more real and solid than where the subject is, in a great measure, indifferent to us. What affects us, we conclude can never be a chimera; and as our passion is engaged on the one side or the other, we naturally think that the question lies within human comprehension; which, in other cases of this nature, we are apt to entertain some doubt of. Without this advantage I never should have ventured upon a third volume of such abstruse philosophy in an age wherein the greatest part of men seem agreed to convert reading into an amusement, and to reject every thing that requires any considerable degree of attention to be comprehended.

It has been observed that nothing is ever present to the mind but its perceptions; and that all the actions of seeing, hearing, judging, loving, hating, and thinking, fall under this denomination. The mind can

---

From the first edition of 1740. Some 18th-century spellings have been modernized. Sections I and II are taken from Part 1, "Of Virtue and Vice in General," of Book III.

never exert itself in any action which we may not comprehend under the term of *perception;* and consequently that term is no less applicable to those judgments by which we distinguish moral good and evil than to every other operation of the mind. To approve of one character, to condemn another, are only so many different perceptions.

Now as perceptions resolve themselves into two kinds, viz. *impressions* and *ideas,* this distinction gives rise to a question, with which we shall open up our present enquiry concerning morals. *Whether it is by means of our ideas or impressions we distinguish between vice and virtue, and pronounce an action blameable or praise-worthy?* This will immediately cut off all loose discourses and declamations, and reduce us to something precise and exact on the present subject.

Those who affirm that virtue is nothing but a conformity to reason; that there are eternal fitnesses and unfitnesses of things, which are the same to every rational being that considers them; that the immutable measures of right and wrong impose an obligation, not only on human creatures, but also on the Deity himself: All these systems concur in the opinion, that morality, like truth, is discerned merely by ideas, and by their juxtaposition and comparison. In order, therefore, to judge of these systems, we need only consider whether it be possible, from reason alone, to distinguish between moral good and evil, or whether there must concur some other principles to enable us to make that distinction.

If morality had naturally no influence on human passions and actions, it were in vain to take such pains to inculcate it; and nothing would be more fruitless than that multitude of rules and precepts, with which all moralists abound. Philosophy is commonly divided into *speculative* and *practical;* and as morality is always comprehended under the latter division, it is supposed to influence our passions and actions, and to go beyond the calm and indolent judgments of the understanding. And this is confirmed by common experience, which informs us that men are often governed by their duties, and are deterred from some actions by the opinion of injustice, and impelled to others by that of obligation.

Since morals, therefore, have an influence on the actions and affections, it follows that they cannot be derived from reason; and that because reason alone, as we have already proved, can never have any such influence. Morals excite passions, and produce or prevent actions. Reason of itself is utterly impotent in this particular. The rules of morality, therefore, are not conclusions of our reason.

No one, I believe, will deny the justness of this inference; nor is there any other means of evading it, than by denying that principle on which it is founded. As long as it is allowed that reason has no influence on our passions and actions, it is in vain to pretend that morality is discovered only by a deduction of reason. An active principle can never be founded on an inactive; and if reason be inactive in itself, it must remain so in all its shapes and appearances, whether it exerts itself in natural or moral subjects, whether it considers the powers of external bodies, or the actions of rational beings.

It would be tedious to repeat all the arguments, by which I have proved that reason is perfectly inert, and can never either prevent or produce any action or affection. It will be easy to recollect what has been said upon that subject. I shall only recall on this occasion one of these arguments, which I shall endeavour to render still more conclusive and more applicable to the present subject.

Reason is the discovery of truth or falsehood. Truth or falsehood consists in an agreement or disagreement either to the *real* relations of ideas, or to *real* existence and matter of fact. Whatever, therefore, is not susceptible of this agreement or disagreement is incapable of being true or false and can never be an object of our reason. Now it is evident our passions, volitions, and actions, are not susceptible of any such agreement or disagreement, being original facts and realities, complete in themselves, and implying no reference to other passions, volitions, and actions. It is impossible, therefore, they can be pronounced either true or false, and be either contrary or conformable to reason.

This argument is of double advantage to our present purpose. For it proves *directly* that actions do not derive their merit from a conformity to reason, nor their blame from a contrariety to it; and it proves the same truth more *indirectly,* by showing us, that as reason can never immediately prevent or produce any action by contradicting or approving of it, it cannot be the source of moral good and evil, which are found to have that influence. Actions may be laudable or blameable; but they cannot be reasonable or unreasonable: Laudable or blameable, therefore, are not the same with reasonable or unreasonable. The merit and demerit of actions frequently contradict, and sometimes control our natural propensities. But reason has no such influence. Moral distinctions, therefore, are not the offspring of reason. Reason is wholly inactive, and can never be the source of so active a principle as conscience, or a sense of morals.

But perhaps it may be said, that though no will or action can be immediately contradictory to reason, yet we may find such contradiction in some of the attendants of the action, that is, in its causes or effects. The action may cause a judgment, or may be *obliquely* caused by one, when the judgment concurs with a passion; and by an abusive way of speaking, which philosophy will scarce allow of, the same contrariety may, upon that account, be ascribed to the action. How far this truth or falsehood may be the source of morals, it will now be proper to consider.

It has been observed that reason, in a strict and philosophical sense, can have an influence on our conduct only after two ways: Either when it excites a passion by informing us of the existence of something which is a proper object of it; or when it discovers the connection of causes and effects, so as to afford us means of exerting any passion. These are the only kinds of judgment which can accompany our actions, or can be said to produce them in any manner; and it must be allowed that these judgments may often be false and erroneous. A person may be affected with passion, by supposing a pain or pleasure to lie in an object which has no tendency to produce either of these sensations, or which produces the contrary to what is imagined. A person may also take false measures for the attaining of his end, and may retard, by his foolish conduct, instead of forwarding the execution of any project. These false judgments may be thought to affect the passions and actions which are connected with them, and may be said to render them unreasonable, in a figurative and improper way of speaking. But though this be acknowledged, it is easy to observe that these errors are so far from being the source of all immorality, that they are commonly very innocent, and draw no manner of guilt upon the person who is so unfortunate as to fall into them. They extend not beyond a mistake of *fact*, which moralists have not generally supposed criminal, as being perfectly involuntary. I am more to be lamented than blamed, if I am mistaken with regard to the influence of objects in producing pain or pleasure, or if I know not the proper means of satisfying my desires. No one can ever regard such errors as a defect in my moral character. A fruit, for instance, that is really disagreeable, appears to me at a distance, and through mistake I fancy it to be pleasant and delicious. Here is one error. I choose certain means of reaching this fruit which are not proper for my end. Here is a second error; nor is there any third one which can ever possibly enter into our reasonings concerning actions. I ask, therefore, if a man, in this situation, and guilty of these two errors, is to be regarded as vicious and criminal, however unavoidable they might have been? Or if it be possible to imagine that such errors are the sources of all immorality?

And here it may be proper to observe that if moral distinctions be derived from the truth or falsehood of those judgments, they must take place wherever we form the judgments; nor will there be any difference, whether the question be concerning an apple or a kingdom, or whether the error be avoidable or unavoidable. For as the very essence of morality is supposed to consist in an agreement or disagreement to reason, the other circumstances are entirely arbitrary, and can never either bestow on any action the character of virtuous or vicious, or deprive it of that character. To which we may add, that this agreement or disagreement, not admitting of degrees, all virtues and vices would of course be equal.

Should it be pretended, that though a mistake of *fact* be not criminal, yet a mistake of *right* often is; and that this may be the source of immorality: I would answer, that it is impossible such a mistake can ever be the original source of immorality, since it supposes a real right and wrong; that is, a real distinction in morals, independent of these judgments. A mistake, therefore, of right may become a species of immorality; but it is only a secondary one, and is founded on some other, antecedent to it.

As to those judgments which are the *effects* of our actions, and which, when false, give occasion to pronounce the actions contrary to truth and reason; we may observe that our actions never cause any judgment, either true or false, in ourselves, and that it is only on others they have such an influence. It is certain that an action, on many occasions, may give rise to false conclusions in others; and that a person, who through a window sees any lewd behavior of mine with my neighbor's wife, may be so simple as to imagine she is certainly my own. In this respect my action resembles somewhat a lie or falsehood; only with this difference, which is material, that I perform not the action with any intention of giving rise to a false judgment in another, but merely to satisfy my lust and passion. It causes, however, a mistake and false judgment by accident; and the falsehood of its effects may be ascribed, by some odd figurative way of speaking, to the action itself. But still I can see no pretext of reason for asserting that the tendency to cause such an error is the first spring or original source of all immorality.[1]

---

[1] One might think it were entirely superfluous to prove this, if a late author [Wollaston], who has had the good fortune to obtain some reputation, had not seriously affirmed that such a falsehood is the foundation of all guilt and moral deformity. That we may discover the fallacy of his hypothesis, we need only consider that a false conclusion is drawn from an action only by means of an obscurity of natural principles, which makes a cause be secretly interrupted in its operation, by contrary causes, and renders the connection between two objects uncertain and variable. Now, as a like uncertainty and variety of causes take place, even in natural objects, and produce a like error in our judgment, if that tendency to produce error were the very essence of vice and immorality, it should follow that even inanimate objects might be vicious and immoral.

It is in vain to urge that inanimate objects act without liberty and choice. For as liberty and choice are not necessary to make an action produce in us an erroneous conclusion, they can be, in no respect, essential to morality; and I do not readily perceive, upon this system, how they can ever come to be regarded by it. If the tendency to cause error be the origin of immorality, that tendency and immorality would in every case be inseparable.

Add to this, that if I had used the precaution of shutting the windows while I indulged myself in those liberties with my neighbour's wife, I should have been guilty of no immorality; and that because my action, being perfectly concealed, would have had no tendency to produce any false conclusion.

For the same reason, a thief, who steals in by a ladder at a window, and takes all imaginable care to cause no disturbance, is in no respect criminal. For either he will not be perceived, or if he be, it is impossible he can produce any error, nor will any one, from these circumstances, take him to be other than what he really is.

It is well known that those who are squint-sighted do very readily cause mis-

Thus upon the whole, it is impossible that the distinction between moral good and evil can be made by reason; since that distinction has an influence upon our actions, of which reason alone is incapable. Reason and judgment may, indeed, be the mediate cause of an action, by prompting or by directing a passion: But it is not pretended, that a judgment of this kind, either in its truth or falsehood, is attended with virtue or vice. And as to the judgments which are caused by our judgments, they can still less bestow those moral qualities on the actions, which are their causes.

But to be more particular, and to show that those eternal immutable fitnesses and unfitnesses of things cannot be defended by sound philosophy, we may weigh the following considerations.

If the thought and understanding were alone capable of fixing the boundaries of right and wrong, the character of virtuous and vicious either must lie in some relations of objects, or must be a matter of fact which is discovered by our reasoning. This consequence is evident. As the operations of human understanding divide themselves into two kinds, the comparing of ideas, and the inferring of matter of fact; were virtue discovered by the understanding, it must be an object of one of these operations, nor is there any third operation of the understanding which can discover it. There has been an opinion very industriously propagated by certain philosophers, that morality is susceptible of dem-

---

takes in others, and that we imagine they salute or are talking to one person, while they address themselves to another. Are they therefore, upon that account, immoral?

Besides, we may easily observe that in all those arguments there is an evident reasoning in a circle. A person who takes possession of *another's* goods, and uses them as his *own*, in a manner declares them to be his own; and this falsehood is the source of the immorality of injustice. But is property, or right, or obligation, intelligible, without an antecedent morality?

A man that is ungrateful to his benefactor, in a manner affirms that he never received any favours from him. But in what manner? Is it because it is his duty to be grateful? But this supposes, that there is some antecedent rule of duty and morals. Is it because human nature is generally grateful, and makes us conclude that a man who does any harm never received any favour from the person he harmed? But human nature is not so generally grateful as to justify such a conclusion. Or if it were, is an exception to a general rule in every case criminal, for no other reason than because it is an exception?

But what may suffice entirely to destroy this whimsical system is that it leaves us under the same difficulty to give a reason why truth is virtuous and falsehood vicious, as to account for the merit or turpitude of any other action. I shall allow, if you please, that all immorality is derived from this supposed falsehood in action, provided you can give me any plausible reason why such a falsehood is immoral. If you consider rightly of the matter, you will find yourself in the same difficulty as at the beginning.

This last argument is very conclusive; because, if there be not an evident merit or turpitude annexed to this species of truth or falsehood, it can never have any influence upon our actions. For, who ever thought of forbearing any action because others might possibly draw false conclusions from it? Or, who ever performed any, that he might give rise to true conclusions?

onstration; and though no one has ever been able to advance a single step in those demonstrations, yet it is taken for granted that this science may be brought to an equal certainty with geometry or algebra. Upon this supposition, vice and virtue must consist in some relations; since it is allowed on all hands that no matter of fact is capable of being demonstrated. Let us, therefore, begin with examining this hypothesis, and endeavour, if possible, to fix those moral qualities which have been so long the objects of our fruitless researches. Point out distinctly the relations, which constitute morality or obligation, that we may know wherein they consist, and after what manner we must judge of them.

If you assert that vice and virtue consist in relations susceptible of certainty and demonstration, you must confine yourself to those *four* relations, which alone admit of that degree of evidence; and in that case you run into absurdities from which you will never be able to extricate yourself. For as you make the very essence of morality to lie in the relations, and as there is no one of the relations but what is applicable, not only to an irrational, but also to an inanimate object; it follows, that even such objects must be susceptible of merit or demerit. *Resemblance, contrariety, degrees in quality,* and *proportions in quantity and number;* all these relations belong as properly to matter, as to our actions, passions and volitions. It is unquestionable, therefore, that morality lies not in any of these relations, nor the sense of it in their discovery.[2]

Should it be asserted that the sense of morality consists in the discovery of some relation distinct from these, and that our enumeration was not complete when we comprehended all demonstrable relations under four general heads: To this I know not what to reply, till some one be so good as to point out to me this new relation. It is impossible to refute a system, which has never yet been explained. In such a manner of fighting in the dark, a man loses his blows in the air, and often places them where the enemy is not present.

I must, therefore, on this occasion, rest contented with requiring

---

2 As a proof, how confused our way of thinking on this subject commonly is, we may observe that those who assert that morality is demonstrable, do not say that morality lies in the relations, and that the relations are distinguishable by reason. They only say that reason can discover such an action, in such relations, to be virtuous, and such another vicious. It seems they thought it sufficient if they could bring the word, Relation, into the proposition, without troubling themselves whether it was to the purpose or not. But here, I think, is plain argument. Demonstrative reason discovers only relations. But that reason, according to this hypothesis, discovers also vice and virtue. These moral qualities, therefore, must be relations. When we blame any action in any situation, the whole complicated object, of action and situation, must form certain relations, wherein the essence of vice consists. This hypothesis is not otherwise intelligible. For what does reason discover, when it pronounces any action vicious? Does it discover a relation or a matter of fact? These questions are decisive, and must not be eluded.

the two following conditions of any one that would undertake to clear up this system. *First,* as moral good and evil belong only to the actions of the mind, and are derived from our situation with regard to external objects, the relations, from which these moral distinctions arise, must lie only between internal actions, and external objects, and must not be applicable either to internal actions, compared among themselves, or to external objects, when placed in opposition to other external objects. For as morality is supposed to attend certain relations, if these relations could belong to internal actions considered singly, it would follow that we might be guilty of crimes in ourselves, and independent of our situation, with respect to the universe: And in like manner, if these moral relations could be applied to external objects, it would follow that even inanimate beings would be susceptible of moral beauty and deformity. Now it seems difficult to imagine that any relation can be discovered between our passions, volitions and actions, compared to external objects, which relation might not belong either to these passions and volitions, or to these external objects, compared among *themselves.*

But it will be still more difficult to fulfill the *second* condition, requisite to justify this system. According to the principles of those who maintain an abstract rational difference between moral good and evil, and a natural fitness and unfitness of things, it is not only supposed that these relations, being eternal and immutable, are the same when considered by every rational creature, but their *effects* are also supposed to be necessarily the same; and it is concluded they have no less, or rather a greater, influence in directing the will of the deity, than in governing the rational and virtuous of our own species. These two particulars are evidently distinct. It is one thing to know virtue, and another to conform the will to it. In order, therefore, to prove that the measures of right and wrong are eternal laws, *obligatory* on every rational mind, it is not sufficient to show the relations upon which they are founded: We must also point out the connection between the relation and the will; and must prove that this connection is so necessary, that in every well-disposed mind, it must take place and have its influence; though the difference between these minds be in other respects immense and infinite. Now besides what I have already proved, that even in human nature no relation can ever alone produce any action; besides this, I say, it has been shown, in treating of the understanding, that there is no connection of cause and effect, such as this is supposed to be, which is discoverable otherwise than by experience, and of which we can pretend to have any security by the simple consideration of the objects. All beings in the universe, considered in themselves, appear entirely loose and independent of each other. It is only by experience we learn their influence and connection; and this influence we ought never to extend beyond experience.

Thus it will be impossible to fulfil the *first* condition required to the system of eternal rational measures of right and wrong; because it is impossible to show those relations, upon which such a distinction may be founded: And it is as impossible to fulfil the *second* condition; because we cannot prove *a priori*, that these relations, if they really existed and were perceived, would be universally forcible and obligatory.

But to make these general reflections more clear and convincing, we may illustrate them by some particular instances, wherein this character of moral good or evil is the most universally acknowledged. Of all crimes that human creatures are capable of committing, the most horrid and unnatural is ingratitude, especially when it is committed against parents, and appears in the more flagrant instances of wounds and death. This is acknowledged by all mankind, philosophers as well as the people; the question only arises among philosophers, whether the guilt or moral deformity of this action be discovered by demonstrative reasoning, or felt by an internal sense, and by means of some sentiment, which the reflecting on such an action naturally occasions. This question will soon be decided against the former opinion, if we can show the same relations in other objects, without the notion of any guilt or iniquity attending them. Reason or science is nothing but the comparing of ideas and the discovery of their relations; and if the same relations have different characters, it must evidently follow that those characters are not discovered merely by reason. To put the affair, therefore, to this trial, let us choose any inanimate object, such as an oak or elm; and let us suppose that by the dropping of its seed, it produces a sapling below it, which springing up by degrees, at last overtops and destroys the parent tree: I ask, if in this instance there be wanting any relation, which is discoverable in parricide or ingratitude? Is not the one tree the cause of another's existence; and the latter the cause of the destruction of the former, in the same manner as when a child murders his parent? It is not sufficient to reply that a choice or will is wanting. For in the case of parricide, a will does not give rise to any *different* relations, but is only the cause from which the action is derived; and consequently produces the *same* relations, that in the oak or elm arise from some other principles. It is a will or choice that determines a man to kill his parent; and they are the laws of matter and motion that determine a sapling to destroy the oak from which it sprung. Here then the same relations have different causes; but still the relations are the same: And as their discovery is not in both cases attended with a notion of immorality, it follows that that notion does not arise from such a discovery.

But to choose an instance still more resembling; I would fain ask any one why incest in the human species is criminal, and why the very same action and the same relations in animals have not the smallest moral turpitude and deformity? If it be answered that this action is innocent in animals, because they have not reason sufficient to discover its turpitude; but that man, being endowed with that faculty which *ought* to restrain him to his duty, the same action instantly becomes criminal to him; should this be said, I would reply, that this is evidently arguing in a circle. For before reason can perceive this turpitude, the turpitude must exist; and consequently is independent of the decisions of our reason, and is their object more properly than their effect. According to this system, then, every animal that has sense, and appetite, and will; that is, every animal must be susceptible of all the same virtues and vices, for which we ascribe praise and blame to human creatures. All the difference is, that our superior reason may serve to discover the vice or virtue, and by that means may augment the blame or praise: But still this discovery supposes a separate being in these moral distinctions, and a being which depends only on the will and appetite, and which, both in thought and reality, may be distinguished from the reason. Animals are susceptible of the same relations with respect to each other as the human species, and therefore would also be susceptible of the same morality, if the essence of morality consisted in these relations. Their want of a degree of reason may hinder them from perceiving the duties and obligations of morality, but can never hinder these duties from existing; since they must antecedently exist, in order to their being perceived. Reason must find them, and can never produce them. This argument deserves to be weighed, as being, in my opinion, entirely decisive.

Nor does this reasoning only prove that morality consists not in any relations that are the objects of science; but if examined will prove with equal certainty, that it consists not in any *matter of fact,* which can be discovered by the understanding. This is the *second* part of our argument; and if it can be made evident, we may conclude that morality is not an object of reason. But can there be any difficulty in proving that vice and virtue are not matters of fact, whose existence we can infer by reason? Take any action allowed to be vicious: Wilful murder, for instance. Examine it in all lights, and see if you can find that matter of fact, or real existence, which you call *vice.* In whichever way you take it, you find only certain passions, motives, volitions and thoughts. There is no other matter of fact in the case. The vice entirely escapes you, as long as you consider the object. You never can find it, till you turn your reflection into your own breast, and find a sentiment of disapprobation which arises in you towards this action. Here is a matter of fact; but it is the object of feeling, not of reason. It lies in yourself, not in the object. So that when you pronounce any action or character to be vicious, you mean nothing but that from the constitution of your nature you have a feeling or sentiment of blame from the contemplation of it. Vice and virtue, therefore, may be compared to sounds, colours, heat and cold, which, according to modern philosophy, are not qualities in objects, but perceptions in the mind: And this discovery in morals, like that other in physics, is to be regarded as a considerable advancement of the speculative sciences; though, like that too, it has little or no influence on practice. Nothing can be more real, or concern us more, than our own sentiments of pleasure and uneasiness; and if these be favourable to virtue, and unfavorable to vice, no more can be requisite to the regulation of our conduct and behaviour.

I cannot forbear adding to these reasonings an observation, which may, perhaps, be found of some importance. In every system of morality which I have hitherto met with, I have always remarked that the author proceeds for some time in the ordinary way of reasoning, and establishes the being of a God, or makes observations concerning human affairs; when of a sudden I am surprised to find, that instead of the usual copulations of propositions, *is* and *is not*, I meet with no proposition that is not connected with an *ought*, or an *ought not*. This change is imperceptible; but is, however, of the last consequence. For as this *ought*, or *ought not*, expresses some new relation or affirmation, it is necessary that it should be observed and explained; and at the same time that a reason should be given for what seems altogether inconceivable, how this new relation can be a deduction from others which are entirely different from it. But as authors do not commonly use this precaution, I shall presume to recommend it to the readers; and am persuaded that this small attention would subvert all the vulgar systems of morality, and let us see that the distinction of vice and virtue is not founded merely on the relations of objects, nor is perceived by reason.

SECTION II **Moral Distinctions Derived from a Moral Sense**

Thus the course of the argument leads us to conclude, that since vice and virtue are not discoverable merely by reason, or the comparison of ideas, it must be by means of some impression or sentiment they occasion, that we are able to mark the difference between them. Our decisions concerning moral rectitude and depravity are evidently perceptions: and as all perceptions are either impressions or ideas, the exclusion of the one is a convincing argument for the other. Morality, therefore, is more properly felt than judged of; though this feeling or sentiment is commonly so soft and gentle that we are apt to confound it with an idea, according to our common custom of taking all things for the same which have any near resemblance to each other.

The next question is, Of what nature are these impressions, and after what manner do they operate upon us? Here we cannot remain long in suspense, but must pronounce the impression arising from virtue, to be agreeable, and that proceeding from vice to be uneasy. Every moment's experience must convince us of this. There is no spectacle so fair and beautiful as a noble and generous action; nor any which gives us more abhorrence than one that is cruel and treacherous. No enjoyment equals the satisfaction we receive from the company of those we love and esteem; as the greatest of all punishment is to be obliged to pass our lives with those we hate or condemn. A very play or romance may afford us instances of this pleasure, which virtue conveys to us; and pain, which arises from vice.

Now since the distinguishing impressions, by which moral good or evil is known, are nothing but *particular* pains or pleasures; it follows, that in all enquiries concerning these moral distinctions, it will be sufficient to show the principles which make us feel a satisfaction or uneasiness from the survey of any character, in order to satisfy us why the character is laudable or blameable. An action, or sentiment, or character is virtuous or vicious; why? because its view causes a pleasure or uneasiness of a particular kind. In giving a reason, therefore, for the pleasure or uneasiness, we sufficiently explain the vice or virtue. To have the sense of virtue is nothing but to *feel* a satisfaction of a particular kind from the contemplation of a character. The very *feeling* constitutes our praise or admiration. We go no farther; nor do we enquire into the cause of the satisfaction. We do not infer a character to be virtuous because it pleases: But in feeling that it pleases after such a particular manner, we in effect feel that it is virtuous. The case is the same as in our judgments concerning all kinds of beauty, and tastes, and sensations. Our approbation is implied in the immediate pleasure they convey to us.

I have objected to the system which establishes eternal rational measures of right and wrong, that it is impossible to show, in the actions of reasonable creatures, any relations which are not found in external objects; and therefore, if morality always attended these relations, it were possible for inanimate matter to become virtuous or vicious. Now it may, in like manner, be objected to the present system that if virtue and vice be determined by pleasure and pain, these qualities must, in every case, arise from the sensations; and consequently any object, whether animate or inanimate, rational or irrational, might become morally good or evil, provided it can excite a satisfaction or uneasiness. But though this objection seems to be the very same, it has by no means the same force in the one case as in the other. For, *first,* it is evident, that under the term *pleasure* we comprehend sensations which are very different from each other, and which have only such a distant resemblance as is requisite to make them be expressed by the same abstract term. A good composition of music and a bottle of good wine equally produce pleasure; and what is more, their goodness is determined merely by the pleasure. But shall we say upon that account that the wine is harmonious or the music of a good flavor? In like manner an inanimate object and the character or sentiments of any person may, both of them, give satisfaction; but as the satisfaction is different, this keeps our sentiments concerning them from being confounded, and makes us ascribe virtue to the one, and not to the other.

Nor is every sentiment of pleasure or pain which arises from characters and actions, of that *peculiar* kind which makes us praise or condemn. The good qualities of an enemy are hurtful to us, but may still command our esteem and respect. It is only when a character is considered in general, without reference to our particular interest, that it causes such a feeling or sentiment as denominates it morally good or evil. It is true, those sentiments, from interest and morals, are apt to be confounded and naturally run into one another. It seldom happens that we do not think an enemy vicious, and can distinguish between his opposition to our interest and real villainy or baseness. But this hinders not, but that the sentiments are, in themselves, distinct; and a man of temper and judgment may preserve himself from these illusions. In like manner, though it is certain a musical voice is nothing but one that naturally gives a *particular* kind of pleasure; yet it is difficult for a man to be sensible that the voice of an enemy is agreeable, or to allow it to be musical. But a person of a fine ear, who has the command of himself, can separate these feelings, and give praise to what deserves it.

Secondly, We may call to remembrance the preceding system of the passions, in order to remark a still more considerable difference among our pains and pleasures. Pride and humility, love and hatred are excited, when there is any thing presented to us that both bears a relation to the object of the passion, and produces a separate sensation related to the sensation of the passion. Now virtue and vice are attended with these circumstances. They must necessarily be placed either in ourselves or others, and excite either pleasure or uneasiness; and therefore must give rise to one of these four passions; which clearly distinguishes them from the pleasure and pain arising from inanimate objects, that often bear no relation to us: And this is, perhaps, the most considerable effect that virtue and vice have upon the human mind.

It may now be asked in *general*, concerning this pain or pleasure, that distinguishes moral good and evil, *From what principles is it derived, and whence does it arise in the human mind?* To this I reply, *first,* that it is absurd to imagine that in every particular instance these sentiments are produced by an *original quality* and *primary* constitution. For as the number of our duties is, in a manner, infinite, it is impossible that our original instincts should extend to each of them, and from our very first infancy impress on the human mind all that multitude of precepts which are contained in the most complete system of ethics. Such a method of proceeding is not conformable to the usual maxims by which nature is conducted, where a few principles produce all that variety we observe in the universe, and everything is carried on in the easiest and most simple manner. It is necessary, therefore, to abridge these primary impulses, and find some more general principles upon which all our notions of morals are founded.

But in the *second* place, should it be asked, Whether we ought to search for these principles in *nature,* or whether we must look for them in some other origin? I would reply, that our answer to this question depends upon the definition of the word, Nature, than which there is none more ambiguous and equivocal. If *nature* be opposed to miracles, not only the distinction between vice and virtue is natural, but also every event which has ever happened in the world, *excepting those miracles, on which our religion is founded.* In saying, then, that the sentiments of vice and virtue are natural in this sense, we make no very extraordinary discovery.

But *nature* may also be opposed to rare and unusual; and in this sense of the word, which is the common one, there may often arise disputes concerning what is natural or unnatural; and one may in general affirm that we are not possessed of any very precise standard, by which these disputes can be decided. Frequent and rare depend upon the number of examples we have observed; and as this number may gradually increase or diminish, it will be impossible to fix any exact boundaries between them. We may only affirm on this head, that if ever there was anything which could be called natural in this sense, the sentiments of morality certainly may; since there never was any nation of the world, nor any single person in any nation who was utterly deprived of them, and who never, in any instance, showed the least approbation or dislike of manners. These sentiments are so rooted in our constitution and temper, that without entirely confounding the human mind by disease or madness, it is impossible to extirpate and destroy them.

But *nature* may also be opposed to artifice, as well as to what is rare and unusual; and in this sense it may be disputed whether the notions of virtue be natural or not. We readily forget, that the designs, and projects, and views of men are principles as necessary in their operation as heat and cold, moist and dry: But taking them to be free and entirely our own, it is usual for us to set them in opposition to the other principles of nature. Should it, therefore, be demanded, whether the sense of virtue be natural or artificial, I am of opinion that it is impossible for me at present to give any precise answer to this question. Perhaps it will appear afterwards that our sense of some virtues is artificial, and that of others natural. The discussion of this question will be more proper, when we enter upon an exact detail of each particular vice and virtue. [3]

Meanwhile it may not be amiss to observe from these definitions of *natural* and *unnatural,* that nothing can be more unphilosophical than those systems, which assert, that virtue is the same with what is

---

[3] In the following discourse *natural* is also opposed sometimes to *civil,* sometimes to *moral.* The opposition will always discover the sense, in which it is taken.

natural, and vice with what is unnatural. For in the first sense of the word, Nature, as opposed to miracles, both vice and virtue are equally natural; and in the second sense, as opposed to what is unusual, perhaps virtue will be found to be the most unnatural. At least it must be owned that heroic virtue, being as unusual, is as little natural as the most brutal barbarity. As to the third sense of the word, it is certain that both vice and virtue are equally artificial, and out of nature. For however it may be disputed, whether the notion of a merit or demerit in certain actions be natural or artificial, it is evident that the actions themselves are artificial, and are performed with a certain design and intention; otherwise they could never be ranked under any of these denominations. It is impossible, therefore, that the character of natural and unnatural can ever, in any sense, mark the boundaries of vice and virtue.

Thus we are still brought back to our first position, that virtue is distinguished by the pleasure, and vice by the pain, that any action, sentiment or character gives us by the mere view and contemplation. This decision is very commodious; because it reduces us to this simple question, *Why any action or sentiment upon the general view or survey, gives a certain satisfaction or uneasiness,* in order to show the origin of its moral rectitude or depravity, without looking for any incomprehensible relations and qualities, which never did exist in nature, nor even in our imagination, by any clear and distinct conception. I flatter myself I have executed a great part of my present design by a state of the question, which appears to me so free from ambiguity and obscurity.

Immanuel Kant (1724-1804)

Immanuel Kant was born in Königsberg, East Prussia, and during his entire life never traveled more than about forty miles from that city. His parents were Pietists, a sect of the Lutheran Church that stressed Protestant devotional ideals, and Kant's earliest academic interest at the University of Königsberg was theology. But his interests ultimately touched on nearly every theoretical subject, and he wrote, usually significantly, on law, astronomy, world government, religion, physical geography, anthropology, and all areas of philosophy. Kant never married and he lived a life of strict routine and earnest propriety.

In 1746 Kant completed his studies and made his living as a tutor until 1755, when he obtained a position in the university. In 1770 he became a full professor in the University of Königsberg. Kant was known as a learned, popular, and witty lecturer and writer, but during the seventies his interests narrowed to fundamental philosophical problems, his attitudes became more earnest, and his thought more laborious. All this culminated in the *Critique of Pure Reason* (1781), a work that proved to have more influence on subsequent philosophy than any written since the time of the ancient Greeks. In the remainder of the decade Kant wrote a succession of books—*Prolegomena to Any Future Metaphysics* (1783), *Fundamental Principles of the Metaphysic of Morals* (1785), *Critique of Practical Reason* (1788), and *Critique of Judgment* (1790).

Kant's main work on ethics is the *Critique of Practical Reason*. Three standard explanatory books are *The Categorical Imperative* (1948) by H. J. Paton, *A Commentary on Kant's Critique of Practical Reason* (1960) by Lewis White Beck, and *Kant's Moral Philosophy* (1970) by H. B. Acton. Also recommended are Chapter 5 of C. D. Broad's *Five Types of Ethical Theory* (1930), and *The Anatomy of Reason: A Commentary on Kant's Groundwork of the Metaphysics of Morals* (1973) by Robert Paul Wolff. Wolff's *Immanuel Kant: Foundations of the Metaphysics of Morals with Critical Essays* (1969) contains nine appraisals by various contemporary writers. An interesting attempt to combine Kantian and utilitarian arguments is *Generalization in Ethics* (1961) by Marcus Singer. Two additional books are *Kant's Ethical Theory* (1954) by W. D. Ross and *Kant* (1955) by S. Körner.

Fundamental Principles of the Metaphysic of Morals

PREFACE

Ancient Greek philosophy was divided into three sciences: Physics, Ethics, and Logic. This division is perfectly suitable to the nature of the thing; and the only improvement that can be made in it is to add the principle on which it is based, so that we may both satisfy ourselves of its completeness, and also be able to determine correctly the necessary subdivisions.

All rational knowledge is either *material* or *formal:* the former considers some object, the latter is concerned only with the form of the understanding and of the reason itself, and with the universal laws of thought in general without distinction of its objects. Formal philosophy is called logic. Material philosophy, however, which has to do with determinate objects and the laws to which they are subject, is again twofold; for these laws are either laws of *nature* or of *freedom.* The science of the former is physics, that of the latter, ethics; they are also called *natural philosophy* and *moral philosophy* respectively.

Logic cannot have any empirical part—that is, a part in which the universal and necessary laws of thought should rest on grounds taken from experience; otherwise it would not be logic, that is, a canon for the understanding or the reason, valid for all thought, and capable of demonstration. Natural and moral philosophy, on the contrary, can each have their empirical part, since the former has to determine the laws of nature as an object of experience, the latter the laws of the human will, so far as it is affected by nature; the former, however, being laws according to which everything does happen, the latter, laws according to which everything ought to happen. Ethics, however, must also consider the conditions under which what ought to happen frequently does not.

We may call all philosophy *empirical,* so far as it is based on

---

Translated by Thomas K. Abbott, 4th ed. (London and New York, 1889). Footnotes enclosed in square brackets are by the translator.

grounds of experience; on the other hand, that which delivers its doctrines from *a priori* principles alone we may call *pure* philosophy. When the latter is merely formal, it is *logic;* if it is restricted to definite objects of the understanding, it is *metaphysic.*

In this way there arises the idea of a twofold metaphysic—a *metaphysic of nature* and a *metaphysic of morals.* Physics will thus have an empirical and also a rational part. It is the same with ethics; but here the empirical part might have the special name of *practical anthropology,* the name *morality* being appropriated to the rational part.

All trades, arts, and handiworks have gained by division of labor, namely, when, instead of one man doing everything, each confines himself to a certain kind of work distinct from others in the treatment it requires, so as to be able to perform it with greater facility and in the greatest perfection. Where the different kinds of work are not so distinguished and divided, where everyone is a jack-of-all-trades, there manufactures remain still in the greatest barbarism. It might deserve to be considered whether pure philosophy in all its parts does not require a man specially devoted to it, and whether it would not be better for the whole business of science if those who, to please the tastes of the public, are wont to blend the rational and empirical elements together, mixed in all sorts of proportions unknown to themselves, and who call themselves independent thinkers, giving the name of minute philosophers to those who apply themselves to the rational part only—if these, I say, were warned not to carry on two employments together which differ widely in the treatment they demand, for each of which perhaps a special talent is required, and the combination of which in one person only produces bunglers. But I only ask here whether the nature of science does not require that we should always carefully separate the empirical from the rational part, and prefix to physics proper (or empirical physics) a metaphysic of nature, and to practical anthropology a metaphysic of morals, which must be carefully cleared of everything empirical so that we may know how much can be accomplished by pure reason in both cases, and from what sources it draws this its *a priori* teaching, and that whether the latter inquiry is conducted by all moralists (whose name is legion), or only by some who feel a calling thereto.

As my concern here is with moral philosophy, I limit the question suggested to this: whether it is not of the utmost necessity to construct a pure moral philosophy, perfectly cleared of everything which is only empirical, and which belongs to anthropology? For that such a philosophy must be possible is evident from the common idea of duty and of the moral laws. Everyone must admit that if a law is to have moral force, that is, to be the basis of an obligation, it must carry with it absolute necessity; that, for example, the precept, 'Thou shalt not lie,' is not valid for men alone, as if other rational beings had no need to observe it; and so with all the other moral laws properly so called; that, therefore, the basis of obligation must not be sought in the nature of man, or in the circumstances in the world in which he is placed, but *a priori* simply in the conceptions of pure reason; and although any other precept which is founded on principles of mere experience may be in certain respects universal, yet in as far as it rests even in the least degree on an empirical basis, perhaps only as to a motive, such a precept, while it may be a practical rule, can never be called a moral law.

Thus not only are moral laws with their principles essentially distinguished from every other kind of practical knowledge in which there is anything empirical, but all moral philosophy rests wholly on its pure part. When applied to man, it does not borrow the least thing from the knowledge of man himself (anthropology), but gives laws *a priori* to him as a rational being. No doubt these laws require a judgment sharpened by experience, in order, on the one hand, to distinguish in what cases they are applicable, and, on the other, to procure for them access to the will of the man, and effectual influence on conduct; since man is acted on by so many inclinations that, though capable of the idea of a practical pure reason, he is not so easily able to make it effective *in concreto* in his life.

A metaphysic of morals is therefore indispensably necessary, not merely for speculative reasons, in order to investigate the sources of the practical principles which are to be found *a priori* in our reason, but also because morals themselves are liable to all sorts of corruption as long as we are without that clue and supreme canon by which to estimate them correctly. For in order that an action should be morally good, it is not enough that it *conform* to the moral law, but it must also be done *for the sake of the law,* otherwise that conformity is only very contingent and uncertain; since a principle which is not moral, although it may now and then produce actions conformable to the law, will also often produce actions which contradict it. Now it is only in a pure philosophy that we can look for the moral law in its purity and genuineness (and, in a practical matter, this is of the utmost consequence): we must, therefore, begin with pure philosophy (metaphysic), and without it there cannot be any moral philosophy at all. That which mingles these pure principles with the empirical does not deserve the name of philosophy (for what distinguishes philosophy from common rational knowledge is that it treats in separate sciences what the latter only comprehends confusedly); much less does it deserve that of moral philosophy, since by this confusion it even spoils the purity of morals themselves and counteracts its own end.

Let it not be thought, however, that what is here demanded is already extant in the propaedeutic prefixed by the celebrated Wolf [1] to his moral philosophy, namely, his so-called *general practical philosophy,* and that, therefore, we have not to strike into an entirely new field. Just because it was to be a general practical philosophy, it has not taken into consideration a will of any particular kind—say, one which should be determined solely from *a priori* principles without any empirical motives, and which we might call a pure will—but volition in general, with all the actions and conditions which belong to it in this general signification. By this it is distinguished from a metaphysic of morals, just as general logic, which treats of the acts and canons of thought *in general,* is distinguished from transcendental philosophy, which treats of the particular acts and canons *of pure* thought, that is, that whose cognitions are altogether *a priori.* For the metaphysic of morals has to examine the idea and the principles of a possible *pure* will, and not the acts and conditions of human volition generally, which for the most part are drawn from psychology. It is true that moral laws and duty are spoken of in the general practical philosophy (contrary indeed to all fitness). But this is no objection, for in this respect also the authors of that science remain true to their idea of it; they do not distinguish the motives which are prescribed as such by reason alone altogether *a priori,* and which are properly moral, from the empirical motives which the understanding raises to general conceptions merely by comparison of experiences; but without noticing the difference of their sources, and looking on them all as homogeneous, they consider only their greater or less amount. It is in this way they frame their notion of *obligation,* which, though anything but moral, is all that can be asked for in a philosophy which passes no judgment at all on the origin of all possible practical concepts, whether they are *a priori* or only *a posteriori.*

Intending to publish hereafter a metaphysic of morals, I issue in the first instance these fundamental principles. Indeed there is properly no other foundation for it than the *critical examination of a pure practical reason;* just as that of metaphysics is the critical examination of the pure speculative reason, already published. But in the first place the former is not so absolutely necessary as the latter, because in moral concerns human reason can easily be brought to a high degree of correctness and completeness, even in the commonest understanding, while on the contrary in its theoretic but pure use it is wholly dialectical; and in the second place, if the critique of a pure practical reason is to be complete, it must be possible at the same time to show its

---

1 [Johann Christian Von Wolf (1679–1754) was the author of treatises on philosophy, mathematics, etc., which were for a long time the standard textbooks in the German universities. His philosophy was founded on that of Leibniz.]

identity with the speculative reason in a common principle, for it can ultimately be only one and the same reason which has to be distinguished merely in its application. I could not, however, bring it to such completeness here without introducing considerations of a wholly different kind, which would be perplexing to the reader. On this account, I have adopted the title of *Fundamental Principles of the Metaphysic of Morals* [*Grundlegung zur Metaphysik der Sitten*] instead of that of a *critical examination of the pure practical reason.*

But in the third place, since a metaphysic of morals, in spite of the discouraging title, is yet capable of being presented in a popular form, and one adapted to the common understanding, I find it useful to separate from it this preliminary treatise on its fundamental principles, in order that I may not hereafter have need to introduce these necessarily subtle discussions into a book of a more simple character.

The present treatise is, however, nothing more than the investigation and establishment of *the supreme principle of morality,* and this alone constitutes a study complete in itself, and one which ought to be kept apart from every other moral investigation. No doubt, my conclusions on this weighty question, which has hitherto been very unsatisfactorily examined, would receive much light from the application of the same principle to the whole system, and would be greatly confirmed by the adequacy which it exhibits throughout; but I must forego this advantage, which indeed would be after all more gratifying than useful, since the easy applicability of a principle and its apparent adequacy give no very certain proof of its soundness, but rather inspire a certain partiality, which prevents us from examining and estimating it strictly in itself, and without regard to consequences.

I have adopted in this work the method which I think most suitable, proceeding analytically from common knowledge to the determination of its ultimate principle, and again descending synthetically from the examination of this principle and its sources to the common knowledge in which we find it employed. The division will, therefore, be as follows:

1. *First section:* Transition from the common rational knowledge of morality to the philosophical.
2. *Second section:* Transition from popular moral philosophy to the metaphysic of morals.
3. *Third section:* Final step from the metaphysic of morals to the critique of the pure practical reason.

FIRST SECTION Transition from the Common Rational Knowledge of Morality to the Philosophical

Nothing can possibly be conceived in the world, or even out of it, which can be called good without qualification, except a *good will*. Intelligence, wit, judgment, and the other *talents* of the mind, however they may be named, or courage, resolution, perseverance, as qualities of temperament, are undoubtedly good and desirable in many respects; but these gifts of nature may also become extremely bad and mischievous if the will which is to make use of them, and which, therefore, constitutes what is called *character,* is not good. It is the same with the *gifts of fortune.* Power, riches, honor, even health, and the general well-being and contentment with one's condition which is called *happiness,* inspire pride, and often presumption, if there is not a good will to correct the influence of these on the mind, and with this also to rectify the whole principle of acting, and adapt it to its end. The sight of a being who is not adorned with a single feature of a pure and good will, enjoying unbroken prosperity, can never give pleasure to an impartial rational spectator. Thus a good will appears to constitute the indispensable condition even of being worthy of happiness.

There are even some qualities which are of service to this good will itself, and may facilitate its action, yet which have no intrinsic unconditional value, but always presuppose a good will, and this qualifies the esteem that we justly have for them, and does not permit us to regard them as absolutely good. Moderation in the affections and passions, self-control, and calm deliberation are not only good in many respects, but even seem to constitute part of the intrinsic worth of the person; but they are far from deserving to be called good without qualification, although they have been so unconditionally praised by the ancients. For without the principles of a good will, they may become extremely bad; and the coolness of a villain not only makes him far more dangerous, but also directly makes him more abominable in our eyes than he would have been without it.

A good will is good not because of what it performs or effects, not by its aptness for the attainment of some proposed end, but simply by virtue of the volition—that is, it is good in itself, and considered by itself is to be esteemed much higher than all that can be brought about by it in favor of any inclination, nay, even of the sum-total of all inclinations. Even if it should happen that, owing to special disfavor of fortune, or the niggardly provision of a step-motherly nature, this will should wholly lack power to accomplish its purpose, if with its greatest efforts it should yet achieve nothing, and there should remain only the good will (not, to be sure, a mere wish, but the summoning of all means in our power), then, like a jewel, it would still shine by its own light, as a thing which has its whole value in itself. Its usefulness or fruitfulness can neither add to nor take away anything from this value. It would be, as it were, only the setting to enable us to handle it the more conveniently in common commerce, or to attract to it the attention of those who are not yet connoisseurs, but not to recommend it to true connoisseurs, or to determine its value.

There is, however, something so strange in this idea of the absolute value of the mere will, in which no account is taken of its utility, that notwithstanding the thorough assent of even common reason to the idea, yet a suspicion must arise that it may perhaps really be the product of mere high-flown fancy, and that we may have misunderstood the purpose of nature in assigning reason as the governor of our will. Therefore we will examine this idea from this point of view.

In the physical constitution of an organized being, that is, a being adapted suitably to the purposes of life, we assume it as a fundamental principle that no organ for any purpose will be found but what is also the fittest and best adapted for that purpose. Now in a being which has reason and a will, if the proper object of nature were its *conservation,* its *welfare,* in a word, its *happiness,* then nature would have hit upon a very bad arrangement in selecting the reason of the creature to carry out this purpose. For all the actions which the creature has to perform with a view to this purpose, and the whole rule of its conduct, would be far more surely prescribed to it by instinct, and that end would have been attained thereby much more certainly than it ever can be by reason. Should reason have been communicated to this favored creature over and above, it must only have served it to contemplate the happy constitution of its nature, to admire it, to congratulate itself thereon, and to feel thankful for it to the beneficent cause, but not that it should subject its desires to that weak and delusive guidance, and meddle bunglingly with the purpose of nature. In a word, nature would have taken care that reason should not break forth into *practical exercise,* nor have the presumption, with its weak insight, to think out for itself the plan of happiness and of the means of attaining it. Nature would not only have taken on herself the choice of the ends but also of the means, and with wise foresight would have entrusted both to instinct.

And, in fact, we find that the more a cultivated reason applies itself with deliberate purpose to the enjoyment of life and happiness, so much the more does the man fail of true satisfaction. And from this circumstance there arises in many, if they are candid enough to confess it, a certain degree of *misology,* that is, hatred of reason, especially in the case of those who are most experienced in the use of it, because after calculating all the advantages they derive—I do not say from the invention of all the arts of common luxury, but even from the sciences (which seem to them to be after all only a luxury of the understanding)—they find that they have, in fact, only brought more trouble on their shoulders rather than gained in happiness; and they end by envying rather than despising the more common stamp of men who keep closer to the guidance of mere instinct, and do not allow their reason much influence on their conduct. And this we must admit, that the judgment of those who would very much lower the lofty eulogies of the advantages which reason gives us in regard to the happiness and satisfaction of life, or who would even reduce them below zero, is by no means morose or ungrateful to the goodness with which the world is governed, but that there lies at the root of these judgments the idea that our existence has a different and far nobler end, for which, and not for happiness, reason is properly intended, and which must, therefore, be regarded as the supreme condition to which the private ends of man must, for the most part, be postponed.

For as reason is not competent to guide the will with certainty in regard to its objects and the satisfaction of all our wants (which it to some extent even multiplies), this being an end to which an implanted instinct would have led with much greater certainty; and since, nevertheless, reason is imparted to us as a practical faculty, that is, as one which is to have influence on the *will*, therefore, admitting that nature generally in the distribution of her capacities has adapted the means to the end, its true destination must be to produce a *will*, not merely good as a *means* to something else, but *good in itself*, for which reason was absolutely necessary. This will then, though not indeed the sole and complete good, must be the supreme good and the condition of every other, even of the desire of happiness. Under these circumstances, there is nothing inconsistent with the wisdom of nature in the fact that the cultivation of the reason, which is requisite for the first and unconditional purpose, does in many ways interfere, at least in this life, with the attainment of the second, which is always conditional—namely, happiness. Nay, it may even reduce it to nothing, without nature thereby failing of her purpose. For reason recognizes the establishment of a good will as its highest practical destination, and in attaining this purpose is capable only of a satisfaction of its own proper kind, namely, that from the attainment of an end, which end again is determined by reason only, notwithstanding that this may involve many a disappointment to the ends of inclination.

We have then to develop the notion of a will which deserves to be highly esteemed for itself, and is good without a view to anything further, a notion which exists already in the sound natural understanding, requiring rather to be cleared up than to be taught, and which in estimating the value of our actions always takes the first place and constitutes the condition of all the rest. In order to do this, we will take the notion of duty, which includes that of a good will, although implying certain subjective restrictions and hindrances. These, however, far from concealing it or rendering it unrecognizable, rather bring it out by contrast and make it shine forth so much the brighter.

I omit here all actions which are already recognized as inconsistent with duty, although they may be useful for this or that purpose, for with these the question whether they are done *from duty* cannot arise at all, since they even conflict with it. I also set aside those actions which really conform to duty, but to which men have *no* direct *inclina-*

tion, performing them because they are impelled thereto by some other inclination. For in this case we can readily distinguish whether the action which agrees with duty is done *from duty* or from a selfish view. It is much harder to make this distinction when the action accords with duty, and the subject has besides a *direct* inclination to it. For example, it is always a matter of duty that a dealer should not overcharge an inexperienced purchaser; and wherever there is much commerce the prudent tradesman does not overcharge, but keeps a fixed price for everyone, so that a child buys of him as well as any other. Men are thus *honestly* served; but this is not enough to make us believe that the tradesman has so acted from duty and from principles of honesty; his own advantage required it; it is out of the question in this case to suppose that he might besides have a direct inclination in favor of the buyers, so that, as it were, from love he should give no advantage to one over another. Accordingly the action was done neither from duty nor from direct inclination, but merely with a selfish view.

On the other hand, it is a duty to maintain one's life; and, in addition, everyone has also a direct inclination to do so. But on this account the often anxious care which most men take for it has no intrinsic worth, and their maxim has no moral import. They preserve their life *as duty requires,* no doubt, but not *because duty requires.* On the other hand, if adversity and hopeless sorrow have completely taken away the relish for life, if the unfortunate one, strong in mind, indignant at his fate rather than desponding or dejected, wishes for death, and yet preserves his life without loving it—not from inclination or fear, but from duty—then his maxim has a moral worth.

To be beneficent when we can is a duty; and besides this, there are many minds so sympathetically constituted that, without any other motive of vanity or self-interest, they find a pleasure in spreading joy around them, and can take delight in the satisfaction of others so far as it is their own work. But I maintain that in such a case an action of this kind, however proper, however amiable it may be, has nevertheless no true moral worth, but is on a level with other inclinations, for example, the inclination to honor, which, if it is happily directed to that which is in fact of public utility and accordant with duty, and consequently honorable, deserves praise and encouragement, but not esteem. For the maxim lacks the moral import, namely, that such actions be done *from duty,* not from inclination. Put the case that the mind of that philanthropist was clouded by sorrow of his own, extinguishing all sympathy with the lot of others, and that while he still has the power to benefit others in distress, he is not touched by their trouble because he is absorbed with his own; and now suppose that he tears himself out of this dead insensibility and performs the action without any inclination to it, but simply from duty, then first has his action its genuine moral worth.

Further still, if nature has put little sympathy in the heart of this or that man, if he, supposed to be an upright man, is by temperament cold and indifferent to the sufferings of others, perhaps because in respect of his own he is provided with the special gift of patience and fortitude, and supposes, or even requires, that others should have the same—and such a man would certainly not be the meanest product of nature—but if nature had not specially framed him for a philanthropist, would he not still find in himself a source from whence to give himself a far higher worth than that of a good-natured temperament could be? Unquestionably. It is just in this that the moral worth of the character is brought out which is incomparably the highest of all, namely, that he is beneficent, not from inclination, but from duty.

To secure one's own happiness is a duty, at least indirectly; for discontent with one's condition, under a pressure of many anxieties and amidst unsatisfied wants, might easily become a great *temptation to transgression of duty*. But here again, without looking to duty, all men have already the strongest and most intimate inclination to happiness, because it is just in this idea that all inclinations are combined in one total. But the precept of happiness is often of such a sort that it greatly interferes with some inclinations, and yet a man cannot form any definite and certain conception of the sum of satisfaction of all of them which is called happiness. It is not then to be wondered at that a single inclination, definite both as to what it promises and as to the time within which it can be gratified, is often able to overcome such a fluctuating idea, and that a gouty patient, for instance, can choose to enjoy what he likes, and to suffer what he may, since, according to his calculation, on this occasion at least, he has [only] not sacrificed the enjoyment of the present moment to a possibly mistaken expectation of a happiness which is supposed to be found in health. But even in this case, if the general desire for happiness did not influence his will, and supposing that in his particular case health was not a necessary element in this calculation, there yet remains in this, as in all other cases, this law—namely, that he should promote his happiness not from inclination but from duty, and by this would his conduct first acquire true moral worth.

It is in this manner, undoubtedly, that we are to understand those passages of Scripture also in which we are commanded to love our neighbor, even our enemy. For love, as an affection, cannot be commanded, but beneficence for duty's sake may, even though we are not impelled to it by any inclination—nay, are even repelled by a natural and unconquerable aversion. This is *practical* love, and not *pathological* —a love which is seated in the will, and not in the propensions of sense—in principles of action and not of tender sympathy; and it is this love alone which can be commanded.

The second [2] proposition is: That an action done from duty derives its moral worth, *not from the purpose* which is to be attained by
it, but from the maxim by which it is determined, and therefore, does
not depend on the realization of the object of the action, but merely
on the *principle of volition* by which the action has taken place, without regard to any object of desire. It is clear from what precedes that
the purposes which we may have in view of our actions, or their effects
regarded as ends and springs of the will, cannot give to actions any unconditional or moral worth. In what, then, can their worth lie if it is
not to consist in the will and in reference to its expected effect? It cannot lie anywhere but in the *principle of the will* without regard to the
ends which can be attained by the action. For the will stands between
its *a priori* principle, which is formal, and its *a posteriori* spring, which
is material, as between two roads, and as it must be determined by
something, it follows that it must be determined by the formal principle of volition when an action is done from duty, in which case every
material principle has been withdrawn from it.

The third proposition, which is a consequence of the two preceding, I would express thus: *Duty is the necessity of acting from respect
for the law.* I may have *inclination* for an object as the effect of my
proposed action, but I cannot have *respect* for it just for this reason
that it is an effect and not an energy of will. Similarly, I cannot have
respect for inclination, whether my own or another's; I can at most, if
my own, approve it; if another's, sometimes even love it, that is, look
on it as favorable to my own interest. It is only what is connected with
my will as a principle, by no means as an effect—what does not subserve my inclination, but overpowers it, or at least in case of choice
excludes it from its calculation—in other words, simply the law of itself,
which can be an object of respect, and hence a command. Now an action done from duty must wholly exclude the influence of inclination,
and with it every object of the will, so that nothing remains which can
determine the will except objectively the *law,* and subjectively *pure
respect* for this practical law, and consequently the maxim[3] that I
should follow this law even to the thwarting of all my inclinations.

Thus the moral worth of an action does not lie in the effect expected from it, nor in any principle of action which requires to borrow
its motive from this expected effect. For all these effects—agreeableness of one's condition, and even the promotion of the happiness of
others—could have been also brought about by other causes, so that

---

2 [The first proposition was that to have moral worth an action must be done
from duty.]

3 A *maxim* is the subjective principle of volition. The objective principle (i.e.,
that which would also serve subjectively as a practical principle to all rational
beings if reason had full power over the faculty of desire) is the practical *law.*

for this there would have been no need of the will of a rational being; whereas it is in this alone that the supreme and unconditional good can be found. The preeminent good which we call moral can therefore consist in nothing else than *the conception of law* in itself, *which certainly is only possible in a rational being,* in so far as this conception, and not the expected effect, determines the will. This is a good which is already present in the person who acts accordingly, and we have not to wait for it to appear first in the result.[4]

But what sort of law can that be the conception of which must determine the will, even without paying any regard to the effect expected from it, in order that this will may be called good absolutely and without qualification? As I have deprived the will of every impulse which could arise to it from obedience to any law, there remains nothing but the universal conformity of its actions to law in general, which alone is to serve the will as a principle, that is, I am never to act otherwise than so *that I could also will that my maxim should become a universal law.* Here, now, it is the simple conformity to law in general, without assuming any particular law applicable to certain actions, that serves the will as its principle, and must so serve it if duty is not to be a vain delusion and a chimerical notion. The common reason of men in its practical judgments perfectly coincides with this, and always has in view the principle here suggested. Let the question be, for example: May I when in distress make a promise with the intention not to keep it? I readily distinguish here between the two significations which the question may have: whether it is prudent or whether it is right to make a false promise? The former may undoubtedly often be

---

[4] It might be here objected to me that I take refuge behind the word *respect* in an obscure feeling, instead of giving a distinct solution of the question by a concept of the reason. But although respect is a feeling, it is not a feeling *received* through influence, but is *self-wrought* by a rational concept, and, therefore, is specifically distinct from all feelings of the former kind, which may be referred either to inclination or fear. What I recognize immediately as a law for me, I recognize with respect. This merely signifies the consciousness that my will is *subordinate* to a law, without the intervention of other influences on my sense. The immediate determination of the will by the law, and the consciousness of this, is called *respect,* so that this is regarded as an *effect* of the law on the subject, and not as the *cause* of it. Respect is properly the conception of a worth which thwarts my self-love. Accordingly it is something which is considered neither as an object of inclination nor of fear, although it has something analogous to both. The *object* of respect is the *law* only, that is, the law which we impose on *ourselves,* and yet recognize as necessary in itself. As a law, we are subjected to it without consulting self-love; as imposed by us on ourselves, it is a result of our will. In the former aspect it has an analogy to fear, in the latter to inclination. Respect for a person is properly only respect for the law (of honesty, etc.) of which he gives us an example. Since we also look on the improvement of our talents as a duty, we consider that we see in a person of talents, as it were, the *example of a law* (viz. to become like him in this by exercise), and this constitutes our respect. All so-called moral *interest* consists simply in *respect* for the law.

the case. I see clearly indeed that it is not enough to extricate myself
from a present difficulty by means of this subterfuge, but it must be
well considered whether there may not hereafter spring from this lie
much greater inconvenience than that from which I now free myself,
and as, with all my supposed *cunning,* the consequences cannot be so
easily foreseen but that credit once lost may be much more injurious
to me than any mischief which I seek to avoid at present, it should be
considered whether it would not be more *prudent* to act herein according to a universal maxim, and to make it a habit to promise nothing
except with the intention of keeping it. But it is soon clear to me that
such a maxim will still only be based on the fear of consequences. Now
it is a wholly different thing to be truthful from duty, and to be so
from apprehension of injurious consequences. In the first case, the very
notion of the action already implies a law for me; in the second case,
I must first look about elsewhere to see what results may be combined
with it which would affect myself. For to deviate from the principle of
duty is beyond all doubt wicked; but to be unfaithful to my maxim of
prudence may often be very advantageous to me, although to abide by
it is certainly safer. The shortest way, however, and an unerring one,
to discover the answer to this question whether a lying promise is consistent with duty, is to ask myself, Should I be content that my maxim
(to extricate myself from difficulty by a false promise) should hold good
as a universal law, for myself as well as for others; and should I be
able to say to myself, 'Every one may make a deceitful promise when
he finds himself in a difficulty from which he cannot otherwise extricate
himself'? Then I presently became aware that, while I can will the lie,
I can by no means will that lying should be a universal law. For with
such a law there would be no promises at all, since it would be in vain
to allege my intention in regard to my future actions to those who
would not believe this allegation, or if they over-hastily did so, would
pay me back in my own coin. Hence my maxim, as soon as it should
be made a universal law, would necessarily destroy itself.

I do not, therefore, need any far-reaching penetration to discern
what I have to do in order that my will may be morally good. Inexperienced in the course of the world, incapable of being prepared for all its
contingencies, I only ask myself: Canst thou also will that thy maxim
should be a universal law? If not, then it must be rejected, and that
not because of a disadvantage accruing from it to myself or even to
others, but because it cannot enter as a principle into a possible universal legislation, and reason extorts from me immediate respect for
such legislation. I do not indeed as yet *discern* on what this respect is
based (this the philosopher may inquire), but at least I understand this
—that it is an estimation of the worth which far outweighs all worth
of what is recommended by inclination, and that the necessity of acting from *pure* respect for the practical law is what constitutes duty, to

which every other motive must give place because it is the condition of a will being good *in itself*, and the worth of such a will is above everything.

Thus, then, without quitting the moral knowledge of common human reason, we have arrived at its principle. And although, no doubt, common men do not conceive it in such an abstract and universal form, yet they always have it really before their eyes and use it as the standard of their decision. Here it would be easy to show how, with this compass in hand, men are well able to distinguish, in every case that occurs, what is good, what bad, conformably to duty or inconsistent with it, if, without in the least teaching them anything new, we only, like Socrates, direct their attention to the principle they themselves employ; and that, therefore, we do not need science and philosophy to know what we should do to be honest and good, yea, even wise and virtuous. Indeed we might well have conjectured beforehand that the knowledge of what every man is bound to do, and therefore also to know, would be within the reach of every man, even the commonest. Here we cannot forbear admiration when we see how great an advantage the practical judgment has over the theoretical in the common understanding of men. In the latter, if common reason ventures to depart from the laws of experience and from the perceptions of the senses, it falls into mere inconceivabilities and self-contradictions, at least into a chaos of uncertainty, obscurity, and instability. But in the practical sphere it is just when the common understanding excludes all sensible springs from practical laws that its power of judgment begins to show itself to advantage. It then becomes even subtle, whether it be that it chicanes with its own conscience or with other claims respecting what is to be called right, or whether it desires for its own instruction to determine honestly the worth of actions; and, in the latter case, it may even have as good a hope of hitting the mark as any philosopher whatever can promise himself. Nay, it is almost more sure of doing so, because the philosopher cannot have any other principle, while he may easily perplex his judgment by a multitude of considerations foreign to the matter, and so turn aside from the right way. Would it not therefore be wiser in moral concerns to acquiesce in the judgment of common reason, or at most only to call in philosophy for the purpose of rendering the system of morals more complete and intelligible, and its rules more convenient for use (especially for disputation), but not so as to draw off the common understanding from its happy simplicity, or to bring it by means of philosophy into a new path of inquiry and instruction?

Innocence is indeed a glorious thing; only, on the other hand, it is very sad that it cannot well maintain itself, and is easily seduced. On this account even wisdom—which otherwise consists more in conduct than in knowledge—yet has need of science, not in order to learn from it, but to secure for its precepts admission and permanence. Against all the commands of duty which reason represents to man as so deserving of respect, he feels in himself a powerful counterpoise in his wants and inclinations, the entire satisfaction of which he sums up under the name of happiness. Now reason issues its commands unyieldingly, without promising anything to the inclinations, and, as it were, with disregard and contempt for these claims, which are so impetuous and at the same time so plausible, and which will not allow themselves to be suppressed by any command. Hence there arises a natural *dialectic,* that is, a disposition to argue against these strict laws of duty and to question their validity, or at least their purity and strictness; and, if possible, to make them more accordant with our wishes and inclinations, that is to say, to corrupt them at their very source and entirely to destroy their worth—a thing which even common practical reason cannot ultimately call good.

Thus is the *common reason of man* compelled to go out of its sphere and to take a step into the field of a *practical philosophy,* not to satisfy any speculative want (which never occurs to it as long as it is content to be mere sound reason), but even on practical grounds, in order to attain in it information and clear instruction respecting the source of its principle, and the correct determination of it in opposition to the maxims which are based on wants and inclinations, so that it may escape from the perplexity of opposite claims, and not run the risk of losing all genuine moral principles through the equivocation into which it easily falls. Thus, when practical reason cultivates itself, there insensibly arises in it a dialectic which forces it to seek aid in philosophy, just as happens to it in its theoretic use; and in this case, therefore, as well as in the other, it will find rest nowhere but in a thorough critical examination of our reason.

SECOND SECTION Transition from Popular Moral Philosophy to the Metaphysic of Morals

If we have hitherto drawn our notion of duty from the common use of our practical reason, it is by no means to be inferred that we have treated it as an empirical notion. On the contrary, if we attend to the experience of men's conduct, we meet frequent and, as we ourselves allow, just complaints that one cannot find a single certain example of the disposition to act from pure duty. Although many things are done in *conformity* with what *duty* prescribes, it is nevertheless always doubtful whether they are done strictly *from duty,* so as to have a moral worth. Hence there have at all times been philosophers who have altogether denied that this disposition actually exists at all in human actions, and have ascribed everything to a more or less refined self-love. Not that they have on that account questioned the soundness of the conception of morality; on the contrary, they spoke with sincere regret of the frailty and corruption of human nature, which, though noble enough to take as its rule an idea so worthy of respect, is yet too weak to follow it; and employs reason, which ought to give it the law only for the purpose of providing for the interest of the inclinations, whether singly or at the best in the greatest possible harmony with one another.

In fact, it is absolutely impossible to make out by experience with complete certainty a single case in which the maxim of an action, however right in itself, rested simply on moral grounds and on the conception of duty. Sometimes it happens that with the sharpest self-examination we can find nothing beside the moral principle of duty which could have been powerful enough to move us to this or that action and to so great a sacrifice; yet we cannot from this infer with certainty that it was not really some secret impulse of self-love, under the false appearance of duty, that was the actual determining cause of the will. We like then to flatter ourselves by falsely taking credit for a more noble motive; whereas in fact we can never, even by the strictest examination, get completely behind the secret springs of action, since, when the question is of moral worth, it is not with the actions which we see that we are concerned, but with those inward principles of them which we do not see.

Moreover, we cannot better serve the wishes of those who ridicule all morality as a mere chimera of human imagination overstepping itself from vanity, than by conceding to them that notions of duty must be drawn only from experience (as from indolence, people are ready to think is also the case with all other notions); for this is to prepare for them a certain triumph. I am willing to admit out of love of humanity that even most of our actions are correct, but if we look closer at them we everywhere come upon the dear self which is always prominent, and it is this they have in view, and not the strict command of duty, which would often require self-denial. Without being an enemy of virtue, a cool observer, one that does not mistake the wish for good, however lively, for its reality, may sometimes doubt whether true virtue is actually found anywhere in the world, and this especially as years increase and the judgment is partly made wiser by experience, and partly also more acute in observation. This being so, nothing can secure us from falling away altogether from our ideas of duty, or maintain in the soul a well-grounded respect for its law, but the clear conviction that although there should never have been actions which really sprang from such pure sources, yet whether this or that takes place is not at all the question; but that reason of itself, independent on all experience, ordains what ought to take place, that accordingly actions of which perhaps the world has hitherto never given an example, the feasibility even of which might be very much doubted by one who founds everything on experience, are nevertheless inflexibly commanded by reason; that, for example, even though there might never yet have been a sincere friend, yet not a whit the less is pure sincerity in friendship required of every man, because, prior to all experience, this duty is involved as duty in the idea of a reason determining the will by *a priori* principles.

When we add further that, unless we deny that the notion of morality has any truth or reference to any possible object, we must admit that its law must be valid, not merely for men, but for all *rational creatures generally*, not merely under certain contingent conditions or with exceptions, but *with absolute necessity*, then it is clear that no experience could enable us to infer even the possibility of such apodictic laws. For with what right could we bring into unbounded respect as a universal precept for every rational nature that which perhaps holds only under the contingent conditions of humanity? Or how could laws of the determination of *our* will be regarded as laws of the determination of the will of rational beings generally, and for us only as such, if they were merely empirical and did not take their origin wholly *a priori* from pure but practical reason?

Nor could anything be more fatal to morality than that we should wish to derive it from examples. For every example of it that is set before me must be first itself tested by principles of morality, whether it is worthy to serve as an original example, that is, as a pattern, but by no means can it authoritatively furnish the conception of morality. Even the Holy One of the Gospels must first be compared with our ideal of moral perfection before we can recognize Him as such; and so He says of Himself, 'Why call ye Me [whom you see] good; none is good [the model of good] but God only [whom ye do not see]?' But whence have we the conception of God as the supreme good? Simply from the *idea* of moral perfection, which reason frames *a priori* and connects inseparably with the notion of a free will. Imitation finds no place at all in morality, and examples serve only for encouragement, that is, they put beyond doubt the feasibility of what the law commands, they make visible that which the practical rule expresses more generally, but they can never authorize us to set aside the true original which lies in reason, and to guide ourselves by examples.

If then there is no genuine supreme principle of morality but what must rest simply on pure reason, independent on all experience, I think it is not necessary even to put the question whether it is good to exhibit these concepts in their generality (in *abstracto*) as they are established *a priori* along with the principles belonging to them, if our knowledge is to be distinguished from the *vulgar* and to be called philosophical. In our times indeed this might perhaps be necessary; for if we collected votes, whether pure rational knowledge separated from everything empirical, that is to say, metaphysic of morals, or whether popular practical philosophy is to be preferred, it is easy to guess which side would preponderate.

This descending to popular notions is certainly very commendable if the ascent to the principles of pure reason has first taken place and been satisfactorily accomplished. This implies that we first *found* Ethics on Metaphysics, and then, when it is firmly established, procure a *hearing* for it by giving it a popular character. But it is quite absurd to try to be popular in the first inquiry, on which the soundness of the principles depends. It is not only that this proceeding can never lay claim to the very rare merit of a true *philosophical popularity,* since there is no art in being intelligible if one renounces all thoroughness of insight; but also it produces a disgusting medley of compiled observations and half-reasoned principles. Shallow pates enjoy this because it can be used for everyday chat, but the sagacious find in it only confusion, and being unsatisfied and unable to help themselves, they turn away their eyes, while philosophers, who see quite well through this delusion, are little listened to when they call men off for a time from this pretended popularity in order that they might be rightfully popular after they have attained a definite insight.

We need only look at the attempts of moralists in that favorite fashion, and we shall find at one time the special constitution of human nature (including, however, the idea of a rational nature generally), at one time perfection, at another happiness, here moral sense, there fear of God, a little of this and a little of that, in marvellous mixture, without its occurring to them to ask whether the principles of morality are to be sought in the knowledge of human nature at all (which we can have only from experience); and, if this is not so—if these principles are to be found altogether *a priori* free from everything empirical, in pure rational concepts only, and nowhere else, not even in the smallest degree—then rather to adopt the method of making this a separate inquiry, as pure practical philosophy, or (if one may use a name so decried) as metaphysic of morals,[5] to bring it by itself to completeness, and to require the public, which wishes for popular treatment, to await the issue of this undertaking.

Such a metaphysic of morals, completely isolated, not mixed with any anthropology, theology, physics, or hyperphysics, and still less with occult qualities (which we might call hypophysical), is not only an

---

[5] Just as pure mathematics are distinguished from applied, pure logic from applied, so if we choose we may also distinguish pure philosophy of morals (metaphysic) from applied (viz., applied to human nature). By this designation we are also at once reminded that moral principles are not based on properties of human nature, but must subsist *a priori* themselves, while from such principles practical rules must be capable of being deduced for every rational nature, and accordingly for that of man.

indispensable substratum of all sound theoretical knowledge of duties, but is at the same time a desideratum of the highest importance to the actual fulfilment of their precepts. For the pure conception of duty, unmixed with any foreign addition of empirical attractions, and, in a word, the conception of the moral law, exercises on the human heart, by way of reason alone (which first becomes aware with this that it can of itself be practical), an influence so much more powerful than all other springs[6] which may be derived from the field of experience that in the consciousness of its worth it despises the latter, and can by degrees become their master; whereas a mixed ethics, compounded partly of motives drawn from feelings and inclinations, and partly also of conceptions of reason, must make the mind waver between motives which cannot be brought under any principle, which lead to good only by mere accident, and very often also to evil.

From what has been said, it is clear that all moral conceptions have their seat and origin completely *a priori* in the reason, and that, moreover, in the commonest reason just as truly as in that which is in the highest degree speculative; that they cannot be obtained by abstraction from any empirical, and therefore merely contingent, knowledge; that it is just this purity of their origin that makes them worthy to serve as our supreme practical principle, and that just in proportion as we add anything empirical, we detract from their genuine influence and from the absolute value of actions; that it is not only of the greatest necessity, in a purely speculative point of view, but is also of the greatest practical importance, to derive these notions and laws from pure reason, to present them pure and unmixed, and even to determine the compass of this practical or pure rational knowledge, that is, to determine the whole faculty of pure practical reason; and, in doing so, we must not make its principles dependent on the particular nature of human reason, though in speculative philosophy this may be permitted, or may even at times be necessary; but since moral laws ought to hold

---

[6] I have a letter from the late excellent Sulzer, in which he asks me what can be the reason that moral instruction, although containing much that is convincing for the reason, yet accomplishes so little? My answer was postponed in order that I might make it complete. But it is simply this, that the teachers themselves have not got their own notions clear, and when they endeavor to make up for this by raking up motives of moral goodness from every quarter, trying to make their physic right strong, they spoil it. For the commonest understanding shows that if we imagine, on the one hand, an act of honesty done with steadfast mind, apart from every view to advantage of any kind in this world or another, and even under the greatest temptations of necessity or allurement, and, on the other hand, a similar act which was affected, in however low a degree, by a foreign motive, the former leaves far behind and eclipses the second; it elevates the soul, and inspires the wish to be able to act in like manner oneself. Even moderately young children feel this impression, and one should never represent duties to them in any other light.

good for every rational creature, we must derive them from the general concept of a rational being. In this way, although for its *application* to man morality has need of anthropology, yet, in the first instance, we must treat it independently as pure philosophy, that is, as metaphysic, complete in itself (a thing which in such distinct branches of science is easily done); knowing well that, unless we are in possession of this, it would not only be vain to determine the moral element of duty in right actions for purposes of speculative criticism, but it would be impossible to base morals on their genuine principles, even for common practical purposes, especially of moral instruction, so as to produce pure moral dispositions, and to engraft them on men's minds to the promotion of the greatest possible good in the world.

But in order that in this study we may not merely advance by the natural steps from the common moral judgment (in this case very worthy of respect) to the philosophical, as has been already done, but also from a popular philosophy, which goes no further than it can reach by groping with the help of examples, to metaphysics (which does not allow itself to be checked by anything empirical and, as it must measure the whole extent of this kind of rational knowledge, goes as far as ideal conceptions, where even examples fail us), we must follow and clearly describe the practical faculty of reason, from the general rules of its determination to the point where the notion of duty springs from it.

Everything in nature works according to laws. Rational beings alone have the faculty of acting according *to the conception* of laws— that is, according to principles, that is, have a *will*. Since the deduction of actions from principles requires *reason,* the will is nothing but practical reason. If reason infallibly determines the will, then the actions of such a being which are recognized as objectively necessary are subjectively necessary also, that is, the will is a faculty to choose *that only* which reason independent on inclination recognizes as practically necessary, that is, as good. But if reason of itself does not sufficiently determine the will, if the latter is subject also to subjective conditions (particular impulses) which do not always coincide with the objective conditions, in a word, if the will does not *in itself* completely accord with reason (which is actually the case with men), then the actions which objectively are recognized as necessary are subjectively contingent, and the determination of such a will according to objective laws is *obligation,* that is to say, the relation of the objective laws to a will that is not thoroughly good is conceived as the determination of the will of a rational being by principles of reason, but which the will from its nature does not of necessity follow.

The conception of an objective principle, in so far as it is obligatory for a will, is called a command (of reason), and the formula of the command is called an Imperative.

All imperatives are expressed by the word *ought* [or *shall*], and thereby indicate the relation of an objective law of reason to a will which from its subjective constitution is not necessarily determined by it (an obligation). They say that something would be good to do or to forbear, but they say it to a will which does not always do a thing because it is conceived to be good to do it. That is practically *good*, however, which determines the will by means of the conceptions of reason, and consequently not from subjective causes, but objectively, that is, on principles which are valid for every rational being as such. It is distinguished from the *pleasant* as that which influences the will only by means of sensation from merely subjective causes, valid only for the sense of this or that one, and not as a principle of reason which holds for every one.[7]

A perfectly good will would therefore be equally subject to objective laws (viz., laws of good), but could not be conceived as *obliged* thereby to act lawfully, because of itself from its subjective constitution it can only be determined by the conception of good. Therefore no imperatives hold for the Divine will, or in general for a *holy* will; *ought* is here out of place because the volition is already of itself necessarily in unison with the law. Therefore imperatives are only formulae to express the relation of objective laws of all volition to the subjective imperfection of the will of this or that rational being, for example, the human will.

Now all *imperatives* command either *hypothetically* or *categorically*. The former represent the practical necessity of a possible action as means to something else that is willed (or at least which one might possibly will). The categorical imperative would be that which represented an action as necessary of itself without reference to another end, that is, as objectively necessary.

Since every practical law represents a possible action as good, and on this account, for a subject who is practically determinable by reason as necessary, all imperatives are formulae determining an action which

---

[7] The dependence of the desires on sensations is called inclination, and this accordingly always indicates a *want*. The dependence of a contingently determinable will on principles of reason is called an *interest*. This, therefore, is found only in the case of a dependent will which does not always of itself conform to reason; in the Divine will we cannot conceive any interest. But the human will can also *take an interest* in a thing without therefore acting *from interest*. The former signifies the *practical* interest in the action, the latter the *pathological* in the object of the action. The former indicates only dependence of the will on principles of reason in themselves; the second, dependence on principles of reason for the sake of inclination, reason supplying only the practical rules how the requirement of the inclination may be satisfied. In the first case the action interests me; in the second the object of the action (because it is pleasant to me). We have seen in the first section that in an action done from duty we must look not to the interest in the object, but only to that in the action itself, and in its rational principle (viz., the law).

is necessary according to the principle of a will good in some respects. If now the action is good only as a means *to something else,* then the imperative is *hypothetical;* if it is conceived as good *in itself* and consequently as being necessarily the principle of a will which of itself conforms to reason, then it is *categorical.*

Thus the imperative declares what action possible by me would be good, and presents the practical rule in relation to a will which does not forthwith perform an action simply because it is good, whether because the subject does not always know that it is good, or because, even if it know this, yet its maxims might be opposed to the objective principles of practical reason.

Accordingly the hypothetical imperative only says that the action is good for some purpose, *possible* or *actual.* In the first case it is a *problematical,* in the second an *assertorial* practical principle. The categorical imperative which declares an action to be objectively necessary in itself without reference to any purpose, that is, without any other end, is valid as an *apodictic* (practical) principle.

Whatever is possible only by the power of some rational being may also be conceived as a possible purpose of some will; and therefore the principles of action as regards the means necessary to attain some possible purpose are in fact infinitely numerous. All sciences have a practical part consisting of problems expressing that some end is possible for us, and of imperatives directing how it may be attained. These may, therefore, be called in general imperatives of *skill.* Here there is no question whether the end is rational and good, but only what one must do in order to attain it. The precepts for the physician to make his patient thoroughly healthy, and for a poisoner to ensure certain death, are of equal value in this respect, that each serves to effect its purpose perfectly. Since in early youth it cannot be known what ends are likely to occur to us in the course of life, parents seek to have their children taught a *great many things,* and provide for their *skill* in the use of means for all sorts of arbitrary ends, of none of which can they determine whether it may not perhaps hereafter be an object to their pupil, but which it is at all events *possible* that he might aim at; and this anxiety is so great that they commonly neglect to form and correct their judgment on the value of the things which may be chosen as ends.

There is *one* end, however, which may be assumed to be actually such to all rational beings (so far as imperatives apply to them, viz., as dependent beings), and, therefore, one purpose which they not merely *may* have, but which we may with certainty assume that they all actually *have* by a natural necessity, and this is *happiness.* The hypothetical imperative which expresses the practical necessity of an action as means to the advancement of happiness is *assertorial.* We are not to present it as necessary for an uncertain and merely possible purpose, but for a purpose which we may presuppose with certainty and *a priori* in every man, because it belongs to his being. Now skill in the choice of means to his own greatest well-being may be called *prudence*,[8] in the narrowest sense. And thus the imperative which refers to the choice of means to one's own happiness, that is, the precept of prudence, is still always *hypothetical;* the action is not commanded absolutely, but only as means to another purpose.

Finally, there is an imperative which commands a certain conduct immediately, without having as its condition any other purpose to be attained by it. This imperative is *categorical.* It concerns not the matter of the action, or its intended result, but its form and the principle of which it is itself a result; and what is essentially good in it consists in the mental disposition, let the consequence be what it may. This imperative may be called that of *morality.*

There is a marked distinction also between the volitions on these three sorts of principles in the *dissimilarity* of the obligation of the will. In order to mark this difference more clearly, I think they would be most suitably named in their order if we said they are either *rules* of skill, or *counsels* of prudence, or *commands* (*laws*) of morality. For it is *law* only that involves the conception of an *unconditional* and objective necessity, which is consequently universally valid; and commands are laws which must be obeyed, that is, must be followed, even in opposition to inclination. *Counsels,* indeed, involve necessity, but one which can only hold under a contingent subjective condition, viz., they depend on whether this or that man reckons this or that as part of his happiness; the categorical imperative, on the contrary, is not limited by any condition, and as being absolutely, although practically, necessary may be quite properly called a command. We might also call the first kind of imperatives *technical* (belonging to art), the second *pragmatic*[9] (belonging to welfare), the third *moral* (belonging to free conduct generally, that is, to morals).

Now arises the question, how are all these imperatives possible? This question does not seek to know how we can conceive the accomplishment of the action which the imperative ordains, but merely how

---

[8] The word *prudence* is taken in two senses: in the one it may bear the name of knowledge of the world, in the other that of private prudence. The former is a man's ability to influence others so as to use them for his own purposes. The latter is the sagacity to combine all these purposes for his own lasting benefit. This latter is properly that to which the value even of the former is reduced, and when a man is prudent in the former sense, but not in the latter, we might better say of him that he is clever and cunning, but, on the whole, imprudent.

[9] It seems to me that the proper signification of the word *pragmatic* may be most accurately defined in this way. For *sanctions* [see *Cr. of Pract. Reas.*, p. 271] are called pragmatic which flow properly, not from the law of the states as necessary enactments, but from *precaution* for the general welfare. A history is composed pragmatically when it teaches *prudence*, that is, instructs the world how it can provide for its interests better, or at least as well as the men of former time.

we can conceive the obligation of the will which the imperative expresses. No special explanation is needed to show how an imperative of skill is possible. Whoever wills the end wills also (so far as reason decides his conduct) the means in his power which are indispensably necessary thereto. This proposition is, as regards the volition, analytical; for in willing an object as my effect there is already thought the casualty of myself as an acting cause, that is to say, the use of the means; and the imperative educes from the conception of volition of an end the conception of actions necessary to this end. Synthetical propositions must no doubt be employed in defining the means to a proposed end; but they do not concern the principle, the act of the will, but the object and its realization. For example, that in order to bisect a line on an unerring principle I must draw from its extremities two intersecting arcs; this no doubt is taught by mathematics only in synthetical propositions; but if I know that it is only by this process that the intended operation can be performed, then to say that if I fully will the operation, I also will the action required for it, is an analytical proposition; for it is one and the same thing to conceive something as an effect which I can produce in a certain way, and to conceive myself as acting in this way.

If it were only equally easy to give a definite conception of happiness, the imperatives of prudence would correspond exactly with those of skill, and would likewise be analytical. For in this case as in that, it could be said whoever wills the end wills also (according to the dictate of reason necessarily) the indispensable means thereto which are in his power. But, unfortunately, the notion of happiness is so indefinite that although every man wishes to attain it, yet he never can say definitely and consistently what it is that he really wishes and wills. The reason of this is that all the elements which belong to the notion of happiness are altogether empirical, that is, they must be borrowed from experience, and nevertheless the idea of happiness requires an absolute whole, a maximum of welfare in my present and all future circumstances. Now it is impossible that the most clear-sighted and at the same time most powerful being (supposed finite) should frame to himself a definite conception of what he really wills in this. Does he will riches, how much anxiety, envy, and snares might he not thereby draw upon his shoulders? Does he will knowledge and discernment, perhaps it might prove to be only an eye so much the sharper to show him so much the more fearfully the evils that are now concealed from him and that cannot be avoided, or to impose more wants on his desires, which already give him concern enough. Would he have long life? Who guarantees to him that it would not be a long misery? Would he at least have health? How often has uneasiness of the body restrained from excesses into which perfect health would have allowed one to fall, and so on? In short, he is unable, on any principle, to determine with certainty what would make him truly happy; because to do so he would need to be omniscient. We cannot therefore act on any definite principles to secure happiness, but only on empirical counsels, for example, of regimen, frugality, courtesy, reserve, etc., which experience teaches do, on the average, most promote well-being. Hence it follows that the imperatives of prudence do not, strictly speaking, command at all, that is, they cannot present actions objectively as practically *necessary;* that they are rather to be regarded as counsels (*consilia*) than precepts (*praecepta*) of reason, that the problem to determine certainly and universally what action would promote the happiness of a rational being is completely insoluble, and consequently no imperative respecting it is possible which should, in the strict sense, command to do what makes happy; because happiness is not an ideal of reason but of imagination, resting solely on empirical grounds, and it is vain to expect that these should define an action by which one could attain the totality of a series of consequences which is really endless. This imperative of prudence would, however, be an analytical proposition if we assume that the means to happiness could be certainly assigned; for it is distinguished from the imperative of skill only by this that in the latter the end is merely *possible,* in the former it is *given;* as, however, both only ordain the means to that which we suppose to be willed as an end, it follows that the imperative which ordains the willing of the means to him who wills the end is in both cases analytical. Thus there is no difficulty in regard to the possibility of an imperative of this kind either.

On the other hand, the question, how the imperative of *morality* is possible, is undoubtedly one, the only one, demanding a solution, as this is not at all hypothetical, and the objective necessity which it presents cannot rest on any hypothesis, as is the case with the hypothetical imperatives. Only here we must never leave out of consideration that we *cannot* make out *by any example,* in other words, empirically, whether there is such an imperative at all; but it is rather to be feared that all those which seem to be categorical may yet be at bottom hypothetical. For instance, when the precept is: Thou shalt not promise deceitfully; and it is assumed that the necessity of this is not a mere counsel to avoid some other evil, so that it should mean; Thou shalt not make a lying promise, lest if it become known thou shouldst destroy thy credit, but that an action of this kind must be regarded as evil in itself, so that the imperative of the prohibition is categorical; then we cannot show with certainty in any example that the will was determined merely by the law, without any other spring of action, although it may appear to be so. For it is always possible that fear of disgrace, perhaps also obscure dread of other dangers, may have a secret influence on the will. Who can prove by experience the nonexistence of a cause when all that experience tells us is that we do not perceive it? But in such a case the so-called moral imperative, which as such appears to be categorical and unconditional, would in reality be only a pragmatic precept, drawing our attention to our own interests, and merely teaching us to take these into consideration.

We shall therefore have to investigate *a priori* the possibility of a categorical imperative, as we have not in this case the advantage of its reality being given in experience, so that [the elucidation of] its possibility should be requisite only for its explanation, not for its establishment. In the meantime it may be discerned beforehand that the categorical imperative alone has the purport of a practical law; all the rest may indeed be called *principles* of the will but not laws, since whatever is only necessary for the attainment of some arbitrary purpose may be considered as in itself contingent, and we can at any time be free from the precept if we give up the purpose; on the contrary, the unconditional command leaves the will no liberty to choose the opposite, consequently it alone carries with it that necessity which we require in a law.

Secondly, in the case of this categorical imperative or law of morality, the difficulty (of discerning its possibility) is a very profound one. It is an *a priori* synthetical practical proposition;[10] and as there is so much difficulty in discerning the possibility of speculative propositions of this kind, it may readily be supposed that the difficulty will be no less with the practical.

In this problem we will first inquire whether the mere conception of a categorical imperative may not perhaps supply us also with the formula of it, containing the proposition which alone can be a categorical imperative; for even if we know the tenor of such an absolute command, yet how it is possible will require further special and laborious study, which we postpone to the last section.

When I conceive a hypothetical imperative, in general I do not know beforehand what it will contain until I am given the condition. But when I conceive a categorical imperative, I know at once what it contains. For as the imperative contains besides the law only the necessity that the maxims[11] shall conform to this law, while the law con-

---

10 I connect the act with the will without presupposing any condition resulting from any inclination, but *a priori,* and therefore necessarily (though only objectively, that is, assuming the idea of a reason possessing full power over all subjective motives). This is accordingly a practical proposition which does not deduce the willing of an action by mere analysis from another already presupposed (for we have not such a perfect will), but connects it immediately with the conception of the will of a rational being, as something not contained in it.

11 A 'maxim' is a subjective principle of action, and must be distinguished from the *objective principle,* namely, practical law. The former contains the practical rule set by reason according to the conditions of the subject (often its ignorance or its inclinations), so that it is the principle on which the subject *acts;* but the law is the objective principle valid for every rational being, and is the principle on which it *ought to act*—that is an imperative.

tains no conditions restricting it, there remains nothing but the general statement that the maxim of the action should conform to a universal law, and it is this conformity alone that the imperative properly represents as necessary.

There is therefore but one categorical imperative, namely this: *Act only on that maxim whereby thou canst at the same time will that it should become a universal law.*

Now if all imperatives of duty can be deduced from this one imperative as from their principle, then, although it should remain undecided whether what is called duty is not merely a vain notion, yet at least we shall be able to show what we understand by it and what this notion *means*.

Since the universality of the law according to which effects are produced constitutes what is properly called *nature* in the most general sense (as to form)—that is, the existence of things so far as it is determined by general laws—the imperative of duty may be expressed thus: *Act as if the maxim of thy action were to become by thy will a universal law of nature.*

We will now enumerate a few duties, adopting the usual division of them into duties to ourselves and to others, and into perfect and imperfect duties.[12]

1. A man reduced to despair by a series of misfortunes feels wearied of life, but is still so far in possession of his reason that he can ask himself whether it would not be contrary to his duty to himself to take his own life. Now he inquires whether the maxim of his action could become a universal law of nature. His maxim is: From self-love I adopt it as a principle to shorten my life when its longer duration is likely to bring more evil than satisfaction. It is asked then simply whether this principle founded on self-love can become a universal law of nature. Now we see at once that a system of nature of which it should be a law to destroy life by means of the very feeling whose special nature it is to impel to the improvement of life would contradict itself, and therefore could not exist as a system of nature; hence that maxim cannot possibly exist as a universal law of nature, and conse-

---

[12] It must be noted here that I reserve the division of duties for a future *metaphysic of morals;* so that I give it here only as an arbitrary one (in order to arrange my examples). For the rest, I understand by a perfect duty one that admits no exception in favor of inclination, and then I have not merely external but also internal perfect duties. This is contrary to the use of the word adopted in the schools; but I do not intend to justify it here, as it is all one for my purpose whether it is admitted or not. [*Perfect* duties are usually understood to be those which can be enforced by external law; *imperfect,* those which cannot be enforced. They are also called respectively *determinate* and *indeterminate, officia juris* and *officia virtutis.*]

quently would be wholly inconsistent with the supreme principle of all duty.[13]

2. Another finds himself forced by necessity to borrow money. He knows that he will not be able to repay it, but sees also that nothing will be lent to him unless he promises stoutly to repay it in a definite time. He desires to make this promise, but he has still so much conscience as to ask himself: Is it not unlawful and inconsistent with duty to get out of a difficulty in this way? Suppose, however, that he resolves to do so, then the maxim of his action would be expressed thus: When I think myself in want of money, I will borrow money and promise to repay it, although I know that I never can do so. Now this principle of self-love or of one's own advantage may perhaps be consistent with my whole future welfare; but the question now is, Is it right? I change then the suggestion of self-love into a universal law, and state the question thus: How would it be if my maxim were a universal law? Then I see at once that it could never hold as a universal law of nature, but would necessarily contradict itself. For supposing it to be a universal law that everyone when he thinks himself in a difficulty should be able to promise whatever he pleases, with the purpose of not keeping his promise, the promise itself would become impossible, as well as the end that one might have in view in it, since no one would consider that anything was promised to him, but would ridicule all such statements as vain pretenses.

3. A third finds in himself a talent which with the help of some culture might make him a useful man in many respects. But he finds himself in comfortable circumstances and prefers to indulge in pleasure rather than to take pains in enlarging and improving his happy natural capacities. He asks, however, whether his maxim of neglect of his natural gifts, besides agreeing with his inclination to indulgence, agrees also with what is called duty. He sees then that a system of nature could indeed subsist with such a universal law, although men (like the South Sea islanders) should let their talents rest and resolve to devote their lives merely to idleness, amusement, and propagation of their species—in a word, to enjoyment; but he cannot possibly *will* that this should be a universal law of nature, or be implanted in us as such by a natural instinct. For, as a rational being, he necessarily wills that his faculties be developed, since they serve him, and have been given him, for all sorts of possible purposes.

4. A fourth, who is in prosperity, while he sees that others have to contend with great wretchedness and that he could help them, thinks: What concern is it of mine? Let everyone be as happy as Heaven

---

13 [On suicide cf. further *Metaphysik der Sitten*, p. 274.]

pleases, or as he can make himself; I will take nothing from him nor even envy him, only I do not wish to contribute anything to his welfare or to his assistance in distress! Now no doubt, if such a mode of thinking were a universal law, the human race might very well subsist, and doubtless even better than in a state in which everyone talks of sympathy and good-will, or even takes care occasionally to put it into practice, but, on the other side, also cheats when he can, betrays the rights of men, or otherwise violates them. But although it is possible that a universal law of nature might exist in accordance with that maxim, it is impossible to *will* that such a principle should have the universal validity of a law of nature. For a will which resolved this would contradict itself, inasmuch as many cases might occur in which one would have need of the love and sympathy of others, and in which, by such a law of nature, sprung from his own will, he would deprive himself of all hope of the aid he desires.

These are a few of the many actual duties, or at least what we regard as such, which obviously fall into two classes on the one principle that we have laid down. We must be *able to will* that a maxim of our action should be a universal law. This is the canon of the moral appreciation of the action generally. Some actions are of such a character that their maxim cannot without contradiction be even *conceived* as a universal law of nature, far from it being possible that we should *will* that it *should* be so. In others, this intrinsic impossibility is not found, but still it is impossible to *will* that their maxim should be raised to the universality of a law of nature, since such a will would contradict itself. It is easily seen that the former violate strict or rigorous (inflexible) duty; the latter only laxer (meritorious) duty. Thus it has been completely shown by these examples how all duties depend as regards the nature of the obligation (not the object of the action) on the same principle.

If now we attend to ourselves on occasion of any transgression of duty, we shall find that we in fact do not will that our maxim should be a universal law, for that is impossible for us; on the contrary, we will that the opposite should remain a universal law, only we assume the liberty of making an *exception* in our own favor or (just for this time only) in favor of our inclination. Consequently, if we considered all cases from one and the same point of view, namely, that of reason, we should find a contradiction in our own will, namely, that a certain principle should be objectively necessary as a universal law, and yet subjectively should not be universal, but admit of exceptions. As however, we at one moment regard our action from the point of view of a will wholly conformed to reason, and then again look at the same action from the point of view of a will affected by inclination, there is not really any contradiction, but an antagonism of inclination to the precept of reason, whereby the universality of the principle is changed into a mere generality, so that the practical principle of reason shall meet the maxim half way. Now, although this cannot be justified in our own impartial judgment, yet it proves that we do really recognize the validity of the categorical imperative and (with all respect for it) only allow ourselves a few exceptions which we think unimportant and forced from us.

We have thus established at least this much—that if duty is a conception which is to have any import and real legislative authority for our actions, it can only be expressed in categorical, and not at all in hypothetical, imperatives. We have also, which is of great importance, exhibited clearly and definitely for every practical application the content of the categorical imperative, which must contain the principle of all duty if there is such a thing at all. We have not yet, however, advanced so far as to prove *a priori* that there actually is such an imperative, that there is a practical law which commands absolutely of itself and without any other impulse, and that the following of this law is duty.

With the view of attaining to this it is of extreme importance to remember that we must not allow ourselves to think of deducing the reality of this principle from the *particular attributes of human nature.* For duty is to be a practical, unconditional necessity of action; it must therefore hold for all rational beings (to whom an imperative can apply at all), and *for this reason only* be also a law for all human wills. On the contrary, whatever is deduced from the particular natural characteristics of humanity, from certain feelings and propensions,[14] nay, even, if possible, from any particular tendency proper to human reason, and which need not necessarily hold for the will of every rational being—this may indeed supply us with a maxim but not with a law; with a subjective principle on which we may have a propension and inclination to act, but not with an objective principle on which we should be *enjoined* to act, even though all our propensions, inclinations, and natural dispositions were opposed to it. In fact, the sublimity and intrinsic dignity of the command in duty are so much the more evident, the less the subjective impulses favor it and the more they oppose it, without being able in the slightest degree to weaken the obligation of the law or to diminish its validity.

Here then we see philosophy brought to a critical position, since it has to be firmly fixed, notwithstanding that it has nothing to support it

---

14 [Kant distinguishes 'Hang (*propensio*)' from 'Neigung (*inclinatio*)' as follows: 'Hang' is a predisposition to the desire of some enjoyment; in other words, it is the subjective possibility of excitement of a certain desire which precedes the conception of its object. When the enjoyment has been experienced, it produces a 'Neigung' (inclination) to it, which accordingly is defined 'habitual sensible desire.'—*Anthropologie,* §§ 72, 79; *Religion,* p. 31.]

in heaven or earth. Here it must show its purity as absolute director of its own laws, not the herald of those which are whispered to it by an implanted sense or who knows what tutelary nature. Although these may be better than nothing, yet they can never afford principles dictated by reason, which must have their source wholly *a priori* and thence their commanding authority, expecting everything from the supremacy of the law and the due respect for it, nothing from inclination, or else condemning the man to self-contempt and inward abhorrence.

Thus every empirical element is not only quite incapable of being an aid to the principle of morality, but is even highly prejudicial to the purity of morals; for the proper and inestimable worth of an absolutely good will consists just in this that the principle of action is free from all influence of contingent grounds, which alone experience can furnish. We cannot too much or too often repeat our warning against this lax and even mean habit of thought which seeks for its principle among empirical motives and laws; for human reason in its weariness is glad to rest on this pillow, and in a dream of sweet illusions (in which, instead of Juno, it embraces a cloud) it substitutes for morality a bastard patched up from limbs of various derivation, which looks like anything one chooses to see in it; only not like virtue to one who has once beheld her in her true form.[15]

The question then is this: Is it a necessary law *for all rational beings* that they should always judge of their actions by maxims of which they can themselves will that they should serve as universal laws? If it is so, then it must be connected (altogether *a priori*) with the very conception of the will of a rational being generally. But in order to discover this connection we must, however reluctantly, take a step into metaphysic, although into a domain of it which is distinct from speculative philosophy—namely, the metaphysic of morals. In a practical philosophy, where it is not the reasons of what *happens* that we have to ascertain, but the laws of what *ought to happen,* even although it never does, that is, objective practical laws, there it is not necessary to inquire into the reasons why anything pleases or displeases, how the pleasure of mere sensation differs from taste, and whether the latter is distinct from a general satisfaction of reason; on what the feeling of pleasure or pain rests, and how from it desires and inclinations arise, and from these again maxims by the cooperation of reason; for all this belongs to an empirical psychology, which would constitute the second part of physics, if we regard physics as the *philosophy* of nature, so far as it is

---

[15] To behold virtue in her proper form is nothing else but to contemplate morality stripped of all admixture of sensible things and of every spurious ornament of reward or self-love. How much she then eclipses everything else that appears charming to the affections, every one may readily perceive with the least exertion of his reason, if it be not wholly spoiled for abstraction.

based on *empirical laws.* But here we are concerned with objective practical laws, and consequently with the relation of the will to itself so far as it is determined by reason alone, in which case whatever has reference to anything empirical is necessarily excluded; since if *reason of itself alone* determines the conduct (and it is the possibility of this that we are now investigating), it must necessarily do so *a priori.*

The will is conceived as a faculty of determining oneself to action *in accordance with the conception of certain laws.* And such a faculty can be found only in rational beings. Now that which serves the will as the objective ground of its self-determination is the *end,* and if this is assigned by reason alone, it must hold for all rational beings. On the other hand, that which merely contains the ground of possibility of the action of which the effect is the end, this is called the *means.* The subjective ground of the desire is the *spring,* the objective ground of the volition is the *motive;* hence the distinction between subjective ends which rest on springs, and objective ends which depend on motives valid for every rational being. Practical principles are *formal* when they abstract from all subjective ends; they are *material* when they assume these, and therefore particular, springs of action. The ends which a rational being proposes to himself at pleasure as *effects* of his actions (material ends) are all only relative, for it is only their relation to the particular desires of the subject that gives them their worth, which therefore cannot furnish principles universal and necessary for all rational beings and for every volition, that is to say, practical laws. Hence all these relative ends can give rise only to hypothetical imperatives.

Supposing, however, that there were something *whose existence* has *in itself* an absolute worth, something which, being *an end in itself,* could be a source of definite laws, then in this and this alone would lie the source of a possible categorical imperative, that is, a practical law.

Now I say: man and generally any rational being *exists* as an end in himself, *not merely as a means* to be arbitrarily used by this or that will, but in all his actions, whether they concern himself or other rational beings, must be always regarded at the same time as an end. All objects of the inclinations have only a conditional worth; for if the inclinations and the wants founded on them did not exist, then their object would be without value. But the inclinations themselves, being sources of want, are so far from having an absolute worth for which they should be desired that, on the contrary, it must be the universal wish of every rational being to be wholly free from them. Thus the worth of any object which is *to be acquired* by our action is always conditional. Beings whose existence depends not on our will but on nature's, have nevertheless, if they are nonrational beings, only a relative value as means, and are therefore called *things;* rational beings, on the contrary, are called *persons,* because their very nature points them out as ends in themselves, that is, as something which must not be used merely as means, and so far therefore restricts freedom of action (and is an object of respect). These, therefore, are not merely subjective ends whose existence has a worth *for us* as an effect of our action, but *objective ends*, that is, things whose existence is an end in itself—an end, moreover, for which no other can be substituted, which they should subserve *merely* as means, for otherwise nothing whatever would possess *absolute worth;* but if all worth were conditioned and therefore contingent, then there would be no supreme practical principle of reason whatever.

If then there is a supreme practical principle or, in respect of the human will, a categorical imperative, it must be one which, being drawn from the conception of that which is necessarily an end for everyone because it is *an end in itself,* constitutes an *objective* principle of will, and can therefore serve as a universal practical law. The foundation of this principle is: *rational nature exists as an end in itself.* Man necessarily conceives his own existence as being so; so far then this is a *subjective* principle of human actions. But every other rational being regards its existence similarly, just on the same rational principle that holds for me, [16] so that it is at the same time an objective principle from which as a supreme practical law all laws of the will must be capable of being deduced. Accordingly the practical imperative will be as follows: *So act as to treat humanity, whether in thine own person or in that of any other, in every case as an end withal, never as means only.* We will now inquire whether this can be practically carried out.

To abide by the previous examples:

First, under the head of necessary duty to oneself: He who contemplates suicide should ask himself whether his action can be consistent with the idea of humanity *as an end in itself.* If he destroys himself in order to escape from painful circumstances, he uses a person merely as *a mean* to maintain a tolerable condition up to the end of life. But a man is not a thing, that is to say, something which can be used merely as means, but must in all his actions be always considered as an end in himself. I cannot, therefore, dispose in any way of a man in my own person so as to mutilate him, to damage or kill him. (It belongs to ethics proper to define this principle more precisely, so as to avoid all misunderstanding, for example, as to the amputation of the limbs in order to preserve myself; as to exposing my life to danger with a view to preserve it, etc. This question is therefore omitted here.)

Secondly, as regards necessary duties, or those of strict obligation, towards others: He who is thinking of making a lying promise to others

[16] This proposition is here stated as a postulate. The ground of it will be found in the concluding section.

will see at once that he would be using another man *merely as a mean,* without the latter containing at the same time the end in himself. For he whom I propose by such a promise to use for my own purposes cannot possibly assent to my mode of acting towards him, and therefore cannot himself contain the end of this action. This violation of the principle of humanity in other men is more obvious if we take in examples of attacks on the freedom and property of others. For then it is clear that he who transgresses the rights of men intends to use the person of others merely as means, without considering that as rational beings they ought always to be esteemed also as ends, that is, as beings who must be capable of containing in themselves the end of the very same action. [17]

Thirdly, as regards contingent (meritorious) duties to oneself: It is not enough that the action does not violate humanity in our own person as an end in itself, it must also *harmonize with* it. Now there are in humanity capacities of greater perfection which belong to the end that nature has in view in regard to humanity in ourselves as the subject; to neglect these might perhaps be consistent with the *maintenance* of humanity as an end in itself, but not with the *advancement* of this end.

Fourthly, as regards meritorious duties towards others: The natural end which all men have is their own happiness. Now humanity might indeed subsist although no one should contribute anything to the happiness of others, provided he did not intentionally withdraw anything from it; but after all, this would only harmonize negatively, not positively, with *humanity as an end in itself,* if everyone does not also endeavor, as far as in him lies, to forward the ends of others. For the ends of any subject which is an end in himself ought as far as possible to be *my* ends also, if that conception is to have its *full* effect with me.

This principle that humanity and generally every rational nature is *an end in itself* (which is the supreme limiting condition of every man's freedom of action), is not borrowed from experience, *first,* because it is universal, applying as it does to all rational beings whatever, and experience is not capable of determining anything about them; *secondly,* because it does not present humanity as an end to men (subjectively), that is, as an object which men do of themselves actually adopt as an end; but as an objective end which must as a law constitute the su-

---

[17] Let it not be thought that the common: *quod tibi non vis fieri, etc.,* could serve here as the rule of principle. For it is only a deduction from the former, though with several limitations; it cannot be a universal law, for it does not contain the principle of duties to oneself, nor of the duties of benevolence to others (for many a one would gladly consent that others should not benefit him, provided only that he might be excused from showing benevolence to them), nor finally that of duties of strict obligation to one another, for on this principle the criminal might argue against the judge who punishes him, and so on.

preme limiting condition of all our subjective ends, let them be what we will; it must therefore spring from pure reason. In fact the objective principle of all practical legislation lies (according to the first principle) in *the rule* and its form of universality which makes it capable of being a law (say, for example, a law of nature); but the *subjective* principle is in the *end;* now by the second principle, the subject of all ends is each rational being inasmuch as it is an end in itself. Hence follows the third practical principle of the will, which is the ultimate condition of its harmony with the universal practical reason, viz., the idea of *the will of every rational being as a universally legislative will.*

On this principle all maxims are rejected which are inconsistent with the will being itself universal legislator. Thus the will is not subject to the law, but so subject that it must be regarded *as itself giving the law,* and on this ground only subject to the law (of which it can regard itself as the author).

In the previous imperatives, namely, that based on the conception of the conformity of actions to general laws, as in a *physical system of nature,* and that based on the universal *prerogative* of rational beings as *ends* in themselves—these imperatives just because they were con- ceived as categorical excluded from any share in their authority all admixture of any interest as a spring of action; they were, however, only *assumed* to be categorical, because such an assumption was neces- sary to explain the conception of duty. But we could not prove inde- pendently that there are practical propositions which command categorically, nor can it be proved in this section; one thing, however, could be done, namely, to indicate in the imperative itself, by some determinate expression, that in the case of volition from duty all interest is renounced, which is the specific criterion of categorical as distinguished from hypothetical imperatives. This is done in the present (third) formula of the principle namely, in the idea of the will of every rational being as a *universally legislating will.*

For although a will *which is subject to laws* may be attached to this law by means of an interest, yet a will which is itself a supreme law-giver, so far as it is such, cannot possibly depend on any interest, since a will so dependent would itself need another law restricting the interest of its self-love by the condition that it should be valid as uni- versal law.

Thus the *principle* that every human will *is a will which in all its maxims gives universal laws,*[18] provided it be otherwise justified, would be very *well adapted* to be the categorical imperative, in this

---

[18] I may be excused from adducing examples to elucidate this principle as those which have already been used to elucidate the categorical imperative and its formula would all serve for the like purpose here.

respect, namely, that just because of the idea of universal legislation it is *not based on any interest,* and therefore it alone among all possible imperatives can be *unconditional.* Or still better, converting the proposition, if there is a categorical imperative (that is, a law for the will of every rational being), it can only command that everything be done from maxims of one's will regarded as a will which could at the same time will that it should itself give universal laws, for in that case only the practical principle and the imperative which it obeys are unconditional, since they cannot be based on any interest.

Looking back now on all previous attempts to discover the principle of morality, we need not wonder why they all failed. It was seen that man was bound to laws by duty, but it was not observed that the laws to which he is subject are *only those of his own giving,* though at the same time they are *universal,* and that he is only bound to act in conformity with his own will—a will, however, which is designed by nature to give universal laws. For when one has conceived man only as subject to a law (no matter what), then this law required some interest, either by way of attraction or constraint, since it did not originate as a law from *his own* will, but this will was according to a law obliged by *something else* to act in a certain manner. Now by this necessary consequence all the labor spent in finding a supreme principle of *duty* was irrevocably lost. For men never elicited duty, but only a necessity of acting from a certain interest. Whether this interest was private or otherwise, in any case the imperative must be conditional, and could not by any means be capable of being a moral command. I will therefore call this the principle of *autonomy* of the will, in contrast with every other which I accordingly reckon as *Heteronomy.*[19]

The conception of every rational being as one which must consider itself as giving in all the maxims of its will universal laws, so as to judge itself and its actions from this point of view—this conception leads to another which depends on it and is very fruitful, namely, that of a *kingdom of ends.*

By a 'kingdom' I understand the union of different rational beings in a system by common laws. Now since it is by laws that ends are determined as regards their universal validity, hence, if we abstract from the personal differences of rational beings, and likewise from all the content of their private ends, we shall be able to conceive all ends combined in a systematic whole (including both rational beings as ends in themselves, and also the special ends which each may propose to himself), that is to say, we can conceive a kingdom of ends, which on the preceding principles is possible.

---

19 [Cp. *Critical Examination of Practical Reason,* p. 184.]

For all rational beings come under the *law* that each of them must treat itself and all others *never merely as means,* but in every case *at the same time as ends in themselves.* Hence results a systematic union of rational beings by common objective laws, that is, a kingdom which may be called a kingdom of ends, since what these laws have in view is just the relation of these beings to one another as ends and means. It is certainly only an ideal.

A rational being belongs as a *member* to the kingdom of ends when, although giving universal laws in it, he is also himself subject to these laws. He belongs to it *as sovereign* when, while giving laws, he is not subject to the will of any other.

A rational being must always regard himself as giving laws either as member or as sovereign in a kingdom of ends which is rendered possible by the freedom of will. He cannot, however, maintain the latter position merely by the maxims of his will, but only in case he is a completely independent being without wants and with unrestricted power adequate to his will.

Morality consists then in the reference of all action to the legislation which alone can render a kingdom of ends possible. This legislation must be capable of existing in every rational being, and of emanating from his will, so that the principle of this will is never to act on any maxim which could not without contradiction be also a universal law, and accordingly always so to act *that the will could at the same time regard itself as giving in its maxims universal laws.* If now the maxims of rational beings are not by their own nature coincident with this objective principle, then the necessity of acting on it is called practical necessitation, that is, *duty.* Duty does not apply to the sovereign in the kingdom of ends, but it does to every member of it and to all in the same degree.

The practical necessity of acting on this principle, that is, duty, does not rest at all on feelings, impulses, or inclinations, but solely on the relation of rational beings to one another, a relation in which the will of a rational being must always be regarded as *legislative,* since otherwise it could not be conceived as *an end in itself.* Reason then refers every maxim of the will, regarding it as legislating universally, to every other will and also to every action towards oneself; and this not on account of any other practical motive or any future advantage, but from the idea of the *dignity* of a rational being, obeying no law but that which he himself also gives.

In the kingdom of ends everything has either *value* or *dignity.* Whatever has a value can be replaced by something else which is *equivalent;* whatever, on the other hand, is above all value, and therefore admits of no equivalent, has a dignity.

Whatever has reference to the general inclinations and wants of mankind has a *market value;* whatever, without presupposing a want, corresponds to a certain taste, that is, to a satisfaction in the mere purposeless play of our faculties, has a *fancy value;* but that which constitutes the condition under which alone anything can be an end in itself, this has not merely a relative worth, that is, value, but an intrinsic worth, that is, *dignity.*

Now morality is the condition under which alone a rational being can be an end in himself, since by this alone it is possible that he should be a legislating member in the kingdom of ends. Thus morality, and humanity as capable of it, is that which alone has dignity. Skill and diligence in labor have a market value; wit, lively imagination, and humor have fancy value; on the other hand, fidelity to promises, benevolence from principle (not from instinct), have an intrinsic worth. Neither nature nor art contains anything which in default of these it could put in their place, for their worth consists not in the effects which spring from them, not in the use and advantage which they secure, but in the disposition of mind, that is, the maxims of the will which are ready to manifest themselves in such actions, even though they should not have the desired effect. These actions also need no recommendation from any subjective taste or sentiment, that they may be looked on with immediate favor and satisfaction; they need no immediate propension or feeling for them; they exhibit the will that performs them as an object of an immediate respect, and nothing but reason is required to *impose* them on the will; not to *flatter* it into them, which, in the case of duties, would be a contradiction. This estimation therefore shows that the worth of such a disposition is dignity, and places it infinitely above all value, with which it cannot for a moment be brought into comparison or competition without as it were violating its sanctity.

What then is it which justifies virtue or the morally good disposition, in making such lofty claims? It is nothing less than the privilege it secures to the rational being of participating in the giving of universal laws, by which it qualifies him to be a member of a possible kingdom of ends, a privilege to which he was already destined by his own nature as being an end in himself, and on that account legislating in the kingdom of ends; free as regards all laws of physical nature, and obeying those only which he himself gives, and by which his maxims can belong to a system of universal law to which at the same time he submits himself. For nothing has any worth except what the law assigns it. Now the legislation itself which assigns the worth of everything must for that very reason possess dignity, that is, an unconditional incomparable worth; and the word *respect* alone supplies a becoming expression for the esteem which a rational being must have for it. *Autonomy* then is the basis of the dignity of human and of every rational nature.

The three modes of presenting the principle of morality that have been adduced are at bottom only so many formulae of the very same law, and each of itself involves the other two. There is, however, a difference in them, but it is rather subjective than objectively practical, intended, namely, to bring an idea of the reason nearer to intuition (by means of a certain analogy), and thereby nearer to feeling. All maxims, in fact, have—

1. A *form,* consisting in universality; and in this view the formula of the moral imperative is expressed thus, that the maxims must be so chosen as if they were to serve as universal laws of nature.

2. A *matter,* namely, an end, and here the formula says that the rational being, as it is an end by its own nature and therefore an end in itself, must in every maxim serve as the condition limiting all merely relative and arbitrary ends.

3. A *complete characterization* of all maxims by means of that formula, namely, that all maxims ought, by their own legislation, to harmonize with a possible kingdom of ends as with a kingdom of nature. [20] There is a progress here in the order of the categories of *unity* of the form of the will (its universality), *plurality* of the matter (the objects, that is, the ends), and *totality* of the system of these. In forming our moral judgment of actions it is better to proceed always on the strict method, and start from the general formula of the categorical imperative: *Act according to a maxim which can at the same time make itself a universal law.* If, however, we wish to gain an *entrance* for the moral law, it is very useful to bring one and the same action under the three specified conceptions, and thereby as far as possible to bring it nearer to intuition.

We can now end where we started at the beginning, namely, with the conception of a will unconditionally good. *That will is absolutely good* which cannot be evil—in other words, whose maxim, if made a universal law, could never contradict itself. This principle, then, is its supreme law: *Act always on such a maxim as thou canst at the same time will to be a universal law;* this is the sole condition under which a will can never contradict itself; and such an imperative is categorical. Since the validity of the will as a universal law for possible actions is analogous to the universal connection of the existence of things by general laws, which is the formal notion of nature in general, the categorical imperative can also be expressed thus: *Act on maxims which can at the same time have for their object themselves as universal laws of nature.* Such then is the formula of an absolutely good will.

---

[20] Teleology considers nature as a kingdom of ends; ethics regards a possible kingdom of ends as a kingdom of nature. In the first case, the kingdom of ends is a theoretical idea, adopted to explain what actually is. In the latter it is a practical idea, adopted to bring about that which is not yet, but which can be realized by our conduct, namely, if it conforms to this idea.

Rational nature is distinguished from the rest of nature by this that it sets before itself an end. This end would be the matter of every good will. But since in the idea of a will that is absolutely good without being limited by any condition (of attaining this or that end) we must abstract wholly from every end *to be effected* (since this would make every will only relatively good), it follows that in this case the end must be conceived, not as an end to be effected, but as an *independently* existing end. Consequently it is conceived only negatively, that is, as that which we must never act against, and which, therefore, must never be regarded merely as means, but must in every volition be esteemed as an end likewise. Now this end can be nothing but the subject of all possible ends, since this is also the subject of a possible absolutely good will; for such a will cannot without contradiction be postponed to any other object. This principle: So act in regard to every rational being (thyself and others) that he may always have place in thy maxim as an end in himself, is accordingly essentially identical with this other: Act upon a maxim which, at the same time, involves its own universal validity for every rational being. For that in using means for every end I should limit my maxim by the condition of its holding good as a law for every subject, this comes to the same thing as that the fundamental principle of all maxims of action must be that the subject of all ends, that is, the rational being himself, be never employed merely as means, but as the supreme condition restricting the use of all means—that is, in every case as an end likewise.

It follows incontestably that, to whatever laws any rational being may be subject, he being an end in himself must be able to regard himself as also legislating universally in respect of these same laws, since it is just this fitness of his maxims for universal legislation that distinguishes him as an end in himself; also it follows that this implies his dignity (prerogative) above all mere physical beings, that he must always take his maxims from the point of view which regards himself, and likewise every other rational being, as lawgiving beings (on which account they are called persons). In this way a world of rational beings (mundus intelligibilis) is possible as a kingdom of ends, and this by virtue of the legislation proper to all persons as members. Therefore, every rational being must so act as if he were by his maxims in every case a legislating member in the universal kingdom of ends. The formal principle of these maxims is: So act as if thy maxim were to serve likewise as the universal law (of all rational beings). A kingdom of ends is thus only possible on the analogy of a kingdom of nature, the former, however, only by maxims—that is, self-imposed rules—the latter only by the laws of efficient causes acting under necessitation from without. Nevertheless, although the system of nature is looked upon as a machine, yet so far as it has reference to rational beings as its ends, it is given on this account the name of a kingdom of nature.

Now such a kingdom of ends would be actually realized by means of maxims conforming to the canon which the categorical imperative pre-scribes to all rational beings, *if they were universally followed.* But although a rational being, even if he punctually follows this maxim himself, cannot reckon upon all others being therefore true to the same, nor expect that the kingdom of nature and its orderly arrangements shall be in harmony with him as a fitting member, so as to form a kingdom of ends to which he himself contributes, that is to say, that it shall favor his expectation of happiness, still that law: Act according to the maxims of a member of a merely possible kingdom of ends legis-lating in it universally, remains in its full force inasmuch as it com-mands categorically. And it is just in this that the paradox lies; that the mere dignity of man as a rational creature, without any other end or advantage to be attained thereby, in other words, respect for a mere idea, should yet serve as an inflexible precept of the will, and that it is precisely in this independence of the maxim on all such springs of action that its sublimity consists; and it is this that makes every rational subject worthy to be a legislative member in the kingdom of ends, for otherwise he would have to be conceived only as subject to the physical law of his wants. And although we should suppose the kingdom of nature and the kingdom of ends to be united under one sovereign, so that the latter kingdom thereby ceased to be a mere idea and acquired true reality, then it would no doubt gain the accession of a strong spring, but by no means any increase of its intrinsic worth. For this sole absolute lawgiver must, notwithstanding this, be always conceived as estimating the worth of rational beings only by their disinterested behavior, as prescribed to themselves from that idea [the dignity of man] alone. The essence of things is not altered by their external rela-tions, and that which, abstracting from these, alone constitutes the absolute worth of man is also that by which he must be judged, who-ever the judge may be, and even by the Supreme Being. *Morality,* then, is the relation of actions to the autonomy of the will, that is, to the potential universal legislation by its maxims. An action that is con-sistent with the autonomy of the will is *permitted;* one that does not agree therewith is *forbidden.* A will whose maxims necessarily coin-cide with the laws of autonomy is a *holy* will, good absolutely. The dependence of a will not absolutely good on the principle of autonomy (moral necessitation) is obligation. This, then, cannot be applied to a holy being. The objective necessity of actions from obligation is called *duty.*

From what has just been said, it is easy to see how it happens that, although the conception of duty implies subjection to the law, we yet ascribe a certain *dignity* and sublimity to the person who fulfils all his duties. There is not, indeed, any sublimity in him, so far as he is *subject* to the moral law; but inasmuch as in regard to that very law he is like-wise a *legislator,* and on that account alone subject to it, he has sublimity. We have also shown above that neither fear nor inclination, but simply respect for the law, is the spring which can give actions a moral worth. Our own will, so far as we suppose it to act only under the condition that its maxims are potentially universal laws, this ideal will which is possible to us is the proper object of respect; and the dignity of humanity consists just in this capacity of being universally legislative, though with the condition that it is itself subject to this same legislation.

The Autonomy of the Will as the Supreme Principle of Morality

Autonomy of the will is that property of it by which it is a law to itself (independently on any property of the objects of volition). The principle of autonomy then is: Always so to choose that the same volition shall comprehend the maxims of our choice as a universal law. We cannot prove that this practical rule is an imperative, that is, that the will of every rational being is necessarily bound to it as a condition, by a mere analysis of the conceptions which occur in it, since it is a synthetical proposition; we must advance beyond the cognition of the objects to a critical examination of the subject, that is, of the pure practical reason, for this synthetic proposition which commands apodictically must be capable of being cognized wholly *a priori*. This matter, however, does not belong to the present section. But that the principle of autonomy in question is the sole principle of morals can be readily shown by mere analysis of the conceptions of morality. For by this analysis we find that its principle must be a categorical imperative, and that what this commands is neither more nor less than this very autonomy.

Heteronomy of the Will as the Source of All Spurious Principles of Morality

If the will seeks the law which is to determine it *anywhere else* than in the fitness of its maxims to be universal laws of its own dictation, consequently if it goes out of itself and seeks this law in the character of any of its objects, there always results *heteronomy*. The will in that case does not give itself the law, but it is given by the object through its relation to the will. This relation, whether it rests on inclination or on conceptions of reason, only admits of hypothetical imperatives: I ought to do something *because I wish for something else*. On the contrary, the moral, and therefore categorical, imperative says: I ought to do so and so, even though I should not wish for anything else. For example, the former says: I ought not to lie if I would retain my reputation; the latter says: I ought not to lie although it should not bring me the least discredit. The latter therefore must so far abstract from all objects that they shall have no *influence* on the will, in order that practical reason (will) may not be restricted to administering an interest not belonging to it, but may simply show its own commanding authority as the supreme legislation. Thus, for example, I ought to endeavor to promote the happiness of others, not as if its realization involved any concern of mine (whether by immediate inclination or by any satisfaction indirectly gained through reason), but simply because a maxim which excludes it cannot be comprehended as a universal law in one and the same volition.

Classification of All Principles of Morality Which Can Be Founded on the Conception of Heteronomy

Here as elsewhere human reason in its pure use, so long as it was not critically examined, has first tried all possible wrong ways before it succeeded in finding the one true way.

All principles which can be taken from this point of view are either *empirical* or *rational*. The *former*, drawn from the principle of *happiness*, are built on physical or moral feelings; the *latter*, drawn from the principle of *perfection*, are built either on the rational conception of perfection as a possible effect, or on that of an independent perfection (the will of God) as the determining cause of our will.

Empirical principles are wholly incapable of serving as a foundation for moral laws. For the universality with which these should hold for all rational beings without distinction, the unconditional practical necessity which is thereby imposed on them is lost when their foundation is taken from the *particular constitution of human nature* or the accidental circumstances in which it is placed. The principle of *private happiness*, however, is the most objectionable, not merely because it is false, and experience contradicts the supposition that prosperity is always proportioned to good conduct, not yet merely because it contributes nothing to the establishment of morality—since it is quite a different thing to make a prosperous man and a good man, or to make one prudent and sharp-sighted for his own interests, and to make him virtuous—but because the springs it provides for morality are such as rather undermine it and destroy its sublimity, since they put the motives to virtue and to vice in the same class, and only teach us to make a better calculation, the specific difference between virtue and vice being entirely extinguished. On the other hand, as to moral feeling, this supposed special sense,[21] the appeal to it is indeed superficial when those who cannot *think* believe that *feeling* will help them out, even in what

---

21 I class the principle of moral feeling under that of happiness, because every empirical interest promises to contribute to our well-being by the agreeableness that a thing affords, whether it be immediately and without a view to profit, or whether profit be regarded. We must likewise, with Hutcheson, class the principle of sympathy with the happiness of others under his assumed moral sense.

concerns general laws; and besides, feelings which naturally differ infinitely in degree cannot furnish a uniform standard of good and evil, nor has anyone a right to form judgments for others by his own feelings; nevertheless this moral feeling is nearer to morality and its dignity in this respect that it pays virtue the honor of ascribing to her *immediately* the satisfaction and esteem we have for her, and does not, as it were, tell her to her face that we are not attached to her by her beauty but by profit.

Among the *rational* principles of morality, the ontological conception of *perfection,* notwithstanding its defects, is better than the theological conception which derives morality from a Divine absolutely perfect will. The former is, no doubt, empty and indefinite, and consequently useless for finding in the boundless field of possible reality the greatest amount suitable for us; moreover, in attempting to distinguish specifically the reality of which we are now speaking from every other, it inevitably tends to turn in a circle and cannot avoid tacitly presupposing the morality which it is to explain; it is nevertheless preferable to the theological view, first, because we have no intuition of the Divine perfection, and can only deduce it from our own conceptions the most important of which is that of morality, and our explanation would thus be involved in a gross circle; and, in the next place, if we avoid this, the only notion of the Divine will remaining to us is a conception made up of the attributes of desire of glory and dominion, combined with the awful conceptions of might and vengeance, and any system of morals erected on this foundation would be directly opposed to morality.

However, if I had to choose between the notion of the moral sense and that of perfection in general (two systems which at least do not weaken morality, although they are totally incapable of serving as its foundation), then I should decide for the latter, because it at least withdraws the decision of the question from the sensibility and brings it to the court of pure reason; and although even here it decides nothing, it at all events preserves the indefinite idea (of a will good in itself) free from corruption, until it shall be more precisely defined.

For the rest I think I may be excused here from a detailed refutation of all these doctrines; that would only be superfluous labor, since it is so easy, and is probably so well seen even by those whose office requires them to decide for one of those theories (because their hearers would not tolerate suspension of judgments). But what interests us more here is to know that the prime foundation of morality laid down by all these principles is nothing but heteronomy of the will, and for this reason they must necessarily miss their aim.

In every case where an object of the will has to be supposed, in order that the rule may be prescribed which is to determine the will, there the rule is simply heteronomy; the imperative is conditional, namely, *if* or *because* one wishes for this object, one should act so and so; hence it can never command morally, that is, categorically. Whether the object determines the will by means of inclination, as in the principle of private happiness, or by means of reason directed to objects of our possible volition generally, as in the principle of perfection, in either case the will never determines itself *immediately* by the conception of the action, but only by the influence which the foreseen effect of the action has on the will; *I ought to do something, on this account, because I wish for something else;* and here there must be yet another law assumed in me as its subject, by which I necessarily will this other thing, and this law again requires an imperative to restrict this maxim. For the influence which the conception of an object within the reach of our faculties can exercise on the will of the subject in consequence of its natural properties, depends on the nature of the subject, either the sensibility (inclination and taste) or the understanding and reason, the employment of which is by the peculiar constitution of their nature attended with satisfaction. It follows that the law would be, properly speaking, given by nature, and as such it must be known and proved by experience, and would consequently be contingent, and therefore incapable of being an apodictic practical rule, such as the moral rule must be. Not only so, but it is *inevitably only heteronomy;* the will does not give itself the law, but it is given by a foreign impulse by means of a particular natural constitution of the subject adapted to receive it. An absolutely good will, then, the principle of which must be a categorical imperative, will be indeterminate as regards all objects, and will contain merely the *form of volition* generally, and that as autonomy, that is to say, the capability of the maxims of every good will to make themselves a universal law, is itself the only law which the will of every rational being imposes on itself, without needing to assume any spring or interest as a foundation.

How such a synthetical practical a priori proposition is possible, and why it is necessary, is a problem whose solution does not lie within the bounds of the metaphysic of morals; and we have not here affirmed its truth, much less professed to have a proof of it in our power. We simply showed by the development of the universally received notion of morality that an autonomy of the will is inevitably connected with it, or rather is its foundation. Whoever then holds morality to be anything real, and not a chimerical idea without any truth, must likewise admit the principle of it that is here assigned. This section, then, like the first, was merely analytical. Now to prove that morality is no creation of the brain, which it cannot be if the categorical imperative and with it the autonomy of the will is true, and as an *a priori* principle absolutely necessary, this supposes the *possibility of a synthetic use of pure practical reason,* which, however, we cannot venture on without first giving a critical examination of this faculty of reason. In the concluding section we shall give the principal outlines of this critical examination as far as is sufficient for our purpose.

John Stuart Mill (1806–1873)

John Stuart Mill had the fortune (or misfortune, as the case may be) to be an intellectual prodigy by both birth and training. In London his father James Mill, also a philosopher, taught young Mill Greek and mathematics when he was three, and Latin, logic, and political economy when he was thirteen. At home Mill was also deeply influenced by Jeremy Bentham, a family friend now famous in the history of philosophy as Mill's predecessor in the development of utilitarianism. Two events ultimately broadened and helped to humanize Mill's life as well as his philosophical outlook: a period of depression that overcame him when he was twenty-one and from which he slowly recovered and his friendship with and ultimate marriage to Harriet Taylor. Jointly they wrote the essay *On Liberty* (1859). Important books that Mill wrote prior to this were his *System of Logic* (1843) and *The Principles of Political Economy* (1848). In his later years Mill became an eloquent spokesman, both in writings and during one term in Parliament, for humanistic reform and liberal open-mindedness. Along with *On Liberty, Utilitarianism,* first published in 1863 in a magazine, exemplifies Mill's enthusiasm and hope that knowledge and clear thinking eventually can remove the ills of human society. Mill's other important works are *Considerations on Representative Government* (1861), *Examination of Sir William Hamilton's Philosophy* (1865), and his *Autobiography* published immediately after his death.

Mill's utilitarianism was influenced by, but critical of, Jeremy Bentham's *An Introduction to the Principles of Morals and Legislation* (1789), especially Chapters I–IV. Book IV of *The Methods of Ethics* (1874) by Henry Sidgwick is a famous examination of utilitarianism. Chapters I and II of G. E. Moore's *Ethics* (1912) comprise a precise statement of a version of utilitarianism. Chapter 3 of W. Frankena's *Ethics* (1963) discusses utilitarianism. *John Stuart Mill: Utilitarianism with Critical Essays* (1971), edited by S. Gorowitz, contains twenty-eight essays on the topic by contemporary philosophers. *Mill's Utilitarianism: Text and Criticism* (1969), edited by James Smith and Ernest Sosa, contains selections from Bentham and Mill, together with seven critical essays. *Forms and Limits of Utilitarianism* (1965) by David Lyons is a relatively technical examination of act and rule utilitarianism. There also is *Utilitarianism: For and Against* (1973) by J. J. C. Smart and Bernard Williams in which Smart defends act utilitarianism and Williams criticizes utilitarianism in general.

Utilitarianism

CHAPTER I **General Remarks**

There are few circumstances among those which make up the present condition of human knowledge more unlike what might have been expected, or more significant of the backward state in which speculation on the most important subjects still lingers, than the little progress which has been made in the decision of the controversy respecting the criterion of right and wrong. From the dawn of philosophy, the question concerning the *summum bonum,* or, what is the same thing, concerning the foundation of morality, has been accounted the main problem in speculative thought, has occupied the most gifted intellects and divided them into sects and schools carrying on a vigorous warfare against one another. And after more than two thousand years the same discussions continue, philosophers are still ranged under the same contending banners, and neither thinkers nor mankind at large seem nearer to being unanimous on the subject than when the youth Socrates listened to the old Protagoras and asserted (if Plato's dialogue be grounded on a real conversation) the theory of utilitarianism against the popular morality of the so-called sophist.

It is true that similar confusion and uncertainty and, in some cases, similar discordance exist respecting the first principles of all the sciences, not excepting that which is deemed the most certain of them— mathematics, without much impairing, generally indeed without impairing at all, the trustworthiness of the conclusions of those sciences. An apparent anomaly, the explanation of which is that the detailed doctrines of a science are not usually deduced from, nor depend for their evidence upon, what are called its first principles. Were it not so, there would be no science more precarious, or whose conclusions were more insufficiently made out, than algebra, which derives none of its certainty from what are commonly taught to learners as its elements, since these, as laid down by some of its most eminent teachers, are as full of fictions as English law, and of mysteries as theology. The truths which are ultimately accepted as the first principles of a science are really the last results of metaphysical analysis practiced on the elementary notions with which the science is conversant; and their relation to the science is not that of foundations to an edifice, but of roots to a tree, which may perform their office equally well though they be

242

never dug down to and exposed to light. But though in science the particular truths precede the general theory, the contrary might be expected to be the case with a practical art, such as morals or legislation. All action is for the sake of some end, and rules of action, it seems natural to suppose, must take their whole character and color from the end to which they are subservient. When we engage in a pursuit, a clear and precise conception of what we are pursuing would seem to be the first thing we need, instead of the last we are to look forward to. A test of right and wrong must be the means, one would think, of ascertaining what is right or wrong, and not a consequence of having already ascertained it.

The difficulty is not avoided by having recourse to the popular theory of a natural faculty, a sense or instinct, informing us of right and wrong. For—besides that the existence of such a moral instinct is itself one of the matters in dispute—those believers in it who have any pretensions to philosophy have been obliged to abandon the idea that it discerns what is right or wrong in the particular case in hand, as our other senses discern the sight or sound actually present. Our moral faculty, according to all those of its interpreters who are entitled to the name of thinkers, supplies us only with the general principles of moral judgments; it is a branch of our reason, not of our sensitive faculty, and must be looked to for the abstract doctrines of morality, not for perception of it in the concrete. The intuitive, no less than what may be termed the inductive, school of ethics insists on the necessity of general laws. They both agree that the morality of an individual action is not a question of direct perception, but of the application of a law to an individual case. They recognize also, to a great extent, the same moral laws, but differ as to their evidence and the source from which they derive their authority. According to the one opinion, the principles of morals are evident *a priori*, requiring nothing to command assent except that the meaning of the terms be understood. According to the other doctrine, right and wrong, as well as truth and falsehood, are questions of observation and experience. But both hold equally that morality must be deduced from principles; and the intuitive school affirm as strongly as the inductive that there is a science of morals. Yet they seldom attempt to make out a list of the *a priori* principles which are to serve as the premises of the science; still more rarely do they make any effort to reduce those various principles to one first principle or common ground of obligation. They either assume the ordinary precepts of morals as of *a priori* authority, or they lay down as the common groundwork of those maxims some generality much less obviously authoritative than the maxims themselves, and which has never succeeded in gaining popular acceptance. Yet to support their pretensions there ought either to be some one fundamental principle or law at the root of all morality, or, if there be several, there should be a determinate order of precedence among them; and the one principle, or the rule for deciding between the various principles when they conflict, ought to be self-evident.

To inquire how far the bad effects of this deficiency have been mitigated in practice, or to what extent the moral beliefs of mankind have been vitiated or made uncertain by the absence of any distinct recognition of an ultimate standard, would imply a complete survey and criticism of past and present ethical doctrine. It would, however, be easy to show that whatever steadiness or consistency these moral beliefs have attained has been mainly due to the tacit influence of a standard not recognized. Although the nonexistence of an acknowledged first principle has made ethics not so much a guide as a consecration of men's actual sentiments, still, as men's sentiments, both of favor and of aversion, are greatly influenced by what they suppose to be the effects of things upon their happiness, the principle of utility, or, as Bentham latterly called it, the greatest happiness principle, has had a large share in forming the moral doctrines even of those who must scornfully reject its authority. Nor is there any school of thought which refuses to admit that the influence of actions on happiness is a most material and even predominant consideration in many of the details of morals however unwilling to acknowledge it as the fundamental principle of morality and the source of moral obligation. I might go much further and say that to all those *a priori* moralists who deem it necessary to argue at all, utilitarian arguments are indispensable. It is not my present purpose to criticize these thinkers; but I cannot help referring, for illustration, to a systematic treatise by one of the most illustrious of them, the *Metaphysics of Ethics* by Kant. This remarkable man, whose system of thought will long remain one of the landmarks in the history of philosophical speculation, does, in the treatise in question, lay down a universal first principle as the origin and ground of moral obligation; it is this: 'So act that the rule on which thou actest would admit of being adopted as a law by all rational beings.' But when he begins to deduce from this precept any of the actual duties of morality, he fails, almost grotesquely, to show that there would be any contradiction, any logical (not to say physical) impossibility, in the adoption by all rational beings of the most outrageously immoral rules of conduct. All he shows is that the *consequences* of their universal adoption would be such as no one would choose to incur.

On the present occasion, I shall, without further discussion of the other theories, attempt to contribute something toward the understanding and appreciation of the 'utilitarian' or 'happiness' theory, and toward such proof as it is susceptible of. It is evident that this cannot be proof in the ordinary and popular meaning of the term. Questions of ultimate ends are not amenable to direct proof. Whatever can be proved to be good must be so by being shown to be a means to something admitted to be good without proof. The medical art is proved to be good by its conducing to health; but how is it possible to prove that health is good? The art of music is good, for the reason, among others, that it produces pleasure; but what proof is it possible to give that pleasure is good? If, then, it is asserted that there is a comprehensive formula, including all things which are in themselves good, and that whatever else is good is not so as an end but as a means, the formula may be accepted or rejected, but is not a subject of what is commonly understood by proof. We are not, however, to infer that its acceptance or rejection must depend on blind impulse or arbitrary choice. There is a larger meaning of the word 'proof,' in which this question is as amenable to it as any other of the disputed questions of philosophy. The subject is within the cognizance of the rational faculty; and neither does that faculty deal with it solely in the way of intuition. Considerations may be presented capable of determining the intellect either to give or withhold its assent to the doctrine; and this is equivalent to proof.

We shall examine presently of what nature are these considerations; in what manner they apply to the case, and what rational grounds, therefore, can be given for accepting or rejecting the utilitarian formula. But it is a preliminary condition of rational acceptance or rejection that the formula should be correctly understood. I believe that the very imperfect notion ordinarily formed of its meaning is the chief obstacle which impedes its reception, and that, could it be cleared even from only the grosser misconceptions, the question would be greatly simplified and a large proportion of its difficulties removed. Before, therefore, I attempt to enter into the philosophical grounds which can be given for assenting to the utilitarian standard, I shall offer some illustrations of the doctrine itself, with the view of showing more clearly what it is, distinguishing it from what it is not, and disposing of such of the practical objections to it as either originate in, or are closely connected with, mistaken interpretations of its meaning. Having thus prepared the ground, I shall afterwards endeavor to throw such light as I can call upon the question considered as one of philosophical theory.

CHAPTER II **What Utilitarianism Is**

A passing remark is all that needs be given to the ignorant blunder of supposing that those who stand up for utility as the test of right and wrong use the term in that restricted and merely colloquial sense in which utility is opposed to pleasure. An apology is due to the philosophical opponents of utilitarianism for even the momentary appearance of confounding them with anyone capable of so absurd a misconception; which is the more extraordinary, inasmuch as the contrary accusation, of referring everything to pleasure, and that, too, in its grossest form, is another of the common charges against utilitarianism: and, as has been pointedly remarked by an able writer, the same sort of persons, and often the very same persons, denounce the theory 'as impracticably dry when the word "utility" precedes the word "pleasure," and as too practicably voluptuous when the word "pleasure" precedes the word "utility." ' Those who know anything about the matter are aware that every writer, from Epicurus to Bentham, who maintained the theory of utility meant by it, not something to be contradistinguished from pleasure, but pleasure itself, together with exemption from pain; and instead of opposing the useful to the agreeable or the ornamental, have always declared that the useful means these, among other things. Yet the common herd, including the herd of writers, not only in newspapers and periodicals, but in books of weight and pretension, are perpetually falling into this shallow mistake. Having caught up the word 'utilitarian,' while knowing nothing whatever about it but its sound, they habitually express by it the rejection or the neglect of pleasure in some of its forms: of beauty, of ornament, or of amusement. Nor is the term thus ignorantly misapplied solely in disparagement, but occasionally in compliment, as though it implied superiority to frivolity and the mere pleasures of the moment. And this perverted use is the only one in which the word is popularly known, and the one from which the new generation are acquiring their sole notion of its meaning. Those who introduced the word, but who had for many years discontinued it as a distinctive appellation, may well feel themselves called upon to resume it if by doing so they can hope to contribute anything toward rescuing it from this utter degradation.[1]

The creed which accepts as the foundation of morals 'utility' or the 'greatest happiness principle' holds that actions are right in proportion as they tend to promote happiness; wrong as they tend to produce the reverse of happiness. By happiness is intended pleasure and the absence of pain; by unhappiness, pain and the privation of pleasure. To give a clear view of the moral standard set up by the theory, much more requires to be said; in particular, what things it includes in the ideas of pain and pleasure, and to what extent this is left an open question. But

---

[1] The author of this essay has reason for believing himself to be the first person who brought the word 'utilitarian' into use. He did not invent it, but adopted it from a passing expression in Mr. Galt's *Annals of the Parish*. After using it as a designation for several years, he and others abandoned it from a growing dislike to anything resembling a badge or watchword of sectarian distinction. But as a name for one single opinion, not a set of opinions—to denote the recognition of utility as a standard, not any particular way of applying it—the term supplies a want in the language, and offers, in many cases, a convenient mode of avoiding tiresome circumlocution.

these supplementary explanations do not affect the theory of life on which this theory of morality is grounded—namely, that pleasure and freedom from pain are the only things desirable as ends; and that all desirable things (which are as numerous in the utilitarian as in any other scheme) are desirable either for pleasure inherent in themselves or as means to the promotion of pleasure and the prevention of pain.

Now such a theory of life excites in many minds, and among them in some of the most estimable in feeling and purpose, inveterate dislike. To suppose that life has (as they express it) no higher end than pleasure —no better and nobler object of desire and pursuit—they designate as utterly mean and groveling, as a doctrine worthy only of swine, to whom the followers of Epicurus were, at a very early period, contemptuously likened; and modern holders of the doctrine are occasionally made the subject of equally polite comparisons by its German, French, and English assailants.

When thus attacked, the Epicureans have always answered that it is not they, but their accusers, who represent human nature in a degrading light, since the accusation supposes human beings to be capable of no pleasures except those of which swine are capable. If this supposition were true, the charge could not be gainsaid, but would then be no longer an imputation; for if the sources of pleasure were precisely the same to human beings and to swine, the rule of life which is good enough for the one would be good enough for the other. The comparison of the Epicurean life to that of beasts is felt as degrading, precisely because a beast's pleasures do not satisfy a human being's conceptions of happiness. Human beings have faculties more elevated than the animal appetites and, when once made conscious of them, do not regard anything as happiness which does not include their gratification. I do not, indeed, consider the Epicureans to have been by any means faultless in drawing out their scheme of consequences from the utilitarian principle. To do this in any sufficient manner, many Stoic, as well as Christian, elements require to be included. But there is no known Epicurean theory of life which does not assign to the pleasures of the intellect, of the feelings and imagination, and of the moral sentiments a much higher value as pleasures than to those of mere sensation. It must be admitted, however, that utilitarian writers in general have placed the superiority of mental over bodily pleasures chiefly in the greater permanency, safety, uncostliness, etc., of the former—that is, in their circumstantial advantages rather than in their intrinsic nature. And on all these points utilitarians have fully proved their case; but they might have taken the other and, as it may be called, higher ground with entire consistency. It is quite compatible with the principle of utility to recognize the fact that some kinds of pleasure are more desirable and more valuable than others. It would be absurd that, while in estimating all other things quality is considered as well as quantity, the estimation of pleasure should be supposed to depend on quantity alone.

If I am asked what I mean by difference of quality in pleasures, or what makes one pleasure more valuable than another, merely as a pleasure, except its being greater in amount, there is but one possible answer. Of two pleasures, if there be one to which all or almost all who have experience of both give a decided preference, irrespective of any feeling of moral obligation to prefer it, that is the more desirable pleasure. If one of the two is, by those who are competently acquainted with both, placed so far above the other that they prefer it, even though knowing it to be attended with a greater amount of discontent, and would not resign it for any quantity of the other pleasure which their nature is capable of, we are justified in ascribing to the preferred enjoyment a superiority in quality so far outweighing quantity as to render it, in comparison, of small account.

Now it is an unquestionable fact that those who are equally acquainted with and equally capable of appreciating and enjoying both do give a most marked preference to the manner of existence which employs their higher faculties. Few human creatures would consent to be changed into any of the lower animals for a promise of the fullest allowance of a beast's pleasures; no intelligent human being would consent to be a fool, no instructed person would be an ignoramus, no person of feeling and conscience would be selfish and base, even though they should be persuaded that the fool, the dunce, or the rascal is better satisfied with his lot than they are with theirs. They would not resign what they possess more than he for the most complete satisfaction of all the desires which they have in common with him. If they ever fancy they would, it is only in cases of unhappiness so extreme that to escape from it they would exchange their lot for almost any other, however undesirable in their own eyes. A being of higher faculties requires more to make him happy, is capable probably of more acute suffering, and certainly accessible to it at more points, than one of an inferior type; but in spite of these liabilities, he can never really wish to sink into what he feels to be a lower grade of existence. We may give what explanation we please of this unwillingness; we may attribute it to pride, a name which is given indiscriminately to some of the most and to some of the least estimable feelings of which mankind are capable; we may refer it to the love of liberty and personal independence, an appeal to which was with the Stoics one of the most effective means for the inculcation of it; to the love of power or to the love of excitement, both of which do really enter into and contribute to it; but its most appropriate appellation is a sense of dignity, which all human beings possess in one form or other, and in some, though by no means in exact, proportion to their higher faculties, and which is so essential a part of the happiness of those in whom it is strong that nothing which conflicts with it could be otherwise than momentarily an object of desire to them. Whoever supposes that this preference takes place at a sacrifice of happiness—that the superior being, in anything like equal circumstances, is not happier than the inferior—confounds the two very different ideas of happiness and content. It is indisputable that the being whose capacities of enjoyment are low has the greatest chance of having them fully satisfied; and a highly endowed being will always feel that any happiness which he can look for, as the world is constituted, is imperfect. But he can learn to bear its imperfections, if they are at all bearable; and they will not make him envy the being who is indeed unconscious of the imperfections, but only because he feels not at all the good which those imperfections qualify. It is better to be a human being dissatisfied than a pig satisfied; better to be Socrates dissatisfied than a fool satisfied. And if the fool, or the pig, are of a different opinion, it is because they only know their own side of the question. The other party to the comparison knows both sides.

It may be objected that many who are capable of the higher pleasures occasionally, under the influence of temptation, postpone them to the lower. But this is quite compatible with a full appreciation of the intrinsic superiority of the higher. Men often, from infirmity of character, make their election for the nearer good, though they know it to be the less valuable; and this no less when the choice is between two bodily pleasures than when it is between bodily and mental. They pursue sensual indulgences to the injury of health, though perfectly aware that health is the greater good. It may be further objected that many who begin with youthful enthusiasm for everything noble, as they advance in years, sink into indolence and selfishness. But I do not believe that those who undergo this very common change voluntarily choose the lower description of pleasures in preference to the higher. I believe that, before they devote themselves exclusively to the one, they have already become incapable of the other. Capacity for the nobler feelings is in most natures a very tender plant, easily killed, not only by hostile influences, but by mere want of sustenance; and in the majority of young persons it speedily dies away if the occupations to which their position in life has devoted them, and the society into which it has thrown them, are not favorable to keeping that higher capacity in exercise. Men lose their high aspirations as they lose their intellectual tastes, because they have not time or opportunity for indulging them; and they addict themselves to inferior pleasures, not because they deliberately prefer them, but because they are either the only ones to which they have access or the only ones which they are any longer capable of enjoying. It may be questioned whether anyone who has remained equally susceptible to both classes of pleasures ever knowingly and calmly preferred the lower, though many, in all ages, have broken down in an ineffectual attempt to combine both.

From this verdict of the only competent judges, I apprehend there can be no appeal. On a question which is the best worth having of two pleasures, or which of two modes of existence is the most grateful to the feelings, apart from its moral attributes and from its consequences, the judgment of those who are qualified by knowledge of both, or, if they differ, that of the majority among them, must be admitted as final. And there needs be the less hesitation to accept this judgment respecting the quality of pleasures, since there is no other tribunal to be referred to even on the question of quantity. What means are there of determining which is the acutest of two pains, or the intensest of two pleasurable sensations, except the general suffrage of those who are familiar with both? Neither pains nor pleasures are homogeneous, and pain is always heterogeneous with pleasure. What is there to decide whether a particular pleasure is worth purchasing at the cost of a particular pain, except the feelings and judgment of the experienced? When, therefore, those feelings and judgment declare the pleasures derived from the higher faculties to be preferable *in kind,* apart from the question of intensity, to those of which the animal nature, disjoined from the higher faculties, is susceptible, they are entitled on this subject to the same regard.

I have dwelt on this point as being a necessary part of a perfectly just conception of utility or happiness considered as the directive rule of human conduct. But it is by no means an indispensable condition to the acceptance of the utilitarian standard; for that standard is not the agent's own greatest happiness, but the greatest amount of happiness altogether; and if it may possibly be doubted whether a noble character is always the happier for its nobleness, there can be no doubt that it makes other people happier, and that the world in general is immensely a gainer by it. Utilitarianism, therefore, could only attain its end by the general cultivation of nobleness of character, even if each individual were only benefited by the nobleness of others, and his own, so far as happiness is concerned, were a sheer deduction from the benefit. But the bare enunciation of such an absurdity as this last renders refutation superfluous.

According to the greatest happiness principle, as above explained, the ultimate end, with reference to and for the sake of which all other things are desirable—whether we are considering our own good or that of other people—is an existence exempt as far as possible from pain, and as rich as possible in enjoyments, both in point of quantity and quality; the test of quality and the rule for measuring it against quantity being the preference felt by those who, in their opportunities of experience, to which must be added their habits of self-consciousness and self-observation, are best furnished with the means of comparison. This, being according to the utilitarian opinion the end of human action, is necessarily also the standard of morality, which may accordingly be defined 'the rules and precepts for human conduct,' by the observance of which an existence such as has been described might be, to the greatest extent possible, secured to all mankind; and not to them only, but, so far as the nature of things admits, to the whole sentient creation.

Against this doctrine, however, arises another class of objectors who say that happiness, in any form, cannot be the rational purpose of human life and action; because, in the first place, it is unattainable; and they contemptuously ask, What right hast thou to be happy?—a question which Mr. Carlyle clinches by the addition, What right, a short time ago, hadst thou even *to be?* Next they say that men can do *without* happiness; that all noble human beings have felt this, and could not have become noble but by learning the lesson of *Entsagen,* or renunciation; which lesson, thoroughly learned and submitted to, they affirm to be the beginning and necessary condition of all virtue.

The first of these objections would go to the root of the matter were it well founded; for if no happiness is to be had at all by human beings, the attainment of it cannot be the end of morality or of any rational conduct. Though, even in that case, something might still be said for the utilitarian theory, since utility includes not solely the pursuit of happiness, but the prevention or mitigation of unhappiness; and if the former aim be chimerical, there will be all the greater scope and more imperative need for the latter, so long at least as mankind think fit to live and do not take refuge in the simultaneous act of suicide recommended under certain conditions by Novalis. When, however, it is thus positively asserted to be impossible that human life should be happy, the assertion, if not something like a verbal quibble, is at least an exaggeration. If by happiness be meant a continuity of highly pleasurable excitement, it is evident enough that this is impossible. A state of exalted pleasure lasts only moments or in some cases, and with some intermissions, hours or days, and is the occasional brilliant flash of enjoyment, not its permanent and steady flame. Of this the philosophers who have taught that happiness is the end of life were as fully aware as those who taunt them. The happiness which they meant was not a life of rapture, but moments of such, in an existence made up of few and transitory pains, many and various pleasures, with a decided predominance of the active over the passive, and having as the foundation of the whole not to expect more from life than it is capable of bestowing. A life thus composed, to those who have been fortunate enough to obtain it, has always appeared worthy of the name of happiness. And such an existence is even now the lot of many during some considerable portion of their lives. The present wretched education and wretched social arrangements are the only real hindrance to its being attainable by almost all.

The objectors perhaps may doubt whether human beings, if taught to consider happiness as the end of life, would be satisfied with such a moderate share of it. But great numbers of mankind have been satisfied with much less. The main constituents of a satisfied life appear to be two, either of which by itself is often found sufficient for the purpose: tranquillity and excitement. With much tranquillity, many find that they can be content with very little pleasure; with much excitement, many can reconcile themselves to a considerable quantity of pain. There is assuredly no inherent impossibility of enabling even the mass of mankind to unite both, since the two are so far from being incompatible that they are in natural alliance, the prolongation of either being a preparation for, and exciting a wish for, the other. It is only those in whom indolence amounts to a vice that do not desire excitement after an interval of repose; it is only those in whom the need of excitement is a disease that feel the tranquillity which follows excitement dull and insipid, instead of pleasurable in direct proportion to the excitement which preceded it. When people who are tolerably fortunate in their outward lot do not find in life sufficient enjoyment to make it valuable to them, the cause generally is caring for nobody but themselves. To those who have neither public nor private affections, the excitements of life are much curtailed, and in any case dwindle in value as the time approaches when all selfish interests must be terminated by death; while those who leave after them objects of personal affection, and especially those who have also cultivated a fellow-feeling with the collective interests of mankind, retain as lively an interest in life on the eve of death as in the vigor of youth and health. Next to selfishness, the principal cause which makes life unsatisfactory is want of mental cultivation. A cultivated mind—I do not mean that of a philosopher, but any mind to which the fountains of knowledge have been opened, and which has been taught, in any tolerable degree, to exercise its faculties—finds sources of inexhaustible interest in all that surrounds it: in the objects of nature, the achievements of art, the imaginations of poetry, the incidents of history, the ways of mankind, past and present, and their prospects in the future. It is possible, indeed, to become indifferent to all this, and that too without having exhausted a thousandth part of it, but only when one has had from the beginning no moral or human interest in these things and has sought in them only the gratification of curiosity.

Now there is absolutely no reason in the nature of things why an amount of mental culture sufficient to give an intelligent interest in these objects of contemplation should not be the inheritance of everyone born in a civilized country. As little is there an inherent necessity that any human being should be a selfish egotist, devoid of every feeling or care but those which center in his own miserable individuality. Something far superior to this is sufficiently common even now, to give ample earnest of what the human species may be made. Genuine private affections and a sincere interest in the public good are possible, though in unequal degrees, to every rightly brought up human being. In a world in which there is so much to interest, so much to enjoy, and so much also to correct and improve, everyone who has this moderate amount of moral and intellectual requisites is capable of an existence which may be called enviable; and unless such a person, through bad laws or subjection to the will of others, is denied the liberty to use the sources of happiness within his reach, he will not fail to find this enviable existence, if he escape the positive evils of life, the great sources of physical and mental suffering—such as indigence, disease, and the unkindness, worthlessness, or premature loss of objects of affection. The main stress of the problem lies, therefore, in the contest with these calamities from which it is a rare good fortune entirely to escape; which, as things now are, cannot be obviated, and often cannot be in any material degree mitigated. Yet no one whose opinion deserves a moment's consideration can doubt that most of the great positive evils of the world are in themselves removable, and will, if human affairs continue to improve, be in the end reduced within narrow limits. Poverty, in any sense implying suffering, may be completely extinguished by the wisdom of society combined with the good sense and providence of individuals. Even that most intractable of enemies, disease, may be indefinitely reduced in dimensions by good physical and moral education and proper control of noxious influences, while the progress of science holds out a promise for the future of still more direct conquests over this detestable foe. And every advance in that direction relieves us from some, not only of the chances which cut short our own lives, but, what concerns us still more, which deprive us of those in whom our happiness is wrapt up. As for vicissitudes of fortune and other disappointments connected with worldly circumstances, these are principally the effect either of gross imprudence, of ill-regulated desires, or of bad or imperfect social institutions. All the grand sources, in short, of human suffering are in a great degree, many of them almost entirely, conquerable by human care and effort; and though their removal is grievously slow—though a long succession of generations will perish in the breach before the conquest is completed, and this world becomes all that, if will and knowledge were not wanting, it might easily be made—yet every mind sufficiently intelligent and generous to bear a part, however small and inconspicuous, in the endeavor will draw a noble enjoyment from the contest itself, which he would not for any bribe in the form of selfish indulgence consent to be without.

And this leads to the true estimation of what is said by the objectors concerning the possibility and the obligation of learning to do without happiness. Unquestionably it is possible to do without happiness; it is done involuntarily by nineteen-twentieths of mankind, even in those parts of our present world which are least deep in barbarism;

and it often has to be done voluntarily by the hero or the martyr, for the sake of something which he prizes more than his individual happiness. But this something, what is it, unless the happiness of others or some of the requisites of happiness? It is noble to be capable of resigning entirely one's own portion of happiness, or chances of it; but, after all, this self-sacrifice must be for some end; it is not its own end; and if we are told that its end is not happiness but virtue, which is better than happiness, I ask, would the sacrifice be made if the hero or martyr did not believe that it would earn for others immunity from similar sacrifices? Would it be made if he thought that his renunciation of happiness for himself would produce no fruit for any of his fellow creatures, but to make their lot like his and place them also in the condition of persons who have renounced happiness? All honor to those who can abnegate for themselves the personal enjoyment of life when by such renunciation they contribute worthily to increase the amount of happiness in the world; but he who does it or professes to do it for any other purpose is no more deserving of admiration than the ascetic mounted on his pillar. He may be an inspiriting proof of what men *can* do, but assuredly not an example of what they *should*.

Though it is only in a very imperfect state of the world's arrangements that anyone can best serve the happiness of others by the absolute sacrifice of his own, yet, so long as the world is in that imperfect state, I fully acknowledge that the readiness to make such a sacrifice is the highest virtue which can be found in man. I will add that in this condition of the world, paradoxical as the assertion may be, the conscious ability to do without happiness gives the best prospect of realizing such happiness as is attainable. For nothing except that consciousness can raise a person above the chances of life by making him feel that, let fate and fortune do their worst, they have not power to subdue him; which, once felt, frees him from excess of anxiety concerning the evils of life and enables him, like many a Stoic in the worst times of the Roman Empire, to cultivate in tranquillity the sources of satisfaction accessible to him, without concerning himself about the uncertainty of their duration any more than about their inevitable end.

Meanwhile, let utilitarians never cease to claim the morality of self-devotion as a possession which belongs by as good a right to them as either to the Stoic or to the Transcendentalist. The utilitarian morality does recognize in human beings the power of sacrificing their own greatest good for the good of others. It only refuses to admit that the sacrifice is itself a good. A sacrifice which does not increase or tend to increase the sum total of happiness, it considers as wasted. The only self-renunciation which it applauds is devotion to the happiness, or to some of the means of happiness, of others, either of mankind collectively or of individuals within the limits imposed by the collective interests of mankind.

I must again repeat what the assailants of utilitarianism seldom have the justice to acknowledge, that the happiness which forms the utilitarian standard of what is right in conduct is not the agent's own happiness but that of all concerned. As between his own happiness and that of others, utilitarianism requires him to be as strictly impartial as a disinterested and benevolent spectator. In the golden rule of Jesus of Nazareth, we read the complete spirit of the ethics of utility. 'To do as you would be done by,' and 'to love your neighbor as yourself,' constitute the ideal perfection of utilitarian morality. As the means of making the nearest approach to this ideal, utility would enjoin, first, that laws and social arrangements should place the happiness or (as, speaking practically, it may be called) the interest of every individual as nearly as possible in harmony with the interest of the whole; and, secondly, that education and opinion, which have so vast a power over human character, should so use that power as to establish in the mind of every individual an indissoluble association between his own happiness and the good of the whole, especially between his own happiness and the practice of such modes of conduct, negative and positive, as regard for the universal happiness prescribes; so that not only he may be unable to conceive the possibility of happiness to himself, consistently with conduct opposed to the general good, but also that a direct impulse to promote the general good may be in every individual one of the habitual motives of action, and the sentiments connected therewith may fill a large and prominent place in every human being's sentient existence. If the impugners of the utilitarian morality represented it to their own minds in this its true character, I know not what recommendation possessed by any other morality they could possibly affirm to be wanting to it; what more beautiful or more exalted developments of human nature any other ethical system can be supposed to foster, or what springs of action, not accessible to the utilitarian, such systems rely on for giving effect to their mandates.

The objectors to utilitarianism cannot always be charged with representing it in a discreditable light. On the contrary, those among them who entertain anything like a just idea of its disinterested character sometimes find fault with its standard as being too high for humanity. They say it is exacting too much to require that people shall always act from the inducement of promoting the general interests of society. But this is to mistake the very meaning of a standard of morals and confound the rule of action with the motive of it. It is the business of ethics to tell us what are our duties, or by what test we may know them; but no system of ethics requires that the sole motive of all we do shall be a feeling of duty; on the contrary, ninety-nine hundredths of all our actions are done from other motives, and rightly so done if the rule of duty does not condemn them. It is the more unjust to utilitarianism that this particular misapprehension should be made a ground of objection to it, inasmuch as utilitarian moralists have gone beyond almost all others in affirming that the motive has nothing to do with the morality of the action, though much with the worth of the agent. He who saves a fellow creature from drowning does what is morally right, whether his motive be duty or the hope of being paid for his trouble; he who betrays the friend that trusts him is guilty of a crime, even if his object be to serve another friend to whom he is under greater obligations. But to speak only of actions done from the motive of duty, and in direct obedience to principle: it is a misapprehension of the utilitarian mode of thought to conceive it as implying that people should fix their minds upon so wide a generality as the world, or society at large. The great majority of good actions are intended not for the benefit of the world, but for that of individuals, of which the good of the world is made up; and the thoughts of the most virtuous man need not on these occasions travel beyond the particular persons concerned, except so far as is necessary to assure himself that in benefiting them he is not violating the rights, that is, the legitimate and authorized expectations, of anyone else. The multiplication of happiness is, according to the utilitarian ethics, the object of virtue: the occasions on which any person (except one in a thousand) has it in his power to do this on an extended scale—in other words, to be a public benefactor—are but exceptional; and on these occasions alone is he called on to consider public utility; in every other case, private utility, the interest or happiness of some few persons, is all he has to attend to. Those alone the influence of whose actions extends to society in general need concern themselves habitually about so large an object. In the case of abstinences indeed—of things which people forbear to do from moral considerations, though the consequences in the particular case might be beneficial—it would be unworthy of an intelligent agent not to be consciously aware that the action is of a class which, if practiced generally, would be generally injurious, and that this is the ground of the obligation to abstain from it. The amount of regard for the public interest implied in this recognition is no greater than is demanded by every system of morals, for they all enjoin to abstain from whatever is manifestly pernicious to society.

The same considerations dispose of another reproach against the doctrine of utility, founded on a still grosser misconception of the purpose of a standard of morality and of the very meaning of the words 'right' and 'wrong.' It is often affirmed that utilitarianism renders men cold and unsympathizing; that it chills their moral feelings toward individuals; that it makes them regard only the dry and hard consideration of the consequences of actions, not taking into their moral estimate the qualities from which those actions emanate. If the assertion means that they do not allow their judgment respecting the rightness or wrongness of an action to be influenced by their opinion of the qualities of the person who does it, this is a complaint not against utilitarianism, but against any standard of morality at all; for certainly no known ethical standard decides an action to be good or bad because it is done by a good or a bad man, still less because done by an amiable, a brave, or a benevolent man, or the contrary. These considerations are relevant, not to the estimation of actions, but of persons; and there is nothing in the utilitarian theory inconsistent with the fact that there are other things which interest us in persons besides the rightness and wrongness of their actions. The Stoics, indeed, with the paradoxical misuse of language which was part of their system, and by which they strove to raise themselves above all concern about anything but virtue, were fond of saying that he who has that has everything; that he, and only he, is rich, is beautiful, is a king. But no claim of this description is made for the virtuous man by the utilitarian doctrine. Utilitarians are quite aware that there are other desirable possessions and qualities besides virtue, and are perfectly willing to allow to all of them their full worth. They are also aware that a right action does not necessarily indicate a virtuous character, and that actions which are blamable often proceed from qualities entitled to praise. When this is apparent in any particular case, it modifies their estimation, not certainly of the act, but of the agent. I grant that they are, notwithstanding, of opinion that in the long run the best proof of a good character is good actions; and resolutely refuse to consider any mental disposition as good of which the predominant tendency is to produce bad conduct. This makes them unpopular with many people, but it is an unpopularity which they must share with everyone who regards the distinction between right and wrong in a serious light; and the reproach is not one which a conscientious utilitarian need be anxious to repel.

If no more be meant by the objection than that many utilitarians look on the morality of actions, as measured by the utilitarian standards, with too exclusive a regard, and do not lay sufficient stress upon the other beauties of character which go toward making a human being lovable or admirable, this may be admitted. Utilitarians who have cultivated their moral feelings, but not their sympathies, nor their artistic perceptions, do fall into this mistake; and so do all other moralists under the same conditions. What can be said in excuse for other moralists is equally available for them, namely, that, if there is to be any error, it is better that it should be on that side. As a matter of fact, we may affirm that among utilitarians, as among adherents of other systems, there is every imaginable degree of rigidity and of laxity in the application of their standard; some are even puritanically rigorous, while others are as indulgent as can possibly be desired by sinner or by sentimentalist. But on the whole, a doctrine which brings prominently forward the interest that mankind have in the repression and prevention of conduct which violates the moral law is likely to be inferior to no other in turning the sanctions of opinion against such violations. It is true, the question 'What does violate the moral law?' is one on which those who recognize different standards of morality are likely now and then to differ. But difference of opinion on moral questions was not first introduced into the world by utilitarianism, while that doctrine does supply, if not always an easy, at all events a tangible and intelligible, mode of deciding such differences.

It may not be superfluous to notice a few more of the common misapprehensions of utilitarian ethics, even those which are so obvious and gross that it might appear impossible for any person of candor and intelligence to fall into them; since persons, even of considerable mental endowment, often give themselves so little trouble to understand the bearings of any opinion against which they entertain a prejudice, and men are in general so little conscious of this voluntary ignorance as a defect that the vulgarest misunderstandings of ethical doctrines are continually met with in the deliberate writings of persons of the greatest pretensions both to high principle and to philosophy. We not uncommonly hear the doctrine of utility inveighed against as a *godless* doctrine. If it be necessary to say anything at all against so mere an assumption, we may say that the question depends upon what idea we have formed of the moral character of the Deity. If it be a true belief that God desires, above all things, the happiness of his creatures, and that this was his purpose in their creation, utility is not only not a godless doctrine, but more profoundly religious than any other. If it be meant that utilitarianism does not recognize the revealed will of God as the supreme law of morals, I answer that a utilitarian who believes in the perfect goodness and wisdom of *God* necessarily believes that whatever God has thought fit to reveal on the subject of morals must fulfill the requirements of utility in a supreme degree. But others besides utilitarians have been of opinion that the Christian revelation was intended, and is fitted, to inform the hearts and minds of mankind with a spirit which should enable them to find for themselves what is right, and incline them to do it when found rather than to tell them except in a very general way, what it is; and that we need a doctrine of ethics, carefully followed out, to *interpret* to us the will of God. Whether this opinion is correct or not, it is superfluous here to discuss; since whatever aid religion, either natural or revealed, can afford to ethical investigation is as open to the utilitarian moralist as to any other. He can use it as the testimony of God to the usefulness or hurtfulness of any given course of action by as good a right as others can use it for the indication of a transcendental law having no connection with usefulness or with happiness.

Again, utility is often summarily stigmatized as an immoral doctrine by giving it the name of 'expediency,' and taking advantage of the popular use of that term to contrast it with principle. But the expedient, in the sense in which it is opposed to the right, generally means that which is expedient for the particular interest of the agent himself; as when a minister sacrifices the interests of his country to keep himself in place. When it means anything better than this, it means that which is expedient for some immediate object, some temporary purpose, but which violates a rule whose observance is expedient in a much higher degree. The expedient, in this sense, instead of being the same thing with the useful, is a branch of the hurtful. Thus it would often be expedient, for the purpose of getting over some momentary embarrassment, or attaining some object immediately useful to ourselves or others, to tell a lie. But inasmuch as the cultivation in ourselves of a sensitive feeling on the subject of veracity is one of the most useful, and the enfeeblement of that feeling one of the most hurtful, things to which our conduct can be instrumental; and inasmuch as any, even unintentional, deviation from truth does that much toward weakening the trustworthiness of human assertion, which is not only the principal support of all present social well-being, but the insufficiency of which does more than any one thing that can be named to keep back civilization, virtue, everything on which human happiness on the largest scale depends—we feel that the violation, for a present advantage, of a rule of such transcendent expediency is not expedient, and that he who, for the sake of convenience to himself or to some other individual, does what depends on him to deprive mankind of the good, and inflict upon them the evil, involved in the greater or less reliance which they can place in each other's word, acts the part of one of their worst enemies. Yet that even this rule, sacred as it is, admits of possible exceptions is acknowledged by all moralists; the chief of which is when the withholding of some fact (as of information from a malefactor, or of bad news from a person dangerously ill) would save an individual (especially an individual other than oneself) from great and unmerited evil, and when the withholding can only be effected by denial. But in order that the exception may not extend itself beyond the need, and may have the least possible effect in weakening reliance on veracity, it ought to be recognized, and, if possible, its limits defined; and, if the principle of utility is good for anything, it must be good for weighing these conflicting utilities against one another and marking out the region within which one or the other preponderates.

Again, defenders of utility often find themselves called upon to reply to such objections as this—that there is not time, previous to action, for calculating and weighing the effects of any line of conduct on the general happiness. This is exactly as if anyone were to say that it is impossible to guide our conduct by Christianity because there is not time, on every occasion on which anything has to be done, to read through the Old and New Testaments. The answer to the objection is that there has been ample time, namely, the whole past duration of the human species. During all that time mankind have been learning by experience the tendencies of actions; on which experience all the prudence as well as all the morality of life are dependent. People talk as if the commencement of this course of experience had hitherto been put off, and as if, at the moment when some man feels tempted to meddle with the property or life of another, he had to begin considering for the first time whether murder and theft are injurious to human happiness. Even then I do not think that he would find the question very puzzling; but, at all events, the matter is now done to his hand. It is truly a whimsical supposition that, if mankind were agreed in considering utility to be the test of morality, they would remain without any agreement as to what *is* useful, and would take no measures for having their notions on the subject taught to the young and enforced by law and opinion. There is no difficulty in proving any ethical standard whatever to work ill if we suppose universal idiocy to be conjoined with it; but on any hypothesis short of that, mankind must by this time have acquired positive beliefs as to the effects of some actions on their happiness; and the beliefs which have thus come down are the rules of morality for the multitude, and for the philosopher until he has succeeded in finding better. That philosophers might easily do this, even now, on many subjects; that the received code of ethics is by no means of divine right; and that mankind have still much to learn as to the effects of actions on the general happiness, I admit or rather earnestly maintain. The corollaries from the principle of utility, like the precepts of every practical art, admit of indefinite improvement, and, in a progressive state of the human mind, their improvement is perpetually going on. But to consider the rules of morality as improvable is one thing; to pass over the intermediate generalization entirely and endeavor to test each individual action directly by the first principle is another. It is a strange notion that the acknowledgement of a first principle is inconsistent with the admission of secondary ones. To inform a traveler respecting the place of his ultimate destination is not to forbid the use of landmarks and direction-posts on the way. The proposition that happiness is the end and aim of morality does not mean that no road ought to be laid down to that goal, or that persons going thither should not be advised to take one direction rather than another. Men really ought to leave off talking a kind of nonsense on this subject, which they would neither talk nor listen to on other matters of practical concernment. Nobody argues that the art of navigation is not founded on astronomy because sailors cannot wait to calculate the Nautical Almanac. Being rational creatures, they go to sea with it ready calculated; and all rational creatures go out upon the sea of life with their minds made up on the common questions of right and wrong, as well as on many of the far more difficult questions of wise and foolish. And this, as long as foresight is a human quality, it is to be presumed they will continue to do. Whatever we adopt as the fundamental principle of morality, we require subordinate principles to apply it by; the impossibility of doing without them, being common to all systems, can afford no argument against any one in particular; but gravely to argue as if no such secondary principles could be had, and as if mankind had remained till now, and always must remain, without drawing any general conclusions from the experience of human life is as high a pitch, I think, as absurdity has ever reached in philosophical controversy.

The remainder of the stock arguments against utilitarianism mostly consist in laying to its charge the common infirmities of human nature, and the general difficulties which embarrass conscientious persons in shaping their course through life. We are told that a utilitarian will be apt to make his own particular case an exception to moral rules, and, when under temptation, will see a utility in the breach of a rule, greater than he will see in its observance. But is utility the only creed which is able to furnish us with excuses for evil-doing and means of cheating our own conscience? They are afforded in abundance by all doctrines which recognize as a fact in morals the existence of conflicting considerations, which all doctrines do that have been believed by sane persons. It is not the fault of any creed, but of the complicated nature of human affairs, that rules of conduct cannot be so framed as to require no exceptions, and that hardly any kind of action can safely be laid down as either always obligatory or always condemnable. There is no ethical creed which does not temper the rigidity of its laws by giving a certain latitude, under the moral responsibility of the agent, for accommodation to peculiarities of circumstances; and under every creed, at the opening thus made, self-deception and dishonest casuistry get in. There exists no moral system under which there do not arise unequivocal cases of conflicting obligation. These are the real difficulties, the knotty points both in the theory of ethics and in the conscientious guidance of personal conduct. They are overcome practically, with greater or with less success, according to the intellect and virtue of the individual; but it can hardly be pretended that anyone will be the less qualified for dealing with them, from possessing an ultimate standard to which conflicting rights and duties can be referred. If utility is the ultimate source of moral obligations, utility may be invoked to decide between them when their demands are incompatible. Though the application of the standard may be difficult, it is better than none at all; while in other systems, the moral laws all claiming independent authority, there is no common umpire entitled to interfere between them; their claims to precedence one over another rest on little better than sophistry, and, unless determined, as they generally are, by the unacknowledged influence of consideration of utility, afford a free scope for the action of personal desires and partialities. We must remember that only in these cases of conflict between secondary principles is it requisite that first principles should be appealed to. There is no case of moral obligation in which some secondary principle is not involved; and if only one, there can seldom be any real doubt which one it is, in the mind of any person by whom the principle itself is recognized.

CHAPTER III **Of the Ultimate Sanction of the Principle of Utility**

The question is often asked, and properly so, in regard to any supposed moral standard—What is its sanction? what are the motives to obey? or, more specifically, what is the source of its obligation? whence does it derive its binding force? It is a necessary part of moral philosophy to provide the answer to this question, which, though frequently assuming the shape of an objection to the utilitarian morality, as if it had some special applicability to that above others, really arises in regard to all standards. It arises, in fact, whenever a person is called on to *adopt* a standard, or refer morality to any basis on which he has not been accustomed to rest it. For the customary morality, that which education and opinion have consecrated, is the only one which presents itself to the mind with the feeling of being *in itself* obligatory; and when a person is asked to believe that this morality *derives* its obligation from some general principle round which custom has not thrown the same halo, the assertion is to him a paradox; the supposed corollaries seem to have a more binding force than the original theorem; the superstructure seems to stand better without than with what is represented as its foundation. He says to himself, I feel that I am bound not to rob or murder, betray or deceive; but why am I bound to promote the general happiness? If my own happiness lies in something else, why may I not give that the preference?

If the view adopted by the utilitarian philosophy of the nature of the moral sense be correct, this difficulty will always present itself until the influences which form moral character have taken the same hold of the principle which they have taken of some of the consequences—until, by the improvement of education, the feeling of unity with our fellow creatures shall be (what it cannot be denied that Christ intended it to be) as deeply rooted in our character, and to our own consciousness as completely a part of our nature, as the horror of crime is in an ordinarily well-brought-up young person. In the meantime, however, the difficulty has no peculiar application to the doctrine of utility, but is inherent in every attempt to analyze morality and reduce it to principles; which, unless the principle is already in men's minds invested with as much sacredness as any of its applications, always seems to divest them of a part of their sanctity.

The principle of utility either has, or there is no reason why it might not have, all the sanctions which belong to any other system of morals. Those sanctions are either external or internal. Of the external sanctions it is not necessary to speak at any length. They are the hope of favor and the fear of displeasure from our fellow creatures or from the Ruler of the universe, along with whatever we may have of sympathy or affection for them, or of love and awe of Him, inclining us to do His will independently of selfish consequences. There is evidently no reason why all these motives for observance should not attach themselves to the utilitarian morality as completely and as powerfully as to any other. Indeed, those of them which refer to our fellow creatures are sure to do so, in proportion to the amount of general intelligence; for whether there be any other ground of moral obligation than the general happiness or not, men do desire happiness; and however imperfect may be their own practice, they desire and commend all conduct in others toward themselves by which they think their happiness is promoted. With regard to the religious motive, if men believe, as most profess to do, in the goodness of God, those who think that conduciveness to the general happiness is the essence or even only the criterion of good must necessarily believe that it is also that which God approves. The whole force therefore of external reward and punishment, whether physical or moral, and whether proceeding from God or from our fellow men, together with all that the capacities of human nature admit of disinterested devotion to either, become available to enforce the utilitarian morality, in proportion as that morality is recognized; and the more powerfully, the more the appliances of education and general cultivation are bent to the purpose.

So far as to external sanctions. The internal sanction of duty, whatever our standard of duty may be, is one and the same—a feeling in our own mind; a pain, more or less intense, attendant on violation of duty, which in properly cultivated moral natures rises, in the more serious cases, into shrinking from it as an impossibility. This feeling, when disinterested and connecting itself with the pure idea of duty, and not with some particular form of it, or with any of the merely accessory circumstances, is the essence of conscience; though in that complex phenomenon as it actually exists, the simple fact is in general all encrusted over with collateral associations derived from sympathy, from love, and still more from fear; from all the forms of religious feeling; from the recollections of childhood and of all our past life; from self-esteem, desire of the esteem of others, and occasionally even self-abasement. This extreme complication is, I apprehend, the origin of the sort of mystical character which, by a tendency of the human mind of which there are many other examples, is apt to be attributed to the idea of moral obligation, and which leads people to believe that the idea cannot possibly attach itself to any other objects that those which, by a supposed mysterious law, are found in our present experience to excite it. Its binding force, however, consists in the existence of a mass of feeling which must be broken through in order to do what violates our standard of right, and which, if we do nevertheless violate that standard, will probably have to be encountered afterwards in the form of remorse. Whatever theory we have of the nature or origin of conscience, this is what essentially constitutes it.

The ultimate sanction, therefore, of all morality (external motives apart) being a subjective feeling in our own minds, I see nothing embarrassing to those whose standard is utility in the question, What is the sanction of that particular standard? We may answer, the same as of all other moral standards—the conscientious feelings of mankind. Undoubtedly this sanction has no binding efficacy on those who do not possess the feelings it appeals to; but neither will these persons be more obedient to any other moral principle than to the utilitarian one. On them morality of any kind has no hold but through the external sanctions. Meanwhile the feelings exist, a fact in human nature, the reality of which, and the great power with which they are capable of acting on those in whom they have been duly cultivated, are proved by experience. No reason has ever been shown why they may not be cultivated to as great intensity in connection with the utilitarian as with any other rule of morals.

There is, I am aware, a disposition to believe that a person who sees in moral obligation a transcendental fact, an objective reality belonging to the province of 'things in themselves,' is likely to be more obedient to it than one who believes it to be entirely subjective, having its seat in human consciousness only. But whatever a person's opinion may be on this point of ontology, the force he is really urged by is his own subjective feeling, and is exactly measured by its strength. No one's belief that duty is an objective reality is stronger than the belief that God is so; yet the belief in God, apart from the expectation of actual reward and punishment, only operates on conduct through, and in proportion to, the subjective religious feeling. The sanction, so far as it is disinterested, is always in the mind itself; and the notion, therefore, of the transcendental moralists must be that this sanction will not exist *in* the mind unless it is believed to have its root out of the mind; and that if a person is able to say to himself, 'That which is restraining me and which is called my conscience is only a feeling in my own mind,' he may possibly draw the conclusion that when the feeling ceases the obligation ceases, and that if he find the feeling inconvenient, he may disregard it and endeavor to get rid of it. But is this danger confined to the utilitarian morality? Does the belief that moral obligation has its seat outside the mind make the feeling of it too strong to be got rid of?

The fact is so far otherwise that all moralists admit and lament the ease with which, in the generality of minds, conscience can be silenced or stifled. The question, 'Need I obey my conscience?' is quite as often put to themselves by persons who never heard of the principle of utility as by its adherents. Those whose conscientious feelings are so weak as to allow of their asking this question, if they answer it affirmatively, will not do so because they believe in the transcendental theory, but because of the external sanctions.

It is not necessary, for the present purpose, to decide whether the feeling of duty is innate or implanted. Assuming it to be innate, it is an open question to what objects it naturally attaches itself; for the philosophic supporters of that theory are now agreed that the intuitive perception is of principles of morality and not of the details. If there be anything innate in the matter, I see no reason why the feeling which is innate should not be that of regard to the pleasures and pains of others. If there is any principle of morals which is intuitively obligatory, I should say it must be that. If so, the intuitive ethics would coincide with the utilitarian, and there would be no further quarrel between them. Even as it is, the intuitive moralists, though they believe that there are other intuitive moral obligations, do already believe this to be one; for they unanimously hold that a large *portion* of morality turns upon the consideration due to the interests of our fellow creatures. Therefore, if the belief in the transcendental origins of moral obligation gives any additional efficacy to the internal sanction, it appears to me that the utilitarian principle has already the benefit of it.

On the other hand, if, as is my own belief, the moral feelings are not innate but acquired, they are not for that reason the less natural. It is natural to man to speak, to reason, to build cities, to cultivate the ground, though these are acquired faculties. The moral feelings are not indeed a part of our nature in the sense of being in any perceptible degree present in all of us; but this, unhappily, is a fact admitted by those who believe the most strenuously in their transcendental origin. Like the other acquired capacities above referred to, the moral faculty, if not a part of our nature, is a natural outgrowth from it; capable, like them, in a certain small degree, of springing up spontaneously; and susceptible of being brought by cultivation to a high degree of development. Unhappily it is also susceptible, by a sufficient use of the external sanctions and of the force of early impressions, of being cultivated in almost any direction, so that there is hardly anything so absurd or so mischievous that it may not, by means of these influences, be made to act on the human mind with all the authority of conscience. To doubt that the same potency might be given by the same means to the principle of utility, even if it had no foundation in human nature, would be flying in the face of all experience.

But moral associations which are wholly of artificial creation, when the intellectual culture goes on, yield by degrees to the dissolving force of analysis; and if the feeling of duty, when associated with utility, would appear equally arbitrary; if there were no leading department of our nature, no powerful class of sentiments, with which that association would harmonize, which would make us feel it congenial and incline us not only to foster it in others (for which we have abundant interested motives), but also to cherish it in ourselves—if there were not, in short, a natural basis of sentiment for utilitarian morality, it might well happen that this association also, even after it had been implanted by education, might be analyzed away.

But there *is* this basis of powerful natural sentiment; and this it is which, when once the general happiness is recognized as the ethical standard, will constitute the strength of the utilitarian morality. This firm foundation is that of the social feelings of mankind—the desire to be in unity with our fellow creatures, which is already a powerful principle in human nature, and happily one of those which tend to become stronger, even without express inculcation, from the influences of advancing civilization. The social state is at once so natural, so necessary, and so habitual to man, that, except in some unusual circumstances or by an effort of voluntary abstraction, he never conceives himself otherwise than as a member of a body; and this association is riveted more and more, as mankind are further removed from the state of savage independence. Any condition, therefore, which is essential to a state of society becomes more and more an inseparable part of every person's conception of the state of things which he is born into, and which is the destiny of a human being. Now society between human beings, except in the relation of master and slave, is manifestly impossible on any other footing than that the interests of all are to be consulted. Society between equals can only exist on the understanding that the interests of all are to be regarded equally. And since in all states of civilization, every person, except an absolute monarch, has equals, everyone is obliged to live on these terms with somebody; and in every age some advance is made toward a state in which it will be impossible to live permanently on other terms with anybody. In this way people grow up unable to conceive as possible to them a state of total disregard of other people's interests. They are under a necessity of conceiving themselves as at least abstaining from all the grosser injuries, and (if only for their own protection) living in a state of constant protest against them. They are also familiar with the fact of co-operating with others and proposing to themselves a collective, not an individual, interest as the aim (at least for the time being) of their actions. So long as they are co-operating, their ends are identified with those of others; there is at least a temporary feeling that the interests of others are their own interests. Not only does all strengthening of social ties, and all healthy growth of society, give to each individual a stronger personal interest in practically consulting the welfare of others, it also leads him to identify his *feelings* more and more with their good, or at least with an even greater degree of practical consideration for it. He comes, as though instinctively, to be conscious of himself as a being who *of course* pays regard to others. The good of others becomes to him a thing naturally and necessarily to be attended to, like any of the physical conditions of our existence. Now, whatever amount of this feeling a person has, he is urged by the strongest motives both of interest and of sympathy to demonstrate it, and to the utmost of his power encourage it in others; and even if he has none of it himself, he is as greatly interested as anyone else that others should have it. Consequently, the smallest germs of the feeling are laid hold of and nourished by the contagion of sympathy and the influences of education; and a complete web of corroborative association is woven round it by the powerful agency of the external sanctions. This mode of conceiving ourselves and human life, as civilization goes on, is felt to be more and more natural. Every step in political improvement renders it more so, by removing the sources of opposition of interest and leveling those inequalities of legal privilege between individuals or classes, owing to which there are large portions of mankind whose happiness it is still practicable to disregard. In any improving state of the human mind, the influences are constantly on the increase which tend to generate in each individual a feeling of unity with all the rest; which, if perfect, would make him never think of, or desire, any beneficial condition for himself in the benefits of which they are not included. If we now suppose this feeling of unity to be taught as a religion, and the whole force of education, of institutions, and of opinion directed, as it once was in the case of religion, to make every person grow up from infancy surrounded on all sides both by the profession and the practice of it, I think that no one who can realize this conception will feel any misgiving about the sufficiency of the ultimate sanction for the happiness morality. To any ethical student who finds the realization difficult, I recommend, as a means of facilitating it, the second of M. Comte's two principal works, the *Traité de politique positive*. I entertain the strongest objections to the system of politics and morals set forth in that treatise, but I think it has superabundantly shown the possibility of giving to the service of humanity, even without the aid of belief in a Providence, both the psychological power and the social efficacy of a religion, making it take hold of human life, and color all thought, feeling, and action in a manner of which the greatest ascendancy ever exercised by any religion may be but a type and foretaste; and of which the danger is, not that it should be insufficient, but that it should be so excessive as to interfere unduly with human freedom and individuality.

Neither is it necessary to the feeling which constitutes the binding force of the utilitarian morality on those who recognize it to wait for those social influences which would make its obligation felt by mankind at large. In the comparatively early state of human advancement in which we now live, a person cannot, indeed, feel that entireness of sympathy with all others which would make any real discordance in the general direction of their conduct in life impossible, but already a person in whom the social feeling is at all developed cannot bring himself to think of the rest of his fellow creatures as struggling rivals with him for the means of happiness, whom he must desire to see defeated in their object in order that he may succeed in his. The deeply rooted conception which every individual even now has of himself as a social being tends to make him feel it one of his natural wants that there should be harmony between his feelings and aims and those of his fellow creatures. If differences of opinion and of mental culture make it impossible for him to share many of their actual feelings—perhaps make him denounce and defy those feelings—he still needs to be conscious that his real aim and theirs do not conflict; that he is not opposing himself to what they really wish for, namely, their own good, but is, on the contrary, promoting it. This feeling in most individuals is much inferior in strength to their selfish feelings, and is often wanting altogether. But to those who have it, it possesses all the characters of a natural feeling. It does not present itself to their minds as a superstition of education or a law despotically imposed by the power of society, but as an attribute which it would not be well for them to be without. This conviction is the ultimate sanction of the greatest happiness morality. This it is which makes any mind of well-developed feelings work with, and not against, the outward motives to care for others, afforded by what I have called the external sanctions; and, when those sanctions are wanting or act in an opposite direction, constitutes in itself a powerful internal binding force, in proportion to the sensitiveness and thoughtfulness of the character, since few but those whose mind is a moral blank could bear to lay out their course of life on the plan of paying no regard to others except so far as their own private interest compels.

CHAPTER IV Of What Sort of Proof the Principle of Utility Is Susceptible

It has already been remarked that questions of ultimate ends do not admit of proof, in the ordinary acceptation of the term. To be incapable of proof by reasoning is common to all first principles, to the first premises of our knowledge, as well as to those of our conduct. But the former, being matters of fact, may be the subject of a direct appeal to the faculties which judge of fact—namely, our senses and our internal consciousness. Can an appeal be made to the same faculties on questions of practical ends? Or by what other faculty is cognizance taken of them?

Questions about ends are, in other words, questions what things are desirable. The utilitarian doctrine is that happiness is desirable, and the only thing desirable, as an end; all other things being only desirable as means to that end. What ought to be required of this doctrine, what conditions is it requisite that the doctrine should fulfill—to make good its claim to be believed?

The only proof capable of being given that an object is visible is that people actually see it. The only proof that a sound is audible is that people hear it; and so of the other sources of our experience. In like manner, I apprehend, the sole evidence it is possible to produce that anything is desirable is that people do actually desire it. If the end which the utilitarian doctrine proposes to itself were not, in theory and in practice, acknowledged to be an end, nothing could ever convince any person that it was so. No reason can be given why the general happiness is desirable, except that each person, so far as he believes it to be attainable, desires his own happiness. This, however, being a fact, we have not only all the proof which the case admits of, but all which it is possible to require, that happiness is a good, that each person's happiness is a good to that person, and the general happiness, therefore, a good to the aggregate of all persons. Happiness has made out its title as *one* of the ends of conduct and, consequently, one of the criteria of morality.

But it has not, by this alone, proved itself to be the sole criterion. To do that, it would seem, by the same rule, necessary to show, not only that people desire happiness, but that they never desire anything else. Now it is palpable that they do desire things which, in common language, are decidedly distinguished from happiness. They desire, for example, virtue and the absence of vice no less really than pleasure and the absence of pain. The desire of virtue is not as universal, but it is as authentic a fact as the desire of happiness. And hence the opponents of the utilitarian standard deem that they have a right to infer that there are other ends of human action besides happiness, and that happiness is not the standard of approbation and disapprobation.

But does the utilitarian doctrine deny that people desire virtue, or maintain that virtue is not a thing to be desired? The very reverse. It maintains not only that virtue is to be desired, but that it is to be desired disinterestedly, for itself. Whatever may be the opinion of utilitarian moralists as to the original conditions by which virtue is made virtue, however they may believe (as they do) that actions and dispositions are only virtuous because they promote another end than virtue, yet this being granted, and it having been decided, from considerations of this description, what *is* virtuous, they not only place virtue at the very head of the things which are good as means to the ultimate end, but they also recognize as a psychological fact the possibility of its being, to the individual, a good in itself, without looking to any end beyond it; and hold that the mind is not in a right state, not in a state comformable to utility, not in the state most conducive to the general happiness, unless it does love virtue in this manner—as a thing desirable in itself, even although, in the individual instance, it should not produce those other desirable consequences which it tends to produce, and on account of which it is held to be virtue. This opinion is not, in the smallest degree, a departure from the happiness principle. The ingredients of happiness are very various, and each of them is desirable in itself, and not merely when considered as swelling an aggregate. The principle of utility does not mean that any given pleasure, as music for instance, or any given exemption from pain, as for example health, is to be looked upon as means to a collective something termed happiness, and to be desired on that account. They are desired and desirable in and for themselves; besides being means, they are a part of the end. Virtue, according to the utilitarian doctrine, is not naturally and originally part of the end, but it is capable of becoming so; and in those who live it disinterestedly it has become so, and is desired and cherished, not as a means to happiness, but as a part of their happiness.

To illustrate this further, we may remember that virtue is not the only thing originally a means, and which if it were not a means to anything else would be and remain indifferent, but which by association with what it is a means to comes to be desired for itself, and that too with the utmost intensity. What, for example, shall we say of the love of money? There is nothing originally more desirable about money than about any heap of glittering pebbles. Its worth is solely that of the things which it will buy; the desires for other things than itself, which it is a means of gratifying. Yet the love of money is not only one of the strongest moving forces of human life, but money is, in many cases, desired in and for itself; the desire to possess it is often stronger than the desire to use it, and goes on increasing when all the desires which point to ends beyond it, to be compassed by it, are falling off. It may, then, be said truly that money is desired not for the sake of an end, but as part of the end. From being a means to happiness, it has come to be itself a principle ingredient of the individual's conception of happiness. The same may be said of the majority of the great objects of human life: power, for example, or fame, except that to each of these there is a certain amount of immediate pleasure annexed, which has at least the semblance of being naturally inherent in them—a thing which cannot be said of money. Still, however, the strongest natural attraction, both of power and of fame, is the immense aid they give to the attainment of our other wishes; and it is the strong association thus generated between them and all our objects of desire which gives to the direct desire of them the intensity it often assumes, so as in some characters to surpass in strength all other desires. In these cases the means have become a part of the end, and a more important part of it than any of the things which they are means to. What was once desired as an instrument for the attainment of happiness has come to be desired for its own sake. In being desired for its own sake it is, however, desired as *part* of happiness. The person is made, or thinks he would be made, happy by its mere possession; and is made unhappy by failure to obtain it. The desire of it is not a different thing from the desire of happiness any more than the love of music or the desire of health. They are included in happiness. They are some of the elements of which the desire of happiness is made up. Happiness is not an abstract idea but a concrete whole; and these are some of its parts. And the utilitarian standard sanctions and approves their being so. Life would be a poor thing, very ill provided with sources of happiness, if there were not this provision of nature by which things originally indifferent, but conductive to, or otherwise associated with, the satisfaction of our primitive desires, become in themselves sources of pleasure more valuable than the primitive pleasures, both in permanency, in the space of human existence that they are capable of covering, and even in intensity.

Virtue, according to the utilitarian conception, is a good of this description. There was no original desire of it, or motive to it, save its conduciveness to pleasure, and especially to protection from pain. But through the association thus formed it may be felt a good in itself, and desired as such with as great intensity as any other good; and with this difference between it and the love of money, of power, or of fame—that all of these may, and often do, render the individual noxious to the other members of the society to which he belongs, whereas there is nothing which makes him so much a blessing to them as the cultivation of the disinterested love of virtue. And consequently, the utilitarian standard, while it tolerates and approves those other acquired desires, up to the point beyond which they would be more injurious to the general happiness than promotive of it, enjoins and requires the cultivation of the love of virtue up to the greatest strength possible, as being above all things important to the general happiness.

It results from the preceding considerations that there is in reality nothing desired except happiness. Whatever is desired otherwise than as a means to some end beyond itself, and ultimately to happiness, is desired as itself a part of happiness, and is not desired for itself until it has become so. Those who desire virtue for its own sake desire it either because the consciousness of it is a pleasure, or because the consciousness of being without it is a pain, or for both reasons united; as in truth the pleasure and pain seldom exist separately, but almost always together—the same person feeling pleasure in the degree of virtue attained, and pain in not having attained more. If one of these gave him no pleasure, and the other no pain, he would not love or desire virtue, or would desire it only for the other benefits which it might produce to himself or to persons whom he cared for.

We have now, then, an answer to the question, of what sort of proof the principle of utility is susceptible. If the opinion which I have now stated is psychologically true—if human nature is so constituted as to desire nothing which is not either a part of happiness or a means of happiness—we can have no other proof, and we require no other, that these are the only things desirable. If so, happiness is the sole end of human action, and the promotion of it the test by which to judge of all human conduct; from whence it necessarily follows that it must be the criterion of morality, since a part is included in the whole.

And now to decide whether this is really so, whether mankind do desire nothing for itself but that which is a pleasure to them, or of which the absence is a pain, we have evidently arrived at a question of fact and experience, dependent like all similar questions, upon evidence. It can only be determined by practiced self-consciousness and self-observation, assisted by observation of others. I believe that these sources of evidence, impartially consulted, will declare that desiring a thing and finding it pleasant, aversion to it and thinking of it as painful, are phenomena entirely inseparable or, rather, two parts of the same phenomenon—in strictness of language, two different modes of naming the same psychological fact; that to think of an object as desirable (unless for the sake of its consequences) and to think of it as pleasant are one and the same thing; and that to desire anything except in proportion as the idea of it is pleasant is a physical and metaphysical impossibility.

So obvious does this appear to me that I expect it will hardly be disputed; and the objection made will be, not that desire can possibly be directed to anything ultimately except pleasure and exemption from pain, but that the will is a different thing from desire, that a person of confirmed virtue or any other person whose purposes are fixed carries out his purposes without any thought of the pleasure he has in contemplating them or expects to derive from their fulfillment, and persists in acting on them, even though these pleasures are much diminished by changes in his character or decay of his passive sensibilities, or are outweighed by the pains which the pursuit of the purposes may bring upon him. All this I fully admit and have stated it elsewhere as positively and emphatically as anyone. Will, the active phenomenon, is a different thing from desire, the state of passive sensibility, and, though originally an offshoot from it, may in time take root and detach itself from the parent stock, so much so that in the case of a habitual purpose, instead of willing the thing because we desire it, we often desire it only because we will it. This, however, is but an instance of that familiar fact, the power of habit, and is nowise confined to the case of virtuous actions. Many different things which men originally did from a motive of some sort they continue to do from habit. Sometimes this is done unconsciously, the consciousness coming only after the action;

at other times with conscious volition, but volition which has become habitual and is put in operation by the force of habit, in opposition perhaps to the deliberate preference, as often happens with those who have contracted habits of vicious or hurtful indulgence. Third and last comes the case in which the habitual act of will in the individual instance is not in contradiction to the general intention prevailing at other times, but in fulfillment of it, as in the case of the person of confirmed virtue and of all who pursue deliberately and consistently any determinate end. The distinction between will and desire thus understood is an authentic and highly important psychological fact; but the fact consists solely in this—that will, like all other parts of our constitution, is amenable to habit, and that we may will from habit what we no longer desire for itself, or desire only because we will it. It is not the less true that will, in the beginning, is entirely produced by desire, including in that term the repelling influence of pain as well as the attractive one of pleasure. Let us take into consideration no longer the person who has a confirmed will to do right, but him in whom that virtuous will is still feeble, conquerable by temptation, and not to be fully relied on; by what means can it be strengthened? How can the will to be virtuous, where it does not exist in sufficient force, be implanted or awakened? Only by making the person *desire* virtue—by making him think of it in a pleasurable light, or of its absence in a painful one. It is by associating the doing right with pleasure, or the wrong with pain, or by eliciting and impressing and bringing home to the person's experience the pleasure naturally involved in the one or the pain in the other, that is possible to call forth that will to be virtuous which, when confirmed, acts without any thought of either pleasure or pain. Will is the child of desire, and passes out of the dominion of its parent only to come under that of habit. That which is the result of habit affords no presumption of being intrinsically good; and there would be no reason for wishing that the purpose of virtue should become independent of pleasure and pain were it not that the influence of the pleasurable and painful associations which prompt to virtue is not sufficiently to be depended on for unerring constancy of action until it has acquired the support of habit. Both in feeling and in conduct, habit is the only thing which imparts certainty; and it is because of the importance to others of being able to rely absolutely on one's feelings and conduct, and to oneself of being able to rely on one's own, that the will to do right ought to be cultivated into this habitual independence. In other words, this state of the will is a means to good, not intrinsically a good; and does not contradict the doctrine that nothing is a good to human beings but in so far as it is either itself pleasurable or a means of attaining pleasure or averting pain.

But if this doctrine be true, the principle of utility is proved. Whether it is so or not must now be left to the consideration of the thoughtful reader.

George Edward Moore
(1873–1958)

G. E. Moore first studied classics at Cambridge University. But he soon turned to philosophy, partly due to the influence of Bertrand Russell. Moore ultimately spent nearly forty years at Cambridge, retiring from active teaching in 1939. His most influential book was *Principia Ethica* (1903), followed by *Ethics* (1912), a less technical book in which Moore developed a version of utilitarianism incorporating his earlier views. Just after the turn of the century G. E. Moore and Bertrand Russell played the main role in inaugurating the philosophical movement, still dominant in English-speaking countries, that goes under the general label "analytical philosophy." Moore insisted on the careful, precise analysis of philosophical claims and after examination often found these claims to be less plausible than those of common sense. Even the style of later philosophical writing was influenced by Moore's painstaking attempts to achieve clarity and avoid ambiguity. Moore's other works include *Philosophical Studies* (1922) and "A Reply to My Critics" in *The Philosophy of G. E. Moore* (1942), a volume of essays about Moore's philosophy edited by P. A. Schilpp.

A classic article is William Frankena's "The Naturalistic Fallacy," in *Mind* (1938), and reprinted in many ethics anthologies. Among selections in this anthology, Hume anticipates Moore when he argues that "ought" judgments cannot be deduced from "is" judgments; Ayer accepts and uses Moore's arguments for a "naturalistic fallacy," and Searle attempts to show that Hume, Moore, and Ayer are mistaken.

A number of recent books set out to explain Moore's position and its significance for twentieth-century ethics. These books also discuss several of our other twentieth-century authors, especially Ayer, Toulmin, and Hare. Some of these works are: *Ethics Since 1900* (1960) by M. Warnock, *Ethics* (1963) by W. Frankena, *The Revolution in Ethical Theory* (1966) by G. Kerner, *Contemporary Moral Philosophy* (1967) by G. J. Warnock, *Modern Moral Philosophy* (1970) by W. D. Hudson, and *Twentieth-Century Ethics* (1974) by Roger Hancock.

Principia Ethica

PREFACE

It appears to me that in Ethics, as in all other philosophical studies, the difficulties and disagreements, of which its history is full, are mainly due to a very simple cause: namely to the attempt to answer questions, without first discovering precisely *what* question it is which you desire to answer. I do not know how far this source of error would be done away, if philosophers would *try* to discover what question they were asking, before they set about to answer it; for the work of analysis and distinction is often very difficult: we may often fail to make the necessary discovery, even though we make a definite attempt to do so. But I am inclined to think that in many cases a resolute attempt would be sufficient to ensure success; so that, if only this attempt were made, many of the most glaring difficulties and disagreements in philosophy would disappear. At all events, philosophers seem, in general, not to make the attempt; and, whether in consequence of this omission or not, they are constantly endeavouring to prove that 'Yes' or 'No' will answer questions, to which *neither* answer is correct, owing to the fact that what they have before their minds is not one question, but several, to some of which the true answer is 'No,' to others 'Yes.'

I have tried in this book to distinguish clearly two kinds of question, which moral philosophers have always professed to answer, but which, as I have tried to show, they have almost always confused both with one another and with other questions. These two questions may be expressed, the first in the form: What kind of things ought to exist for their own sakes? the second in the form: What kind of actions ought we to perform? I have tried to shew exactly what it is that we ask about a thing, when we ask whether it ought to exist for its own sake, is good in itself or has intrinsic value; and exactly what it is that we ask about an action, when we ask whether we ought to do it, whether it is a right action or a duty.

But from a clear insight into the nature of these two questions,

---

Reprinted from *Principia Ethica* by George E. Moore by permission of Cambridge University Press. Published by the Syndics of the Cambridge University Press, 1960.

there appears to me to follow a second most important result: namely, what is the nature of the evidence, by which alone any ethical proposition can be proved or disproved, confirmed or rendered doubtful. Once we recognise the exact meaning of the two questions, I think it also becomes plain exactly what kind of reasons are relevant as arguments for or against any particular answer to them. It becomes plain that, for answers to the *first* question, no relevant evidence whatever can be adduced: from no other truth, except themselves alone, can it be inferred that they are either true or false. We can guard against error only by taking care, that, when we try to answer a question of this kind, we have before our minds that question only, and not some other or others; but that there is great danger of such errors of confusion I have tried to shew, and also what are the chief precautions by the use of which we may guard against them. As for the *second* question, it becomes equally plain, that any answer to it *is* capable of proof or disproof—that, indeed, so many different considerations are relevant to its truth or falsehood, as to make the attainment of probability very difficult, and the attainment of certainty impossible. Nevertheless the *kind* of evidence, which is both necessary and alone relevant to such proof and disproof, is capable of exact definition. Such evidence must contain propositions of two kinds and of two kinds only: it must consist, in the first place, of truths with regard to the results of the action in question—of *causal* truths—but it must *also* contain ethical truths of our first or self-evident class. Many truths of both kinds are necessary to the proof that any action ought to be done; and any other kind of evidence is wholly irrelevant. It follows that, if any ethical philosopher offers for propositions of the first kind any evidence whatever, or if, for propositions of the second kind, he either fails to adduce both causal and ethical truths, or adduces truths that are neither, his reasoning has not the least tendency to establish his conclusions. But not only are his conclusions totally devoid of weight: we have, moreover, reason to suspect him of the error of confusion; since the offering of irrelevant evidence generally indicates that the philosopher who offers it has had before his mind, not the question which he professes to answer, but some other entirely different one. Ethical discussion, hitherto, has perhaps consisted chiefly in reasoning of this totally irrelevant kind.

One main object of this book may, then, be expressed by slightly changing one of Kant's famous titles. I have endeavoured to write 'Prolegomena to any future Ethics that can possibly pretend to be scientific.' In other words, I have endeavoured to discover what are the fundamental principles of ethical reasoning; and the establishment of these principles, rather than of any conclusions which may be attained by their use, may be regarded as my main object. I have, however, also attempted, in Chapter VI, to present some conclusions, with regard to the proper answer of the question 'What is good in itself?' which are very different from any which have commonly been advocated by philosophers. I have tried to define the classes within which all great goods and evils fall; and I have maintained that very many different things are good and evil in themselves, and that neither class of things possesses any other property which is both common to all its members and peculiar to them.

In order to express the fact that ethical propositions of my *first* class are incapable of proof or disproof, I have sometimes followed Sidgwick's usage in calling them 'Intuitions.' But I beg it may be noticed that I am not an 'Intuitionist,' in the ordinary sense of the term. Sidgwick himself seems never to have been clearly aware of the immense importance of the difference which distinguishes his Intuitionism from the common doctrine, which has generally been called by that name. The Intuitionist proper is distinguished by maintaining that propositions of my *second* class—propositions which assert that a certain action is *right* or a *duty*—are incapable of proof or disproof by any enquiry into the results of such actions. I, on the contrary, am no less anxious to maintain that propositions of *this* kind are *not* 'Intuitions,' than to maintain that propositions of my *first* class *are* Intuitions.

Again, I would wish it observed that, when I call such propositions 'Intuitions,' I mean *merely* to assert that they are incapable of proof; I imply nothing whatever as to the manner or origin of our cognition of them. Still less do I imply (as most Intuitionists have done) that any proposition whatever is true, *because* we cognise it in a particular way or by the exercise of any particular faculty: I hold, on the contrary, that in every way in which it is possible to cognise a true proposition, it is also possible to cognise a false one.

CHAPTER I **The Subject-Matter of Ethics**

1. It is very easy to point out some among our every-day judgments, with the truth of which Ethics is undoubtedly concerned. Whenever we say, 'So and so is a good man,' or 'That fellow is a villain'; whenever we ask, 'What ought I to do?' or 'Is it wrong for me to do like this?'; whenever we hazard such remarks as 'Temperance is a virtue and drunkenness a vice'—it is undoubtedly the business of Ethics to discuss such questions and such statements; to argue what is the true answer when we ask what it is right to do, and to give reasons for thinking that our statements about the character of persons or the morality of actions are true or false. In the vast majority of cases, where we make statements involving any of the terms 'virtue,' 'vice,' 'duty,' 'right,' 'ought,' 'good,' 'bad,' we are making ethical judgments; and if we wish to discuss their truth, we shall be discussing a point of Ethics.

So much as this is not disputed; but it falls very far short of defining the province of Ethics. That province may indeed be defined as
the whole truth about that which is at the same time common to all
such judgments and peculiar to them. But we have still to ask the
question: What is it that is thus common and peculiar? And this is a
question to which very different answers have been given by ethical
philosophers of acknowledged reputation, and none of them, perhaps,
completely satisfactory.

2. If we take such examples as those given above, we shall not be
far wrong in saying that they are all of them concerned with the question of 'conduct'—with the question, what, in the conduct of us, human
beings, is good, and what is bad, what is right, and what is wrong. For
when we say that a man is good, we commonly mean that he acts
rightly; when we say that drunkenness is a vice, we commonly mean
that to get drunk is a wrong or wicked action. And this discussion of
human conduct is, in fact, that with which the name 'Ethics' is most
intimately associated. It is so associated by derivation; and conduct is
undoubtedly by far the commonest and most generally interesting object
of ethical judgments.

Accordingly, we find that many ethical philosophers are disposed
to accept as an adequate definition of 'Ethics' the statement that it deals
with the question what is good or bad in human conduct. They hold
that its enquiries are properly confined to 'conduct' or to 'practice';
they hold that the name 'practical philosophy' covers all the matter
with which it has to do. Now, without discussing the proper meaning
of the word (for verbal questions are properly left to the writers of
dictionaries and other persons interested in literature; philosophy, as
we shall see, has no concern with them), I may say that I intend to use
'Ethics' to cover more than this—a usage, for which there is, I think,
quite sufficient authority. I am using it to cover an enquiry for which, at
all events, there is no other word: the general enquiry into what is good.

Ethics is undoubtedly concerned with the question what good
conduct is; but being concerned with this, it obviously does not start at
the beginning, unless it is prepared to tell us what is good as well as
what is conduct. For 'good conduct' is a complex notion: all conduct
is not good; for some is certainly bad and some may be indifferent. And
on the other hand, other things, besides conduct, may be good; and if
they are so, then, 'good' denotes some property, that is common to
them and conduct; and if we examine good conduct alone of all good
things, then we shall be in danger of mistaking for this property, some
property which is not shared by those other things: and thus we shall
have made a mistake about Ethics even in this limited sense; for we
shall not know what good conduct really is. This is a mistake which
many writers have actually made, from limiting their enquiry to conduct. And hence I shall try to avoid it by considering first what is good

in general; hoping, that if we can arrive at any certainty about this, it will be much easier to settle the question of good conduct: for we all know pretty well what 'conduct' is. This, then, is our first question: What is good? and What is bad? and to the discussion of this question (or these questions) I give the name of Ethics, since that science must, at all events, include it.

3. But this is a question which may have many meanings. If, for example, each of us were to say 'I am doing good now' or 'I had a good dinner yesterday,' these statements would each of them be some sort of answer to our question, although perhaps a false one. So, too, when A asks B what school he ought to send his son to, B's answer will certainly be an ethical judgment. And similarly all distribution of praise or blame to any personage or thing that has existed, now exists, or will exist, does give some answer to the question 'What is good?' In all such cases some particular thing is judged to be good or bad: the question 'What?' is answered by ''This.' But this is not the sense in which a scientific Ethics asks the question. Not one, of all the many million answers of this kind, which must be true, can form a part of an ethical system; although that science must contain reasons and principles sufficient for deciding on the truth of all of them. There are far too many persons, things and events in the world, past, present, or to come, for a discussion of their individual merits to be embraced in any science. Ethics, therefore, does not deal at all with facts of this nature, facts that are unique, individual, absolutely particular; facts with which such studies as history, geography, astronomy, are compelled, in part at least, to deal. And, for this reason, it is not the business of the ethical philosopher to give personal advice or exhortation.

4. But there is another meaning which may be given to the question 'What is good?' 'Books are good' would be an answer to it, though an answer obviously false; for some books are very bad indeed. And ethical judgments of this kind do indeed belong to Ethics; though I shall not deal with many of them. Such is the judgment 'Pleasure is good'—a judgment, of which Ethics should discuss the truth, although it is not nearly as important as that other judgment, with which we shall be much occupied presently—'Pleasure *alone* is good.' It is judgments of this sort, which are made in such books on Ethics as contain a list of 'virtues'—in Aristotle's 'Ethics' for example. But it is judgments of precisely the same kind, which form the substance of what is commonly supposed to be a study different from Ethics, and one much less respectable—the study of Casuistry. We may be told that Casuistry differs from Ethics, in that it is much more detailed and particular, Ethics much more general. But it is most important to notice that Casuistry does not deal with anything that is absolutely particular— particular in the only sense in which a perfectly precise line can be drawn between it and what is general. It is not particular in the sense just noticed, the sense in which this book is a particular book, and A's friend's advice particular advice. Casuistry may indeed be *more* particular and Ethics *more* general; but that means that they differ only in degree and not in kind. And this is universally true of 'particular' and 'general,' when used in this common, but inaccurate, sense. So far as Ethics allows itself to give lists of virtues or even to name constituents of the Ideal, it is indistinguishable from Casuistry. Both alike deal with what is general, in the sense in which physics and chemistry deal with what is general. Just as chemistry aims at discovering what are the properties of oxygen, *wherever it occurs,* and not only of this or that particular specimen of oxygen; so Casuistry aims at discovering what actions are good, *whenever they occur.* In this respect Ethics and Casuistry alike are to be classed with such sciences as physics, chemistry and physiology, in their absolute distinction from those of which history and geography are instances. And it is to be noted that, owing to their detailed nature, casuistical investigations are actually nearer to physics and to chemistry than are the investigations usually assigned to Ethics. For just as physics cannot rest content with the discovery that light is propagated by waves of ether, but must go on to discover the particular nature of the ether-waves corresponding to each several colour; so Casuistry, not content with the general law that charity is a virtue must attempt to discover the relative merits of every different form of charity. Casuistry forms, therefore, part of the ideal of ethical science: Ethics cannot be complete without it. The defects of Casuistry are not defects of principle; no objection can be taken to its aim and object. It has failed only because it is far too difficult a subject to be treated adequately in our present state of knowledge. The casuist has been unable to distinguish, in the cases which he treats, those elements upon which their value depends. Hence he often thinks two cases to be alike in respect of value, when in reality they are alike only in some other respect. It is to mistakes of this kind that the pernicious influence of such investigations has been due. For Casuistry is the goal of ethical investigation. It cannot be safely attempted at the beginning of our studies, but only at the end.

5. But our question 'What is good?' may have still another meaning. We may, in the third place, mean to ask, not what thing or things are good, but how 'good' is to be defined. This is an enquiry which belongs only to Ethics, not to Casuistry; and this is the enquiry which will occupy us first.

It is an enquiry to which most special attention should be directed; since this question, how 'good' is to be defined, is the most fundamental question in all Ethics. That which is meant by 'good' is, in fact, except its converse 'bad,' the *only* simple object of thought which is peculiar to Ethics. Its definition is, therefore, the most essential point in the definition of Ethics; and moreover a mistake with regard to it entails a far larger number of erroneous ethical judgments than any other. Unless this first question be fully understood, and its true answer clearly recognised, the rest of Ethics is as good as useless from the point of view of systematic knowledge. True ethical judgments, of the two kinds last dealt with, may indeed be made by those who do not know the answer to this question as well as by those who do; and it goes without saying that the two classes of people may lead equally good lives. But it is extremely unlikely that the *most general* ethical judgments will be equally valid, in the absence of a true answer to this question: I shall presently try to shew that the gravest errors have been largely due to beliefs in a false answer. And, in any case, it is impossible that, till the answer to this question be known, any one should know *what is the evidence* for any ethical judgment whatsoever. But the main object of Ethics, as a systematic science, is to give correct *reasons* for thinking that this or that is good; and, unless this question be answered, such reasons cannot be given. Even, therefore, apart from the fact that a false answer leads to false conclusions, the present enquiry is a most necessary and important part of the science of Ethics.

6. What, then, is good? How is good to be defined? Now, it may be thought that this is a verbal question. A definition does indeed often mean the expressing of one word's meaning in other words. But this is not the sort of definition I am asking for. Such a definition can never be of ultimate importance in any study except lexicography. If I wanted that kind of definition I should have to consider in the first place how people generally used the word 'good'; but my business is not with its proper usage, as established by custom. I should, indeed, be foolish, if I tried to use it for something which it did not usually denote: if, for instance, I were to announce that, whenever I used the word 'good,' I must be understood to be thinking of that object which is usually denoted by the word 'table.' I shall, therefore, use the word in the sense in which I think it is ordinarily used; but at the same time I am not anxious to discuss whether I am right in thinking that it is so used. My business is solely with that object or idea, which I hold, rightly or wrongly, that the word is generally used to stand for. What I want to discover is the nature of that object or idea, and about this I am extremely anxious to arrive at an agreement.

But, if we understand the question in this sense, my answer to it may seem a very disappointing one. If I am asked 'What is good?' my answer is that good is good, and that is the end of the matter. Or if I am asked 'How is good to be defined?' my answer is that it cannot be defined, and that is all I have to say about it. But disappointing as these answers may appear, they are of the very last importance. To readers who are familiar with philosophic terminology, I can express their importance by saying that they amount to this: That propositions about the good are all of them synthetic and never analytic; and that is plainly no trivial matter. And the same thing may be expressed more popularly, by saying that, if I am right, then nobody can foist upon us such an axiom as that 'Pleasure is the only good' or that 'The good is the desired' on the pretence that this is 'the very meaning of the word.'

7. Let us, then, consider this position. My point is that 'good' is a simple notion, just as 'yellow' is a simple notion; that, just as you cannot, by any manner of means, explain to any one who does not already know it, what yellow is, so you cannot explain what good is. Definitions of the kind that I was asking for, definitions which describe the real nature of the object or notion denoted by a word, and which do not merely tell us what the word is used to mean, are only possible when the object or notion in question is something complex. You can give a definition of a horse, because a horse has many different properties and qualities, all of which you can enumerate. But when you have enumerated them all, when you have reduced a horse to his simplest terms, then you can no longer define those terms. They are simply something which you think of or perceive, and to any one who cannot think of or perceive them, you can never, by any definition, make their nature known. It may perhaps be objected to this that we are able to describe to others, objects which they have never seen or thought of. We can, for instance, make a man understand what a chimaera is, although he has never heard of one or seen one. You can tell him that it is an animal with a lioness's head and body, with a goat's head growing from the middle of its back, and with a snake in place of a tail. But here the object which you are describing is a complex object; it is entirely composed of parts, with which we are all perfectly familiar—a snake, a goat, a lioness; and we know, too, the manner in which those parts are to be put together, because we know what is meant by the middle of a lioness's back, and where her tail is wont to grow. And so it is with all objects, not previously known, which we are able to define: they are all complex; all composed of parts, which may themselves, in the first instance, be capable of similar definition, but which must in the end be reducible to simplest parts, which can no longer be defined. But yellow and good, we say, are not complex: they are notions of that simple kind, out of which definitions are composed and with which the power of further defining ceases.

8. When we say, as Webster says, 'The definition of horse is "A hoofed quadruped of the genus Equus," we may, in fact, mean three different things. (1) We may mean merely: 'When I say "horse," you are to understand that I am talking about a hoofed quadruped of the genus Equus.' This might be called the arbitrary verbal definition: and I do not mean that good is indefinable in that sense. (2) We may mean, as Webster ought to mean: 'When most English people say "horse," they mean a hoofed quadruped of the genus Equus.' This may be called the verbal definition proper, and I do not say that good is indefinable in this sense either; for it is certainly possible to discover how people use a word: otherwise, we could never have known that 'good' may be translated by 'gut' in German and by 'bon' in French. But (3) we may, when we define horse, mean something much more important. We may mean that a certain object, which we all of us know, is composed in a certain manner: that it has four legs, a head, a heart, a liver, etc., etc., all of them arranged in definite relations to one another. It is in this sense that I deny good to be definable. I say that it is not composed of any parts, which we can substitute for it in our minds when we are thinking of it. We might think just as clearly and correctly about a horse, if we thought of all its parts and their arrangement instead of thinking of the whole: we could, I say, think how a horse differed from a donkey just as well, just as truly, in this way, as now we do, only not so easily; but there is nothing whatsoever which we could so substitute for good; and that is what I mean, when I say that good is indefinable.

9. But I am afraid I have still not removed the chief difficulty which may prevent acceptance of the proposition that good is indefinable. I do not mean to say that *the* good, that which is good, is thus indefinable; if I did think so, I should not be writing on Ethics, for my main object is to help towards discovering that definition. It is just because I think there will be less risk of error in our search for a definition of 'the good,' that I am now insisting that *good* is indefinable. I must try to explain the difference between these two. I suppose it may be granted that 'good' is an adjective. Well 'the good,' 'that which is good,' must therefore be the substantive to which the adjective 'good' will apply: it must be the whole of that to which the adjective will apply, and the adjective must *always* truly apply to it. But if it is that to which the adjective will apply, it must be something different from that adjective itself; and the whole of that something different, whatever it is, will be our definition of *the* good. Now it may be that this something will have other adjectives, beside 'good,' that will apply to it. It may be full of pleasure, for example; it may be intelligent: and if these two adjectives are really part of its definition, then it will certainly be true, that pleasure and intelligence are good. And many people appear to think that, if we say 'Pleasure and intelligence are good,' or if we say 'Only pleasure and intelligence are good,' we are defining 'good.' Well, I cannot deny that propositions of this nature may sometimes be called definitions; I do not know well enough how the word is generally used to decide upon this point. I only wish it to be understood that that is not what I mean when I say there is no possible definition of good, and that I shall not mean this if I use the word again. I do most fully believe that some true proposition of the form 'Intelligence is good and intelligence alone is good' can be found; if none could be found, our definition of *the* good would be impossible. As it is, I believe *the* good to be definable; and yet I still say that good itself is indefinable.

10. 'Good,' then, if we mean by it that quality which we assert to belong to a thing, when we say that the thing is good, is incapable of any definition, in the most important sense of that word. The most important sense of 'definition' is that in which a definition states what are the parts which invariably compose a certain whole; and in this sense 'good' has no definition because it is simple and has no parts. It is one of those innumerable objects of thought which are themselves incapable of definition, because they are the ultimate terms by reference to which whatever *is* capable of definition must be defined. That there must be an indefinite number of such terms is obvious, on reflection; since we cannot define anything except by an analysis, which, when carried as far as it will go, refers us to something, which is simply different from anything else, and which by that ultimate difference explains the peculiarity of the whole which we are defining: for every whole contains some parts which are common to other wholes also. There is, therefore, no intrinsic difficulty in the contention that 'good' denotes a simple and indefinable quality. There are many other instances of such qualities.

Consider yellow, for example. We may try to define it, by describing its physical equivalent; we may state what kind of light-vibrations must stimulate the normal eye, in order that we may perceive it. But a moment's reflection is sufficient to show that those light-vibrations are not themselves what we mean by yellow. *They* are not what we perceive. Indeed we should never have been able to discover their existence, unless we had first been struck by the patent difference of quality between the different colours. The most we can be entitled to say of those vibrations is that they are what corresponds in space to the yellow which we actually perceive.

Yet a mistake of this simple kind has commonly been made about 'good.' It may be true that all things which are good are *also* something else, just as it is true that all things which are yellow produce a certain kind of vibration in the light. And it is a fact, that Ethics aims at discovering what are those other properties belonging to all things which are good. But far too many philosophers have thought that when they named those other properties they were actually defining good; that these properties, in fact, were simply not 'other,' but absolutely and entirely the same with goodness. This view I propose to call the 'naturalistic fallacy' and of it I shall now endeavour to dispose.

11. Let us consider what it is such philosophers say. And first it is to be noticed that they do not agree among themselves. They not only say that they are right as to what good is, but they endeavour to prove that other people who say that it is something else, are wrong. One, for instance, will affirm that good is pleasure, another, perhaps, that good is that which is desired; and each of these will argue eagerly to prove that the other is wrong. But how is that possible? One of them says that good is nothing but the object of desire, and at the same time tries to prove that it is not pleasure. But from his first assertion, that good just means the object of desire, one of two things must follow as regards his proof:

(1) He may be trying to prove that the object of desire is not pleasure. But, if this be all, where is his Ethics? The position he is maintaining is merely a psychological one. Desire is something which occurs in our minds, and pleasure is something else which so occurs; and our would-be ethical philosopher is merely holding that the latter is not the object of the former. But what has that to do with the question in dispute? His opponent held the ethical proposition that pleasure was the good, and although he should prove a million times over the psychological proposition that pleasure is not the object of desire, he is no nearer proving his opponent to be wrong. The position is like this. One man says a triangle is a circle: another replies 'A triangle is a straight line, and I will prove to you that I am right: *for*' (this is the only argument) 'a straight line is not a circle.' 'That is quite true,' the other may reply; 'but nevertheless a triangle is a circle, and you have said nothing whatever to prove the contrary. What is proved is that one of us is wrong, for we agree that a triangle cannot be both a straight line and a circle: but which is wrong, there can be no earthly means of proving, since you define triangle as straight line and I define it as circle.'— Well, that is one alternative which any naturalistic Ethics has to face; if good is *defined* as something else, it is then impossible either to prove that any other definition is wrong or even to deny such definition.

(2) The other alternative will scarcely be more welcome. It is that the discussion is after all a verbal one. When A says 'Good means pleasant' and B says 'Good means desired,' they may merely wish to assert that most people have used the word for what is pleasant and for what is desired respectively. And this is quite an interesting subject for discussion: only it is not a whit more an ethical discussion than the last was. Nor do I think that any exponent of naturalistic Ethics would be willing to allow that this was all he meant. They are all so anxious to persuade us that what they call the good is what we really ought to do. 'Do, pray, act so, because the word "good" is generally used to denote actions of this nature': such, on this view, would be the substance of their teaching. And in so far as they tell us how we ought to act, their teaching is truly ethical, as they mean it to be. But how perfectly absurd is the reason they would give for it! 'You are to do this, because most people use a certain word to denote conduct such as this.' 'You are to say the thing which is not, because most people call it lying.' That is an argument just as good!—My dear sirs, what we want to

know from you as ethical teachers, is not how people use a word; it is not even, what kind of actions they approve, which the use of this word 'good' may certainly imply: what we want to know is simply what *is* good. We may indeed agree that what most people do think good, is actually so; we shall at all events be glad to know their opinions: but when we say their opinions about what *is* good, we do mean what we say; we do not care whether they call that thing which they mean 'horse' or 'table' or 'chair', 'gut' or 'bon' or 'ἀγαθός'; we want to know what it is that they so call. When they say 'Pleasure is good,' we cannot believe that they merely mean 'Pleasure is pleasure' and nothing more than that.

12. Suppose a man says 'I am pleased'; and suppose that is not a lie or a mistake but the truth. Well, if it is true, what does that mean? It means that his mind, a certain definite mind, distinguished by certain definite marks from all others, has at this moment a certain definite feeling called pleasure. 'Pleased' *means* nothing but having pleasure, and though we may be more pleased or less pleased, and even, we may admit for the present, have one or another kind of pleasure; yet in so far as it is pleasure we have, whether there be more or less of it, and whether it be of one kind or another, what we have is one definite thing, absolutely indefinable, some one thing that is the same in all the various degrees and in all the various kinds of it that there may be. We may be able to say how it is related to other things: that, for example, it is in the mind, that it causes desire, that we are conscious of it, etc., etc. We can, I say, describe its relations to other things, but define it we can *not*. And if anybody tried to define pleasure for us as being any other natural object; if anybody were to say, for instance, that pleasure *means* the sensation of red, and were to proceed to deduce from that that pleasure is a colour, we should be entitled to laugh at him and to distrust his future statements about pleasure. Well, that would be the same fallacy which I have called the naturalistic fallacy. That 'pleased' does not mean 'having the sensation of red,' or anything else whatever, does not prevent us from understanding what it does mean. It is enough for us to know that 'pleased' does mean 'having the sensation of pleasure,' and though pleasure is absolutely indefinable, though pleasure is pleasure and nothing else whatever, yet we feel no difficulty in saying that we are pleased. The reason is, of course, that when I say 'I am pleased,' I do *not* mean that 'I' am the same thing as 'having pleasure.' And similarly no difficulty need be found in my saying that 'pleasure is good' and yet not meaning that 'pleasure' is the same thing as 'good,' that pleasure *means* good, and that good *means* pleasure. If I were to imagine that when I said 'I am pleased,' I meant that I was exactly the same thing as 'pleased,' I should not indeed call that a naturalistic fallacy, although it would be the same fallacy as I have called naturalistic with reference to Ethics. The reason of this is obvious enough. When a man confuses two natural objects with one another, defining the one by the other, if for instance, he confuses himself, who is one natural object, with 'pleased' or with 'pleasure' which are others, then there is no reason to call the fallacy naturalistic. But if he confuses 'good,' which is not in the same sense a natural object, with any natural object whatever, then there is a reason for calling that a naturalistic fallacy; its being made with regard to 'good' marks it as something quite specific, and this specific mistake deserves a name because it is so common. As for the reasons why good is not to be considered a natural object, they may be reserved for discussion in another place. But, for the present, it is sufficient to notice this: Even if it were a natural object, that would not alter the nature of the fallacy nor diminish its importance one whit. All that I have said about it would remain quite equally true: only the name which I have called it would not be so appropriate as I think it is. And I do not care about the name: what I do care about is the fallacy. It does not matter what we call it, provided we recognise it when we meet with it. It is to be met with in almost every book on Ethics; and yet it is not recognised: and that is why it is necessary to multiply illustrations of it, and convenient to give it a name. It is a very simple fallacy indeed. When we say that an orange is yellow, we do not think our statement binds us to hold that 'orange' means nothing else than 'yellow,' or that nothing can be yellow but an orange. Supposing the orange is also sweet! Does that bind us to say that 'sweet' is exactly the same thing as 'yellow,' that 'sweet' must be defined as 'yellow'? And supposing it be recognised that 'yellow' just means 'yellow' and nothing else whatever, does that make it any more difficult to hold that oranges are yellow? Most certainly it does not: on the contrary, it would be absolutely meaningless to say that oranges were yellow, unless yellow did in the end mean just 'yellow' and nothing else whatever—unless it was absolutely indefinable. We should not get any very clear notion about things, which are yellow—we should not get very far with our science, if we were bound to hold that everything which was yellow, *meant* exactly the same thing as yellow. We should find we had to hold that an orange was exactly the same thing as a stool, a piece of paper, a lemon, anything you like. We could prove any number of absurdities; but should we be the nearer to the truth? Why, then, should it be different with 'good'? Why, if good is good and indefinable, should I be held to deny that pleasure is good? Is there any difficulty in holding both to be true at once? On the contrary, there is no meaning in saying that pleasure is good, unless good is something different from pleasure. It is absolutely useless, so far as Ethics is concerned, to prove, as Mr. Spencer tries to do, that increase of pleasure coincides with increase of life, unless good *means* something different from either life or pleasure. He might just as well try to prove that an orange is yellow by shewing that it always is wrapped up in paper.

13. In fact, if it is not the case that 'good' denotes something simple and indefinable, only two alternatives are possible: either it is a complex, a given whole, about the correct analysis of which there may be disagreement; or else it means nothing at all, and there is no such subject as Ethics. In general, however, ethical philosophers have attempted to define good, without recognizing what such an attempt must mean. They actually use arguments which involve one or both of the absurdities considered in § 11. We are, therefore, justified in concluding that the attempt to define good is chiefly due to want of clearness as to the possible nature of definition. There are, in fact, only two serious alternatives to be considered, in order to establish the conclusion that 'good' does denote a simple and indefinable notion. It might possibly denote a complex, as 'horse' does; or it might have no meaning at all. Neither of these possibilities has, however, been clearly conceived and seriously maintained, as such, by those who presume to define good; and both may be dismissed by a simple appeal to facts.

(1) The hypothesis that disagreement about the meaning of good is disagreement with regard to the correct analysis of a given whole, may be most plainly seen to be incorrect by consideration of the fact that, whatever definition be offered, it may be always asked, with significance, of the complex so defined, whether it is itself good. To take, for instance, one of the more plausible, because one of the more complicated, of such proposed definitions, it may easily be thought, at first sight, that to be good may mean to be that which we desire to desire. Thus if we apply this definition to a particular instance and say 'When we think that A is good, we are thinking that A is one of the things which we desire to desire,' our proposition may seem quite plausible. But, if we carry the investigation further, and ask ourselves 'Is it good to desire to desire A?' it is apparent, on a little reflection, that this question is itself as intelligible, as the original question 'Is A good?'—that we are, in fact, now asking for exactly the same information about the desire to desire A, for which we formerly asked with regard to A itself. But it is also apparent that the meaning of this second question cannot be correctly analysed into 'Is the desire to desire A one of the things which we desire to desire?': we have not before our minds anything so complicated as the question 'Do we desire to desire to desire to desire A?' Moreover any one can easily convince himself by inspection that the predicate of this proposition—'good'—is positively different from the notion of 'desiring to desire' which enters into its subject: 'That we should desire to desire A is good' is *not* merely equivalent to 'That A should be good is good.' It may indeed be true

that what we desire to desire is always also good; perhaps, even the converse may be true: but it is very doubtful whether this is the case, and the mere fact that we understand very well what is meant by doubting it, shews clearly that we have two different notions before our minds.

(2) And the same consideration is sufficient to dismiss the hypothesis that 'good' has no meaning whatsoever. It is very natural to make the mistake of supposing that what is universally true is of such a nature that its negation would be self-contradictory: the importance which has been assigned to analytic propositions in the history of philosophy shews how easy such a mistake is. And thus it is very easy to conclude that what seems to be a universal ethical principle is in fact an identical proposition; that, if, for example, whatever is called 'good' seems to be pleasant, the proposition 'Pleasure is the good' does not assert a connection between two different notions, but involves only one, that of pleasure, which is easily recognised as a distinct entity. But whoever will attentively consider with himself what is actually before his mind when he asks the question 'Is pleasure (or whatever it may be) after all good?' can easily satisfy himself that he is not merely wondering whether pleasure is pleasant. And if he will try this experiment with each suggested definition in succession, he may become expert enough to recognise that in every case he has before his mind a unique object, with regard to the connection of which with any other object, a distinct question may be asked. Every one does in fact understand the question 'Is this good?' When he thinks of it, his state of mind is different from what it would be, were he asked 'Is this pleasant, or desired, or approved?' It has a distinct meaning for him, even though he may not recognise in what respect it is distinct. Whenever he thinks of 'intrinsic value,' or 'intrinsic worth,' or says that a thing 'ought to exist,' he has before his mind the unique object—the unique property of things— which I mean by 'good.' Everybody is constantly aware of this notion, although he may never become aware at all that it is different from other notions of which he is also aware. But, for correct ethical reasoning, it is extremely important that he should become aware of this fact; and, as soon as the nature of the problem is clearly understood, there should be little difficulty in advancing so far in analysis.

14. 'Good,' then, is indefinable; and yet, so far as I know, there is only one ethical writer, Prof. Henry Sidgwick, who has clearly recognised and stated this fact. We shall see, indeed, how far many of the most reputed ethical systems fall short of drawing the conclusions which follow from such a recognition. At present I will only quote one instance, which will serve to illustrate the meaning and importance of this principle that 'good' is indefinable, or, as Prof. Sidgwick says, an 'unanalysable notion.' It is an instance to which Prof. Sidgwick himself refers in a note on the passage, in which he argues that 'ought' is unanalysable[1].

'Bentham,' says Sidgwick, 'explains that his fundamental principle "states the greatest happiness of all those whose interest is in question as being the right and proper end of human action"'; and yet 'his language in other passages of the same chapter would seem to imply' that he *means* by the word "right" "conducive to the general happiness." Prof. Sidgwick sees that, if you take these two statements together, you get the absurd result that 'greatest happiness is the end of human action, which is conducive to the general happiness'; and so absurd does it seem to him to call this result, as Bentham calls it, 'the fundamental principle of a moral system,' that he suggests that Bentham cannot have meant it. Yet Prof. Sidgwick himself states elsewhere[2] that Psychological Hedonism is 'not seldom confounded with Egoistic Hedonism'; and that confusion, as we shall see, rests chiefly on that same fallacy, the naturalistic fallacy, which is implied in Bentham's statements. Prof. Sidgwick admits therefore that this fallacy is sometimes committed, absurd as it is; and I am inclined to think that Bentham may really have been one of those who committed it. Mill, as we shall see, certainly did commit it. In any case, whether Bentham committed it or not, his doctrine, as above quoted, will serve as a very good illustration of this fallacy, and of the importance of the contrary proposition that good is indefinable.

Let us consider this doctrine. Bentham seems to imply, so Prof. Sidgwick says, that the word 'right' *means* 'conducive to general happiness.' Now this, by itself, need not necessarily involve the naturalistic fallacy. For the word 'right' is very commonly appropriated to actions which lead to the attainment of what is good; which are regarded as *means* to the ideal and not as ends-in-themselves. This use of 'right,' as denoting what is good as a means, whether or not it be also good as an end, is indeed the use to which I shall confine the word. Had Bentham been using 'right' in this sense, it might be perfectly consistent for him to *define* right as 'conducive to the general happiness,' *provided only* (and notice this proviso) he had already proved, or laid down as an axiom, that general happiness was *the* good, or (what is equivalent to this) that general happiness alone was good. For in that case he would have already defined *the* good as general happiness (a position perfectly consistent, as we have seen, with the contention that 'good' is indefinable), and, since right was to be defined as 'conducive to *the* good,' it would actually *mean* 'conducive to general happiness.' But this method of escape from the charge of having committed the natural-

---

[1] *Methods of Ethics*, Bk. 1, Chap. iii, § 1 (6th edition).
[2] *Methods of Ethics*, Bk. 1, Chap. iv, § 1.

istic fallacy has been closed by Bentham himself. For his fundamental principle is, we see, that the greatest happiness of all concerned is the *right* and proper *end* of human action. He applies the word 'right,' therefore, to the end, as such, not only to the means which are conducive to it; and, that being so, right can no longer be defined as 'conducive to the general happiness,' without involving the fallacy in question. For now it is obvious that the definition of right as conducive to general happiness can be used by him in support of the fundamental principle that general happiness is the right end; instead of being itself derived from that principle. If right, by definition, means conducive to general happiness, then it is obvious that general happiness is the right end. It is not necessary now first to prove or assert that general happiness is the right end, before right is defined as conducive to general happiness—a perfectly valid procedure; but on the contrary the definition of right as conducive to general happiness proves general happiness to be the right end—a perfectly invalid procedure, since in this case the statement that 'general happiness is the right end of human action' is not an ethical principle at all, but either, as we have seen, a proposition about the meaning of words, or else a proposition about the *nature* of general happiness, not about its rightness or goodness.

Now, I do not wish the importance I assign to this fallacy to be misunderstood. The discovery of it does not at all refute Bentham's contention that greatest happiness is the proper end of human action, if that be understood as an ethical proposition, as he undoubtedly intended it. That principle may be true all the same; we shall consider whether it is so in succeeding chapters. Bentham might have maintained it, as Prof. Sidgwick does, even if the fallacy had been pointed out to him. What I am maintaining is that the *reasons* which he actually gives for his ethical proposition are fallacious ones so far as they consist in a definition of right. What I suggest is that he did not perceive them to be fallacious; that, if he had done so, he would have been led to seek for other reasons in support of his Utilitarianism; and that, had he sought for other reasons, he *might* have found none which he thought to be sufficient. In that case he would have changed his whole system—a most important consequence. It is undoubtedly also possible that he would have thought other reasons to be sufficient, and in that case his ethical system, in its main results, would still have stood. But, even in this latter case, his use of the fallacy would be a serious objection to him as an ethical philosopher. For it is the business of Ethics, I must insist, not only to obtain true results, but also to find valid reasons for them. The direct object of Ethics is knowledge and not practice; and any one who uses the naturalistic fallacy has certainly not fulfilled this first object, however correct his practical principles may be.

My objections to Naturalism are then, in the first place, that it offers no reason at all, far less any valid reason, for any ethical principle whatever; and in this it already fails to satisfy the requirements of Ethics, as a scientific study. But in the second place I contend that, though it gives a reason for no ethical principle, it is a *cause* of the acceptance of false principles—it deludes the mind into accepting ethical principles, which are false; and in this it is contrary to every aim of Ethics. It is easy to see that if we start with a definition of right conduct as conduct conducive to general happiness; then, knowing that right conduct is universally conduct conducive to the good, we very easily arrive at the result that the good is general happiness. If, on the other hand, we once recognise that we must start our Ethics without a definition, we shall be much more apt to look about us, before we adopt any ethical principle whatever; and the more we look about us, the less likely are we to adopt a false one. It may be replied to this: Yes, but we shall look about us just as much, before we settle on our definition, and are therefore just as likely to be right. But I will try to shew that this is not the case. If we start with the conviction that a definition of good can be found, we start with the conviction that good *can mean* nothing else than some one property of things; and our only business will then be to discover what that property is. But if we recognise that, so far as the meaning of good goes, anything whatever may be good, we start with a much more open mind. Moreover, apart from the fact that, when we think we have a definition, we cannot logically defend our ethical principles in any way whatever, we shall also be much less apt to defend them well, even if illogically. For we shall start with the conviction that good must mean so and so, and shall therefore be inclined either to misunderstand our opponent's arguments or to cut them short with the reply, 'This is not an open question: the very meaning of the word decides it; no one can think otherwise except through confusion.'

15. Our first conclusion as to the subject-matter of Ethics is, then, that there is a simple, indefinable, unanalysable object of thought by reference to which it must be defined. By what name we call this unique object is a matter of indifference, so long as we clearly recognise what it is and that it does differ from other objects. The words which are commonly taken as the signs of ethical judgments all do refer to it; and they are expressions of ethical judgments solely because they do so refer. But they may refer to it in two different ways, which it is very important to distinguish, if we are to have a complete definition of the range of ethical judgments. Before I proceeded to argue that there was such an indefinable notion involved in ethical notions, I stated (§ 4) that it was necessary for Ethics to enumerate all true universal judgments, asserting that such and such a thing was good, whenever it occurred. But, although all such judgments do refer to that unique notion which I have called 'good,' they do not all refer to it in the same way. They may either assert that this unique property does always attach to the thing in question, or else they may assert only that the thing in question is *a cause or necessary condition* for the existence of other things to which this unique property does attach. The nature of these two species of universal ethical judgments is extremely different; and a great part of the difficulties, which are met with in ordinary ethical speculation, are due to the failure to distinguish them clearly. Their difference has, indeed, received expression in ordinary language by the contrast between the terms 'good as means' and 'good in itself,' 'value as a means' and 'intrinsic value.' But these terms are apt to be applied correctly only in the more obvious instances; and this seems to be due to the fact that the distinction between the conceptions which they denote has not been made a separate object of investigation. . . .

Alfred Jules Ayer (b. 1910)

Alfred Jules Ayer was educated at Oxford University, served in the British Military Intelligence during World War II, and since 1946 has been Grote Professor of the Philosophy of Mind and Logic at the University of London. His book *Language, Truth and Logic* was published in 1936. Its criticism of traditional metaphysics, theology, and ethics caused great controversy, and the book has become the best-known exposition of the philosophical movement known as logical positivism. Ayer has published many books, including *The Foundations of Empirical Knowledge* (1940), *Philosophical Essays* (1954), *The Problem of Knowledge* (1956), *The Concept of a Person and Other Essays* (1963), *Metaphysics and Common Sense* (1969), *Russell and Moore: The Analytical Heritage* (1971), and *The Central Questions of Philosophy* (1974).

The most thorough and detailed defense of the emotive theory of ethics is *Ethics and Language* (1945) by Charles L. Stevenson. The view that ethical terms cannot be defined by means of nonethical terms is presented in our selection from Moore's *Principia Ethica* (1903). The following books contain useful expositions and appraisals of emotivism, including Ayer's version: *Ethics* (1954) by P. H. Nowell-Smith, *Ethics Since 1900* (1960) by M. Warnock, *The Revolution in Ethical Theory* (1966) by G. Kerner, *Contemporary Moral Philosophy* (1967) by G. J. Warnock, and *Twentieth-Century Ethics* (1974) by Roger Hancock.

Language, Truth and Logic

FROM: VI **Critique of Ethics**

There is still one objection to be met before we can claim to have justified our view that all synthetic propositions are empirical hypotheses. This objection is based on the common supposition that our speculative knowledge is of two distinct kinds—that which relates to questions of empirical fact, and that which relates to questions of value. It will be said that 'statements of value' are genuine synthetic propositions, but that they cannot with any show of justice be represented as hypotheses, which are used to predict the course of our sensations; and, accordingly, that the existence of ethics and aesthetics as branches of speculative knowledge presents an insuperable objection to our radical empiricist thesis.

In face of this objection, it is our business to give an account of 'judgments of value' which is both satisfactory in itself and consistent with our general empiricist principles. We shall set ourselves to show that in so far as statements of value are significant, they are ordinary 'scientific' statements; and that in so far as they are not scientific, they are not in the literal sense significant, but are simply expressions of emotion which can be neither true nor false. In maintaining this view, we may confine ourselves for the present to the case of ethical statements. What is said about them will be found to apply, *mutatis mutandis,* to the case of aesthetic statements also.

The ordinary system of ethics, as elaborated in the works of ethical philosophers, is very far from being a homogeneous whole. Not only is it apt to contain pieces of metaphysics, and analyses of non-ethical concepts: its actual ethical contents are themselves of very different kinds. We may divide them, indeed, into four main classes. There are, first of all, propositions which express definitions of ethical terms, or judgements about the legitimacy or possibility of certain definitions. Secondly, there are propositions describing the phenomena of moral experience, and their causes. Thirdly, there are exhortations to moral virtue. And, lastly, there are actual ethical judgements. It is unfortunately the case that the distinction between these four classes, plain as it is, is commonly ignored by ethical philosophers; with the result that

---

From *Language, Truth and Logic* by Alfred J. Ayer. Reprinted by permission of Victor Gollancz, Ltd.

it is often very difficult to tell from their works what it is that they are seeking to discover or prove.

In fact, it is easy to see that only the first of our four classes, namely that which comprises the propositions relating to the definitions of ethical terms, can be said to constitute ethical philosophy. The propositions which describe the phenomena of moral experience, and their causes, must be assigned to the science of psychology, or sociology. The exhortations to moral virtue are not propositions at all, but ejaculations or commands which are designed to provoke the reader to action of a certain sort. Accordingly, they do not belong to any branch of philosophy or science. As for the expressions of ethical judgements, we have not yet determined how they should be classified. But inasmuch as they are certainly neither definitions nor comments upon definitions, nor quotations, we may say decisively that they do not belong to ethical philosophy. A strictly philosophical treatise on ethics should therefore make no ethical pronouncements. But it should, by giving an analysis of ethical terms, show what is the category to which all such pronouncements belong. And this is what we are now about to do.

A question which is often discussed by ethical philosophers is whether it is possible to find definitions which would reduce all ethical terms to one or two fundamental terms. But this question, though it undeniably belongs to ethical philosophy, is not relevant to our present enquiry. We are not now concerned to discover which term, within the sphere of ethical terms, is to be taken as fundamental; whether, for example, 'good' can be defined in terms of 'right' or 'right' in terms of 'good,' or both in terms of 'value.' What we are interested in is the possibility of reducing the whole sphere of ethical terms to non-ethical terms. We are enquiring whether statements of ethical value can be translated into statements of empirical fact.

That they can be so translated is the contention of those ethical philosophers who are commonly called subjectivists, and of those who are known as utilitarians. For the utilitarian defines the rightness of actions, and the goodness of ends, in terms of the pleasure, or happiness, or satisfaction, to which they give rise; the subjectivist, in terms of the feelings of approval which a certain person, or group of people, has towards them. Each of these types of definition makes moral judgements into a sub-class of psychological or sociological judgements; and for this reason they are very attractive to us. For, if either was correct, it would follow that ethical assertions were not generically different from the factual assertions which are ordinarily contrasted with them; and the account which we have already given of empirical hypotheses would apply to them also.

Nevertheless we shall not adopt either a subjectivist or a utilitarian analysis of ethical terms. We reject the subjectivist view that to call an action right, or a thing good, is to say that it is generally approved of, because it is not self-contradictory to assert that some actions which are generally approved of are not right, or that some things which are generally approved of are not good. And we reject the alternative subjectivist view that a man who asserts that a certain action is right, or that a certain thing is good, is saying that he himself approves of it, on the ground that a man who confessed that he sometimes approved of what was bad or wrong would not be contradicting himself. And a similar argument is fatal to utilitarianism. We cannot agree that to call an action right is to say that of all the actions possible in the circumstances it would cause, or be likely to cause, the greatest happiness, or the greatest balance of pleasure over pain, or the greatest balance of satisfied over unsatisfied desire, because we find that it is not self-contradictory to say that it is sometimes wrong to perform the action which would actually or probably cause the greatest happiness, or the greatest balance of pleasure over pain, or of satisfied over unsatisfied desire. And since it is not self-contradictory to say that some pleasant things are not good, or that some bad things are desired, it cannot be the case that the sentence 'x is good' is equivalent to 'x is pleasant,' or to 'x is desired.' And to every other variant of utilitarianism with which I am acquainted the same objection can be made. And therefore we should, I think, conclude that the validity of ethical judgements is not determined by the felicific tendencies of actions, any more than by the nature of people's feelings; but that it must be regarded as 'absolute' or 'intrinsic,' and not empirically calculable.

If we say this, we are not, of course, denying that it is possible to invent a language in which all ethical symbols are definable in non-ethical terms, or even that it is desirable to invent such a language and adopt it in place of our own; what we are denying is that the suggested reduction of ethical to non-ethical statements is consistent with the conventions of our actual language. That is, we reject utilitarianism and subjectivism, not as proposals to replace our existing ethical notions by new ones, but as analyses of our existing ethical notions. Our contention is simply that, in our language, sentences which contain normative ethical symbols are not equivalent to sentences which express psychological propositions, or indeed empirical propositions of any kind.

It is advisable here to make it plain that it is only normative ethical symbols, and not descriptive ethical symbols, that are held by us to be indefinable in factual terms. There is a danger of confusing these two types of symbols, because they are commonly constituted by signs of the same sensible form. Thus a complex sign of the form 'x is wrong' may constitute a sentence which expresses a moral judgement concerning a certain type of conduct, or it may constitute a sentence which states that a certain type of conduct is repugnant to the moral sense of a particular society. In the latter case, the symbol 'wrong' is a descriptive ethical symbol, and the sentence in which it occurs expresses an ordinary sociological proposition; in the former case, the symbol 'wrong' is a normative ethical symbol, and the sentence in which it occurs does not, we maintain, express an empirical proposition at all. It is only with normative ethics that we are at present concerned; so that whenever ethical symbols are used in the course of this argument without qualification, they are always to be interpreted as symbols of the normative type.

In admitting that normative ethical concepts are irreducible to empirical concepts, we seem to be leaving the way clear for the 'absolutist' view of ethics—that is, the view that statements of value are not controlled by observation, as ordinary empirical propositions are, but only by a mysterious 'intellectual intuition.' A feature of this theory, which is seldom recognized by its advocates, is that it makes statements of value unverifiable. For it is notorious that what seems intuitively certain to one person may seem doubtful, or even false, to another. So that unless it is possible to provide some criterion by which one may decide between conflicting intuitions, a mere appeal to intuition is worthless as a test of a proposition's validity. But in the case of moral judgements, no such criterion can be given. Some moralists claim to settle the matter by saying that they 'know' that their own moral judgements are correct. But such an assertion is of purely psychological interest, and has not the slightest tendency to prove the validity of any moral judgement. For dissentient moralists may equally well 'know' that their ethical views are correct. And, as far as subjective certainty goes, there will be nothing to choose between them. When such differences of opinion arise in connection with an ordinary empirical proposition, one may attempt to resolve them by referring to, or actually carrying out, some relevant empirical test. But with regard to ethical statements, there is, on the 'absolutist' or 'intuitionist' theory, no relevant empirical test. We are therefore justified in saying that on this theory ethical statements are held to be unverifiable. They are, of course, also held to be genuine synthetic propositions.

Considering the use which we have made of the principle that a synthetic proposition is significant only if it is empirically verifiable, it is clear that the acceptance of an 'absolutist' theory of ethics would undermine the whole of our main argument. And as we have already rejected the 'naturalistic' theories which are commonly supposed to provide the only alternative to 'absolutism' in ethics, we seem to have reached a difficult position. We shall meet the difficulty by showing that the correct treatment of ethical statements is afforded by a third theory, which is wholly compatible with our radical empiricism.

We begin by admitting that the fundamental ethical concepts are unanalysable, inasmuch as there is no criterion by which one can test the validity of the judgements in which they occur. So far we are in agreement with the absolutists. But, unlike the absolutists, we are able to give an explanation of this fact about ethical concepts. We say that the reason why they are unanalysable is that they are mere pseudo-concepts. The presence of an ethical symbol in a proposition adds nothing to its factual content. Thus if I say to someone, 'You acted wrongly in stealing that money,' I am not stating anything more than if I had simply said, 'You stole that money.' In adding that this action is wrong I am not making any further statement about it. I am simply evincing my moral disapproval of it. It is as if I had said, 'You stole that money,' in a peculiar tone of horror, or written it with the addition of some special exclamation marks. The tone, or the exclamation marks, adds nothing to the literal meaning of the sentence. It merely serves to show that the expression of it is attended by certain feelings in the speaker.

If now I generalise my previous statement and say, 'Stealing money is wrong,' I produce a sentence which has no factual meaning—that is, expresses no proposition which can be either true or false. It is as if I had written 'Stealing money!!'—where the shape and thickness of the exclamation marks show, by a suitable convention, that a special sort of moral disapproval is the feeling which is being expressed. It is clear that there is nothing said here which can be true or false. Another man may disagree with me about the wrongness of stealing, in the sense that he may not have the same feelings about stealing as I have, and he may quarrel with me on account of my moral sentiments. But he cannot strictly speaking, contradict me. For in saying that a certain type of action is right or wrong, I am not making any factual statement, not even a statement about my own state of mind. I am merely expressing certain moral sentiments. And the man who is ostensibly contradicting me is merely expressing his moral sentiments. So that there is plainly no sense in asking which of us is in the right. For neither of us is asserting a genuine proposition.

What we have just been saying about the symbol 'wrong' applies to all normative ethical symbols. Sometimes they occur in sentences which record ordinary empirical facts besides expressing ethical feeling about those facts: sometimes they occur in sentences which simply express ethical feeling about a certain type of action, or situation, without making any statement of fact. But in every case in which one would commonly be said to be making an ethical judgement, the function of the relevant ethical word is purely 'emotive.' It is used to express feeling about certain objects, but not to make any assertion about them.

It is worth mentioning that ethical terms do not serve only to express feeling. They are calculated also to arouse feeling, and so to stimulate action. Indeed some of them are used in such a way as to give the sentences in which they occur the effect of commands. Thus the sentence 'It is your duty to tell the truth' may be regarded both as the expression of a certain sort of ethical feeling about truthfulness and as the expression of the command 'Tell the truth.' The sentence 'You ought to tell the truth' also involves the command 'Tell the truth,' but here the tone of the command is less emphatic. In the sentence 'It is good to tell the truth' the command has become little more than a suggestion. And thus the 'meaning' of the word 'good,' in its ethical usage, is differentiated from that of the word 'duty' or the word 'ought.' In fact we may define the meaning of the various ethical words in terms both of the different feelings they are ordinarily taken to express, and also the different responses which they are calculated to provoke.

We can now see why it is impossible to find a criterion for determining the validity of ethical judgements. It is not because they have an 'absolute' validity which is mysteriously independent of ordinary sense-experience, but because they have no objective validity whatsoever. If a sentence makes no statement at all, there is obviously no sense in asking whether what it says is true or false. And we have seen that sentences which simply express moral judgements do not say anything. They are pure expressions of feeling and as such do not come under the category of truth and falsehood. They are unverifiable for the same reason as a cry of pain or a word of command is unverifiable—because they do not express genuine propositions.

Thus, although our theory of ethics might fairly be said to be radically subjectivist, it differs in a very important respect from the orthodox subjectivist theory. For the orthodox subjectivist does not deny, as we do, that the sentences of a moralizer express genuine propositions. All he denies is that they express propositions of a unique nonempirical character. His own view is that they express propositions about the speaker's feelings. If this were so, ethical judgements clearly would be capable of being true or false. They would be true if the speaker had the relevant feelings, and false if he had not. And this is a matter which is, in principle, empirically verifiable. Furthermore they could be significantly contradicted. For if I say, 'Tolerance is a virtue,' and someone answers, 'You don't approve of it,' he would, on the ordinary subjectivist theory, be contradicting me. On our theory, he would not be contradicting me, because, in saying that tolerance was a virtue, I should not be making any statement about my own feelings or about anything else. I should simply be evincing my feelings, which is not at all the same thing as saying that I have them.

The distinction between the expression of feeling and the assertion of feeling is complicated by the fact that the assertion that one has a certain feeling often accompanies the expression of that feeling, and is then, indeed, a factor in the expression of that feeling. Thus I may simultaneously express boredom and say that I am bored, and in that case my utterance of the words, 'I am bored,' is one of the circumstances which make it true to say that I am expressing or evincing boredom. But I can express boredom without actually saying that I am bored. I can express it by my tone and gestures, while making a statement about something wholly unconnected with it, or by an ejaculation, or without uttering any words at all. So that even if the assertion that one has a certain feeling always involves the expression of that feeling, the expression of a feeling assuredly does not always involve the assertion that one has it. And this is the important point to grasp in considering the distinction between our theory and the ordinary subjectivist theory. For whereas the subjectivist holds that ethical statements actually assert the existence of certain feelings, we hold that ethical statements are expressions and excitants of feeling which do not necessarily involve any assertion.

We have already remarked that the main objection to the ordinary subjectivist theory is that the validity of ethical judgements is not determined by the nature of their author's feelings. And this is an objection which our theory escapes. For it does not imply that the existence of any feelings is a necessary and sufficient condition of the validity of an ethical judgement. It implies, on the contrary, that ethical judgements have no validity.

There is, however, a celebrated argument against subjectivist theories which our theory does not escape. It has been pointed out by Moore that if ethical statements were simply statements about the speaker's feelings, it would be impossible to argue about questions of value.[1] To take a typical example: if a man said that thrift was a virtue, and another replied that it was a vice, they would not, on this theory, be disputing with one another. One would be saying that he approved of thrift, and the other that he didn't; and there is no reason why both these statements should not be true. Now Moore held it to be obvious that we do dispute about questions of value, and accordingly concluded that the particular form of subjectivism which he was discussing was false.

It is plain that the conclusion that it is impossible to dispute about questions of value follows from our theory also. For as we hold that such sentences as 'Thrift is a virtue' and 'Thrift is a vice' do not express propositions at all, we clearly cannot hold that they express incompatible propositions. We must therefore admit that if Moore's argument really refutes the ordinary subjectivist theory, it also refutes ours. But, in fact, we deny that it does refute even the ordinary sub-

---

[1] Cf. *Philosophical Studies*, 'The Nature of Moral Philosophy.'

jectivist theory. For we hold that one really never does dispute about questions of value.

This may seem, at first sight, to be a very paradoxical assertion. For we certainly do engage in disputes which are ordinarily regarded as disputes about questions of value. But, in all such cases, we find, if we consider the matter closely, that the dispute is not really about a question of value, but about a question of fact. When someone disagrees with us about the moral value of a certain action or type of action, we do admittedly resort to argument in order to win him over to our way of thinking. But we do not attempt to show by our arguments that he has the 'wrong' ethical feeling towards a situation whose nature he has correctly apprehended. What we attempt to show is that he is mistaken about the facts of the case. We argue that he has misconceived the agent's motive; or that he has misjudged the effects of the action, or its probable effects in view of the agent's knowledge; or that he has failed to take into account the special circumstances in which the agent was placed. Or else we employ more general arguments about the effects which actions of a certain type tend to produce, or the qualities which are usually manifested in their performance. We do this in the hope that we have only to get our opponent to agree with us about the nature of the empirical facts for him to adopt the same moral attitude towards them as we do. And as the people with whom we argue have generally received the same moral education as ourselves, and live in the same social order, our expectation is usually justified. But if our opponent happens to have undergone a different process of moral 'conditioning' from ourselves, so that, even when he acknowledges all the facts, he still disagrees with us about the moral value of the actions under discussion, then we abandon the attempt to convince him by argument. We say that it is impossible to argue with him because he has a distorted or undeveloped moral sense; which signifies merely that he employs a different set of values from our own. We feel that our own system of values is superior, and therefore speak in such derogatory terms of his. But we cannot bring forward any arguments to show that our system is superior. For our judgement that it is so is itself a judgement of value, and accordingly outside the scope of argument. It is because argument fails us when we come to deal with pure questions of value, as distinct from questions of fact, that we finally resort to mere abuse.

In short, we find that argument is possible on moral questions only if some system of values is presupposed. If our opponent concurs with us in expressing moral disapproval of all actions of a given type t, then we may get him to condemn a particular action A, by bringing forward arguments to show that A is of type t. For the question whether A does or does not belong to that type is a plain question of fact. Given that a man has certain moral principles, we argue that he must, in order to be consistent, react morally to certain things in a certain way. What we do not and cannot argue about is the validity of these moral principles. We merely praise or condemn them in the light of our own feelings.

If anyone doubts the accuracy of this account of moral disputes, let him try to construct even an imaginary argument on a question of value which does not reduce itself to an argument about a question of logic or about an empirical matter of fact. I am confident that he will not succeed in producing a single example. And if that is the case, he must allow that its involving the impossibility of purely ethical arguments is not, as Moore thought, a ground of objection to our theory, but rather a point in favour of it.

Having upheld our theory against the only criticism which appeared to threaten it, we may now use it to define the nature of all ethical enquiries. We find that ethical philosophy consists simply in saying that ethical concepts are pseudo-concepts and therefore unanalysable. The further task of describing the different feelings that the different ethical terms are used to express, and the different reactions that they customarily provoke, is a task for the psychologist. There cannot be such a thing as ethical science, if by ethical science one means the elaboration of a 'true' system of morals. For we have seen that, as ethical judgements are mere expressions of feeling, there can be no way of determining the validity of any ethical system, and, indeed, no sense in asking whether any such system is true. All that one may legitimately enquire in this connection is, What are the moral habits of a given person or group of people, and what causes them to have precisely those habits and feelings? And this enquiry falls wholly within the scope of the existing social sciences.

It appears, then, that ethics, as a branch of knowledge, is nothing more than a department of psychology and sociology. And in case anyone thinks that we are overlooking the existence of casuistry, we may remark that casuistry is not a science, but is a purely analytical investigation of the structure of a given moral system. In other words, it is an exercise in formal logic.

When one comes to pursue the psychological enquiries which constitute ethical science, one is immediately enabled to account for the Kantian and hedonistic theories of morals. For one finds that one of the chief causes of moral behavior is fear, both conscious and unconscious, of a god's displeasure, and fear of the enmity of society. And this, indeed, is the reason why moral precepts present themselves to some people as 'categorical' commands. And one finds, also, that the moral code of a society is partly determined by the beliefs of that society concerning the conditions of its own happiness—or, in other words, that a society tends to encourage or discourage a given type of conduct by the use of moral sanctions according as it appears to promote or detract from the contentment of the society as a whole. And this is the reason why altruism is recommended in most moral codes and egotism condemned. It is from the observation of this connection between morality and happiness that hedonistic or eudaemonistic theories of morals ultimately spring, just as the moral theory of Kant is based on the fact, previously explained, that moral precepts have for some people the force of inexorable commands. As each of these theories ignores the fact which lies at the root of the other, both may be criticized as being one-sided; but this is not the main objection to either of them. Their essential defect is that they treat propositions which refer to the causes and attributes of our ethical feelings as if they were definitions of ethical concepts. And thus they fail to recognise that ethical concepts are pseudo-concepts and consequently indefinable.

As we have already said, our conclusions about the nature of ethics apply to aesthetics also. Aesthetic terms are used in exactly the same way as ethical terms. Such aesthetic words as 'beautiful' and 'hideous' are employed, as ethical words are employed, not to make statements of fact, but simply to express certain feelings and evoke a certain response. It follows, as in ethics, that there is no sense in attributing objective validity to aesthetic judgements, and no possibility of arguing about questions of value in aesthetics, but only about questions of fact. A scientific treatment of aesthetics would show us what in general were the causes of aesthetic feeling, why various societies produced and admired the works of art they did, why taste varies as it does within a given society, and so forth. And these are ordinary psychological or sociological questions. They have, of course, little or nothing to do with aesthetic criticism as we understand it. But that is because the purpose of aesthetic criticism is not so much to give knowledge as to communicate emotion. The critic, by calling attention to certain features of the work under review, and expressing his own feelings about them, endeavours to make us share his attitude towards the work as a whole. The only relevant propositions that he formulates are propositions describing the nature of the work. And these are plain records of fact. We conclude, therefore, that there is nothing in aesthetics, any more than there is in ethics, to justify the view that it embodies a unique type of knowledge.

It should now be clear that the only information which we can legitimately derive from the study of our aesthetic and moral experiences is information about our own mental and physical make-up. We take note of these experiences as providing data for our psychological and sociological generalisations. And this is the only way in which they serve to increase our knowledge. It follows that any attempt to make our use of ethical and aesthetic concepts the basis of a metaphysical theory concerning the existence of a world of values, as distinct from the world of facts, involves a false analysis of these concepts. Our own analysis has shown that the phenomena of moral experience cannot fairly be used to support any rationalist or metaphysical doctrine whatsoever. In particular, they cannot, as Kant hoped, be used to establish the existence of a transcendent god.

Stephen Edelston Toulmin (b. 1922)

Stephen Toulmin attended Kings College, Cambridge, where he received a Ph.D. in 1948. He was a Fellow of Kings College from 1947 to 1951, University Lecturer in the Philosophy of Science at Oxford University from 1949 to 1955, and Professor of Philosophy at the University of Leeds from 1955 to 1959. In 1960 Toulmin became director of the Nuffield Foundation Unit for the History of Ideas. His first book, *An Examination of the Place of Reason in Ethics* (1950), quickly became very influential. Rule utilitarianism, of which Toulmin is the first explicit exponent, is currently the most generally accepted version of utilitarianism. His subsequent books mostly concern the history and philosophy of science: *The Philosophy of Science: An Introduction* (1953), *The Uses of Argument* (1958), a three-volume work called *The Ancestry of Science* (1961, 1962, 1965), *Foresight and Understanding* (1961), *Human Understanding*, vol. 1 (1972), and *Wittgenstein's Vienna* (1973).

An influential article that develops and explains the basis of Toulmin's distinction between particular actions and general practices is "Two Concepts of Rules," by John Rawls (*The Philosophical Review*, vol. 64, 1955). George Kerner's *The Revolution in Ethical Theory* (1966) contains an explanatory and appraisive chapter on Toulmin, as well as chapters on Moore and Hare.

An Examination of
the Place of Reason in Ethics

CHAPTER 10 **The Function and Development of Ethics**

'The function of scientific judgements is to alter one's expectations:
that of ethical judgements, by contrast, is to alter one's feelings and
behaviour.' If this were the only result of all that we have gone through,
one might justifiably complain of having been dragged twice round the
world only to be left in exactly the same position as one started from.
For the question we posed in the very first section took all this for
granted. Given that 'ethical' arguments are those designed to influence
behavior, we asked, to which arguments ('ethical,' needless to say) are
we to pay attention, and which are we to reject, when making up our
minds what to do? That 'ethical' arguments are arguments designed
to influence behaviour seems hardly worth mentioning; the real problem, which (you may protest) remains as unanswered as ever, is not
whether but *in what respects* we are to let them influence our behavior.

   The defence of this is the same as the defence of all round trips:
it broadens the mind. Although, geographically speaking, the place you
come back to is the 'same' place as that you set out from, you understand it better, feel more at ease in it, and can be more intelligently
critical of the things that go on there.[1] So now, although all the real
work lies ahead of us, we know very much better what it will involve,
what kinds of approach are sure to be vain, and which are at all likely
to be fruitful.

10.1 The Question at Issue

The first step towards solving our problem is to set it into its background; to see what it means in terms of our life and activities. The key
to the logic of ethical arguments and sentences is to be found in the

---

   Reprinted from *An Examination of the Place of Reason in Ethics* by Stephen
Toulmin, Chapters 10 and 11, by permission of the Cambridge University Press.
Published by the Syndics of the Cambridge University Press, 1960.
   [1] Cf. T. S. Eliot, *Little Gidding*:

   'We shall not cease from exploration
   And the end of all our exploring
   Will be to arrive where we started
   And know the place for the first time.'

way in which we come to allow reasons to affect our choice of actions. If we are to discover how to select 'valid' ethical arguments from 'invalid' ones, we must first answer the question, 'How is it that we come to let reasoning affect what we do at all?'

Now this question can be interpreted, and so answered, in a number of different ways. All the interpretations and answers are of interest to us, but only one of them is our direct concern. To mention four possibilities:

(i) It might be taken historically, as calling for a description of the course of events by which our ancestors passed from purely impulsive, unreasoning behaviour to the present, limited degree of rational behaviour; for a record of the different kinds of moral code which have existed, of the attitude, at various stages in the development, to conscience, tyranny and the reform of the moral code; and so on.

(ii) It might be taken psychologically, as calling for a description of the course of events accompanying the development of an individual's powers of moral reasoning; for a factual comparison of the different methods of education; for a study of the relation between poverty and vice; and so on.

(iii) It might be taken logically, as an enquiry about the kinds of change in behaviour characteristic of a decision based on 'moral' grounds; about the way in which reasoning must be designed to influence behaviour if it is to be called 'ethical'; and so on.

(iv) It might be interpreted philosophically, as a demand for a 'justification' of ethics; as asking why reasoning should be allowed to influence our behaviour at all.

Neither of the first two interpretations (nor the anthropological one, which can be regarded as a cross between them) is our immediate business. Answers to all these forms of the question will be interesting as illustrating what we are after, but the nature of the logical criteria applicable to ethics is manifestly independent of them. It cannot matter to us exactly what Socrates said, what attitude the sect of Thugs adopts towards ritual murder, how this or that degree of malnutrition affects individual moral standards, or at what age one first sees that there is a difference between 'wrong' and 'what Daddy forbids.' [2] The truth of what we are now after must be independent of whether Socrates even existed. We must therefore concentrate on the third interpretation mentioned—on the kinds of change in behaviour at which reasoning

---

[2] We may of course be influenced by the results of historical, psychological or anthropological research when discussing whether the moral code needs to be altered; but that is another matter.

must be aimed, if we are to call it 'moral' or 'ethical.' If this investigation is a success, its results should help us, by the way, to understand and deal with the fourth, philosophical form of the question.

10.2 The Notion of 'Duty'

Suppose, then, that two people are arguing about what to do. The one (A) begins by advocating course α the other (B) rejects α and proposes β instead. They continue to argue, bringing forward all kinds of reasons for and against α and β. Finally, they come to a decision, agreeing that γ and δ are *really* the right things to do. What kinds of reasons would they have to bring for and against α, β, γ and δ in order for us to say that 'ethical' considerations had affected their decisions, and that they had refrained from α and β in favour of γ and δ because they recognised that it would be 'morally wrong' to do otherwise?

The answer to this question must, in the first place, be twofold. Two types of consideration, not at first sight comparable, cry out to be called 'moral':

(i) arguments showing that γ and δ fulfil a 'duty' in the 'moral code' of the community to which A and B belong, whereas α and β contravene this part of the 'code';

(ii) arguments showing that γ and δ will avoid causing to other members of the community some inconvenience, annoyance or suffering which would be caused by α and β.

The second type of consideration suggests that ethics and ethical language can be regarded as part of the process whereby, as members of a community, we moderate our impulses and adjust our demands so as to reconcile them as far as possible with those of our fellows. But what about the first type of consideration—arguments from 'duty'? How far does it falsify our notions to regard these as a part of the same process? And does it derogate from the 'absoluteness' of 'duty' to characterise it in terms of this process?

The answer is that the only context in which the concept of 'duty' is straightforwardly intelligible is one of communal life—it is, indeed, completely bound up with this very feature of communal life, that we learn to renounce our claims and alter our aims where they conflict with those of our fellows. If this is not immediately obvious, it will become clear when we examine our use of the concept of 'duty' in a concrete case.

Suppose, therefore, that someone declares that he has made an 'anthropological discovery'—the discovery that, whereas there is no single 'duty' which is currently accepted in *all* communities, there·is no community in which *some* 'duties' are not recognised: 'Particular moral principles are Relative,' he may say; 'but all communities recognise the

Absolute Value of Duty.'[3] What kind of evidence shall we require him to cite, if he is to establish his discovery?

One sort of testimony will be no good at all: namely, the reports of an anthropologist who has asked the members of all the communities he has visited, 'Do you recognise the Absolute Value of Duty?' The majority of them would not speak his language, and could not understand his question. An unavoidable preliminary to asking them about it would therefore be to discover what their word for 'duty' was (if they had one). Now this is not nearly as simple a matter as it may seem. More than mere 'translation' is required, and it is all too easy to overlook the steps involved.

In order to discover what word these people used for 'duty,' he would have to watch their behaviour, and identify the word required, if there were one, by reference to the use they made of it in their relations with one another. And, given this, he would hardly need to ask the question. What features of their behaviour would one have to point to, therefore, in order to justify the discovery?

First, one would presumably remark on the fact that, in all the communities visited, *some* kinds of conduct were rewarded and reprobated respectively: secondly, that the exact kinds of conduct so treated varied from community to community. But one would require more than this. In all communities, there are many types of behaviour which are socially expected and yet which, taken singly, are hardly what we should call 'duties.' I should not say that I was 'morally' bound to wear white flannels for tennis, even though that is the 'expected' thing, and even though I might risk some slight degree of ostracism if I were to wear grey ones at a polite tennis party. Nor should I regard a single public belch, or ignorance of the formal modes of address, as grounds for a 'moral' reproach.

It is true that one does recognise a duty to conform on the whole: a man who always dresses eccentrically, never shows any respect for persons, and habitually belches in public does seem to invite criticism— and 'moral' criticism at that. But, in recognising this, we are concerned less with the eccentric behaviour itself than with the fact that it gives offence to others, and with the inconsiderateness of a man who can consistently ignore that fact.

Suppose, for example, that a Patagonian were giving a list of the 'duties' current among the English. He would not start off his list with points of dress or etiquette: still less would he class our going in for crossword puzzles, and giving a prize to the sender of the first correct

---

[3] Cf. A. Macbeath's contribution to the symposium on 'Ethics and Anthropology,' in *Aristotelian Soc. Suppl. Vol.* xx (1946).

solution opened, as a striking example of our recognition of the value of 'duty.' His interest would be more in types of behaviour which, if given up generally, would lead to distress in the society. Further, if winning competitions or wearing the right-coloured trousers were the only type of behaviour he found rewarded or punished among the inhabitants of our island; and if we let murder and rape, robbery and lying go by unnoticed, he would hesitate before saying that we provided a confirming instance of the law at all. But then, if that were the way we carried on, he could hardly call us a 'community' either!

This fact is most important: it shows us the nature of the 'discovery,' and (by implication) that of our concept of 'duty,' too. For consider what kinds of thing we require before we agree to call any collection of people a 'community.' Suppose, for example, that we visit an island, and find that its inhabitants all habitually avoid types of behaviour particularly liable to inconvenience their fellows: then we shall be prepared to refer to the inhabitants of the island as forming a single 'community.' And we shall also say that the members of the community 'recognise a duty to one another,' and 'have a moral code.' But if, instead, we find that we have to divide the inhabitants into two classes, C_1 and C_2—such that members of C_1 are scrupulous only in so far as their conduct affects other members of C_1, but ignore the interests of those of C_2; and those of C_2 respect the interests of other members of C_2 but ignore those of C_1— we shall not be able to call them 'members of a single community' at all. In fact, we shall call the two sets of people, C_1 and C_2, 'separate communities.' Likewise, we shall not be able to say that members of C_1 'recognise any duty' to members of C_2, or vice versa. But we shall have to agree that, within C_1 and C_2, duties are recognised: only in the extreme case, if C_2 consists of one man only, who has 'cut himself off from all communal life,' and carries on regardless of anyone else, can we say that there is anyone on the island who 'recognises *no* duties.' [4]

The degree of mutual respect we find between members of the two classes decides the extent to which we can call them parts of 'a single community.' The same degree of mutual respect decides how far we can say that the inhabitants 'recognise common duties.' Only if we found no such respect between any of the people on the island, and so no semblance of a 'community,' could we say that there was no recognition of the value of duty.

The 'anthropological discovery' that 'all communities recognise the Absolute Value of Duty' is therefore not a discovery at all, but some-

---

[4] Even he may be described as recognising 'duties towards himself' and, perhaps, 'duties towards his God'—but to say this is to shift our ground somewhat.

thing which an anthropologist could safely announce before he ever set out: it only explains, in an obscure and roundabout way, part of what we mean by the notion of a 'community.' 'In all "communities" (i.e., groups of people living together, and respecting one another's interests),' our informant is saying, in effect, 'people control their behaviour so as to have regard for one another's interests.' His 'law of human nature' is a truism, admitting of only one possible exception—a 'community' of angels, who always managed to do what was right instinctively and so had no need for a moral code. They might conceivably be said 'not to recognise the Absolute Value of Duty,' but this would be the case only because they never had cause to stop and 'recognise' it. No less talented 'community' could be so placed.

Even if 5000 supporters of the 'imperative doctrine'—all of them so enlightened as to realise the 'irrational' nature of morality, and all of them vowing to renounce ethical words and arguments as 'mere rationalisation'—even if they tried to live together as a community, they would soon have to adopt rules of behaviour; and, when it came to educating their children, some of their words would perforce become 'ethical.' 'You'll burn yourself if you play with fire,' uttered as the child was pulled away from it, would acquire the meaning of our own, 'You mustn't play with the fire, or you'll harm yourself'; 'It's annoying of you to cut holes in Daddy's trousers' accompanied by the removal of trousers and scissors, would come to mean, 'It's naughty of you to cut holes in Daddy's trousers'; and so on. And, after 20 years, either their 'community' would have ceased to exist, or it would have developed a code as 'moral' as any other—and the fact that the familiar words, 'good,' 'bad,' 'wicked' and 'virtuous,' had been given up would be irrelevant. This sort of thing does happen (I am told) in 'progressive schools,' whose products grow up using words like 'co-operative,' 'undesirable' and 'anti-social,' with all the rhetorical force and emotional associations commonly belonging to 'good,' 'wrong' and 'wicked.'

The concept of 'duty,' in short, is inextricable from the 'mechanics' of social life, and from the practices adopted by different communities in order to make living together in proximity tolerable or even possible. We need not therefore worry about the apparent duality of ethical arguments—about the contrast between arguments from 'duty' and arguments from the welfare of our fellows. And we can fairly characterise ethics as a part of the process whereby the desires and actions of the members of a community are harmonised.

The central importance of 'disposition' in ethics is now understandable: there would be no use for ethical reasoning, either among people whose feelings were wholly unalterable (and who would therefore behave exactly the same whether exhorted to change or not) or, on the other hand, among angels, whose dispositions were always of the best (and who would therefore have no need to inquire or discuss what to do).

Further, the analysis of what I have called the 'function' of ethics can now be completed; we can provisionally define it as being 'to correlate our feelings and behaviour in such a way as to make the fulfilment of everyone's aims and desires as far as possible compatible.'

It is in the light of this function, and of its context of communal living, that we must examine

(i) the development of morality and of ethical reasoning, and
(ii) the logical rules to be applied to ethical arguments.[5]

10.3 The Development of Ethics. (I)

Historically and psychologically alike, the development of ethics is most conveniently described in two contrasted stages. This division we shall find later reflected in the logic of ethics.

The first and most obvious way of preventing conflicts of interest in a community (whether a tribe or a family) is for all its members to have the same aims, the same interests, the same desires, hopes and fears; in fact the same dispositions. In its early stage, therefore, morality boils down to 'doing the done thing': and this is true, both of the way in which a child learns from its parents, and, in social prehistory, of moral codes. Primitive ethics is 'deontological,' a matter of rigid duties, taboos, customs and commandments. It prevents conflicts of interest by keeping the dispositions of all concerned aligned, and condemns behavior directed away from the prescribed aims. Further, these aims are not advocated but imposed, the use of ethical language being part of the behaviour adopted by 'those in authority' for enforcing co-operation: so no wonder if ethical utterances are often 'rhetorical.'

Respect for fixed 'social practices' (or 'done things'), though most

---

5 'Ah!' you may say, 'But compatibility of aims and desires takes one only a certain distance, since it could be achieved on various levels of excellence. Pushpin, to use Bentham's illustration, is as good as poetry, as an example of a non-competitive good.' It is true that we should deplore the taste of a community whose members did not discriminate between poetry and parlour games; but we could not condemn them on *moral* grounds. It is also true that, when discussing the arts, we often say things like, 'You *ought* to hear his violin concerto'; but again the notion of obligation is involved only by transference. So also is it when, in talking to a friend with a busy evening before him, we say, 'You *ought* to have a rest this afternoon.' One would never think of using examples of this kind when teaching anyone the notion of what he 'ought' and 'ought not' to do: the idea of obligation, as it affects our decisions, is primarily moral. In consequence, the present discussion must elucidate the notion of *moral* obligation first: less primitive and transferred uses of the notion will be touched on later—e.g. in §§ 11.8 and 12.1. On Bentham, see § 13.6.

characteristic of primitive morality, continues throughout the later stages of development, and can be recognised in our own societies. Although 'doing the done thing' may be merely conventionalism, it may equally be anything but that; especially in those situations in which *some* common practice must be adopted and, within limits, it does not matter what.

The Rule of the Road is a good example. By appealing to this practice, the statements, 'It is right to drive on the left in England' and 'You ought to be driving on the left,' may be used to alter the hearer's disposition, so that in the future he drives on the left (The ethical judgements are here used 'persuasively.') But the same utterances can also be used simply to draw attention to the rule, or to evince the speaker's displeasure.

Now consider two more subtle examples: first, that of the schoolboy who hears that he has been given his cricket colours. His immediate reaction will probably be one of pleasure, and he will cry out, 'Why, that is good news!' But his school-fellows may feel differently about it, especially if they suspect that he has been given them only because the cricket captain is fond of him. Then they will do their best to make him feel that his rejoicing is misplaced, pointing out (for example) that another, better batsman has had to go without colours as a result. If the schoolboy has a tender conscience, accepts the 'principle' that cricket colours should go to the best cricketers, and not just to the captain's favourites, and admits both that he is rather a friend of the captain's, and that the man who has had to go without has the better batting record and more 1st XI matches to his credit; then he may eventually say, 'Well, naturally I was pleased at the time, but I see now that I *ought not really* to have been given them.'

In this example, several of the most characteristic features of ethics are displayed. To start with, an ethical term is used simply to evince pleasure. Next, contrary feelings are aroused in, and evinced by others. These are concerned at the way in which the schoolboy's award has cut across another's interests—in this case, someone's 'natural right' to colours, based on a generally accepted practice. (The conflict between one schoolboy's winning his colours, and the other's failure to obtain them, is a typically ethical one, in that it is only possible for one of them to have them.) Reasons are advanced for the view that the award was not *really good*. The principle is appealed to as authority. Finally, the schoolboy admits the facts, accepts the principle, and agrees that, though the news originally *seemed* good to him, it was not *really* good.

Again, suppose that I am already rich, and then win £10,000 in a lottery. At first, I may excusably rejoice. But now someone may try to persuade me that I *ought not* to be so glad. He may remind me of all the shillings paid by labourers out of their wages, that went to make up my prize; he may point out that I already have as much money as I have any use for; and he may insist that the prize-money would do more good anywhere but in my bank. In the end, I may come to admit that, however pleased I was to win the prize, it was, all in all, not a good thing that I did. Though it *seemed* good to me at first, it was not *really* good. In this case, a number of 'principles' may be appealed to —for instance, the 'principles' that opportunities for satisfying people's needs should not be neglected; that no one should retain more than he needs of anything while others suffer through going without; and that one should not accept anything which has been got by unnecessary suffering.

Appeal to a 'principle' in ethics is like appeal to a 'law' in science: 'principles' and 'laws of nature' may both be thought of as shorthand summaries of experience—as condensed comparisons. If I explain the 'bending' of a stick in water by reference to the laws of optics, my purpose is to relate the present experience to past observations and experiments; the explanation in terms of 'Snells' Law' is then shorthand for, 'If you had put the stick above a bonfire, you'd have expected it to shimmer in the heated air, wouldn't you? And if.... And if.... So you see, the look of bentness in this case was to be expected.' Likewise, appeal to the 'principle' that you should not accept anything got by unnecessary suffering can be thought of as shorthand for, 'If you found out that your garden was being cultivated by a team of slaves, who were whipped until they produced all the flowers and vegetables you asked for, you wouldn't ask for them any more, would you? And if.... And if.... So, you see, winning £10,000 in this lottery was nothing to be so pleased about.'

Like scientific theories again, all principles are not equally well established; some refer to wider, some to narrower ranges of experience. There is an air of conventionality about the principle that the best cricketers shall be given their colours, which is absent from the principles involved in the second example. The principle that all promises ought to be kept may seem less compelling than the principle that unnecessary suffering ought to be prevented; but, equally, it is less conventional than the rules by which colours are distributed. We shall have to return to these differences in discussing the next stage of development.

10.4 *The Development of Ethics.* (II)

In any particular community, certain principles are current—that is to say, attention is paid to certain types of argument, as appealing to accepted criteria of 'real goodness,' 'real rightness,' 'real obligation,' etc. From these, the members of the community are expected to try and regulate their lives and judgements. And such a set of principles, of 'prima facie obligations,' [6] of 'categorical imperatives,' [7] is what we call the 'moral code' of the community.

At the primitive stage of development, this is something fixed and unalterable.[8] There is no room for criticism of the moral code as a whole, as there is of a particular action, expression of pleasure, or ethical judgement. However, the methods used in primitive communities to harmonise the desires and actions of their members are very crude and, although at first they may do their job, something always happens to throw doubt on them. New opportunities emerge. People discover that different principles of the code conflict. As a result of contact with other peoples having different codes, or of changes within the community, they begin to question not only the rightness of particular actions but also the standards laid down in the code. They realise that, as a result of these changes, the present code is causing frustration and suffering which, by making a specific alteration in the practices of the community, could be avoided—and avoided without incurring any comparable evil.

The same situation arises within the family, when the growing child, having learnt to accept appeal to a principle as an argument for and against actions, begins to question the need for some of the principles with which he has been brought up, and to argue that they cause needless annoyance. When this happens, he ceases to accept authority as the sole moral argument, and becomes himself a 'responsible being.'

At this stage, there are two possible reactions: either for those in authority—those who enforce the existing 'code'—to assert its absolute rightness, and to attempt to legislate for every possibility; or for them to agree, first to criticism, and eventually to modification of the code, so as to remove its objectionable features. If the first course is adopted, the continual changes in the circumstances of the community tend only to aggravate the situation: the second course, on the other hand, represents a natural extension of the process by which moral codes themselves grow out of conflicts of interest—i.e. it takes account of the function of ethics.

When it is recognised that the members of a community have the right to criticise the existing practices, and to suggest new ones, a new phase in the development of ethics begins. In this phase, it is the *mo-*

---

[6] W. D. Ross, *The Right and the Good*, p. 19.

[7] Kant, *Fundamental Principles of the Metaphysics of Ethics*, tr. Abbott (10th ed., 1926), p. 37.

[8] As a matter of anthropology, this is not altogether exact: the features characteristic of my 'second phase of development' are probably present to a limited extent in all communities. The division I adopt is, however, an illuminating one; and this inaccuracy is not one which can affect the validity of the logical considerations of Chapter 11, to which we are leading up.

tives of actions and the *results* of social practices, rather than 'the letter of the law,' which are emphasised. The 'deontological' [9] code was at first supreme; the 'teleological' [10] criterion now amplifies it, and provides a standard by which to criticise it. This does not mean that morality becomes wholly teleological, as Utilitarianism[11] would suggest. All that happens is that the initially inflexible system of taboos is transformed into a *developing* moral code—a code which, in unambiguous cases, remains mandatory, but whose interpretation in equivocal cases and whose future development are controlled by appeal to the function of ethics; that is, to the general requirement that preventable suffering shall be avoided.

The contrast between the two main phases of development is strikingly reflected in the contrast between the Old and New Testaments. The moral code of the Israelites—a nomadic tribe in a hostile environment—was understandably strict; but, in the more settled atmosphere of Palestine under Roman rule, anomalies arose in this code. Jesus was therefore able to criticise contemporary ethical practices in a spirit to which the Pharisees could hardly take open exception. Whatever form their questions took, they could not get him to say that his teaching was meant to *supersede* the Law and the Prophets: in fact, whenever there was any discussion of the Jewish code, he made it clear that he took it as his starting-point. Instead, it was his aim throughout to get the existing code applied in a more intelligent manner: to point out that the prevention of human suffering is more important than formal respect for obsolete customs. Thus, when challenged in the Temple about the propriety of healing the sick on the Sabbath, he asked, 'Whether is it lawful on the sabbath day to do good or to do evil? to save life or for to destroy it?,' [12] and went on to heal the man with a withered hand. Again, in a phrase echoed by Kant[13] he declared, 'Whatsoever ye would that men should do to you, even so do ye to them. This is the law and the Prophets.' [14] He was ready to criticise the existing code, certainly; but only by reference to its function—the func-

---

9 'Deontological theories hold that there are ethical propositions of the form: "Such and such a kind of action would always be right (or wrong) in such and such circumstances, no matter what its consequences might be." ' (Broad, *Five Types of Ethical Theory*, p. 206.)

10 'Teleological theories hold that the rightness or wrongness of an action is always determined by its tendency to produce certain consequences which are intrinsically good or bad.' (Broad, *op. cit.* p. 207.)

11 'The doctrine that it is the duty of each to aim at the maximum happiness of all, and to subordinate everything else to this end.' (Broad, *op. cit.* p. 183.)

12 Luke vi.

13 Cf. *Fundamental Principles of the Metaphysics of Ethics* (tr. Abbott), p. 66: 'Act always on such a maxim as thou canst at the same time will to be a universal law.'

14 Matt. vii.

tion which he expressed, in his own way, as the 'New Commandment,' to love one another.

We can trace the beginnings of this new outlook further back: it is clearly to be seen, breaking through the old, rigid morality, in the more 'advanced' of the Greek tragedies. Contrast, for example, the approaches which different dramatists adopted towards the same traditional stories, and the lessons which they drew from them. Both Sophocles and Euripides wrote plays, which have survived, using the story of Electra and Orestes as their foundation. Sophocles produced an archaic 'drama of duty.' In his play, the central figures perform their ritual act of vengeance—the murder of their own mother, Clytemnestra—without emotion: 'there is no shrinking back, no question of conscience at all.' [15] Euripides' play is in vivid contrast: it is a psychological 'drama of motive.' After the murder, Orestes and Electra suffer 'a long agony of remorse';[16] and even the gods, through the mouth of Castor, are made to condemn the act. For Euripides, the blood-feud has lost its absolute authority. For Sophocles, however, old ways held good, and there could be no question of blame.

We can now see how it is that different 'moral principles' have such different degrees of 'conventionality.' To return to the three examples discussed before: the 'duty' to give cricket-colours to the best cricketers, the 'duty' to keep a promise, and the 'duty' to prevent avoidable suffering. The reason why the first of these appears comparatively conventional, the last comparatively compelling, is clear, when we bear in mind the overall requirement that, wherever we can, we shall prevent suffering from being inflicted upon others. To abolish the custom of giving cricket-colours would have a trivial effect by these standards; to abandon the social practice of promise-keeping might, by the same standards, be expected to have intolerable results; and the third principle cannot be rejected, without completely abandoning the very ideas of 'duty' and of 'ethics.'

CHAPTER 11 The Logic of Moral Reasoning

It is in relation to this background that we have to discuss the logic of ethical reasoning. I do not mean that the validity of our results will depend at all on the truth of any historical and psychological facts that I have quoted: this will not be the case. Such facts will be useful more as illustrating the parts which different kinds of ethical question and statement play in our lives. The only facts, upon which the truth of what

---

15 Gilbert Murray, *Euripides and his Age*, p. 154.

16 *Op. cit.* p. 156: the whole discussion of the contrast between Sophocles' and Euripides' treatments of the story is well worth study (*op. cit.* pp. 152–7).

we have to say will depend, are those more familiar, unquestionable facts of usage—of the kind that we found obliquely expressed in the 'anthropological law,' 'All communities recognise the absolute value of duty'—namely, facts about the ways in which we do recognise a 'duty,' a 'community' and so on.

Bearing this background in mind, then, what questions shall we expect to find arising in ethical contexts, and how are they to be answered?

11.1 Questions about the Rightness of Actions

Consider, first, the simplest and commonest ethical question, 'Is this the right thing to do?' We are taught when young to behave in ways laid down as appropriate to the situations we are in. Sometimes there is a doubt whether or no a proposed action conforms to the moral code. It is to resolve such doubts that we are taught to use the question, 'Is this the right thing to do?,' and, provided the code contains a relevant principle, the answer is 'Yes' or 'No,' according as the proposed action does or does not conform. Questions like, 'What is the right thing to do?,' 'What ought really to have been done?' and 'Was this the correct decision?' do similar jobs, and can be understood in similar ways.

In consequence, if someone complains, 'That wasn't the thing to do' or 'That was hardly the way of going about things, was it?,' his remark may have a genuinely ethical force. And this remains the case, although the only *fact* at issue is whether the action in question belongs to a class of actions generally approved of in the speaker's community. Some people have been misled by this into arguing that many so-called 'ethical' statements are just disguised statements of fact; that 'what seems to be an ethical judgement is very often a factual classification of an action.' [17] But this is a mistake. What makes us call a judgement 'ethical' is the fact that it is used to harmonise people's actions (rather than to give a recognisable description of a state of affairs, for instance); judgements of the kind concerned are unquestionably 'ethical' by this standard; and the fact that the action belongs to a certain class of actions is not so much the 'disguised meaning of' as the 'reason for' the ethical judgement.

Furthermore, the test for answering questions of this simple kind remains the accepted practice, even though the particular action may have unfortunate results. Suppose that I am driving along a winding, country road, and deliberately keep on the left-hand side going round the blind corners. It may happen that a driver going the other way is cutting his corners, so that we collide head-on; but this does not affect

---

17 Ayer, *Language, Truth and Logic* (2nd ed.), p. 21.

the propriety of my driving. My care to keep to the left remains 'right,' my decision not to take any risks on the corners remains 'correct,' in spite of the fact that the consequences, in the event, were unfortunate. Provided that I had no reason to expect such an upset, provided that I was not to know how the other man was behaving—knowledge which would have made a material difference to my decision, and would have taken my situation out of the straightforward class to which the rule applies—the existence of the Rule of the Road is all that is needed to make my decision 'correct.'

11.2 Reasoning about the Rightness of Actions

This brings us to questions about one's 'reasons' for a decision or an action.

If the policeman investigating the accident asks the other driver, 'Why were you driving on the right-hand side of the road?,' he will have to produce a long story in order to justify himself. If, however, I am asked why I was driving on the *left,* the only answer I can give is that the left-hand side is the one on which one *does* drive in England—that the Rule of the Road *is* to drive on the left.

Again, the schoolboy who gets his colours through favouritism may ask, 'And why shouldn't I have been given them?' If he does so, his schoolfellows will point out that it is the practice (and in fact the whole point of colours) for them to go to the best cricketers; and that there were better cricketers to whom they could have been given. And this will be all the justification needed.

Finally, an example in which the logical structure of this type of 'reasoning' is fully set out: suppose that I say, 'I feel that I ought to take this book and give it back to Jones' (so reporting on my feelings). You may ask me, 'But ought you really to do so?' (turning the question into an ethical one), and it is up to me to produce my 'reasons,' if I have any. To begin with, then, I may reply that I ought to take it back to him, 'because I promised to let him have it back before midday'—so classifying my position as one of type S_1. 'But ought you *really?*,' you may repeat. If you do, I can relate S_1 to a more general S_2, explaining, 'I ought to, because I promised to let him have it back.' And if you continue to ask, 'But why ought you really?,' I can answer, in succession, 'Because I ought to do whatever I promise him to do' (S_3), 'Because I ought to do whatever I promise anyone to do' (S_4), and 'Because anyone ought to do whatever he promises anyone else that he will do' or 'Because it was a promise' (S_5). Beyond this point, however, the question cannot arise: there is no more general 'reason' to be given beyond one which relates the action in question to an accepted social practice.

11.3 Conflicts of Duties

This straightforward method of answering the questions, 'Is this the right thing to do?' and 'Why ought you to do that?,' can apply only in situations to which a rule of action is unambiguously appropriate. The most interesting practical questions, however, always arise in those situations in which one set of facts drives us one way, and another pulls us in the opposite direction.

If the muck-heap at the bottom of my garden bursts into flames in midsummer, and someone says, 'There's nothing to be surprised at in that: it's a simple case of spontaneous combustion. Surely you've heard of ricks burning in the same kind of way?,' his explanation may satisfy me: the analogy between the burning of my muck-heap and the spontaneous combustion of a hayrick is close enough for it to be plausible. But, if it is late January, I may reject the explanation, and protest, 'That's all very well in July or August, but not in midwinter: whoever heard of a hayrick catching fire with snow on the ground?,' and, unless he can assure me that it does quite frequently happen, I shall continue to hanker after a different explanation.

In much the same way, the fact that I promised to let Jones have his book back will seem to me reason enough for taking it to him on time— if that is all that there is to it. But, if I have a critically ill relative in the house, who cannot be left, the issue is complicated. The situation is not sufficiently unambiguous for reasoning from the practice of promise-keeping to be conclusive: I may therefore argue, 'That's all very well in the ordinary way, but not when I've got my grandmother to look after: whoever heard of risking someone else's life just to return a borrowed book?' Unless evidence is produced that the risks involved in breaking my promise to Jones are even greater than those attending my grandmother, if she is left alone, I shall conclude that it is my duty to remain with her.

Given two conflicting claims, that is to say, one has to weigh up, as well as one can, the risks involved in ignoring either, and choose 'the lesser of the two evils.' Appeal to a single current principle, though the primary test of the rightness of an action, cannot therefore be relied on as a universal test: where this fails, we are driven back upon our estimate of the probable consequences. And this is the case, not only where there is a conflict of duties, but also, for instance, in circumstances in which, although no matter of principle is involved, some action of ours can nevertheless meet another's need. Here again we naturally and rightly conclude that the action is one that we 'ought' to perform, but we record in our usage the difference between such circumstances and those in which a matter of principle *is* involved: although we should say that we 'ought' to perform the action, we should not usually say that we had a 'moral obligation' to perform it, or even that it was our 'duty.' We here appeal to consequences in the absence of a relevant principle, or 'duty.' [18]

So it comes about that we can, in many cases, justify an individual action by reference to its estimated consequences. Such a reference is no substitute for a principle, where any principle is at issue: but moral reasoning is so complex, and has to cover such a variety of types of situation, that no one logical test (such as 'appeal to an accepted principle') can be expected to meet every case.

11.4 *Reasoning about the Justice of Social Practices*

All these types of question are intelligible by reference to the primitive stage in the development of ethics. As soon as we turn to the second stage, however, there is room for questions of a radically different type.

Recall our analysis of 'explanation.' There I pointed out that, although on most occasions the question, 'Is this really straight?,' has a use, situations might be encountered in which the question, in its ordinary sense, simply cannot be asked. These occasions were of two kinds:[19]

(i) those on which the criterion of straightness is itself questioned, within the framework of a particular theory, and

(ii) those on which the criteria of straightness used in alternative theories are found to be different.

The same kinds of situation arise (and, indeed, are more familiar) in ethics. To give an example of the first: so long as one confines oneself to a particular moral code, no more general 'reason' can be given for an action than one which relates it to a practice (or principle) within that code. If an astronomer, who is discussing light-rays in outer space in terms of non-Euclidean geometry, is asked what reason he has for saying that they are straight, he can only reply, 'Well, they just *are*': in the same way, if I am asked why one ought to keep a particular promise, all that I can say is, 'Well, one just *ought*.' Within the framework of a particular scientific theory, one can ask of most things, 'Is *this* really straight?,' but the *criterion* of straightness cannot be questioned: within the framework of a particular moral code, one can ask of most individual actions, 'Is *this* really right?,' but the *standards* of rightness cannot be questioned.

As an example of the second type of situation: the question, 'Which

---

[18] We can, and sometimes do, employ the language of 'duty' in this case also, by treating the reference to consequences as a reference to a completely general 'duty' to help one another in need. For our present purposes, the difference between these two ways of putting it is purely verbal.

[19] See § 8.5.

is it really right to do—to have only one wife like a Christian, or to have anything up to four like the Mohammedans,' is odd in the same way as the question, 'Is a light-ray going past the sun really straight, as a non-Euclidean theorist declares, or deflected, as a Euclidean theorist says?' If corresponding standards in two moral codes are found to be different, the question, 'Which of these is really right?,' cannot arise. Or rather (to put the same thing in another way), if the question *does* arise, it arises in a very different way, serves a different purpose, and requires an answer of a different sort.

What kind of purpose does it serve, and what kind of answer does it require? In science, if I insist on asking of the standard of straightness, 'But is *it* really straight?,' I am going outside the framework of that particular scientific theory. To question the standard is to question the theory—to criticise the theory *as a whole*—not to ask for an explanation of the phenomenon ostensibly under discussion (the properties of light-rays in outer space). So again in ethics: if I ask of the behavior prescribed in any standard of conduct, 'Is *it* really right?,' I am going outside the moral code; and my question is a criticism of the practice *as a practice,* not a request for a justification of a particular case of promise-keeping (or whatever it may be).

To question the rightness of a particular action is one thing: to question the justice of a practice *as a practice* is another. It is this second type of question which becomes intelligible when we turn to the second stage of development. If a society has a developing moral code, changes in the economic, social, political or psychological situation may lead people to regard the existing practices as unnecessarily restrictive, or as dangerously lax. If this happens, they may come to ask, for instance, 'Is it right that women should be debarred from smoking in public?,' or 'Would it not be better if there were no mixed bathing after dark?,' in each case questioning the practice concerned *as a whole.* The answer to be given will (remembering the function of ethics) be reached by estimating the probable consequences

    (i) of retaining the present practice, and

    (ii) of adopting the suggested alternative.

If, as a matter of fact, there is good reason to suppose that the sole consequences of making the proposed change would be to avoid some existing distresses, then, as a matter of ethics, there is certainly a good reason for making the change. As usual, however, the logically straightforward case is a comparatively uninteresting one: in practice, the interesting problems are those which arise when the happy consequences of the change are not so certain, or when they are likely to be accompanied by new, though perhaps less serious, distresses. And what stake may reasonably be risked for any particular likelihood of gain is something only to be settled with confidence—if then—by appeal to experience.

11.5 The Two Kinds of Moral Reasoning

Two cautions are necessary. Although, as a matter of logic, it makes sense to discuss the justice of any social practice, some practices will in fact always remain beyond question. It is inconceivable (for instance) that any practice will ever be suggested, to replace promising and promise-keeping, which would be anything like as effective. Even in the most 'advanced' stages of morality, therefore, promise-keeping will remain right.

Again, the fact that I can discuss the rightness of promise-keeping as a practice, in this way, does not imply that there is any way of calling in question the rightness of keeping individual promises. In arguing that promise-keeping will remain right at all stages, 'because its abolition would lead to suffering,' I am doing something different in important respects from what I am doing, if I say that I ought to take this book back to Jones now, 'because I promised to.' I can justify the latter statement by pointing out that I am in any of the situations S_1 to S_5:[20] and such reasons will be acceptable in any community which expects promises to be fulfilled. But I cannot further justify it by saying, 'Because one must not inflict avoidable suffering': this kind of reason is appropriate only when discussing whether a social practice should be retained or changed.

The two kinds of moral reasoning which we have encountered are, therefore, distinct. Each provides its own logical criteria—criteria which are appropriate to the criticism of indvidual actions, or social practices, but not both. It was this distinction between the 'reasons' for an individual action and the 'reasons' for a social practice which Socrates made as he waited for the hemlock: he was ready to die rather than repudiate it—refusing, when given the chance, to escape from the prison and so avoid execution. As an Athenian citizen, he saw that it was his duty (regardless of the actual consequences in his particular case) to respect the verdict and sentence of the court. To have escaped would have been to ignore this duty. By doing so, he would not merely have questioned the justice of the verdict in his case: he would have renounced the Athenian constitution and moral code as a whole. This he was not prepared to do.

The history of Socrates illustrates the nature of the distinction, and the kind of situation in which it is important: the kind of situation in which it ceases to be of value can be seen from the story of Hampden and the 'ship-money.' It is those principles which we recognise as just which we have to respect most scrupulously: if we are prepared to dispute the justice of a principle, everything is altered. One of the most striking ways of disputing the justice of a principle is, indeed, by re-

---

[20] See § 11.2.

fusing to conform on a particular occasion: and such refusals give rise, in law and morality alike, to the notion of a 'test case.'

Over 'test cases,' the distinction between the two sorts of moral reasoning vanishes. In justifying the action concerned, one no longer refers to the current practice: it is the injustice of the accepted code, or the greater justice of some alternative proposal, which is now important. The justification of the action is made 'a matter of principle' and the change in the logical criteria appropriate follows accordingly. In making an action a test case one must, however, take care that one's intentions are clear. If this is not done, the action may be criticised on the wrong level. It may be condemned, either by reference to the very principle it was intended to dispute, or as self-interested, or both; and the question of principle may go against one by default. There is an element of pathos about a test case which goes wrong for this reason; but those men whose protests are carried off successfully are often remembered as heroes.

11.6 The Limited Scope of Comparisons between Social Practices

The scope of ethical reasoning is limited as well as defined by the framework of activities in which it plays its part. We have already encountered one limitation: that, in unequivocal cases, once it has been shown that an action is in accordance with an established practice, there is no further room for the question, 'But is this *really* the right thing to do?' The other questions which we have been discussing are, however, limited in similar ways, which we must now turn and consider.

Consider, first, the kinds of circumstance in which we question the rightness of a social practice. If, for example, it is regarded as disgusting for women to smoke in public, and I ask, 'But ought they really to be debarred from doing so?,' the nature of my inquiry is clear: I am suggesting that in future, when a lady lights a cigarette, people need not turn away in disapproval, look horrified, or cut her from their acquaintance. The change I propose is quite sufficiently indicated in my question for us to be able to discuss it as it stands, and even reach a decision about it, on its merits.

If, on the other hand, I ask, 'Is it really right to have only one wife, like the Christians, or would it be better to have anything up to four, according to the old Mohammedan practice?,' my question is a good deal less intelligible. In the first place, there seems to be a suggestion that we abandon our present practice in favour of an alternative one; but the exact nature of the change proposed is not clear; so how can one begin to estimate its probable consequences? Secondly, it is questionable whether the practices compared can be regarded as 'alternatives' at all. The ramifications, both in Christian and in Muslim societies, of the institution of marriage, its relations to the institutions of property, of parenthood and so on, are so complex that there is no question of simply replacing the one institution by the other. Such different parts does the institution of 'marriage' play in the ways of life of a Christian society and of a Muslim one that we might even feel it hardly right to describe Christian and Muslim marriage as being instances of the 'same' institution at all.

The question, 'Which of these institutions is "right"?,' is therefore an unreal one, and there is no conceivable way of answering it—as it stands. The only way of understanding it is to regard it as an even more general question, in a disguised form. As we saw, the question, 'Is this the right thing to do?,' when persisted in beyond a certain point, has to be understood as an inquiry about the justice of the social practice of which 'this' is an instance—but an inquiry couched in an inappropriate form: so now the question, 'Is it right for me to marry one wife or four?,' has to be transformed, first into, 'Is Christian marriage or Muslim marriage the better practice?'; and then again into, 'Is the Christian or the Muslim *way of life* the better?'

When someone asks of two superficially similar institutions, from different ways of life, 'Which is the better?' one may have to say that, by themselves, they are not comparable: all that can be compared are the ways of life *as wholes*. And *this* comparison is, if anything, a private one: which is to say, not that it *cannot* be reasoned about, but that, reason as you may, the final decision is personal. There is no magic wand which will turn the English social system into a Muslim one overnight: the only practical use for the question, 'Which way of life is the better?,' is in the service of a personal decision—for example, whether to remain here in our society, such as it is, or to go and live as an Arab tribesman in the desert.

In general, then, if one is to *reason* about social practices, the only occasions on which one can discuss the question which of two practices is the better are those on which they are genuine alternatives: when it would be practicable to change from one to the other *within one society*. Given this, the question, 'Which is the better?,' has the force of, 'If we changed from one to the other, would the change have happy or unhappy consequences on the whole?' But, if this condition is not satisfied, there is, morally speaking, no reasoning about the question, and pretended arguments about the merits of rival systems—personal preferences apart—are of value only as rhetoric. (More of this later.)[21]

11.7 The Limits to the Analysis of Ethical Concepts

Consider, secondly, the musty old conundrum over which moral philosophers have battled for so long; namely, whether the 'real' analy-

---

21 See § 13.6.

sis of 'X is right' is 'X is an instance of a rule of action (or maxim, or prima facie obligation),' or 'X is the alternative which of all those open to us is likely to have the best results.' [22] If the scope of ethical reasoning is limited by its function, does this question fall within or outside the limits?

To begin with, it must be clear from our discussion that, in talking of the 'analysis' of 'X is right,' philosophers cannot be referring to the 'meaning' of 'X is right.' The 'meaning' of 'X is right' is certainly neither of the alternatives proposed: it is 'X is the thing to do in these circumstances, to encourage others to do in similar circumstances, etc. etc.' To suppose otherwise is to be trapped into the 'naturalistic fallacy' [23]— that is to say, it is to confuse facts and values (the reasons for an ethical judgement, and the judgement itself), by attempting to express the 'meaning' of an *ethical* judgement in *factual* form. The question which the 'analysis' of 'X is right' *can* answer is the question, 'Which kinds of reason are required in order to show that something is right (i.e. the thing to do, to encourage others to do, etc.)—(i) that it is an instance of a rule of action, or (ii) that it is the alternative likely to have the best results?'

The answer, with comparatively little over-simplification, is that it depends upon the nature of the 'thing.' If it is an action which is an unambiguous instance of a maxim generally accepted in the community concerned, it will be right just because it *is* an instance of such a maxim; but, if it is an action over which there is a 'conflict of duties,' or is itself a principle (or social practice) as opposed to a particular action, it will be right or wrong according as its consequences are likely to be good or bad.

When we bear in mind the function of ethics, therefore, we see that the answer to the philosophers' question is, 'Either, depending on the nature of the case.' The question, in other words, falls within the logical limits set by the function of ethics—provided only that you are prepared to accept 'Either' as an answer.

As a matter of history, philosophers have not been so prepared: they have tended to demand an 'unequivocal' answer—'The first' or 'The second,' and not 'Either'—and to assume that either the 'deontological' or the 'teleological' answer must be 'true,' and the other 'false.' [24] But

---

22 Cf. Broad, *Five Types of Ethical Theory*, pp. 206–7.

23 See § 4.5.

24 And the consequences of this demand have been interesting, especially in the cases of the more honest and self-critical philosophers. Notice, for example, the comment made by A. E. Duncan-Jones on the second of the alternatives which I have quoted above (see *Mind*, n.s. XLII, p. 472): 'I believe it in a peculiar way, so that sometimes the theory strikes me as undeniable and sometimes I am sceptical about it.' This seems to me the kind of predicament into which a candid man is bound to find his way, if he demands an 'unambiguous' answer to the present question.

this is to mistake the nature of the problem. Questions presenting a pair of alternants, 'Which is true—*A* or *B*?' are of two kinds: those to which the answer can sensibly be 'Either' or 'Neither,' and those to which the only possible answers are '*A*' and '*B*.' If I report to the police that I have seen a stolen car being driven along the Bath Road, and they ask me, 'In which direction was it going?,' the only positive answers I can give are 'Eastwards' and 'Westwards.' I can, of course, say, 'I didn't notice,' but I *cannot* say 'Either' or 'Neither': if it was being driven along the Bath Road at all, it *must* have been going in the one direction or the other. This seems to be the kind of model which philosophers have had before them when attempting to answer their question, 'Which is the analysis of "X is right"—*A* or *B*?' In any case, they have certainly overlooked the resemblance of their question to the other, verbally-similar type of question, represented in the extreme case by the algebraic query, 'Which is the correct solution of the equation $x^2 - 5x + 6 = 0$, $x = 2$ or $x = 3$?'—the answer to which is, 'Either, depending on the conditions of the particular problem.'

If we must answer the philosophers' question about the 'analysis' of 'X is right,' it will be along the lines of the algebraic query, rather than along those of the policeman's enquiry. It is, in fact, only as long as one is prepared to accept this kind of answer that the function of ethics leaves one room to ask the question at all.

11.8 The Limits to Questions about the Rightness of Actions

Let us return, next, to the simplest and most primitive types of ethical question, 'Is this the right thing to do?' and 'Which of these actions ought I to do?' What limits are there to the circumstances in which we can ask these questions?

Once more we can get some guidance from the parallel between science and ethics. The question, 'What is the scientific explanation of this?,' can be answered in a great variety of circumstances, but one comes across some situations in which science cannot help to still the surprise which prompts the question. The instance I gave as an illustration of this was that of the family all of whom died on their birthdays.[25] When, after the first two children have died on their birthdays, the third does also, you may well be surprised; but the fact that it happens is one to be accepted, not to be explained. None of the laws of nature, which we have developed as a summary of experience, could have led you to anticipate the event: none can show you now that it was to have been expected. There it is—and the pathologists cannot help you. The range of things for which it makes sense to talk of a 'scientific explanation' is

---

[25] See § 7.5.

limited: there is a point up to which science can take you, but beyond that point it cannot go.

In ethics, too, the range of decisions for which it makes sense to talk of a 'moral justification' is limited: again there is a point up to which morality can take you, but beyond which it cannot go. If you ask me, 'Which of these two courses of action ought I to choose?,' we can see which of the accepted social practices are relevant and, if no 'matter of principle' is involved, estimate (as best we can) the effects which either course of action will have on the other members of the community. These considerations may lead us to rule out one of the two courses as 'morally wrong'—that is, as one which, on moral grounds, you ought not to choose. But they may leave us where we were: no matter of principle may be involved, and the foreseeable consequences to others may be neither better nor worse in the one case than in the other. If this happens, and you persist in asking me, 'But which *ought* I to choose?,' I can only reply, '*Morally* speaking, there's nothing to choose between them, so there's no "ought" about it. It's entirely up to you now which you do.'

The notions of 'duty,' of 'obligation,' of 'morality,' are derived from situations in which the conduct of one member of a community preju- dices the interests of another, and are to be understood as part of the procedure for minimising the effects of such conflicts. Provided that two courses of action are equally acceptable according to the established code, and their foreseeable effects on others are equally tolerable, the notions of 'duty' and 'obligation' no longer apply in their primitive senses. If one is to choose between the two courses of action, it is on grounds of a different kind, for 'moral grounds' are no longer conclusive.

What kind of grounds will be relevant? It would be going beyond the scope of this book to discuss this question in detail, but we can take a quick look. At any given time, one can answer the question, 'What, at this moment, do you wish to do?,' and, if at that instant this wish were granted, one would, for the moment, be satisfied. (You do not have to be a psychologist to know this: it is just in the nature of a 'wish.') But we soon find out that to get what we wish for each instant, quite apart from its effects on others, may bring no deep or lasting satisfaction. We therefore begin to bend our energies, less towards those things for which we have a momentary desire, and more towards other things—things which we expect to bring deeper and more lasting contentment. In doing so, we develop a 'rule of life,' a personal 'code' with the help of which, when moral considerations are no longer relevant, we can choose be- tween different courses of action. In developing this 'rule of life,' we have, of course, not only our own experience to guide us; we have the records which others have left of their attempts, failures and successes in the same quest, and the advice of friends and relatives to help us—or confuse us. Given all this mass of experience, we can now 'reason' about proposed courses of action, even when moral considerations are no longer conclusive. At this stage, however, the decision must be a personal one. The argument will be of the form, 'a_1, a_2, . . . (the reasons): so, if I were you, I should choose this course'; and the test of the argument concerns the future of the person concerned. If the course recommended was, as a matter of fact, likely to lead to his deepest and most permanent happiness, the advice was *good* advice—that is, advice worthy of acceptance: and, if the reasoning was such as to establish the true value of the advice, it was *good* reasoning—that is, reasoning worthy of notice.

Passing beyond the scope of 'morality' means passing out of the reach of those principles which find their rightful place in 'morality'— principles which can be formulated in terms independent of person and occasion. In the new field, every argument depends for its validity on an explicit or implicit 'If I were you.' Here the agent's 'feelings' and 'attitudes' enter in, not as the cardboard creatures of philosophical theory, but as logically indispensable participants. And if there is little space in a book of this kind to discuss this new field of argument, there is no reason to suppose that it is less worth discussing than those to which space has been given. It is simply a field in which less can be formalised; and therefore one in which the logician has less to contribute. Perhaps it is more important. Perhaps the chief value of discovering how much of the logic of ethics can be formalised lies in seeing why so much of it cannot—in seeing how (as E. M. Forster suggests in *Howards End*) the formal world of 'moral principles,' of 'telegrams and anger,' pales by comparison with the richer world of 'personal relations.' In some respects logic must be content to lag one step behind discovery: 'form,' at any rate, is created always after the event. 'Moral principles' carry us only so far: it is only rarely that we can go all the way with their help. And when their job is done, the harder task remains of seeing the right answer to a question beginning 'If you were me. . . .'

All this, though a matter of logic rather than of 'empirical fact,' was seen by Socrates and strikingly expressed by Plato. With his help, we can characterise, figuratively, the formal difference between the two kinds of reasoning relevant to the choice of an action. One is 'reasoning on moral grounds,' aimed at the Harmony of Society: the other, to which we turn when reasoning on moral grounds does not lead to a decision by itself, is concerned with each man's own Pursuit of the Good. And the Good?—

> *The Good differs from everything else in a certain respect.... A creature that possesses it permanently, completely and absolutely, has never any need of anything else; its satisfaction is perfect.*[26]

---

[26] *Philebus*, 60 B–C (tr. Hackforth); see *Plato's Examination of Pleasure*, p. 125.

But this is not the end of the matter. The second type of reasoning about the choice of individual actions—that concerned with Happiness rather than with Harmony—has its counterpart in social ethics just as much as the first; and it is one which comes into the picture in similar circumstances. If we took a restricted view of 'ethics,' it might seem to be the case that, when the existing social practices were causing no positive hardship, so that people did not actually complain about them, then there was nothing to be said against them; and that the institutions were therefore 'perfect'—by definition, as it were. This is a position which few people would wish to maintain. Over individual actions, to say that it does not matter what one decides to do, as long as it is within the moral code, is simply to shirk a proper decision—for often enough moral considerations do not take us all the way—and so also is it if one says that it does not matter what the present institutions and social practices are, as long as they do not cause positive and avoidable hardship. Certainly this is the first thing we must ask of our institutions; but, when we have satisfied ourselves about this, they are not necessarily exempt from all criticism. We can now inquire whether, if some specific change were made, the members of our community would lead fuller and happier lives. And again, if there are reasonable grounds for believing that they would, the change is surely justified.

One might naturally and properly argue that our definition of the 'function' of ethics should take account of these considerations too. And we could extend it to do so, if we chose. It is important, however, if we are going to do so, to notice one thing: namely, that this *is* an extension. Our ideas of 'right,' of 'justice,' of 'duty,' of 'obligation,' are manifold: each word covers a genus of concepts. But some members of each genus are more characteristically ethical than others. 'You ought to rest this afternoon, as you've a busy evening ahead of you,' 'You ought to hear his violin concerto,' 'You ought to visit him, if you promised to': these remarks all make use of the notion of 'obligation,' but only in the last of the three does it carry its full force. If you used instances of this last kind to teach someone the notion, you might expect him to recognise that the other uses were natural extensions of it; but you would never expect him to understand the full nature of 'moral obligation' if given only instances of the first and second kinds—instances having hardly more force than that of 'You'll enjoy his violin concerto if you hear it' and 'If you don't rest this afternoon, you'll regret it later.' The notions of 'obligation,' 'right,' 'justice,' 'duty,' and 'ethics' apply in the first place where our actions or institutions may lead to avoidable misery for others; but it is a natural and familiar extension to use them also where the issue concerns the chance of deeper happiness for others, and even for ourselves.

11.9 Is any 'Justification' of Ethics Needed?

In talking about the logic of ethical reasoning in the light of the function of ethics, I have tried to indicate two things:

(i) the different types of question which naturally arise in ethical contexts, and the ways in which they are answered; and

(ii) the limits of ethical reasoning—that is, the kinds of occasion on which questions and considerations of an ethical kind can no longer arise.

So far, however, I have not given an explicit answer to the question from which we set out: namely, 'What is it, in an ethical discussion, that makes a reason a good reason, or an argument a valid argument?'

In previous chapters this question has always caused trouble. When discussing the objective doctrine of ethics, we found it impossible even to reach it without first mastering some highly mysterious arguments about 'non-natural' properties; even more surprisingly, the advocates of the subjective and imperative doctrines tried to dismiss it as vain. But now we are in the opposite position. In this chapter, I have not attempted to give a 'theory of ethics'; I have simply tried to describe the occasions, on which we are in fact prepared to call judgements 'ethical' and decisions 'moral,' and the part which reasoning plays on such occasions. This description has led us to see how, in *particular types* of ethical question and argument, good reasoning is distinguished from bad, and valid argument from invalid—to be specific, by applying to individual judgements the test of principle, and to principles the test of general fecundity.

Now we have to ask, 'Is any further answer needed? Given particular rules applicable to different kinds of ethical judgement and question, have we not all we want? And, if any more were needed, could it not be supplied from an account, more detailed and accurate than has been given, but of the same kind?'

I myself do not feel the need for any *general* answer to the question, 'What makes some ethical reasoning "good" and some ethical arguments "valid"?': answers applicable to particular types of argument are enough. In fact, it seems to me that the demand for any such general answer (however it is to be obtained) must lead one to paradox as surely as did the corresponding demand over science.[27] For either such a general answer will, in particular cases, be equivalent to the rules which we have found, or it will contradict them. In the first case, it can do one of two things. Either it can distort our account, so that one of the criteria alone seems important; or else it can point out, in a more or less roundabout way, the advantages—indeed, 'the absolute necessity to the ex-

---

[27] See § 7.6.

istence of society' [28]—of harmonious co-operation. Instead, however, it may contradict our results. What then? What if we try to adopt the new rules for criticising arguments about conduct, which this general answer lays down?

If we do adopt these new criteria, then it will no longer be 'ethical' reasoning, 'moral' considerations, arguments from 'duty' and questions about what we 'ought' to do that we are criticising: it will be questions, arguments and considerations of another kind—in fact, a different mode of reasoning. This can be shown quite quickly. For suppose that, far from radically changing our criteria, all that the new rules do is to select one of them as the *universal* criterion. If the test of principle is chosen, so that we are never to be allowed to question the pronouncements of those who administer the moral code, then it is not 'morality' to which they apply—it is 'authority,' and authority of a kind which may reasonably be expected to develop rapidly into tyranny. And conversely, if the test of principle is itself ruled out in favour of a universal test of consequence (of the estimated effects on others), then we are faced with something which is no more 'morality' than the other—it would now be better described as 'expediency.' But arguments from expediency and arguments from authority are no more 'ethical' than experienced guess-work is 'scientific.' Consequently, even if all we do is to give up one or other of our present logical criteria, we turn ethics into something other than it is. And if this is the case there is no need for us to go on and consider more drastic alterations: they can be ruled out at once.

No doubt those philosophers who search for more general rules will not be satisfied. No doubt they will still feel that they want an explicit and unique answer to our central question. And no doubt they will object that, in all this, I have not even 'justified' our using reason in ethics at all. 'It's all very well your laying down the law about particular types of ethical argument,' they will say; 'but what is the justification for letting *any* reasoning affect how we decide to behave? Why *ought* one to do what is right, anyway?'

They are sufficiently answered by the peculiarity of their own questions. For let us consider what kind of answer they want when they ask, 'Why ought one to do what is right?' There is no room *within* ethics for such a question. Ethical reasoning may be able to show why we ought to do this action as opposed to that, or advocate this social practice as opposed to that, but it is no help where there can be no choice. And their question does not present us with genuine alternatives at all. For, since the notions of 'right' and of 'obligation' originate in the same situations and serve similar purposes, it is a self-contradiction (taking 'right' and 'ought' in their simplest senses) to suggest that we 'ought' to

---

[28] Hume, *Natural History of Religion*, § xiii, *ad fin.*

do anything but what is 'right.' This suggestion is as unintelligible as the suggestion that some emerald objects might not be green, and the philosophers' question is on a level with the question, 'Why are all scarlet things red?' We can therefore parry it only with another question—'What else "ought" one to do?'

Similar oddities are displayed by all their questions—as long as we take them literally. Ethics may be able to 'justify' one of a number of courses of action, or one social practice as opposed to another: but it does not extend to the 'justification' of all reasoning about conduct. One course of action can be opposed to another: one social practice can be opposed to another. But to what are we expected to oppose 'ethics-as-a-whole'? There can be no discussion about the proposition, 'Ethics is ethics'; any argument treating 'ethics' as something other than it is must be false; and, if those who call for a 'justification' of ethics want 'the case for morality,' as opposed to 'the case for expediency,' etc., then they are giving philosophy a job which is not its own. To show that you ought to choose certain actions is one thing: to make you *want to do* what you ought to do is another, and not a philosopher's task.

11.10 Reason and Self-Love

Hume ran sharply into this difficulty. He had, in fact, to confess (of a man in whom self-love overpowered the sense of right), 'It would be a little difficult to find any [reasoning] which will appear to him satisfactory and convincing.'[29] This confession of his was, however, a masterpiece of understatement. The difficulty he speaks of is of no 'little' one: indeed, it is an 'absolute and insuperable' one, an 'impossibility.' But note the reason: it is not a *practical* impossibility at all, but a *logical* one. A man's ignoring all ethical arguments is just the kind of thing which would lead us to say that his self-love *had* overpowered his sense of right. As long, and only as long, as he continued to ignore all moral reasoning, we should say that his self-love continued in the ascendant: but once he began to accept such considerations as a guide to action, we should begin to think that 'the sense of right' had won.

It is always possible that, when faced with a man whose self-love initially overpowered his sense of right, we might hit upon some reasoning which appeared to him 'satisfactory and convincing.' The result, however, would not be 'a man in whom self-love was dominant, but who was satisfied and convinced by ethical reasoning' (for this is a contradiction in terms); it would be 'a man in whom self-love was dominant, until reasoning beat it down and reinstated the sense of right.'

There is, in this respect, an interesting parallel to be drawn be-

---

29 Hume, *Enquiries* (ed. Selby-Bigge), p. 283.

tween the notion of 'rational belief' in science, and that of 'reasonable belief' in ethics. We call the belief that (for instance) sulphonamides will control pneumonia a 'rational belief,' because it is arrived at by the procedure found reliable in clinical research. The same applies to any belief held as a result of a series of properly conducted scientific experiments. Any such belief is strengthened as a result of further confirmatory observations. These observations (we say) increase the 'probability' of any hypothesis with which they are consistent: that is, they increase the degree of confidence with which it is rational to entertain the hypothesis. In practice, of course, we do not always adopt the most reliable methods of argument—we generalise hastily, ignore conflicting evidence, misinterpret ambiguous observations and so on. We know very well that there are reliable standards of evidence to be observed, but we do not always observe them. In other words, we are not always rational; for to be 'rational' is to employ always these reliable, self-consistent methods of forming one's scientific beliefs, and to fail to be 'rational' is to entertain the hypothesis concerned with a degree of confidence out of proportion to its 'probability.' [30]

As with the 'rational' and the 'probable,' so with the 'reasonable' and the 'desirable.' (the 'desirable,' that is, in its usual sense of what ought to be pursued): the belief that I ought to pay the bill which my bookshop has sent me is a 'reasonable' belief, and the bookseller's demand for payment is a 'reasonable' demand, because they represent a practice which has been found acceptable in such circumstances. Any ethical judgement, held as a result of properly interpreted moral experience, is also 'reasonable.' Any such judgement is strengthened by further experiences which confirm the fecundity of the principle from which the judgement derives. Such experiences increase the 'desirability' of the principle: that is, they increase the degree of conviction with which it is reasonable to advocate and act upon the principle. In practice, of course, we do not always adopt the most satisfactory methods of reaching moral decisions —we jump to conclusions, ignore the suffering of 'inferior' people, misinterpret ambiguous experiences, and so on. We know very well that there are reliable standards to be observed in shaping our principles and institutions, but we do not always observe them. That is to say, we are not always reasonable; for to be 'reasonable' is to employ these reliable, self-consistent methods in reaching all our moral decisions, and to fail to be 'reasonable' is to advocate and act upon our principles with a degree of conviction out of proportion to their desirability.

Consider the light which this parallel throws on Hume's difficulties and on the 'justification' of ethics. It is sometimes suggested that the

---

[30] In connection with this discussion, see Ayer (*op. cit.,* pp. 99–102), whose argument I paraphrase.

'probability' of a hypothesis is just a matter of our confidence in it, as measured by our willingness to rely on it in practice. This account is over-simplified, for it would be completely acceptable only if we always related belief to observation in a 'rational' way. 'Probability' is, rather, a matter of the degree of confidence with which it is rational to adopt a hypothesis. In an analogous way, Hume's theory of ethics makes the 'desirability' of a moral principle a matter of the conviction with which all fully-informed people do hold to it.[31] This likewise would be true— provided that we always related our moral judgements to experience in a 'reasonable' way. . . .

But this clears up the problem. The truth is that, if different people are to agree in their ethical judgements, it is not enough for them all to be fully informed. They must all be *reasonable,* too. (Even this may not be enough: when it comes to controversial questions, they may reasonably differ.) Unfortunately, people are not always reasonable. And this is a sad fact, which philosophers just have to accept. It is absurd and paradoxical of them to suppose that we need produce a 'reasoned argument' capable of convincing the 'wholly unreasonable,' for this would be a self-contradiction.[32]

If, therefore, the request for a 'justification' of ethics is equivalent to this demand, there is no room for a 'justification'; and the question used to express this demand, 'Why ought one to do what is right?', has no literal answer. There may yet be room for answers of a *different* kind: but, if there is, it is certainly not the business of a logician, and probably not the business of any kind of philosopher, to give them. (What kinds of answer might be given, and whose business it would be to give them, are questions I shall return to later.)[33]

---

[31] See § 2.5.

[32] I should have thought it unnecessary to formulate such an obvious truth, had I not found it overlooked, in practice, by eminent philosophers. For instance, I recall a conversation with Bertrand Russell in which he remarked, as an objection to the present account of ethics, that it would not have convinced Hitler. But whoever supposed that it should? We do not prescribe logic as a treatment for lunacy, or expect philosophers to produce panaceas for psychopaths.

[33] In Chapter 14.

Richard Mervyn Hare (b.1919)

R. M. Hare was educated at Oxford University. During World War II he served in the Far East, where he was taken prisoner by the Japanese. Since 1966 Hare has been White's Professor of Moral Philosophy and Fellow of Corpus Christi College at Oxford. He is one of the best-known "neo-Kantian" moral philosophers, and his two most influential books are *The Language of Morals* (1952) and *Freedom and Reason* (1963). Hare has become interested in the applications of ethical theory to practical moral problems, and the title of his recent books reflect this interest: *Essays on Philosophical Method, Practical Inferences, Essays on the Moral Concepts,* and *Applications of Moral Philosophy,* all published in 1972.

An early account of one element of Hare's theory appears in his article "Universalizability" (*Aristotelean Society Proceedings,* 1954–1955). A critical appraisal of Hare's view is Robert Holmes's "Descriptivism, Supervenience, and Universalizability" (*Journal of Philosophy,* 1963). Another neo-Kantian theory that combines universalizability with rational self-interest is John Rawls' *A Theory of Justice* (1971). A related neo-Kantian theory that combines universalizability with utilitarianism (rather than with self-interest as Hare's theory does) is Marcus Singer's *Generalization in Ethics* (1961). Also see the general criticisms of emotivism that are listed with the Ayer selection (page 295).

Freedom and Reason

PART II **MORAL REASONING**

And as ye would that men should do to you, do ye also to them likewise.

ST. LUKE, VI, 31

6. A Moral Argument

6.1. Historically, one of the chief incentives to the study of ethics has been the hope that it findings might be of help to those faced with difficult moral problems. That this is still a principal incentive for many people is shown by the fact that modern philosophers are often reproached for failing to make ethics relevant to morals.[1] This is because one of the main tenets of many recent moral philosophers has been that the most popular method by which it was sought to bring ethics to bear on moral problems was not feasible—namely the method followed by the group of theories loosely known as 'naturalist'.

The method of naturalism is so to characterize the *meanings* of the key moral terms that, given certain factual premises, not themselves moral judgements, moral conclusions can be deduced from them. If this could be done, it was thought that it would be of great assistance to us in making moral decisions; we should only have to find out the non-moral facts, and the moral conclusion as to what we ought to do would follow. Those who say that it cannot be done leave themselves the task of giving an alternative account of moral reasoning.

Naturalism seeks to make the findings of ethics *relevant* to moral decisions by making the former not morally *neutral*. It is a very natural assumption that if a statement of ethics is relevant to morals, then it cannot be neutral as between different moral judgements; and naturalism is a tempting view for those who make this assumption. Naturalistic definitions are not morally neutral, because with their aid we could

---

[1] I have tried to fill in some of the historical background of these reproaches, and to assess the justification for them, in my article in *The Philosophy of C. D. Broad*, ed. P. Schilpp.

show that statements of non-moral facts *entailed* moral conclusions. And some have thought that unless such an entailment can be shown to hold, the moral philosopher has not made moral reasoning possible.

One way of escaping this conclusion is to say that the relation linking a set of non-moral premises with a moral conclusion is not one of entailment, but that some other logical relation, peculiar to morals, justifies the inference. This is the view put forward, for example, by Mr. Toulmin.[2] Since I have argued elsewhere against this approach, I shall not discuss it here. Its advocates have, however, hit upon an important insight: that moral reasoning does not necessarily proceed by way of *deduction* of moral conclusions from non-moral premises. Their further suggestion, that therefore it makes this transition by means of some other, peculiar, nondeductive kind of inference, is not the only possibility. It may be that moral reasoning is not, typically, any kind of 'straight-line' or 'linear' reasoning from premises to conclusion.

6.2. A parallel from the philosophy of science will perhaps make this point clear. It is natural to suppose that what the scientist does is to reason from premises, which are the data of observation, to conclusions, which are his 'scientific laws', by means of a special sort of inference called 'inductive'. Against this view, Professor Popper has forcibly argued that in science there are no inferences other than deductive; the typical procedure of scientists is to propound hypotheses, and then look for ways of testing them—i.e. experiments which, if they are false, will show them to be so. A hypothesis which, try as we may, we fail to falsify, we accept provisionally, though ready to abandon it if, after all, further experiment refutes it; and of those that are so accepted we rate highest the ones which say most, and which would, therefore, be most likely to have been falsified if they were false. The only inferences which occur in this process are deductive ones, from the truth of certain observations to the falsity of a hypothesis. There is no reasoning which proceeds from the data of observation to the *truth* of a hypothesis. Scientific inquiry is rather a kind of *exploration*, or looking for hypotheses which will stand up to the test of experiment.[3]

We must ask whether moral reasoning exhibits any similar features. I want to suggest that it too is a kind of exploration, and not a kind of linear inference, and that the only inferences which take place in it are deductive. What we are doing in moral reasoning is to look for moral judgements and moral principles which, when we have considered their logical consequences and the facts of the case, we can still accept. As we shall see, this approach to the problem enables us to reject the as-

---

[2] S. E. Toulmin, *The Place of Reason in Ethics*, esp. pp. 38–60. See my review in *Philosophical Quarterly*, i (1950/1), 372, and LM 3.4.

[3] K. R. Popper, *The Logic of Scientific Discovery* (esp. pp. 32 f.). See also his article in C. A. Mace (ed.), *British Philosophy in the Mid-Century*, p. 155.

sumption, which seemed so natural, that ethics cannot be relevant to moral decisions without ceasing to be neutral. This is because we are not going to demand any inferences in our reasoning other than deductive ones, and because none of these deductive inferences rely for their validity upon naturalistic definitions of moral terms.

Two further parallels may help to make clear the sense in which ethics is morally neutral. In the kind of scientific reasoning just described, mathematics plays a major part, for many of the deductive inferences that occur are mathematical in character. So we are bound to admit that mathematics is relevant to scientific inquiry. Nevertheless, it is also neutral, in the sense that no discoveries about matters of physical fact can be made with the aid of mathematics alone, and that no mathematical inference can have a conclusion which says more, in the way of prediction of observations, than its premisses implicitly do.

An even simpler parallel is provided by the rules of games. The rules of a game are neutral as between the players, in the sense that they do not, by themselves, determine which player is going to win. In order to decide who wins, the players have to play the game in accordance with the rules, which involves their making, themselves, a great many individual decisions. On the other hand, the 'neutrality' of the rules of a game does not turn it into a game of chance, in which the bad player is as likely to win as the good.

Ethical theory, which determines the meanings and functions of the moral words, and thus the 'rules' of the moral 'game', provides only a clarification of the conceptual framework within which moral reasoning takes place; it is therefore, in the required sense, neutral as between different moral opinions. But it is highly relevant to moral reasoning because, as with the rules of a game, there could be no such thing as moral reasoning without this framework, and the framework dictates the form of the reasoning. It follows that naturalism is not the only way of providing for the possibility of moral reasoning; and this may, perhaps, induce those who have espoused naturalism as a way of making moral thought a rational activity to consider other possibilities.

The rules of moral reasoning are, basically, two, corresponding to the two features of moral judgements which I argued for in the first half of this book, prescriptivity and universalizability. When we are trying, in a concrete case, to decide what we ought to do, what we are looking for (as I have already said) is an action to which we can commit ourselves (prescriptivity) but which we are at the same time prepared to accept as exemplifying a principle of action to be prescribed for others in like circumstances (universalizability). If, when we consider some proposed action, we find that, when universalized, it yields prescriptions which we cannot accept, we reject this action as a solution to our moral problem—if we cannot universalize the prescription, it cannot become an 'ought'.

It is to be noticed that, troublesome as was the problem of moral weakness when we were dealing theoretically with the logical character of the moral concepts, it cannot trouble us here. For if a person is going to reason seriously at all about a moral question, he has to presuppose that the moral concepts are going, in his reasoning, to be used prescriptively. One cannot start a moral argument about a certain proposal on the basis that, whatever the conclusion of it, it makes no difference to what anybody is to do. When one has arrived at a conclusion, one may then be too weak to put it into practice. But *in arguing* one has to discount this possibility; for, as we shall see, to abandon the prescriptivity of one's moral judgements is to unscrew an essential part of the logical mechanism on which such arguments rely. This is why, if a person were to say 'Let's have an argument about this grave moral question which faces us, but let's not think of any conclusion we may come to as requiring anybody to *do* one thing rather than another', we should be likely to accuse him of flippancy, or worse.

6.3. I will now try to exhibit the bare bones of the theory of moral reasoning that I wish to advocate by considering a very simple (indeed over-simplified) example. As we shall see, even this very simple case generates the most baffling complexities; and so we may be pardoned for not attempting anything more difficult to start with.

The example is adapted from a well-known parable.[4] *A* owes money to *B,* and *B* owes money to *C,* and it is the law that creditors may exact their debts by putting their debtors into prison. *B* asks himself, 'Can I say that I ought to take this measure against *A* in order to make him pay?' He is no doubt *inclined* to do this, or *wants* to do it. Therefore, if there were no question of universalizing his prescriptions, he would assent readily to the *singular* prescription 'Let me put *A* into prison' (4.3). But when he seeks to turn this prescription into a moral judgement, and say, 'I *ought* to put *A* into prison because he will not pay me what he owes', he reflects that this would involve accepting the principle 'Anyone who is in my position ought to put his debtor into prison if he does not pay'. But then he reflects that *C* is in the same position of unpaid creditor with regard to himself (*B*), and that the cases are otherwise identical; and that if anyone in this position ought to put his debtors into prison, then so ought *C* to put him (*B*) into prison. And to accept the moral prescription '*C* ought to put me into prison' would commit him (since, as we have seen, he must be using the word 'ought' prescriptively) to accepting the singular prescription 'Let *C* put me into prison'; and this he is not ready to accept. But if he is not, then neither can he accept the original judgement that he (*B*) ought to put *A* into prison for debt. Notice that the whole of this argu-

---

4 Matthew xviii. 23.

ment would break down if 'ought' were not being used both universaliz-ably *and prescriptively;* for if it were not being used prescriptively, the step from '*C* ought to put me into prison' to 'Let *C* put me into prison' would not be valid.

The structure and ingredients of this argument must now be ex-amined. We must first notice an analogy between it and the Popperian theory of scientific method. What has happened is that a provisional or suggested moral principle has been rejected because one of its particular consequences proved unacceptable. But an important difference be-tween the two kinds of reasoning must also be noted; it is what we should expect, given that the data of scientific observation are recorded in descriptive statements, whereas we are here dealing with prescrip-tions. What knocks out a suggested hypothesis, on Popper's theory, is a singular statement of fact: the hypothesis has the consequence that *p;* but not-*p*. Here the logic is just the same, except that in place of the observation-statements '*p*' and 'not-*p*' we have the singular *prescriptions* 'Let *C* put *B* into prison for debt' and its contradictory. Nevertheless, given that *B* is disposed to reject the first of these prescriptions, the argument against him is just as cogent as in the scientific case.

We may carry the parallel further. Just as science, seriously pur-sued, is the search for hypotheses and the testing of them by the at-tempt to falsify their particular consequences, so morals, as a serious endeavour, consists in the search for principles and the testing of them against particular cases. Any rational activity has its discipline, and this is the discipline of moral thought: to test the moral principles that sug-gest themselves to us by following out their consequences and seeing whether we can accept *them.*

No argument, however, starts from nothing. We must therefore ask what we have to have before moral arguments of the sort of which I have given a simple example can proceed. The first requisite is that the facts of the case should be given; for all moral discussion is about some particular set of facts, whether actual or supposed. Secondly we have the logical framework provided by the meaning of the word 'ought' (i.e. prescriptivity and universalizability, both of which we saw to be neces-sary). Because moral judgements have to be universalizable, *B* cannot say that he ought to put *A* into prison for debt without committing him-self to the view that *C,* who is *ex hypothesi* in the same position *vis-à-vis* himself, ought to put *him* into prison; and because moral judgements are prescriptive, this would be, in effect, prescribing to *C* to put him into prison; and this he is unwilling to do, since he has a strong inclina-tion not to go to prison. This inclination gives us the third necessary ingredient in the argument: if *B* were a completely apathetic person, who literally did not mind what happened to himself or to anybody else, the argument would not touch him. The three necessary ingredients which we have noticed, then, are (1) facts; (2) logic; (3) inclinations.

These ingredients enable us, not indeed to arrive at an evaluative conclusion, but to *reject* an evaluative proposition. We shall see later that these are not, in all cases, the only necessary ingredients.

6.4. In the example which we have been using, the position was deliberately made simpler by supposing that *B* actually stood to some other person in exactly the same relation as *A* does to him. Such cases are unlikely to arise in practice. But it is not necessary for the force of the argument that *B* should *in fact* stand in this relation to anyone; it is sufficient that he should consider hypothetically such a case, and see what would be the consequences in it of those moral principles between whose acceptance and rejection he has to decide. Here we have an important point of difference from the parallel scientific argument, in that the crucial case which leads to rejection of the principle can itself be a supposed, not an observed, one. That hypothetical cases will do as well as actual ones is important, since it enables us to guard against a possible misinterpretation of the argument which I have outlined. It might be thought that what moves *B* is the *fear* that *C* will actually do to him as he does to *A*—as happens in the gospel parable. But this fear is not only irrelevant to the moral argument; it does not even provide a particularly strong non-moral motive unless the circumstances are somewhat exceptional. *C* may, after all, not find out what *B* has done to *A*; or *C*'s moral principles may be different from *B*'s, and independent of them, so that what moral principle *B* accepts makes no difference to the moral principles on which *C* acts.

Even, therefore, if *C* did not exist, it would be no answer to the argument for *B* to say 'But in my case there is no fear that anybody will ever be in a position to do to me what I am proposing to do to *A*'. For the argument does not rest on any such fear. All that is essential to it is that *B* should disregard the fact that he plays the particular role in the situation which he does, without disregarding the inclinations which people have in situations of this sort. In other words, he must be prepared to give weight to *A*'s inclinations and interests as if they were his own. This is what turns selfish prudential reasoning into moral reasoning. It is much easier, psychologically, for *B* to do this if he is actually placed in a situation like *A*'s vis-à-vis somebody else; but this is not necessary, provided that he has sufficient imagination to envisage what it is like to be *A*. For our first example, a case was deliberately chosen in which little imagination was necessary; but in most normal cases a certain power of imagination and readiness to use it is a fourth necessary ingredient in moral arguments, alongside those already mentioned, viz. logic (in the shape of universalizability and prescriptivity), the facts, and the inclinations or interests of the people concerned.

It must be pointed out that the absence of even one of these ingredients may render the rest ineffective. For example, impartiality by itself is not enough. If, in becoming impartial, *B* became also completely dispassionate and apathetic, and moved as little by other people's interests as by his own, then, as we have seen, there would be nothing to make him accept or reject one moral principle rather than another. That is why those who, like Adam Smith and Professor Kneale, advocate what have been called 'Ideal Observer Theories' of ethics, sometimes postulate as their imaginary ideal observer not merely an impartial spectator, but an impartially *sympathetic* spectator.[1] To take another example, if the person who faces the moral decision has no imagination, then even the fact that someone can do the very same thing to him may pass him by. If, again, he lacks the readiness to universalize, then the vivid imagination of the sufferings which he is inflicting on others may only spur him on to intensify them, to increase his own vindictive enjoyment. And if he is ignorant of the material facts (for example about what is likely to happen to a person if one takes out a writ against him), then there is nothing to tie the moral argument to particular choices. . . .

6.7. We must next consider a way of escape which may seem much more respectable than those which I have so far mentioned. Let us suppose that *B* is a firm believer in the rights of property and the sanctity of contracts. In this case he may say roundly that debtors ought to be imprisoned by their creditors whoever they are, and that, specifically, *C* ought to imprison him (*B*), and he (*B*) ought to imprison *A*. And he may, unlike the superficially similar person described earlier, be meaning by 'ought' just what we usually mean by it—i.e. he may be using the word prescriptively, realizing that in saying that *C* ought to put him into prison, he is prescribing that *C* put him in prison. *B*, in this case, is perfectly ready to go to prison for his principles, in order that the sanctity of contracts may be enforced. In real life, *B* would be much more likely to take this line if the situation in which he himself played the role of debtor were not actual but only hypothetical; but this, as we saw earlier, ought not to make any difference to the argument.

We are not yet, however, in a position to deal with this escape-route. All we can do is to say why we cannot now deal with it, and leave this loose end to be picked up later. *B*, if he is sincere in holding the principle about the sanctity of contracts (or any other universal moral principle which has the same effect in this particular case), may

---

[1] It will be plain that there are affinities, though there are also differences, between this type of theory and my own. For such theories see W. C. Kneale, *Philosophy*, xxv (1950), 162; R. Firth and R. B. Brandt, *Philosophy and Phenomenological Research*, xii (1951/2), 317, and xv (1954/5), 407, 414, 422; and J. Harrison, *Aristotelian Society*, supp. vol. xxviii (1954), 132. Firth, unlike Kneale, says that the observer must be 'dispassionate', but see Brandt, op. cit., p. 411 n. For a shorter discussion see Brandt, *Ethical Theory*, p. 173. Since for many Christians God occupies the role of 'ideal observer,' the moral judgements which they make may be expected to coincide with those arrived at by the method of reasoning which I am advocating.

have two sorts of grounds for it. He may hold it on utilitarian grounds, thinking that, unless contracts are rigorously enforced, the results will be so disastrous as to outweigh any benefits that A, or B himself, may get from being let off. This could, in certain circumstances, be a good argument. But we cannot tell whether it is, until we have generalized the type of moral argument which has been set out in this chapter, to cover cases in which the interests of more than two parties are involved. As we saw, it is only the interests of A and B that come into the argument as so far considered (the interests of the third party, C, do not need separate consideration, since C was introduced only in order to show B, if necessary fictionally, a situation in which the roles were reversed; therefore C's interests, being a mere replica of B's, will vanish, as a separate factor, once the A/B situation, and the moral judgements made on it, are universalized). But if utilitarian grounds of the sort suggested are to be adduced, they will bring with them a reference to all the other people whose interests would be harmed by laxity in the enforcement of contracts. This escape-route, therefore, if this is its basis, introduces considerations which cannot be assessed until we have generalized our form of argument to cover 'multilateral' moral situations (7.2 ff.). At present, it can only be said that if B can show that leniency in the enforcement of contracts would really have the results he claims for the community at large, he might be justified in taking the severer course. This will be apparent after we have considered in some detail an example (that of the judge and the criminal) which brings out these considerations even more clearly.

On the other hand, B might have a quite different, nonutilitarian kind of reason for adhering to his principle. He might be moved, not by any weight which he might attach to the interests of other people, but by the thought that to enforce contracts of this sort is necessary in order to conform to some moral or other *ideal* that he has espoused. Such ideals might be of various sorts. He might be moved, for example, by an ideal of abstract justice, of the *fiat justitia, ruat caelum* variety. We have to distinguish such an ideal of justice, which pays no regard to people's interests, from that which is concerned merely to do justice *between* people's interests. It is very important, if considerations of justice are introduced into a moral argument, to know of which sort they are. Justice of the second kind can perhaps be accommodated within a moral view which it is not misleading to call utilitarian (7.4). But this is not true of an ideal of the first kind. It is characteristic of this sort of non-utilitarian ideals that, when they are introduced into moral arguments, they render ineffective the appeal to universalized self-interest which is the foundation of the argument that we have been considering. This is because the person who has whole-heartedly espoused such an ideal (we shall call him the 'fanatic') does not mind if people's interests—even his own—are harmed in the pursuit of it (8.6, 9.1).

It need not be justice which provides the basis of such an escape-route as we are considering. Any moral ideal would do, provided that it were pursued regardless of other people's interests. For example, *B* might be a believer in the survival of the fittest, and think that, in order to promote this, he (and everyone else) ought to pursue their own interests by all means in their power and regardless of everyone else's interests. This ideal might lead him, in this particular case, to put *A* in prison, and he might agree that *C* ought to do the same to him, if he were not clever enough to avoid this fate. He might think that universal obedience to such a principle would maximize the production of supermen and so make the world a better place. If these were his grounds, it is possible that we might argue with him factually, showing that the universal observance of the principle would not have the results he claimed. But we might be defeated in this factual argument if he had an ideal which made him call the world 'a better place' when the jungle law prevailed; he could then agree to our factual statements, but still maintain that the condition of the world described by us as resulting from the observance of his principle would be better than its present condition. In this case, the argument might take two courses. If we could get him to imagine himself in the position of the weak, who went to the wall in such a state of the world, we might bring him to realize that to hold his principle involved prescribing that things should be done to him, in hypothetical situations, which he could not sincerely prescribe. If so, then the argument would be on the rails again, and could proceed on lines which we have already sketched. But he might stick to his principle and say 'If I were weak, then I ought to go to the wall'. If he did this, he would be putting himself beyond the reach of what we shall call 'golden-rule' or 'utilitarian' arguments by becoming what we shall call a 'fanatic'. Since a great part of the rest of this book will be concerned with people who take this sort of line, it is unnecessary to pursue their case further at this point.

6.8. The remaining manœuvre that *B* might seek to practise is probably the commonest. It is certainly the one which is most frequently brought up in philosophical controversies on this topic. This consists in a fresh appeal to the facts—i.e. in asserting that there are in fact morally relevant differences between his case and that of others. In the example which we have been considering, we have artificially ruled out this way of escape by assuming that the case of *B* and *C* is exactly similar to that of *A* and *B*; from this it follows a *fortiori* that there are no morally relevant differences. Since the *B/C* case may be a hypothetical one, this condition of exact similarity can always be fulfilled, and therefore this manœuvre is based on a misconception of the type of argument against which it is directed. Nevertheless it may be useful, since this objection is so commonly raised, to deal with it at this point, although nothing further will be added thereby to what has been said already.

It may be claimed that no two actual cases would ever be exactly similar; there would always be some differences, and *B* might allege that some of these were morally relevant. He might allege, for example, that, whereas his family would starve if *C* put him into prison, this would not be the case if he put *A* into prison, because *A*'s family would be looked after by *A*'s relatives. If such a difference existed, there might be nothing logically disreputable in calling it morally relevant, and such arguments are in fact often put forward and accepted.

The difficulty, however, lies in drawing the line between those arguments of this sort which are legitimate, and those which are not. Suppose that *B* alleges that the fact that *A* has a hooked nose or a black skin entitles him, *B*, to put him in prison, but that *C* ought not to do the same thing to him, *B*, because his nose is straight and his skin white. Is this an argument of equal logical respectability? Can I say that the fact that I have a mole in a particular place on my chin entitles me to further my own interests at others' expense, but that they are forbidden to do this by the fact that they lack this mark of natural pre-eminence?

The answer to this manœuvre is implicit in what has been said already about the relevance, in moral arguments, of hypothetical as well as of actual cases. The fact that no two actual cases are ever identical has no bearing on the problem. For all we have to do is to imagine an identical case in which the roles are reversed. Suppose that my mole disappears, and that my neighbour grows one in the very same spot on his chin. Or, to use our other example, what does *B* say about a hypothetical case in which he has a black skin or a hooked nose, and *A* and *C* are both straight-nosed and white-skinned (9.4; 11.7)? Since this is the same argument, in essentials, as we used at the very beginning, it need not be repeated here. *B* is in fact faced with a dilemma. Either the property of his own case, which he claims to be morally relevant, is a properly universal property (i.e. one describable without reference to individuals), or it is not. If it is a universal property, then, because of the meaning of the word 'universal', it is a property which might be possessed by another case in which he played a different role (though in fact it may not be); and we can therefore ask him to ignore the fact that it is he himself who plays the role which he does in this case. This will force him to count as morally relevant only those properties which he is prepared to allow to be relevant even when other people have them. And this rules out all the attractive kinds of special pleading. On the other hand, if the property in question is not a properly universal one, then he has not met the demand for universalizability, and cannot claim to be putting forward a moral argument at all.

6.9. It is necessary, in order to avoid misunderstanding, to add two notes to the foregoing discussion. The misunderstanding arises through a too literal interpretation of the common forms of expression—which constantly recur in arguments of this type—'How would you like it

if . . . ?' and 'Do as you would be done by'. Though I shall later, for convenience, refer to the type of arguments here discussed as 'golden-rule'
arguments, we must not be misled by these forms of expression.

First of all, we shall make the nature of the argument clearer if,
when we are asking *B* to imagine himself in the position of his victim,
we phrase our question, never in the form 'What *would* you say, or feel,
or think, or how *would* you like it, if you were he?', but always in the
form 'What *do* you say (*in propria persona*) about a hypothetical case
in which you are in your victim's position?' The importance of this way
of phrasing the question is that, if the question were put in the first way,
B might reply 'Well, of course, if anybody did this to me I should resent
it very much and make all sorts of adverse moral judgements about the
act; but this has absolutely no bearing on the validity of the moral
opinion which I am *now* expressing'. To involve him in contradiction,
we have to show that he *now* holds an opinion about the hypothetical
case which is inconsistent with his opinion about the actual case.

The second thing which has to be noticed is that the argument, as
set out, does not involve any sort of deduction of a moral judgement, or
even of the negation of a moral judgement, from a factual statement
about people's inclinations, interests, &c. We are not saying to *B* 'You
are as a matter of fact averse to this being done to you in a hypothetical
case; and from this it follows logically that you ought not to do it to
another'. Such a deduction would be a breach of Hume's Law ('No
"ought" from an "is" '), to which I have repeatedly declared my ad-
herence (*LM* 2.5). The point is, rather, that because of his aversion to its
being done to him in the hypothetical case, he cannot accept the singular *prescription* that in the hypothetical case it should be done to him;
and this, because of the logic of 'ought', precludes him from accepting
the moral judgement that he ought to do likewise to another in the
actual case. It is not a question of a factual statement about a person's
inclinations being inconsistent with a moral judgement; rather, his inclinations being what they are, he cannot assent sincerely to a certain
singular prescription, and if he cannot do this, he cannot assent to a
certain universal prescription which entails it, when conjoined with
factual statements about the circumstances whose truth he admits. Because of this entailment, if he assented to the factual statements and to
the universal prescription, but refused (as he must, his inclinations being what they are) to assent to the singular prescription, he would be
guilty of a logical inconsistency.

If it be asked what the relation is between his aversion to being
put in prison in the hypothetical case, and his inability to accept the
hypothetical singular prescription that if he were in such a situation he
should be put into prison, it would seem that the relation is not unlike
that between a belief that the cat is on the mat, and an inability to accept the proposition that the cat is not on the mat. Further attention to

this parallel will perhaps make the position clearer. Suppose that somebody advances the hypothesis that cats never sit on mats, and that we refute him by pointing to a cat on a mat. The logic of our refutation proceeds in two stages. Of these, the second is: 'Here is a cat sitting on a mat, so it is not the case that cats never sit on mats'. This is a piece of logical deduction; and to it, in the moral case, corresponds the step from 'Let this not be done to me' to 'It is not the case that I ought to do it to another in similar circumstances'. But in both cases there is a first stage whose nature is more obscure, and different in the two cases, though there is an analogy between them.

In the 'cat' case, it is logically possible for a man to look straight at the cat on the mat, and yet believe that there is no cat on the mat. But if a person with normal eyesight and no psychological aberrations does this, we say that he does not understand the meaning of the words, 'The cat is on the mat'. And even if he does not have normal eyesight, or suffers from some psychological aberration (such a phobia of cats, say, that he just *cannot* admit to himself that he is face to face with one), yet, if we can convince him that everyone else can see a cat there, he will have to admit that there *is* a cat there, or be accused of misusing the language.

If, on the other hand, a man says 'But I *want* to be put in prison, if ever I am in that situation', we can, indeed, get as far as accusing him of having eccentric desires; but we cannot, when we have proved to him that nobody else has such a desire, face him with the choice of either saying, with the rest, 'Let this not be done to me', or else being open to the accusation of not understanding what he is saying. For it is not an incorrect use of words to want eccentric things. Logic does not prevent me wanting to be put in a gas chamber if a Jew. It is perhaps true that I logically cannot want for its own sake an experience which I think of as *unpleasant;* for to say that I think of it as unpleasant may be logically inconsistent with saying that I want it for its own sake. If this is so, it is because 'unpleasant' is a prescriptive expression. But 'to be put in prison' and 'to be put in a gas chamber if a Jew', are not prescriptive expressions; and therefore th3se things can be wanted without offence to logic. It is, indeed, in the logical possibility of wanting *any-thing* (neutrally described) that the 'freedom' which is alluded to in my title essentially consists. And it is this, as we shall see, that lets by the person whom I shall call the 'fanatic' (9.1 ff.).

There is not, then, a complete analogy between the man who says 'There is no cat on the mat' when there is, and the man who wants things which others do not. But there is a partial analogy, which, having noticed this difference, we may be able to isolate. The analogy is between two relations: the relations between, in both cases, the 'mental state' of these men and what they say. If I believe that there is a cat on the mat I cannot sincerely say that there is not; and, if I want not to be put into prison more than I want anything else, I cannot sincerely say 'Let me be put into prison'. When, therefore, I said above 'His inclinations being what they are, he cannot assent sincerely to a certain singular prescription', I was making an analytic statement (although the 'cannot' is not a logical 'cannot'); for if he were to assent sincerely to the prescription, that would entail *ex vi terminorum* that his inclinations had changed—in the very same way that it is analytically true that, if the other man were to say sincerely that there was a cat on the mat, when before he had sincerely denied this, he must have changed his belief.

If, however, instead of writing 'His inclinations being what they are, he cannot . . .', we leave out the first clause and write simply 'He cannot . . .', the statement is no longer analytic; we are making a statement about his psychology which might be false. For it is logically possible for inclinations to change; hence it is possible for a man to come sincerely to hold an ideal which requires that he himself should be sent to a gas chamber if a Jew. That is the price we have to pay for our freedom. But, as we shall see, in order for reason to have a place in morals it is not necessary for us to close this way of escape by means of a logical barrier; it is sufficient that, men and the world being what they are, we can be very sure that hardly anybody is going to take it with his eyes open. And when we are arguing with one of the vast majority who are not going to take it, the reply that somebody else *might* take it does not help his case against us. In this respect, all moral arguments are *ad hominem*.[6]

9. Toleration and Fanaticism

9.1. In Chapters 6 and 7 morality appeared as a way of arbitrating between conflicting interests. Put as briefly as possible, to think morally is, at least, to subject one's own interests, where they conflict with those of other people, to a principle which one can accept as governing anyone's conduct in like circumstances. But it is more than this: in the broadest sense, morality includes the pursuit of ideals as well as the reconciliation of interests. And although we have suggested that there are some conflicts of ideal with ideal which are not amenable to argument, and that this is no scandal, it would indeed be a scandal if no arguments could be brought against a person who, in pursuit of his own ideals, trampled ruthlessly on other people's interests, including that

---

[6] The above discussion may help to atone for what is confused or even wrong in *LM* 3.3 (p. 42). The remarks there about the possibility or impossibility of accepting certain moral principles gave the impression of creating an impasse; I can, however, plead that in *LM* 4.4 (p. 69) there appeared a hint of the way out which is developed in this book.

interest which consists in the freedom to pursue varying ideals. We require, therefore, to look for such arguments; and for this purpose it will be helpful to examine more closely the difference between ideals and interests, and the relations between them.

As was suggested earlier (7.4), we might say that to have an interest is for there to be something which one wants (or may want), or which is (or may be) a means, necessary or sufficient, for the attainment of something which one wants (or may want). Now it is, as we have seen (5.4), characteristic of desires that they are not universalizable. For although it is perfectly possible to have a universal desire (a desire that in a certain kind of circumstances some event of a certain kind should always take place), desires do not have to be universal. To want to have something does not commit the wanter to wanting other people, in the same circumstances, to have it. A moderately selfish man may want to have enough to eat without wanting everyone, or even everyone in like circumstances, to have enough to eat. It follows that interests likewise are not universalizable; what it is in one person's interests to have, it is not necessarily in his interest that anyone else should have.

Because interests are not universalizable in themselves, they fall a ready victim to the requirement of universalizability which morality imposes. It is therefore relatively easy, in principle, to use moral thinking to achieve a resolution of a conflict of interests (though in practice the selfishness of people in the pursuit of their interests often obstructs their moral thinking in the way described in 5.4). Where an ideal is involved in the conflict, on the other hand, the situation is much more difficult; for ideals, as we have seen, have a universalizability of their own, and therefore resist the attempts of morality to reconcile them with one another. This is most clearly evident in international politics. If two nations, or their governments, have conflicting interests, the conflict may be more or less easily resoluble in one of two ways: either by a completely non-moral piece of bargaining, whereby each forgoes part of its interests on condition that another part is safeguarded, and thus safeguards, also, that major interest which consists in the avoidance of conflict; or else by the introduction of moral considerations, whereby each limits itself to the pursuit of those interests whose pursuit by any nation in like circumstances it can accept. If international relations could be conducted in the first of these two ways, there would now, given a moderate degree of competence and clear thinking in governments, be little danger of war; and in the adoption of the second approach to international conflicts lies our chief hope of a lasting peace. But where ideals are introduced into international politics, neither of these methods is so easy of application, and conflicts become much more intractable. The chief cause of the Second World War, for example, was a conflict of ideals between Nazism and democracy; and the chief cause of the next World War, if there is one, will be a conflict of ideals between communism and Western liberalism.

If we are to understand these tensions, therefore, it is most important for us to see what, in their barest logical bones, is involved in conflicts between ideals and either other ideals or interests, and wherein such conflicts differ from mere conflicts between the interests of two parties. The chief difference, and the source of all the rest, lies in the universalizability of ideals.

To have an ideal (speaking very crudely and remembering the qualifications just made in 8.6) is to think of some kind of thing as pre-eminently good within some larger class. Thus, if I have a conception of the ideal sports car, this is to think of some particular description of sports car as pre-eminently good within the kind, sports car—I might say, 'The ideal sports car would have precise steering, vivid acceleration, powerful and reliable brakes, &c.' To have a moral ideal is to think of some type of man as a pre-eminently good type of man, or, possibly, of some type of society as a pre-eminently good one. The intractability of the conflict between the Nazis and at any rate their Western opponents was due to the fact that the Nazis' ideals of man and of society were utterly different from those of, for example, liberal Englishmen or Americans. If it had been a question merely of conflicting national interests, a reconciliation might, given patience, have been arrived at by each side saying to itself 'Which of our interests have to be sacrificed in the major interest of peace?' (bargaining); or by saying 'Which of our interests is such that its pursuit by any nation in like circumstances is a principle that we can accept?' (morality). But what the Nazis and their opponents were in conflict about were themselves principles. The Nazis thought a certain kind of society and a certain kind of man pre-eminently good—and it was a kind of man and of society which liberals, with their different ideals, could not but abhor.

Now I have maintained that some conflicts of ideals, as such, cannot be made the subject of arguments of the golden-rule type, nor perhaps of any other kind of argument that could lead to a settlement in all cases. This was so where no other parties' interests were involved. But the case of the Nazis is different in this respect; for they not only pursued a certain ideal, but pursued it because of the sort of ideal that it was, in contempt and defiance of both the interests and the ideals of others. If the ideals of the Nazis and the liberals had been such that they could be pursued without interfering with each other, argument might have been impossible and war unnecessary (*LM* 9.2). But to have an ideal is *eo ipso* to have an interest in not being frustrated in the pursuit of it; if, therefore, the ideal of one man or nation requires him or it to interfere with others' pursuits of their ideals, or with any other of their interests, the essential condition for living and letting live is absent, and the kind of conflict arises in which argument is again in place and in which, in the absence of such rational argument, violence is almost inevitable.

Let us, as briefly as possible, consider what might be said in such an argument between a liberal and a Nazi. The liberal might try, first, drawing the Nazi's attention to the consequences of his actions for large numbers of people (Jews for example) who did not share his ideals, and asking him whether he was prepared to assent to a universal principle that people (or even people having the characteristics of Jews) should be caused to suffer thus. Now if only interests were being considered, the liberal would have a strong argument; for, if so, the Nazi would not assent to the judgement that, were he himself to be a Jew, or have the characteristics of Jews, he should be treated in this way. If ideals are left out of consideration, there is absolutely no reason why he should assent to such a judgement, and every reason why he should dissent from it; he will certainly agree that it is against the interests of Jews and of everybody else to be so treated. And thus, by applying the arguments of Chapter 6, the liberal might lead the Nazi to reject the moral judgement that it is right to treat Jews (or anybody else) in this manner. But the Nazi has a universal principle of his own which gets in the way of the liberal's argument. He accepts the principle that the characteristics which Jews have are incompatible with being an ideal or pre-eminently good (or even a tolerably good) man; and that the ideal, or even a tolerably good, society cannot be realized unless people having these characteristics are eliminated. It might therefore seem *prima facie* that it is no use asking him to imagine himself having the characteristics of Jews and to consider what his interests would then be; for he thinks that, even if the other interests of people (including his own) are sacrificed, the ideal state of society ought to be pursued by producing ideal men and eliminating those that fall short of the ideal.

A person who was moved by considerations of self-interest, and was prepared to universalize the judgements based on it, but had no ideals of this fanatical kind, could not think this; and it might plausibly be said that a man who professes to think this is usually either insincere or lacking in imagination—for on the whole such fanaticism is rare. But it exists. The person who has ideals of the sort described is not necessarily defective in either of these ways. His ideals have, on the face of it, nothing to do with self-interest or with a morality which can be generated by universalizing self-interest; they seem much more akin to the aesthetic evaluations discussed in the last chapter. The enormity of Nazism is that it extends an aesthetic style of evaluation into a field where the bulk of mankind think that such evaluations should be subordinated to the interests of other people. The Nazis were like the emperor Heliogabalus, who, I have been told, had people slaughtered because he thought that red blood on green grass looked beautiful.[7]

---

[7] I have been unable to find the source of this story, and cannot therefore say whether it is true.

There is another way of indicating the superior strength of the idealist's position. We saw in 6.6 that there was a way of escaping from the golden-rule argument that was open to anybody, viz. by abstaining from making any moral judgements at all. This way of escape, however, involves a resignation from the argument, considered as a moral one; and it does not seem in any way a defeat for the moralist that he cannot get the better in argument of someone who is not competing in that game, any more than a mathematician need feel worsted if he cannot prove that six eggs and five more make eleven to a man who will not make any mathematical judgements at all. But our Nazi is able to perform what is essentially a very similar manœuvre, while still claiming to play the moral game; for he is still making prescriptive universal judgements, and the only difference between himself and his opponent is that the Nazi sticks to his judgements even when they conflict with his own interest in hypothetical cases (for example the case where he himself is imagined as having the characteristics of Jews). In this respect he might even claim to be morally superior to his opponent, in that the latter abandons his principles when they conflict with his own hypothetical interests; the Nazi might say that one should stick to one's principles regardless of questions of interest.

9.4. Let us first notice that neither aesthetic preferences nor moral ideals could have the bearing that they do upon our actions unless they were prescriptive. Here again the prescriptivity of value-judgements is crucial to our argument. The same point, substantially, can be put in terms of *wanting* or *desiring,* if we use those words in sufficiently wide senses. To have either an aesthetic preference or an ideal is, at least, to want something (e.g., to want not to see scarlet next to magenta; or to want a society free from Jews). We saw above that ideals and aesthetic judgements are not just like desires (9.1); for there is no universalizability-requirement in the case of desires, whereas there is in the case of both aesthetic judgements and ideals. But this does not prevent ideals and aesthetic judgements (again like other value-judgements) sharing with desires their characteristic of being dispositions to action (5.3); and indeed, if we use the word 'desire' in a wide sense, we can say that any evaluation, just because it is prescriptive, incorporates the desire to have or do something rather than something else. The wide sense in which we are here using 'desire' is that in which *any* felt disposition to action counts as a desire; there is also a narrower and commoner sense in which desires are contrasted with other dispositions to action, such as a feeling of obligation (which in the wider sense of 'desire' could be called a desire to do what one ought.) [8]

---

[8] Aristotle used the two terms *orexis* and *epithumia* to mark this distinction between wider and narrower senses of 'desire' (*De Anima,* 414[b]2, 432[b]5).

The important thing for our present argument is that, in this wider sense, the Nazi is desiring that the Jews should be exterminated; and, because the desire is a universal one corresponding to an ideal, he desires that *anyone* having the characteristics which make him want to exterminate Jews should likewise be exterminated. And from this it follows that, if he is sincere and clear-headed, he desires that he himself should be exterminated if he were to come to have the characteristics of Jews. And Heliogabalus, too, must, if he is consistent, desire that anyone (even if it be he himself) should be slaughtered, if that is necessary in order to gratify the taste of somebody who likes to see red and green juxtaposed. At least, Heliogabalus must desire this, if he is really, like the Nazi, doing what he does in pursuit of an ideal.

There is, it is hardly necessary to point out, a more plausible interpretation of Heliogabalus' actions. This is, that he has no such ideal, but only a selfish desire. He does not desire that *anybody* (including himself) should be slaughtered to gratify the colour-preferences of *anybody*; he only desires that people should be slaughtered to gratify *his own* colour-preferences. If his conduct is interpreted in this way, he is open to arguments which we have already outlined in Chapters 6 and 7; and so is a Nazi who is acting from mere self-interest. We have, however, to ignore such people, in order to confine our attention to the hard core of Nazism, if it exists; and to find a parallel to *this*, we have to attribute to Heliogabalus the very extraordinary desire specified in the preceding paragraph—a desire whose fulfilment demands that even he, were it necessary, should be slaughtered to please somebody's aesthetic taste. That we have to look for such a far-fetched parallel as this indicates that we have at least diminished the problem of dealing in argument with the Nazi. For it shows that really intractable Nazis are perhaps rarer than might be thought.

In order to bring out the extraordinary nature of the really fanatical Nazi's desires, let us imagine that we are able to perform on him the following trick, comparable to another which we shall devise later for a different sort of racialist (11.7). We say to him 'You may not know it, but we have discovered that you are not the son of your supposed parents, but of two pure Jews; and the same is true of your wife'; and we produce apparently cast-iron evidence to support this allegation. Is he at all likely to say—as he logically *can* say—'All right then, send me and all my family to Buchenwald!'? And then let us imagine saying to him 'That was only a deception; the evidence we produced was forged. But now, having really faced this possibility, do you still think as you used to about the extermination of Jews?'

The purpose of this manœuvre is to get him, at the end of it, to make—in his own person, as of now—a universalizable prescription in which he really believes. The first stage of the argument is, by itself, of no help to us; it is no good convincing him that a Jew, or a person who believes himself to be a Jew, would make a certain judgement; for Nazis can always say 'Jews can think what they may think, but that is not our opinion' (6.9). But having really imagined himself as a Jew, our Nazi is unlikely to say this. This is not a matter of logic; he would not be contradicting himself if he said 'Jews are such an abomination that I and my whole family, if we were Jews, should be sent to the gas-chamber'. Our argument, as we are going to develop it, will rest, not upon logic by itself—though without logic we should never have got to this point—but upon the fortunate contingent fact that people who would take this logically possible view, after they had really imagined themselves in the other man's position, are extremely rare.

Nevertheless, the position which seems to us so extraordinary, when clarified, that nobody but a madman would hold it, can get adopted by a whole people, or by the influential part of it, if the opinion is jumbled up with other opinions, each of which, severally, is controvertible, but which, taken together, form an amalgam which is able to convince. The contribution of moral philosophy is to take this amalgam to pieces and, having disposed of the logically unsound pieces, to display the logically incontrovertible remainder for what it is—something which only very few people would accept. If somebody wants to send himself and his whole family to the gas-chamber simply on the ground that they are descended from people with hooked noses, is there, or could there possibly be, any moral philosophy that could argue with him? Yet this is what he has to want, if, as morality demands, he is going to treat hypothetical cases as if they were actual.

Let us compare the case of somebody who really wants to kill everybody, himself included. Should it disturb us, as moral philosophers, that no argument can stop him wanting to do this, if his desire is sufficiently intense and unshakeable? Should we not rather say 'Well, at any rate, thank goodness not many people feel like that'? This is not an appeal to the principle *securus judicat orbis terrarum* in order to prove a moral conclusion—such an appeal I earlier stigmatized as pernicious (3.9). It is rather a drawing of comfort from the happy fact that most people want to live. We are not saying 'Nearly everybody holds a certain moral opinion, so it must be right'; in moral arguments we are never entitled to beg questions by assuming that our opponent must hold a moral opinion because it is so common. But it is useful to see what can be done in argument, given that the *desires* of our opponent are normal (even if selfish) ones—though if his desires were sufficiently eccentric they might lead him to hold eccentric moral opinions against which argument would be impossible.

John Rogers Searle (b. 1932)

Searle has been a member of the Philosophy Department at the University of California at Berkeley since 1959. A Rhodes Scholar and a Guggenheim Fellow, he has authored numerous philosophical articles and *Speech Acts* (1969), a much discussed work about the philosophy of language. Searle has been active in many areas outside of professional philosophy, and has concerned himself with university, societal, and political problems. He wrote *The Campus War* (1971) and has been a panelist on the National Educational Television Network.

Several recent textbooks discuss "constitutive rules" and "institutional facts" as Searle uses these notions. A critical article is "How Not to Derive 'Ought' from 'Is' " by James and Judith Thomson (*The Philosophical Review*, 1964). *The Is-Ought Question* (1969), edited by W. D. Hudson, is a collection of twenty-two essays by contemporary writers.

How to Derive "Ought" from "Is"

I

It is often said that one cannot derive an "ought" from an "is."[1] This thesis, which comes from a famous passage in Hume's *Treatise,* while not as clear as it might be, is at least clear in broad outline: there is a class of statements of fact which is logically distinct from a class of statements of value. No set of statements of fact by themselves entails any statement of value. Put in more contemporary terminology, no set of *descriptive* statements can entail an *evaluative* statement without the addition of at least one evaluative premise. To believe otherwise is to commit what has been called the naturalistic fallacy.

I shall attempt to demonstrate a counterexample to this thesis.[2] It is not of course to be supposed that a single counterexample can refute a philosophical thesis, but in the present instance if we can present a plausible counterexample and can in addition give some account or explanation of how and why it is a counterexample, and if we can further offer a theory to back up our counterexample—a theory which will generate an indefinite number of counterexamples—we may at the very least cast considerable light on the original thesis; and possibly, if we can do all these things, we may even incline ourselves to the view that the scope of that thesis was more restricted than we had originally supposed. A counterexample must proceed by taking a statement or statements which any proponent of the thesis would grant were purely factual or "descriptive" (they need not actually contain the word "is") and show how they are logically related to a statement which a proponent of the thesis would regard as clearly "evaluative." (In the present instance it will contain an "ought.") [3]

Reprinted by permission of the author and the publisher, from *The Philosophical Review,* LXXIII (1964).

[1] Earlier versions of this paper were read before the Stanford Philosophy Colloquium and the Pacific Division of the American Philosophical Association. I am indebted to many people for helpful comments and criticisms, especially Hans Herzberger, Arnold Kaufmann, Benson Mates, A. I. Melden, and Dagmar Searle.

[2] In its modern version. I shall not be concerned with Hume's treatment of the problem.

[3] If this enterprise succeeds, we shall have bridged the gap between "evaluative" and "descriptive" and consequently have demonstrated a weakness in this very terminology. At present, however, my strategy is to play along with the

Consider the following series of statements:

(1) Jones uttered the words "I hereby promise to pay you, Smith, five dollars."
(2) Jones promised to pay Smith five dollars.
(3) Jones placed himself under (undertook) an obligation to pay Smith five dollars.
(4) Jones is under an obligation to pay Smith five dollars.
(5) Jones ought to pay Smith five dollars.

I shall argue concerning this list that the relation between any statement and its successor, while not in every case one of "entailment," is nonetheless not just a contingent relation; and the additional statements necessary to make the relationship one of entailment do not need to involve any evaluative statements, moral principles, or anything of the sort.

Let us begin. How is (1) related to (2)? In certain circumstances, uttering the words in quotation marks in (1) is the act of making a promise. And it is a part of or a consequence of the meaning of the words in (1) that in those circumstances uttering them is promising. "I hereby promise" is a paradigm device in English for performing the act described in (2), promising.

Let us state this fact about English usage in the form of an extra premise:

(1a) Under certain conditions C anyone who utters the words (sentence) "I hereby promise to pay you, Smith, five dollars" promises to pay Smith five dollars.

What sorts of things are involved under the rubric "conditions C?" What is involved will be all those conditions, those states of affairs, which are necessary and sufficient conditions for the utterance of the words (sentence) to constitute the successful performance of the act of promising. The conditions will include such things as that the speaker is in the presence of the hearer Smith, they are both conscious, both speakers of English, speaking seriously. The speaker knows what he is doing, is not under the influence of drugs, not hypnotized or acting in a play, not telling a joke or reporting an event, and so forth. This list will no doubt be somewhat indefinite because the boundaries of the concept of a promise, like the boundaries of most concepts in a natural language, are a bit loose.[4] But one thing is clear; however loose the

---

terminology, pretending that the notions of evaluative and descriptive are fairly clear. At the end of the paper I shall state in what respects I think they embody a muddle.

[4] In addition the concept of a promise is a member of a class of concepts which suffer from looseness of a peculiar kind, viz. defeasibility. Cf. H. L. A. Hart, "The Ascription of Responsibility and Rights," *Logic and Language*, First Series, ed. by A. Flew (Oxford, 1951).

boundaries may be, and however difficult it may be to decide marginal cases, the conditions under which a man who utters "I hereby promise" can correctly be said to have made a promise are straightforwardly empirical conditions.

So let us add as an extra premise the empirical assumption that these conditions obtain.

(1b) Conditions C obtain.

From (1), (1a), and (1b) we derive (2). The argument is of the form: If C then (if U then P): C for conditions, U for utterance, P for promise. Adding the premises U and C to this hypothetical we derive (2). And as far as I can see, no moral premises are lurking in the logical wood-pile. More needs to be said about the relation of (1) to (2), but I reserve that for later.

What is the relation between (2) and (3)? I take it that promising is, by definition, an act of placing oneself under an obligation. No analysis of the concept of promising will be complete which does not include the feature of the promiser placing himself under or under-taking or accepting or recognizing an obligation to the promisee, to perform some future course of action, normally for the benefit of the promisee. One may be tempted to think that promising can be analyzed in terms of creating expectations in one's hearers, or some such, but a little reflection will show that the crucial distinction between state-ments of intention on the one hand and promises on the other lies in the nature and degree of commitment or obligation undertaken in promising.

I am therefore inclined to say that (2) entails (3) straight off, but I can have no objection if anyone wishes to add—for the purpose of formal neatness—the tautological premise:

(2a) All promises are acts of placing oneself under (undertaking) an obligation to do the thing promised.

How is (3) related to (4)? If one has placed oneself under an obligation, then, other things being equal, one is under an obligation. That I take it also is a tautology. Of course it is possible for all sorts of things to happen which will release one from obligations one has under-taken and hence the need for the *ceteris paribus* rider. To get an en-tailment between (3) and (4) we therefore need a qualifying statement to the effect that:

(3a) Others things are equal.

Formalists, as in the move from (2) to (3), may wish to add the tauto-logical premise:

(3b) All those who place themselves under an obligation are, other things being equal, under an obligation.

The move from (3) to (4) is thus of the same form as the move from (1) to (2): If E then (if PUO then UO): E for other things are equal, PUO for place under obligation and UO for under obligation. Adding the two premises E and PUO we derive UO.

Is (3a), the *ceteris paribus* clause, a concealed evaluative premise? It certainly looks as if it might be, especially in the formulation I have given it, but I think we can show that, though questions about whether other things are equal frequently involve evaluative considerations, it is not logically necessary that they should in every case. I shall postpone discussion of this until after the next step.

What is the relation between (4) and (5)? Analogous to the tautology which explicates the relation of (3) and (4) there is here the tautology that, other things being equal, one ought to do what one is under an obligation to do. And here, just as in the previous case, we need some premise of the form:

(4a) Other things are equal.

We need the *ceteris paribus* clause to eliminate the possibility that something extraneous to the relation of "obligation" to "ought" might interfere.[5] Here, as in the previous two steps, we eliminate the appearance of enthymeme by pointing out that the apparently suppressed premise is tautological and hence, though formally neat, it is redundant. If, however, we wish to state it formally, this argument is of the same form as the move from (3) to (4): If E then (if UO then O); E for other things are equal, UO for under obligation, O for ought. Adding the premises E and UO we derive O.

Now a word about the phrase "other things being equal" and how it functions in my attempted derivation. This topic and the closely related topic of defeasibility are extremely difficult and I shall not try to do more than justify my claim that the satisfaction of the condition does not necessarily involve anything evaluative. The force of the expression "other things being equal" in the present instance is roughly this. Unless we have some reason (that is, unless we are actually prepared to give some reason) for supposing the obligation is void (step 4) or the agent ought not to keep the promise (step 5), then the obligation holds and he ought to keep the promise. It is not part of the force of the phrase "other things being equal" that in order to satisfy it we need to establish a universal negative proposition to the effect that no

---

[5] The *ceteris paribus* clause in this step excludes somewhat different sorts of cases from those excluded in the previous step. In general we say, "He undertook an obligation, but nonetheless he is not (now) under an obligation" when the obligation has been *removed*, e.g., if the promisee says, "I release you from your obligation." But we say, "He is under an obligation, but nonetheless ought not to fulfill it" in cases where the obligation is *overridden* by some other considerations, e.g., a prior obligation.

reason could ever be given by anyone for supposing the agent is not under an obligation or ought not to keep the promise. That would be impossible and would render the phrase useless. It is sufficient to satisfy the condition that no reason to the contrary can in fact be given.

If a reason is given for supposing the obligation is void or that the promiser ought not to keep a promise, then characteristically a situation calling for an evaluation arises. Suppose, for example, we consider a promised act wrong, but we grant that the promiser did undertake an obligation. Ought he to keep the promise? There is no established procedure for objectively deciding such cases in advance, and an evaluation (if that is really the right word) is in order. But unless we have some reason to the contrary, the *ceteris paribus* condition is satisfied, no evaluation is necessary, and the question whether he ought to do it is settled by saying "he promised." It is always an open possibility that we may have to make an evaluation in order to derive "he ought" from "he promised," for we may have to evaluate a counterargument. But an evaluation is not logically necessary in every case, for there may as a matter of fact be no counterarguments. I am therefore inclined to think that there is nothing necessarily evaluative about the *ceteris paribus* condition, even though deciding whether it is satisfied will frequently involve evaluations.

But suppose I am wrong about this: would that salvage the belief in an unbridgeable logical gulf between "is" and "ought"? I think not, for we can always rewrite my steps (4) and (5) so that they include the *ceteris paribus* clause as part of the conclusion. Thus from our premises we would then have derived "Other things being equal Jones ought to pay Smith five dollars," and that would still be sufficient to refute the tradition, for we would still have shown a relation of entailment between descriptive and evaluative statements. It was not the fact that extenuating circumstances can void obligations that drove philosophers to the naturalistic fallacy fallacy; it was rather a theory of language, as we shall see later on.

We have thus derived (in as strict a sense of "derive" as natural languages will admit of) an "ought" from an "is." And the extra premises which were needed to make the derivation work were in no cause moral or evaluative in nature. They consisted of empirical assumptions, tautologies, and descriptions of word usage. It must be pointed out also that the "ought" is a "categorical" not a "hypothetical" ought. (5) does not say that Jones ought to pay up if he wants such and such. It says he ought to pay up, period. Note also that the steps of the derivation are carried on in the third person. We are not concluding "I ought" from "I said 'I promise,'" but "he ought" from "he said 'I promise.'"

The proof unfolds the connection between the utterance of certain words and the speech act of promising and then in turn unfolds promising into obligation and moves from obligation to "ought." The step from (1) to (2) is radically different from the others and requires special comment. In (1) we construe "I hereby promise . . ." as an English phrase having a certain meaning. It is a consequence of that meaning that the utterance of that phrase under certain conditions is the act of promising. Thus by presenting the quoted expressions in (1) and by describing their use in (1a) we have as it were already invoked the institution of promising. We might have started with an even more ground-floor premise than (1) by saying:

(1b) Jones uttered the phonetic sequence: /ai+hirbai+pramis+təpei+ yu+smiθ+faiv+dalərz/

We would then have needed extra empirical premises stating that this phonetic sequence was associated in certain ways with certain meaningful units relative to certain dialects.

The moves from (2) to (5) are relatively easy. We rely on definitional connections between "promise," "obligate," and "ought," and the only problem which arises is that obligations can be overridden or removed in a variety of ways and we need to take account of that fact. We solve our difficulty by adding further premises to the effect that there are no contrary considerations, that other things are equal.

II

In this section I intend to discuss three possible objections to the derivation.

First Objection

Since the first premise is descriptive and the conclusion evaluative, there must be a concealed evaluative premise in the description of the conditions in (1b).

So far, this argument merely begs the question by assuming the logical gulf between descriptive and evaluative which the derivation is designed to challenge. To make the objection stick, the defender of the distinction would have to show how exactly (1b) must contain an evaluative premise and what sort of premise it might be. Uttering certain words in certain conditions just *is* promising and the description of these conditions needs no evaluative element. The essential thing is that in the transition from (1) to (2) we move from the specification of a certain utterance of words to the specification of a certain speech act. The move is achieved because the speech act is a conventional act; and the utterance of the words, according to the conventions, constitutes the performance of just that speech act.

A variant of this first objection is to say: all you have shown is that "promise" is an evaluative, not a descriptive, concept. But this objection again begs the question and in the end will prove disastrous to the original distinction between descriptive and evaluative. For that a man uttered certain words and that these words have the meaning they do are surely objective facts. And if the statement of these two objective facts plus a description of the conditions of the utterance is sufficient to entail the statement (2) which the objector alleges to be an evaluative statement (Jones promised to pay Smith five dollars), then an evaluative conclusion is derived from descriptive premises without even going through steps (3), (4), and (5).

Second Objection

Ultimately the derivation rests on the principle that one ought to keep one's promises and that is a moral principle, hence evaluative.

I don't know whether "one ought to keep one's promises" is a "moral" principle, but whether or not it is, it is also tautological; for it is nothing more than a derivation from the two tautologies:

> All promises are (create, are undertakings of, are acceptances of) obligations,

and

> One ought to keep (fulfill) one's obligations.

What needs to be explained is why so many philosophers have failed to see the tautological character of this principle. Three things I think have concealed its character from them.

The first is a failure to distinguish external questions about the institution of promising from internal questions asked within the framework of the institution. The questions "Why do we have such an institution as promising?" and "Ought we to have such institutionalized forms of obligation as promising?" are external questions asked about and not within the institution of promising. And the question "Ought one to keep one's promises?" can be confused with or can be taken as (and I think has often been taken as) an external question roughly expressible as "Ought one to accept the institution of promising?" But taken literally, as an internal question, as a question about promises and not about the institution of promising, the question "Ought one to keep one's promises?" is as empty as the question "Are triangles three-sided?" To recognize something as a promise is to grant that, other things being equal, it ought to be kept.

A second fact which has clouded the issue is this. There are many situations, both real and imaginable, where one ought not to keep a promise, where the obligation to keep a promise is overridden by some further considerations, and it was for this reason that we needed those clumsy *ceteris paribus* clauses in our derivation. But the fact that obligations can be overridden does not show that there were no obligations in the first place. On the contrary. And these original obligations are all that is needed to make the proof work.

Yet a third factor is the following. Many philosophers still fail to realize the full force of saying that "I hereby promise" is a performative expression. In uttering it one performs but does not describe the act of promising. Once promising is seen as a speech act of a kind different from describing, then it is easier to see that one of the features of the act is the undertaking of an obligation. But if one thinks the utterance of "I promise" or "I hereby promise" is a peculiar kind of description—for example, of one's mental state—then the relation between promising and obligation is going to seem very mysterious.

Third Objection

The derivation uses only a factual or inverted-commas sense of the evaluative terms employed. For example, an anthropologist observing the behavior and attitudes of the Anglo-Saxons might well go through these derivations, but nothing evaluative would be included. Thus step (2) is equivalent to "He did what they call promising" and step (5) to "According to them he ought to pay Smith five dollars." But since all of the steps (2) to (5) are in *oratio obliqua* and hence disguised statements of fact, the fact-value distinction remains unaffected.

This objection fails to damage the derivation, for what it says is only that the steps *can* be reconstrued as in *oratio obliqua*, that we can construe them as a series of external statements, that we can construct a parallel (or at any rate related) proof about reported speech. But what I am arguing is that, taken quite literally, without any *oratio obliqua* additions or interpretations, the derivation is valid. That one can construct a similar argument which would fail to refute the fact-value distinction does not show that this proof fails to refute it. Indeed it is irrelevant.

III

So far I have presented a counterexample to the thesis that one cannot derive an "ought" from an "is" and considered three possible objections to it. Even supposing what I have said so far is true, still one feels a certain uneasiness. One feels there must be some trick involved somewhere. We might state our uneasiness thus: How can my granting a mere fact about a man, such as the fact that he uttered certain words or that he made a promise, commit *me* to the view that *he* ought to do something? I now want briefly to discuss what broader philosophic significance my attempted derivation may have, in such a way as to give us the outlines of an answer to this question.

I shall begin by discussing the grounds for supposing that it cannot be answered at all.

The inclination to accept a rigid distinction between "is" and "ought," between descriptive and evaluative, rests on a certain picture of the way words relate to the world. It is a very attractive picture, so attractive (to me at least) that it is not entirely clear to what extent the mere presentation of counterexamples can challenge it. What is needed is an explanation of how and why this classical empiricist picture fails to deal with such counterexamples. Briefly, the picture is constructed something like this: first we present examples of so-called descriptive statements ("my car goes eighty miles an hour," "Jones is six feet tall," "Smith has brown hair"), and we contrast them with so-called evaluative statements ("my car is a good car," "Jones ought to pay Smith five dollars," "Smith is a nasty man"). Anyone can see that they are different. We articulate the difference by pointing out that for the descriptive statements the question of truth or falsity is objectively decidable, because to know the meaning of the descriptive expressions is to know under what objectively ascertainable conditions the statements which contain them are true or false. But in the case of evaluative statements the situation is quite different. To know the meaning of the evaluative expressions is not by itself sufficient for knowing under what conditions the statements containing them are true or false, because the meaning of the expressions is such that the statements are not capable of objective or factual truth or falsity at all. Any justification a speaker can give of one of his evaluative statements essentially involves some appeal to attitudes he holds, to criteria of assessment he has adopted, or to moral principles by which he has chosen to live and judge other people. Descriptive statements are thus objective, evaluative statements subjective, and the difference is a consequence of the different sorts of terms employed.

The underlying reason for these differences is that evaluative statements perform a completely different job from descriptive statements. Their job is not to describe any features of the world but to express the speaker's emotions, to express his attitudes, to praise or condemn, to laud or insult, to commend, to recommend, to advise, and so forth. Once we see the different jobs the two perform, we see that there must be a logical gulf between them. Evaluative statements must be different from descriptive statements in order to do their job, for if they were objective they could no longer function to evaluate. Put metaphysically, values cannot lie in the world, for if they did they would cease to be values and would just be another part of the world. Put in the formal mode, one cannot define an evaluative word in terms of descriptive words, for if one did, one would no longer be able to use the evaluative word to commend, but only to describe. Put yet another way, any effort to derive an "ought" from an "is" must be a waste of time, for all it could show even if it succeeded would be that the "is" was not a real "is" but only a disguised "ought" or, alternatively, that the "ought" was not a real "ought" but only a disguised "is."

This summary of the traditional empirical view has been very brief, but I hope it conveys something of the power of this picture. In the hands of certain modern authors, especially Hare and Nowell-Smith, the picture attains considerable subtlety and sophistication.

What is wrong with this picture? No doubt many things are wrong with it. In the end I am going to say that one of the things wrong with it is that it fails to give us any coherent account of such notions as commitment, responsibility, and obligation.

In order to work toward this conclusion I can begin by saying that the picture fails to account for the *different types* of "descriptive" statements. Its paradigms of descriptive statements are such utterances as "my car goes eighty miles an hour," "Jones is six feet tall," "Smith has brown hair," and the like. But it is forced by its own rigidity to construe "Jones got married," "Smith made a promise," "Jackson has five dollars," and "Brown hit a home run" as descriptive statements as well. It is so forced, because whether or not someone got married, made a promise, has five dollars, or hit a home run is as much a matter of objective fact as whether he has red hair or brown eyes. Yet the former kind of statement (statements containing "married," "promise," and so forth) seem to be quite different from the simple empirical paradigms of descriptive statements. How are they different? Though both kinds of statements state matters of objective fact, the statements containing words such as "married," "promise," "home run," and "five dollars" state facts whose existence presupposes certain institutions: a man has five dollars, given the institution of money. Take away the institution and all he has is a rectangular bit of paper with green ink on it. A man hits a home run only given the institution of baseball; without the institution he only hits a sphere with a stick. Similarly, a man gets married or makes a promise only within the institutions of marriage and promising. Without them, all he does is utter words or makes gestures. We might characterize such facts as institutional facts, and contrast them with noninstitutional, or brute, facts: that a man has a bit of paper with green ink on it is a brute fact, that he has five dollars is an institutional fact.[6] The classical picture fails to account for the differences between statements of brute fact and statements of institutional fact.

The word "institution" sounds artificial here, so let us ask: what sorts of institutions are these? In order to answer that question I need

---

[6] For a discussion of this distinction see G. E. M. Anscombe, "Brute Facts," *Analysis* (1958).

to distinguish between two different kinds of rules or conventions. Some rules regulate antecedently existing forms of behavior. For example, the rules of polite table behavior regulate eating, but eating exists independently of these rules. Some rules, on the other hand, do not merely regulate but create or define new forms of behavior: the rules of chess, for example, do not merely regulate an antecedently existing activity called playing chess; they, as it were, create the possibility of or define that activity. The activity of playing chess is constituted by action in accordance with these rules. Chess has no existence apart from these rules. The distinction I am trying to make was foreshadowed by Kant's distinction between regulative and constitutive principles, so let us adopt his terminology and describe our distinction as a distinction between regulative and constitutive rules. Regulative rules regulate activities whose existence is independent of the rules; constitutive rules constitute (and also regulate) forms of activity whose existence is logically dependent on the rules.[7]

Now the institutions that I have been talking about are systems of constitutive rules. The institutions of marriage, money, and promising are like the institutions of baseball or chess in that they are systems of such constitutive rules or conventions. What I have called institutional facts are facts which presuppose such institutions.

Once we recognize the existence of and begin to grasp the nature of such institutional facts, it is but a short step to see that many forms of obligations, commitments, rights, and responsibilities are similarly institutionalized. It is often a matter of fact that one has certain obligations, commitments, rights, and responsibilities, but it is a matter of institutional, not brute, fact. It is one such institutionalized form of obligation, promising, which I invoked above to derive an "ought" from an "is." I started with a brute fact, that a man uttered certain words, and then invoked the institution in such a way as to generate institutional facts by which we arrived at the institutional fact that the man ought to pay another man five dollars. The whole proof rests on an appeal to the constitutive rule that to make a promise is to undertake an obligation.

We are now in a position to see how we can generate an indefinite number of such proofs. Consider the following vastly different example. We are in our half of the seventh inning and I have a big lead off second base. The pitcher whirls, fires to the shortstop covering, and I am tagged out a good ten feet down the line. The umpire shouts "Out!" I, however, being a positivist, hold my ground. The umpire tells me to return to the dugout. I point out to him that you can't derive an

---

[7] For a discussion of a related distinction see J. Rawls, "Two Concepts of Rules," *Philosophical Review,* LXIV (1955).

"ought" from an "is." No set of descriptive statements describing matters of fact, I say, will entail any evaluative statements to the effect that I should or ought to leave the field. "You just can't get orders or recommendations from facts alone." What is needed is an evaluative major premise. I therefore return to and stay on second base (until I am carried off the field). I think everyone feels my claims here to be preposterous, and preposterous in the sense of logically absurd. Of course you can derive an "ought" from an "is," and though to actually set out the derivation in this case would be vastly more complicated than in the case of promising, it is in principle no different. By undertaking to play baseball I have committed myself to the observation of certain constitutive rules.

We are now also in a position to see that the tautology that one ought to keep one's promises is only one of a class of similar tautologies concerning institutionalized forms of obligation. For example, "one ought not to steal" can be taken as saying that to recognize something as someone else's property necessarily involves recognizing his right to dispose of it. This is a constitutive rule of the institution of private property.[8] "One ought not to tell lies" can be taken as saying that to make an assertion necessarily involves undertaking an obligation to speak truthfully. Another constitutive rule. "One ought to pay one's debts" can be construed as saying that to recognize something as a debt is necessarily to recognize an obligation to pay it. It is easy to see how all these principles will generate counterexamples to the thesis that you cannot derive an "ought" from an "is."

My tentative conclusions, then, are as follows:

1. The classical picture fails to account for institutional facts.
2. Institutional facts exist within systems of constitutive rules.
3. Some systems of constitutive rules involve obligations, commitments, and responsibilities.
4. Within those systems we can derive "ought's" from "is's" on the model of the first derivation.

With these conclusions we now return to the question with which I began this section: How can my stating a fact about a man, such as

---

8 Proudhon said: "Property is theft." If one tries to take this as an internal remark it makes no sense. It was intended as an external remark attacking and rejecting the institution of private property. It gets its air of paradox and its force by using terms which are internal to the institution in order to attack the institution.

Standing on the deck of some institutions one can tinker with constitutive rules and even throw some other institutions overboard. But could one throw all institutions overboard (in order perhaps to avoid ever having to derive an "ought" from an "is")? One could not and still engage in those forms of behavior we consider characteristically human. Suppose Proudhon had added (and tried to live by): "Truth is a lie, marriage is infidelity, language is uncommunicative, law is a crime," and so on with every possible institution.

the fact that he made a promise, commit me to a view about what he ought to do? One can begin to answer this question by saying that for me to state such an institutional fact is already to invoke the constitutive rules of the institution. It is those rules that give the word "promise" its meaning. But those rules are such that to commit myself to the view that Jones made a promise involves committing myself to what he ought to do (other things being equal).

If you like, then, we have shown that "promise" is an evaluative word, but since it is also purely descriptive, we have really shown that the whole distinction needs to be re-examined. The alleged distinction between descriptive and evaluative statements is really a conflation of at least two distinctions. On the one hand there is a distinction between different kinds of speech acts, one family of speech acts including evaluations, another family including descriptions. This is a distinction between different kinds of illocutionary force.[9] On the other hand there is a distinction between utterances which involve claims objectively decidable as true or false and those which involve claims not objectively decidable, but which are "matters of personal decision" or "matters of opinion." It has been assumed that the former distinction is (must be) a special case of the latter, that if something has the illocutionary force of an evaluation, it cannot be entailed by factual premises. Part of the point of my argument is to show that this contention is false, that factual premises can entail evaluative conclusions. If I am right, then the alleged distinction between descriptive and evaluative utterances is useful only as a distinction between two kinds of illocutionary force, describing and evaluating, and it is not even very useful there, since if we are to use these terms strictly, they are only two among hundreds of kinds of illocutionary force; and utterances of sentences of the form (5)—"Jones ought to pay Smith five dollars"—would not characteristically fall in either class.

---

[9] See J. L. Austin, *How to Do Things with Words* (Cambridge, Mass., 1962), for an explanation of this notion.

Philippa Foot (b.1920)

Philippa Foot received her M.A. from Oxford University in 1947. A University Lecturer there from 1954 to 1969, she has been Senior Research Fellow at Somerville College, Oxford, since 1969. Since 1972, she also has held the position of Professor in Residence at the University of California at Los Angeles and has been a visiting professor at several other American universities. Foot edited *Theories of Ethics* (1967), published *Morality and Art* (1970), and has contributed many articles to philosophical journals.

Her view is similar in some important respects to Aristotle's conception of the virtues as what are necessary for Man to achieve his good or end (see Books I and II of our Aristotle selection). Also relevant is Foot's article "Moral Arguments," published in the journal *Mind* (1958). Her article "Moral Beliefs" is criticized in two essays, one by M. Tanner and one by D. Z. Phillips, and both can be found in the *Proceedings of the Aristotelian Society* (1964–1965).

Moral Beliefs

To many people it seems that the most notable advance in moral philosophy during the past 50 years or so has been the refutation of naturalism; and they are a little shocked that at this late date such an issue should be reopened. It is easy to understand their attitude: given certain apparently unquestionable assumptions, it would be about as sensible to try to reintroduce naturalism as to try to square the circle. Those who see it like this have satisfied themselves that they know in advance that any naturalistic theory must have a catch in it somewhere, and are put out at having to waste more time exposing an old fallacy. This paper is an attempt to persuade them to look critically at the premises on which their arguments are based.

It would not be an exaggeration to say that the whole of moral philosophy, as it is now widely taught, rests on a contrast between statements of fact and evaluations, which runs something like this: "The truth or falsity of statements of fact is shewn by means of evidence; and what counts as evidence is laid down in the meaning of the expressions occurring in the statement of fact. (For instance, the meaning of 'round' and 'flat' made Magellan's voyages evidence for the roundness rather than the flatness of the Earth; someone who went on questioning whether the evidence was evidence could eventually be shewn to have made some linguistic mistake.) It follows that no two people can make the same statement and count completely different things as evidence; in the end one at least of them could be convicted of linguistic ignorance. It also follows that if a man is given good evidence for a factual conclusion he cannot just refuse to accept the conclusion on the ground that in his scheme of things this evidence is not evidence at all. With evaluations, however, it is different. An evaluation is not connected logically with the factual statements on which it is based. One man may say that a thing is good because of some fact about it, and another may refuse to take that fact as any evidence at all, for nothing is laid down in the meaning of 'good' which connects it with one piece of 'evidence' rather than another. It follows that a moral eccentric could argue to moral conclusions from quite idiosyncratic premises; he could say, for instance, that a man was a good man be-

From Philippa Foot, "Moral Beliefs," reprinted by courtesy of the Editor of The Aristotelian Society. © 1958/59 The Aristotelian Society.

cause he clasped and unclasped his hands, and never turned N.N.E. after turning S.S.W. He could also reject someone else's evaluation simply by denying that his evidence was evidence at all.

"The fact about 'good' which allows the eccentric still to use this term without falling into a morass of meaninglessness, is its 'action-guiding' or 'practical' function. This it retains; for like everyone else he considers himself bound to choose the things he calls 'good' rather than those he calls 'bad'. Like the rest of the world he uses 'good' in connexion only with a 'pro-attitude'; it is only that he has pro-attitudes to quite different things, and therefore calls them good."

There are here two assumptions about 'evaluations', which I will call assumption (1) and assumption (2).

Assumption (1) is that some individual may, without logical error, base his beliefs about matters of value entirely on premises which no one else would recognise as giving any evidence at all. Assumption (2) is that, given the kind of statement which other people regard as evidence for an evaluative conclusion, he may refuse to draw the conclusion because *this* does not count as evidence for *him*.

Let us consider assumption (1). We might say that this depends on the possibility of keeping the meaning of 'good' steady through all changes in the facts about anything which are to count in favour of its goodness. (I do not mean, of course, that a man can make changes as fast as he chooses; only that, whatever he has chosen, it will not be possible to rule him out of order.) But there is a better formulation, which cuts out trivial disputes about the meaning which 'good' happens to have in some section of the community. Let us say that the assumption is that the evaluative function of 'good' can remain constant through changes in the evaluative principle; on this ground it could be said that even if no one can call a man *good* because he clasps and unclasps his hands, he can commend him or express his *pro-attitude* towards him, and if necessary can invent a new moral vocabulary to express his unusual moral code.

Those who hold such a theory will naturally add several qualifications. In the first place, most people now agree with Hare, against Stevenson, that such words as 'good' only apply to individual cases through the application of general principles, so that even the extreme moral eccentric must accept principles of commendation. In the second place 'commending', 'having a pro-attitude', and so on, are supposed to be connected with doing and choosing, so that it would be impossible to say, e.g., that a man was a good man only if he lived for a thousand years. The range of evaluation is supposed to be restricted to the range of possible action and choice. I am not here concerned to question these supposed restrictions on the use of evaluative terms, but only to argue that they are not enough.

The crucial question is this. Is it possible to extract from the meaning of words such as 'good' some element called 'evaluative meaning' which we can think of as externally related to its objects? Such an element would be represented, for instance, in the rule that when any action was 'commended' the speaker must hold himself bound to accept an imperative 'let me do these things'. This is externally related to its object because, within the limitation which we noticed earlier, to possible actions, it would make sense to think of anything as the subject of such 'commendation'. On this hypothesis a moral eccentric could be described as commending the clasping of hands as the action of a good man, and we should not have to look for some background to give the supposition sense. That is to say, on this hypothesis the clasping of hands could be commended without any explanation; it could be what those who hold such theories call 'an ultimate moral principle'.

I wish to say that this hypothesis is untenable, and that there is no describing the evaluative meaning of 'good', evaluation, commending, or anything of the sort, without fixing the object to which they are supposed to be attached. Without first laying hands on the proper object of such things as evaluation, we shall catch in our net either something quite different such as accepting an order or making a resolution, or else nothing at all.

Before I consider this question, I shall first discuss some other mental attitudes and beliefs which have this internal relation to their object. By this I hope to clarify the concept of internal relation to an object, and incidentally, if my examples arouse resistance, but are eventually accepted, to show how easy it is to overlook an internal relation where it exists.

Consider, for instance, pride.

People are often surprised at the suggestion that there are limits to the things a man can be proud of, about which indeed he can feel pride. I do not know quite what account they want to give of pride; perhaps something to do with smiling and walking with a jaunty air, and holding an object up where other people can see it; or perhaps they think that pride is a kind of internal sensation, so that one might naturally beat one's breast and say 'pride is something I feel *here*'. The difficulties of the second view are well known; the logically private object cannot be what a name in the public language is the name of.[1] The first view is the more plausible, and it may seem reasonable to say that given certain behaviour a man can be described as showing that he is proud of something, whatever that something may be. In one sense this is true, and in another sense not. Given any description of an object, action, personal characteristic, etc., it is not possible to rule it out as an object of pride. Before we can do so we need to know what would be said about it by the man who is to be proud of it, or feels proud of it; but if he does not hold the right beliefs about it then whatever his at-

---

[1] See Wittgenstein, *Philosophical Investigations*, especially §§243–315.

titude is it is not pride. Consider, for instance, the suggestion that someone might be proud of the sky or the sea: he looks at them and what he feels is *pride*, or he puffs out his chest and gestures with *pride* in their direction. This makes sense only if a special assumption is made about his beliefs, for instance, that he is under some crazy delusion and believes that he has saved the sky from falling, or the sea from drying up. The characteristic object of pride is something seen (*a*) as in some way a man's own, and (*b*) as some sort of achievement or advantage; without this object pride cannot be described. To see that the second condition is necessary, one should try supposing that a man happens to feel proud because he has laid one of his hands on the other, three times in an hour. Here again the supposition that it is pride that he feels will make perfectly good sense if a special background is filled in. Perhaps he is ill, and it is an achievement even to do this; perhaps this gesture has some religious or political significance, and he is a brave man who will so defy the gods or the rulers. But with no special background there can be no pride, not because no one could psychologically speaking feel pride in such a case, but because whatever he did feel could not logically be pride. Of course, people can see strange things as achievements, though not just anything, and they can identify themselves with remote ancestors, and relations, and neighbours, and even on occasions with Mankind. I do not wish to deny there are many far-fetched and comic examples of pride.

We could have chosen many other examples of mental attitudes which are internally related to their object in a similar way. For instance, fear is not just trembling, and running, and turning pale; without the thought of some menacing evil no amount of this will add up to fear. Nor could anyone be said to feel dismay about something he did not see as bad; if his thoughts about it were that it was altogether a good thing, he could not say that (oddly enough) what he felt about it was dismay. "How odd, I feel dismayed when I ought to be pleased" is the prelude to a hunt for the adverse aspect of the thing, thought of as lurking behind the pleasant facade. But someone may object that pride and fear and dismay are feelings or emotions and therefore not a proper analogy for 'commendation', and there will be an advantage in considering a different kind of example. We could discuss, for instance, the belief that a certain thing is dangerous, and ask whether this could logically be held about anything whatsoever. Like 'this is good', 'this is dangerous' is an assertion, which we should naturally accept or reject by speaking of its truth or falsity; we seem to support such statements with evidence, and moreover there may seem to be a 'warning function' connected with the word 'dangerous' as there is supposed to be a 'commending function' connected with the word 'good'. For suppose that philosophers, puzzled about the property of dangerousness, decided that the word did not stand for a property at all, but was essentially a practical or action-guiding term, used for *warning*. Unless used in an 'inverted comma

sense' the word 'dangerous' was used to warn, and this meant that anyone using it in such a sense committed himself to avoiding the things
he called dangerous, to preventing other people from going near them,
and perhaps to running in the opposite direction. If the conclusion were
not obviously ridiculous, it would be easy to infer that a man whose application of the term was different from ours throughout might say that
the oddest things were dangerous without fear of disproof; the idea
would be that he could still be described as 'thinking them dangerous',
or at least as 'warning', because by his attitude and actions he would
have fulfilled the conditions for these things. This is nonsense because
without its proper object *warning,* like *believing dangerous,* will not be
there. It is logically impossible to warn about anything not thought of
as threatening evil, and for danger we need a particular kind of serious
evil such as injury or death.

There are, however, some differences between thinking a thing
dangerous and feeling proud, frightened or dismayed. When a man says
that something is dangerous he must support his statement with a special
kind of evidence; but when he says that he feels proud or frightened or
dismayed the description of the object of his pride or fright or dismay
does not have quite this relation to his original statement. If he is shewn
that the thing he was proud of was not his after all, or was not after all
anything very grand, he may have to say that his pride was not justified,
but he will not have to take back the statement that he was proud. On
the other hand, someone who says that a thing is dangerous, and later
sees that he made a mistake in thinking that an injury might result from
it, has to go back on his original statement and admit that he was wrong.
In neither case, however, is the speaker able to go on as before. A man
who discovered that it was not his pumpkin but someone else's which
had won the prize could only say that he still felt proud, if he could
produce some other ground for pride. It is in this way that even feelings
are logically vulnerable to facts.

It will probably be objected against these examples that for part of
the way at least they beg the question. It will be said that indeed a man
can only be proud of something he thinks a good action, or an achievement, or a sign of noble birth; as he can only feel dismay about something which he sees as bad, frightened at some threatened evil; similarly he can only warn if he is also prepared to speak, for instance, of
injury. But this will only limit the range of possible objects of those attitudes and beliefs if the range of these terms is limited in its turn. To
meet this objection I shall discuss the meaning of 'injury' because this
is the simplest case. Anyone who feels inclined to say that anything
could be counted as an achievement, or as the evil of which people
were afraid, or about which they felt dismayed, should just try this out.
I wish to consider the proposition that anything could be thought of as
dangerous, because if it causes injury it is dangerous, and anything

could be counted as an injury. I shall consider bodily injury because this is the injury connected with danger; it is not correct to put up a notice by the roadside reading 'Danger!' on account of bushes which might scratch a car. Nor can a substance be labelled 'dangerous' on the ground that it can injure delicate fabrics; although we can speak of the danger that it may do so, that is not the use of the word which I am considering here.

When a body is injured it is changed for the worse in a special way, and we want to know which changes count as injuries. First of all, it matters how an injury comes about; e.g., it cannot be caused by natural decay. Then it seems clear that not just any kind of thing will do, for instance, any unusual mark on the body, however much trouble a man might take to have it removed. By far the most important class of injuries are injuries to a part of the body, counting as injuries because there is interference with the function of that part; injury to a leg, an eye, an ear, a hand, a muscle, the heart, the brain, the spinal cord. An injury to an eye is one that affects, or is likely to affect, its sight; an injury to a hand one which makes it less well able to reach out and grasp, and perform other operations of this kind. A leg can be injured because its movements and supporting power can be affected; a lung because it can become too weak to draw in the proper amount of air. We are most ready to speak of an injury where the function of a part of the body is to perform a characteristic operation, as in these examples. We might hesitate to say that a skull can be injured, and might prefer to speak of damage to it, since although there is indeed a function (a protective function) there is no operation. But thinking of the protective function of the skull we may want to speak of injury here. In so far as the concept of *injury* depends on that of *function* it is narrowly limited, since not even every use to which a part of the body is put will count as its function. Why is it that, even if it is the means by which they earn their living, we would never consider the removal of the dwarf's hump or the bearded lady's beard as a bodily injury? It will be tempting to say that these things are disfigurements, but this is not the point; if we suppose that a man who had some invisible extra muscle made his living as a court jester by waggling his ears, the ear would not have been injured if this were made to disappear. If it were natural to men to communicate by movements of the ear, then ears would have the function of signalling (we have no word for this kind of 'speaking') and an impairment of this function would be an injury; but things are not like this. This court jester would use his ears to make people laugh, but this is not the function of ears.

No doubt many people will feel impatient when such facts are mentioned, because they think that it is quite unimportant that this or that *happens* to be the case, and it seems to them arbitrary that the loss of the beard, the hump, or the ear muscle would not be called an injury.

Isn't the loss of that by which one makes one's living a pretty cata-strophic loss? Yet it seems quite natural that these are not counted as injuries if one thinks about the conditions of human life, and contrasts the loss of a special ability to make people gape or laugh with the ability to see, hear, walk, or pick things up. The first is only needed for one very special way of living; the other in any foreseeable future for any man. This restriction seems all the more natural when we observe what other threats besides that of injury can constitute danger: of death, for instance, or mental derangement. A shock which could cause mental instability or impairment of memory would be called dangerous, because a man needs such things as intelligence, memory, and concentration as he needs sight or hearing or the use of hands. Here we do not speak of injury unless it is possible to connect the impairment with some physi-cal change, but we speak of danger because there is the same loss of a capacity which any man needs.

There can be injury outside the range we have been considering; for a man may sometimes be said to have received injuries where no part of his body has had its function interfered with. In general, I think that any blow which disarranged the body in such a way that there was lasting pain would inflict an injury, even if no other ill resulted, but I do not know of any other important extension of the concept.

It seems therefore that since the range of things which can be called injuries is quite narrowly restricted, the word 'dangerous' is restricted in so far as it is connected with injury. We have the right to say that a man cannot decide to call just anything dangerous, however much he puts up fences and shakes his head.

So far I have been arguing that such things as pride, fear, dismay, and the thought that something is dangerous have an internal relation to their object, and hope that what I mean is becoming clear. Now we must consider whether those attitudes or beliefs which are the moral philosopher's study are similar, or whether such things as 'evaluation' and 'thinking something good' and 'commendation' could logically be found in combination with any object whatsoever. All I can do here is to give an example which may make this suggestion seem implausible, and to knock away a few of its supports. The example will come from the range of trivial and pointless actions such as we were considering in speaking of the man who clasped his hands three times an hour, and we can point to the oddity of the suggestion that this can be called a good action. We are bound by the terms of our question to refrain from adding any special background, and it should be stated once more that the question is about what can count in favour of the goodness or bad-ness of a man or an action, and not what could be, or be thought, good or bad with a special background. I believe that the view I am attacking often seems plausible only because the special background is surrep-titiously introduced.

Someone who said that clasping the hands three times in an hour was a good action would first have to answer the question 'How do you mean?' For the sentence 'this is a good action' is not one which has a clear meaning. Presumably, since our subject is moral philosophy, it does not here mean 'that was a good thing to do' as this might be said of a man who had done something sensible in the course of any enterprise whatever; we are to confine our attention to 'the moral use of "good" '. I am not clear that it makes sense to speak of 'a moral use of "good" ', but we can pick out a number of cases which raise moral issues. It is because these are so diverse and because 'this is a good action' does not pick out any one of them, that we must ask 'How do you mean?' For instance, some things that are done fulfil a duty, such as the duty of parents to children or children to parents. I suppose that when philosophers speak of good actions they would include these. Some come under the heading of a virtue such as charity, and they will be included too. Others again are actions which require the virtues of courage or temperance, and here the moral aspect is due to the fact that they are done in spite of fear or the temptation of pleasure; they must indeed be done for the sake of some real or fancied good, but not necessarily what philosophers would want to call a moral good. Courage is not *particularly* concerned with saving other people's lives, or temperance with leaving them their share of the food and drink, and the goodness of *what is done* may here be all kinds of usefulness. It is because there are these very diverse cases included (I suppose) under the expression 'a good action' that we should refuse to consider applying it without asking what is meant, and we should now ask what is intended when someone is supposed to say that 'clasping the hands three times in an hour is a good action'. Is it supposed that this action fulfils a duty? Then in virtue of what does a man have this duty, and to whom does he owe it? We have promised not to slip in a special background, but he cannot possibly have a *duty* to clasp his hands unless such a background exists. Nor could it be an act of charity, for it is not thought to do anyone any good, nor again a gesture of humility unless a special assumption turns it into this. The action could be courageous, but only if it were done both in the face of fear and for the sake of a good, and we are not allowed to put in special circumstances which could make this the case.

I am sure that the following objection will now be raised. "Of course clasping one's hands three times in an hour cannot be brought under one of the virtues which we recognise, but that is only to say that it is not a good action by our current moral code. It is logically possible that in a quite different moral code quite different virtues should be recognised, for which we have not even got a name." I cannot answer this objection properly, for that would need a satisfactory account of the concept of a virtue. But anyone who thinks it would be easy to describe a new virtue connected with clasping the hands three times in an hour should just try. I think he will find that he has to cheat, and suppose that in the community concerned the clasping of hands has been given some special significance, or is thought to have some special effect. The difficulty is obviously connected with the fact that without a special background there is no possibility of answering the question 'What's the point?' It is no good saying that there would be a point in doing the action because the action was a morally good action: the question is how it can be given any such description if we cannot first speak about the point. And it is just as crazy to suppose that we can call *anything* the point of doing something without having to say what the point of *that* is. In clasping one's hands one may make a slight sucking noise, but what is the point of that? It is surely clear that moral virtues must be connected with human good and harm, and that it is quite impossible to call anything you like good or harm. Consider, for instance, the suggestion that a man might say he had been harmed because a bucket of water had been taken out of the sea. As usual it would be possible to think up circumstances in which this remark would make sense; for instance, when coupled with a belief in magical influences; but then the harm would consist in what was done by the evil spirits, not in the taking of the water from the sea. It would be just as odd if someone were supposed to say that harm had been done to him because the hairs of his head had been reduced to an even number.[2]

I conclude that assumption (1) is very dubious indeed, and that no one should be allowed to speak as if we can understand 'evaluation', 'commendation', or 'pro-attitude', whatever the actions concerned.

II

I propose now to consider what was called Assumption (2), which said that a man might always refuse to accept the conclusion of an argument about values, because what counted as evidence for other people did not count for him. Assumption (2) could be true even if Assumption (1) were false, for it might be that once a particular question of values— say a moral question—had been accepted, any disputant was bound to accept particular pieces of evidence as relevant, the same pieces as everyone else, but that he could always refuse to draw any moral conclusions whatsoever or to discuss any questions which introduced moral terms. Nor do we mean 'he might refuse to draw the conclusion' in the trivial sense in which anyone can perhaps refuse to draw *any* conclu-

---

[2] In face of this sort of example many philosophers take refuge in the thicket of aesthetics. It would be interesting to know if they are willing to let their whole case rest on the possibility that there might be aesthetic objections to what was done.

sion; the point is that any statement of value always seems to go beyond any statement of fact, so that he might have a reason for accepting the factual premises but refusing to accept the evaluative conclusion. That this is so seems to those who argue in this way to follow from the practical implications of evaluation. When a man uses a word such as 'good' in an 'evaluative' and not an 'inverted comma' sense, he is supposed to commit his will. From this it has seemed to follow inevitably that there is a logical gap between fact and value; for is it not one thing to say that a thing is so, and another to have a particular attitude towards its being so; one thing to see that certain effects will follow from a given action, and another to care? Whatever account was offered of the essential feature of evaluation—whether in terms of feelings, attitudes, the acceptance of imperatives or what not—the fact remained that with an evaluation there was a committal in a new dimension, and that this was not guaranteed by any acceptance of facts.

I shall argue that this view is mistaken; that the practical implication of the use of moral terms has been put in the wrong place, and that if it is described correctly the logical gap between factual premises and moral conclusion disappears.

In this argument it will be useful to have as a pattern the practical or 'action-guiding' force of the word 'injury', which is in some, though not all, ways similar to that of moral terms. It is clear I think that an injury is necessarily something bad and therefore something which as such anyone always has a reason to avoid, and philosophers will therefore be tempted to say that anyone who uses 'injury' in its full 'action-guiding' sense commits himself to avoiding the things he calls injuries. They will then be in the usual difficulties about the man who says he knows he ought to do something but does not intend to do it; perhaps also about weakness of the will. Suppose that instead we look again at the kinds of things which count as injuries, to see if the connexion with the will does not start here. As has been shown, a man is injured whenever some part of his body, in being damaged, has become less well able to fulfil its ordinary function. It follows that he suffers a disability, or is liable to do so; with an injured hand he will be less well able to pick things up, hold on to them, tie them together or chop them up, and so on. With defective eyes there will be a thousand other things he is unable to do, and in both cases we should naturally say that he will often be unable to get what he wants to get or avoid what he wants to avoid.

Philosophers will no doubt seize on the word 'want', and say that if we suppose that a man happens to want the things which an injury to his body prevents him from getting, we have slipped in a supposition about a 'pro-attitude' already; and that anyone who does not happen to have these wants can still refuse to use 'injury' in its prescriptive, or 'action-guiding' sense. And so it may seem that the only way to make a *necessary* connexion between 'injury' and the things that are to be avoided, is to say that it is only used in an 'action-guiding sense' when applied to something the speaker intends to avoid. But we should look carefully at the crucial move in that argument, and query the suggestion that someone might happen not to want anything for which he would need the use of hands or eyes. Hands and eyes, like ears and legs, play a part in so many operations that a man could only be said not to need them if he had no wants at all. That such people exist, in asylums, is not to the present purpose at all; the proper use of his limbs is something a man has reason to want if he wants anything.

I do not know just what someone who denies this proposition could have in mind. Perhaps he is thinking of changing the facts of human existence, so that merely wishing, or the sound of the voice, will bring the world to heel? More likely he is proposing to rig the circumstances of some individual's existence within the framework of the ordinary world, by supposing for instance that he is a prince whose servants will sow and reap and fetch and carry for him, and so use their hands and eyes in his service that he will not need the use of his. Let us suppose that such a story could be told about a man's life; it is wildly implausible, but let us pretend that it is not. It is clear that in spite of this we could say that any man had a reason to shun injury; for even if at the end of his life it could be said that by a strange set of circumstances he had never needed the use of his eyes, or his hands, this could not possibly be foreseen. Only by once more changing the facts of human existence, and supposing every vicissitude foreseeable, could such a supposition be made.

This is not to say that an injury might not bring more incidental gain than necessary harm; one has only to think of times when the order has gone out that able-bodied men are to be put to the sword. Such a gain might even, in some peculiar circumstances, be reliably foreseen, so that a man would have even better reason for seeking than for avoiding injury. In this respect the word 'injury' differs from terms such as 'injustice'; the practical force of 'injury' means only that anyone has *a* reason to avoid injuries, not that he has an over-riding reason to do so.

It will be noticed that this account of the 'action-guiding' force of 'injury' links it with reasons for acting rather than with actually doing something. I do not think, however, that this makes it a less good pattern for the 'action-guiding' force of moral terms. Philosophers who have supposed that actual action was required if 'good' were to be used in a sincere evaluation have got into difficulties over weakness of will, and they should surely agree that enough has been done if we can show that any man has reason to aim at virtue and avoid vice. But is this impossibly difficult if we consider the kinds of things that count as virtue and vice? Consider, for instance, the cardinal virtues, prudence, temperance, courage and justice. Obviously any man needs prudence, but does he not also need to resist the temptation of pleasure when there is harm involved? And how could it be argued that he would never need to face what was fearful for the sake of some good? It is not obvious what someone would mean if he said that temperance or courage were not good qualities, and this not because of the 'praising' sense of these *words*, but because of the things that courage and temperance are.

I should like to use these examples to show the artificiality of the notions of 'commendation' and of 'pro-attitudes' as these are commonly employed. Philosophers who talk about these things will say that after the facts have been accepted—say that X is the kind of man who will climb a dangerous mountain, beard an irascible employer for a rise in pay, and in general face the fearful for the sake of something he thinks worth while—there remains the question of 'commendation' or 'evaluation'. If the word 'courage' is used they will ask whether or not the man who speaks of another as having courage is supposed to have commended him. If we say 'yes' they will insist that the judgement about courage *goes beyond the facts*, and might therefore be rejected by someone who refused to do so; if we say 'no' they will argue that 'courage' is being used in a purely descriptive or 'inverted comma sense', and that we have not got an example of the evaluative use of language which is the moral philosopher's special study. What sense can be made, however, of the question 'does he commend?' What is this extra element which is supposed to be present or absent after the facts have been settled? It is not a matter of liking the man who has courage, or of thinking him altogether good, but of 'commending him for his courage'. How are we supposed to do that? The answer that will be given is that we only commend someone else in speaking of him as courageous if we accept the imperative 'let me be courageous' for ourselves. But this is quite unnecessary. I can speak of someone else as having the virtue of courage, and of course recognise it as a virtue in the proper sense, while knowing that I am a complete coward, and making no resolution to reform. I know that I should be better off if I were courageous, and so have a reason to cultivate courage, but I may also know that I will do nothing of the kind.

If someone were to say that courage was not a virtue he would have to say that it was not a quality by which a man came to act well. Perhaps he would be thinking that someone might be worse off for his courage, which is true, but only because an incidental harm might arise. For instance, the courageous man might have underestimated a risk, and run into some disaster which a cowardly man would have avoided because he was not prepared to take any risk at all. And his courage, like any other virtue, could be the cause of harm to him because possessing it he fell into some disastrous state of pride.[3] Similarly, those who

---

[3] Cp. Aquinas, *Summa Theologica*, I–II, q. 55, Art. 4.

question the virtue of temperance are probably thinking not of the virtue itself but of men whose temperance has consisted in resisting pleasure for the sake of some illusory good, or those who have made this virtue their pride.

But what, it will be asked, of justice? For while prudence, courage and temperance are qualities which benefit the man who has them, justice seems rather to benefit others, and to work to the disadvantage of the just man himself. Justice as it is treated here, as one of the cardinal virtues, covers all those things owed to other people: it is under injustice that murder, theft and lying come, as well as the withholding of what is owed for instance by parents to children and by children to parents, as well as the dealings which would be called unjust in everyday speech. So the man who avoids injustice will find himself in need of things he has returned to their owner, unable to obtain an advantage by cheating and lying; involved in all those difficulties painted by Thrasymachus in the first book of the Republic, in order to show that injustice is more profitable than justice to a man of strength and wit. We will be asked how, on our theory, justice can be a virtue and injustice a vice, since it will surely be difficult to show that any man whatsoever must need to be just as he needs the use of his hands and eyes, or needs prudence, courage and temperance?

Before answering this question I shall argue that if it cannot be answered, then justice can no longer be recommended as a virtue. The point of this is not to show that it must be answerable, since justice is a virtue, but rather to suggest that we should at least consider the possibility that justice is not a virtue. This suggestion was taken seriously by Socrates in the Republic, where it was assumed by everyone that if Thrasymachus could establish his premiss—that injustice was more profitable than justice—his conclusion would follow: that a man who had the strength to get away with injustice had reason to follow this as the best way of life. It is a striking fact about modern moral philosophy that no one sees any difficulty in accepting Thrasymachus' premiss and rejecting his conclusion and it is because Nietzsche's position is at this point much closer to that of Plato that he is remote from academic moralists of the present day.

In the Republic it is assumed that if justice is not a good to the just man, moralists who recommend it as a virtue are perpetrating a fraud. Agreeing with this, I shall be asked where exactly the fraud comes in; where the untruth that justice is profitable to the individual is supposed to be told? As a preliminary answer we might ask how many people are prepared to say frankly that injustice is more profitable than justice? Leaving aside, as elsewhere in this paper, religious beliefs which might complicate the matter, we will suppose that some tough atheistical character has asked 'Why should I be just?' (Those who believe that this question has something wrong with it can employ their favourite device for sieving out 'evaluating meaning', and suppose that the question is 'Why should I be "just"?') Are we prepared to reply 'As far as you are concerned you will be better off if you are unjust, but it matters to the rest of us that you should be just, so we are trying to get you to be just'? He would be likely to enquire into our methods, and then take care not to be found out, and I do not think that many of those who think that it is not necessary to show that justice is profitable to the just man would easily accept that there was nothing more they could say.

The crucial question is: 'Can we give anyone, strong or weak, a reason why he should be just?'—and it is no help at all to say that since 'just' and 'unjust' are 'action-guiding words' no one can even ask 'Why should I be just?' Confronted with that argument the man who wants to do unjust things has only to be careful to avoid the *word*, and he has not been given a reason why he should not do the things which other people call 'unjust'. Probably it will be argued that he has been given a reason so far as anyone can ever be given a reason for doing or not doing anything, for the chain of reasons must always come to an end somewhere, and it may seem that one man may always reject the reason which another man accepts. But this is a mistake; some answers to the question 'why should I?' bring the series to a close and some do not. Hume showed how *one* answer closed the series in the following passage:

"Ask a man *why he uses exercise:* he will answer *because he desires to keep his health.* If you then enquire, *why he desires health,* he will readily reply, *because sickness is painful.* If you push your enquiries farther, and desire a reason *why he hates pain,* it is impossible he can ever give any. This is an ultimate end, and is never referred to any other object." (*Enquiries,* Appendix I, V.) Hume might just as well have ended this series with boredom: sickness often brings boredom, and no one is required to give a reason why he does not want to be bored, any more than he has to give a reason why he does want to pursue what interests him. In general, anyone is given a reason for acting when he is shewn the way to something he wants; but for some wants the question 'Why do you want that?' will make sense, and for others it will not.[4] It seems clear that in this division justice falls on the opposite side from pleasure and interest and such things. 'Why shouldn't I do that?' is not answered by the words 'because it is unjust' as it is answered by showing that the action will bring boredom, loneliness, pain, discomfort or certain kinds of incapacity, and this is why it is not true to say that 'it's unjust' gives a reason in so far as any

---

4 For an excellent discussion of reasons for action, see G. E. M. Anscombe, *Intention* §34—40.

reasons can ever be given. 'It's unjust' gives a reason only if the nature of justice can be shown to be such that it is necessarily connected with what a man wants.

This shows why a great deal hangs on the question of whether justice is or is not a good to the just man, and why those who accept Thrasymachus' premiss and reject his conclusion are in a dubious position. They recommend justice to each man, as something he has a reason to follow, but when challenged to show why he should do so they will not always be able to reply. This last assertion does not depend on any 'selfish theory of human nature' in the philosophical sense. It is often possible to give a man a reason for acting by showing him that someone else will suffer if he does not; someone else's good may really be more to him than his own. But the affection which mothers feel for children, and lovers for each other, and friends for friends, will not take us far when we are asked for reasons why a man should be just; partly because it will not extend far enough, and partly because the actions dictated by benevolence and justice are not always the same. Suppose that I owe someone money; '. . . what if he be my enemy, and has given me just cause to hate him? What if he be a vicious man, and deserves the hatred of all mankind? What if he be a miser, and can make no use of what I would deprive him of? What if he be a profligate debauchee, and would rather receive harm than benefit from large possessions?' [5] Even if the general practice of justice could be brought under the motive of universal benevolence—the desire for the greatest happiness of the greatest number—many people certainly do not have any such desire. So that if justice is only to be recommended on these grounds a thousand tough characters will be able to say that they have been given no reason for practising justice, and many more would say the same if they were not too timid or too stupid to ask questions about the code of behaviour which they have been taught. Thus, given Thrasymachus' premiss Thrasymachus' point of view is reasonable; we have no particular reason to admire those who practise justice through timidity or stupidity.

It seems to me, therefore, that if Thrasymachus' thesis is accepted things cannot go on as before; we shall have to admit that the belief on which the status of justice as a virtue was founded is mistaken, and if we still want to get people to be just we must recommend justice to them in a new way. We shall have to admit that injustice is more profitable than justice, at least for the strong, and then do our best to see that hardly anyone can get away with being unjust. We have, of course, the alternative of keeping quiet, hoping that for the most part people will follow convention into a kind of justice, and not ask awkward

---

[5] Hume, *Treatise* Book III, Part II, Sect. 1.

questions, but this policy might be overtaken by a vague scepticism even on the part of those who do not know just what is lacking; we should also be at the mercy of anyone who was able and willing to expose our fraud.

Is it true, however, to say that justice is not something a man needs in his dealings with his fellows, supposing only that he be strong? Those who think that he can get on perfectly well without being just should be asked to say exactly how such a man is supposed to live. We know that he is to practise injustice whenever the unjust act would bring him advantage; but what is he to say? Does he admit that he does not recognise the rights of other people, or does he pretend? In the first case even those who combine with him will know that on a change of fortune, or a shift of affection, he may turn to plunder them, and he must be as wary of their treachery as they are of his. Presumably the happy unjust man is supposed, as in Book II of the Republic, to be a very cunning liar and actor, combining complete injustice with the appearance of justice: he is prepared to treat others ruthlessly, but pretends that nothing is further from his mind. Philosophers often speak as if a man could thus hide himself even from those around him, but the supposition is doubtful, and in any case the price in vigilance would be colossal. If he lets even a few people see his true attitude he must guard himself against them; if he lets no one into the secret he must always be careful in case the least spontaneity betray him. Such facts are important because the need a man has for justice in dealings with other men depends on the fact that they are men and not inanimate objects or animals. If a man only needed other men as he needs household objects, and if men could be manipulated like household objects, or beaten into a reliable submission like donkeys, the case would be different. As things are, the supposition that injustice is more profitable than justice is very dubious, although like cowardice and intemperance it might turn out incidentally to be profitable.

The reason why it seems to some people so impossibly difficult to show that justice is more profitable than injustice is that they consider in isolation particular just acts. It is perfectly true that if a man is just it follows that he will be prepared, in the event of very evil circumstances, even to face death rather than to act unjustly—for instance, in getting an innocent man convicted of a crime of which he has been accused. For him it turns out that his justice brings disaster on him, and yet like anyone else he had good reason to be a just and not an unjust man. He could not have it both ways and while possessing the virtue of justice hold himself ready to be unjust should any great advantage accrue. The man who has the virtue of justice is not ready to do certain things, and if he is too easily tempted we shall say that he was ready after all.

Lawrence Kohlberg (b. 1927)

Lawrence Kohlberg was educated at the University of Chicago and became Professor of Psychology and Human Development there. Since 1967 he has been Professor of Educational and Social Psychology at Harvard University. Kohlberg is famous for developing the cognitive-developmental theory of moral development; an earlier and simpler version of this theory can be found in the writings of the Swiss psychologist Jean Piaget. Kohlberg's theory has been applied to problems of moral education by both himself and others, and he is the author of *Moral Development and Moral Education* (1973), as well as many articles. Two essays by Kohlberg, together with several critiques of Kohlberg's theory, are contained in *Moral Education . . . It Comes with the Territory* (1976), edited by David Purple and Kevin Ryan.

Stage and Sequence:
The Cognitive-Developmental
Approach to Socialization

... Turning to morality, "resistance to temptation" has a moderate but clearly documented correlation with IQ.[1] These findings are not too helpful, however, since resistance to temptation does not define any dimension of age-development of morality. We shall now attempt to show that more "cognitive" dimensions of moral judgment do define moral age-development, and that once moral judgment development is understood, the development of moral action and moral affect becomes much more intelligible and predictable. The assertion that moral judgment undergoes regular age-development and that this development is in some sense cognitive has seldom been questioned since the work of Hartshorne and May (1928–30) and Piaget (1948). However, extreme proponents of the cultural relativism of values must logically question both these contentions, as Bronfenbrenner (1962) has recently done. Bronfenbrenner has claimed that class, sex, and culture are more important determinants of Piaget-type moral judgment than is age-development. Examination of this claim may usefully clarify the sense in which moral judgment is said to have a cognitive-developmental component. One sense of the assertion that moral judgment development is cognitive is that it involves an increase in the child's knowledge of the content of conventional standards and values of his group. This is indeed the nature of moral judgment as measured by conventional "moral knowledge" tests like those of Hartshorne and May (1928–30). In this sense, it is plausible to assert that insofar as the content of standards and value labels differs by class, sex, and culture, so will the development of

---

Excerpted from Lawrence Kohlberg, "Stage and Sequence: The Cognitive-Developmental Approach to Socialization," in David A. Goslin (ed.), *Handbook of Socialization Theory and Research*. Copyright © 1969 by Rand McNally College Publishing Company, Chicago, pp. 373–375, 384–386, 387–388. The tables have been renumbered.

[1] All findings on moral development discussed are documented and referenced in Kohlberg, 1969; some are to be found in Kohlberg, 1963a, 1964; so they will not be referenced in this chapter.

moral judgment. In another sense, however, moral judgments change in cognitive form with development. As an example, it is generally recognized that conceptions and sentiments of justice ("giving each his due") are based on conceptions of reciprocity and of equality. Reciprocity and equality are, however, cognitive as well as moral forms. Piaget (1947) has done a number of studies suggesting that the awareness of logical reciprocity (e.g., recognition that I am my brother's brother) develops with the formation of concrete operations at age 6-7. Our studies (Kohlberg, 1969) indicate that use of reciprocity as a moral reason first appears at the same age.

Another example of cognitive form in moral judgment is the consideration of intentions as opposed to physical consequences in judging the badness of action. According to Piaget (1948), the development of moral intentionality corresponds to the more general cognitive differentiation of objective and subjective, physical and mental, discussed in Section I. Accordingly, it is not surprising to find that in every culture, in every social class, in every sex group, and in every subculture studied (Switzerland, United States, Belgium, Chinese, Malaysian-aboriginal, Mexican, Israel, Hopi, Zuni, Sioux, Papago) age trends toward increased intentionality are found. It is also not surprising to find this trend is always correlated with intelligence or mental development in all groups where intelligence measures have been available. Finally, it is not surprising to find that such cultural or subcultural differences as exist are explainable as due to the amount of social and cognitive stimulation provided by the culture in question.

As an example, in all nations studied, there are social-class differences in the direction of earlier intentionality for the middle class. These are not class differences in values, but class differences in the cognitive and social stimulation of development. In each class, the older and more intelligent children are more intentional. If the "retardation" of the lower-class child were to be explained as due to a different adult subcultural value system, the older and brighter lower-class children would have to be more "retarded" than the younger and duller lower-class children, since they should have learned the lower-class value system better. Intentionality, then, is an example of a culturally universal developmental trend, which is universal and regular in its development because it has a "cognitive form" base in the differentiation of the physical and the mental. . . .

In summary, then, universal and regular age trends of development may be found in moral judgment, and these have a formal-cognitive base. Many aspects of moral judgment do not have such a cognitive base, but these aspects do not define universal and regular trends of moral development.

Using the Piaget (1948) material, we have indicated that there are "natural" culturally universal trends of age-development in moral judgment with a cognitive-formal base. Age trends, however, are not in themselves sufficient to define stages with the properties discussed in our first section. While Piaget attempted to define two stages of moral judgment (the heteronomous and the autonomous), extensive empirical study and logical analysis indicate that his moral stages have not met the criteria of stage he proposes (summarized in our first section), as his cognitive stages do.

Taking cognizance of Piaget's notions as well as those of others such as Hobhouse (1906), J. M. Baldwin (1906), Peck and Havighurst (1960), and McDougall (1908), I have attempted to define stages of moral judgment which would meet these criteria. A summary characterization of the stages is presented in Table II. 1. . . .

. . . Table II.2 presents the definition of moral motives characteristic of each stage. . . . As Table II.2 indicates, each stage involves a differentiation not present at the preceding stage.

The importance of the sequentiality issue may be brought out from two points of view. With regard to the definition of moral development, it is not at all clear that Stages 5 and 6 should be used to define developmental end points in morality. . . . It is possible to view Stages 4, 5, and 6 as alternative types of mature response rather than as a sequence. Indeed, this is the view of some writers who view conventional-authoritarian (Stage 4) adult character types as opposed to humanistic (Stages 5 and 6) character types as representing alternative channels of personality crystallization. If Stages 5 and 6 persons can be shown to have gone through Stage 4 while Stage 4 persons have gone through Stages 5 and 6, it can be argued that the stage hierarchy constitutes more than a value judgment by the investigator.

Our age trends indicate that large groups of moral concepts and ways of thought only attain meaning at successively advanced ages and require the extensive background of social experience and cognitive growth represented by the age factor. From usual views of the moralization process, these age changes in modes of moral thought would simply be interpreted as successive acquisitions or internalizations of cultural moral concepts. Our six types of thought would represent six patterns of verbal morality in the adult culture which are successively absorbed as the child grows more verbally sophisticated. The age order involved might simply represent the order in which the culture presented the various concepts involved, or might simply reflect that greater mental age is required to learn the higher type of concept.

In contrast, we have advocated the developmental interpretation that these types of thought represent structures emerging from the interaction of the child with his social environment, rather than directly reflecting external structures given by the child's culture. Awareness of the basic prohibitions and commands of the culture, as well as some behavioral "internalization" of them, exists from the first of our stages and does not define their succession. Movement from stage to stage represents rather the way in which these prohibitions, as well as much

Table II.1 Classification of Moral Judgment into Levels and Stages of Development

Levels	Basis of Moral Judgment	Stages of Development
I [*The Preconventional*]	Moral value resides in external, quasi-physical happenings, in bad acts, or in quasi-physical needs rather than in persons and standards.	Stage 1: Obedience and punishment orientation. Egocentric deference to superior power or prestige, or a trouble-avoiding set. Objective responsibility. Stage 2: Naively egoistic orientation. Right action is that instrumentally satisfying the self's needs and occasionally others'. Awareness of relativism of value to each actor's needs and perspective. Naive egalitarianism and orientation to exchange and reciprocity.
II [*The Conventional*]	Moral value resides in performing good or right roles, in maintaining the conventional order and the expectancies of others.	Stage 3: Good-boy orientation. Orientation to approval and to pleasing and helping others. Conformity to stereotypical images of majority or natural role behavior, and judgment by intentions. Stage 4: Authority and social-order maintaining orientation. Orientation to "doing duty" and to showing respect for authority and maintaining the given social order for its own sake. Regard for earned expectations of others.
III [*The Postconventional*]	Moral value resides in conformity by the self to shared or shareable standards, rights, or duties.	Stage 5: Contractual legalistic orientation. Recognition of an arbitrary element or starting point in rules or expectations for the sake of agreement. Duty defined in terms of contract, general avoidance of violation of the will or rights of others, and majority will and welfare. Stage 6: Conscience or principle orientation. Orientation not only to actually ordained social rules but to principles of choice involving appeal to logical universality and consistency. Orientation to conscience as a directing agent and to mutual respect and trust.

Source: From "Moral and Religious Education and the Public Schools" by Lawrence Kohlberg, in *Religion and Public Education* by T. Sizer. Copyright © 1967 by Houghton Mifflin Company.

Table II.2 Motives for Engaging in Moral Action in Response to a Moral Dilemma

---

In Europe, a woman was near death from cancer. One drug might save her, a form of radium that a druggist in the same town had recently discovered. The druggist was charging $2,000, ten times what the drug cost him to make. The sick woman's husband, Heinz, went to everyone he knew to borrow the money, but he could only get together about half of what it cost. He told the druggist that his wife was dying and asked him to sell it cheaper or let him pay later. But the druggist said, "No." The husband got desperate and broke into the man's store to steal the drug for his wife. Should the husband have done that? Why?

Stage 1. Action is motivated by avoidance and punishment and "conscience" is irrational fear of punishment.

> Pro—If you let your wife die, you will get in trouble. You'll be blamed for not spending the money to save her and there'll be an investigation of you and the druggist for your wife's death.

> Con—You shouldn't steal the drug because you'll be caught and sent to jail if you do. If you do get away, your conscience would bother you thinking how the police would catch up with you at any minute.

Stage 2. Action motivated by desire for reward or benefit. Possible guilt reactions are ignored and punishment viewed in a pragmatic manner. (Differentiates own fear, pleasure, or pain from punishment-consequences.)

> Pro—If you do happen to get caught you could give the drug back and you wouldn't get much of a sentence. It wouldn't bother you much to serve a little jail term, if you have your wife when you get out.

> Con—He may not get much of a jail term if he steals the drug, but his wife will probably die before he gets out so it won't do him much good. If his wife dies, he shouldn't blame himself, it wasn't his fault she has cancer.

Stage 3. Action motivated by anticipation of disapproval of others, actual or imagined-hypothetical (e.g., guilt). (Differentiation of disapproval from punishment, fear, and pain.)

> Pro—No one will think you're bad if you steal the drug but your family will think you're an inhuman husband if you don't. If you let your wife die, you'll never be able to look anybody in the face again.

> Con—It isn't just the druggist who will think you're a criminal, everyone else will too. After you steal it, you'll feel bad thinking how you've brought dishonor on your family and yourself; you won't be able to face anyone again.

Stage 4. Action motivated by anticipation of dishonor, i.e., institutionalized blame for failure of duty, and by guilt over concrete harm done to others. (Differentiates formal dishonor from informal disapproval. Differentiates guilt for bad consequences from disapproval.)

> Pro—If you have any sense of honor, you won't let your wife die because you're afraid to do the only thing that will save her. You'll always feel guilty that you caused her death if you don't do your duty to her.

> Con—You're desperate and you may not know you're doing wrong when you steal the drug. But you'll know you did wrong after you're punished and sent to jail. You'll always feel guilty for your dishonesty and lawbreaking.

Table II.2   (continued)

Stage 5. Concern about maintaining respect of equals and of the community (assuming their respect is based on reason rather than emotions). Concern about own self-respect, i.e., to avoid judging self as irrational, inconsistent, non-purposive. (Discriminates between institutionalized blame and community disrespect or self-disrespect.)

> Pro—You'd lose other people's respect, not gain it, if you don't steal. If you let your wife die, it would be out of fear, not out of reasoning it out. So you'd just lose self-respect and probably the respect of others too.

> Con—You would lose your standing and respect in the community and violate the law. You'd lose respect for yourself if you're carried away by emotion and forget the long-range point of view.

Stage 6. Concern about self-condemnation for violating one's own principles. (Differentiates between community respect and self-respect. Differentiates between self-respect for achieving rationality and self-respect for maintaining moral principles.)

> Pro—If you don't steal the drug and let your wife die, you'd always condemn yourself for it afterward. You wouldn't be blamed and you would have lived up to the outside rule of the law but you wouldn't have lived up to your own standards of conscience.

> Con—If you stole the drug, you wouldn't be blamed by other people but you'd condemn yourself because you wouldn't have lived up to your own conscience and standards of honesty.

Source: Rest, 1968.

wider aspects of the social structure, are taken up into the child's organization of a moral order. This order may be based upon power and external compulsion (Stage 1), upon a system of exchanges and need satisfactions (Stage 2), upon the maintenance of legitimate expectations (Stages 3 and 4), or upon ideals or general logical principles of social organization (Stages 5 and 6). While these successive bases of a moral order do spring from the child's awareness of the external social world, they also represent active processes of organizing or ordering this world. . . .

The pattern of usage of different stages becomes intelligible when it is recalled that, in a certain sense, all the lower stages are available or at least comprehensible to the S. The pattern of usage, then, is dictated by a hierarchical preference for the highest stage a subject can produce. While S's have difficulty comprehending stages above their own, and do not have difficulty with stages below their own, they prefer higher stages to the lower stages. If they can comprehend a statement two stages above their own, they prefer it to a statement one above. If they comprehend statements one stage but not two above their own, they prefer them to statements either two above or one below their own. If hypothetical statements at their own stage are presented to S's, and

Table II.3   Scoring of Moral Judgments of Eichmann for Developmental Stage

Moral Judgments	Score (Stage)
In actual fact, I was merely a little cog in the machinery that carried out the directives of the German Reich.	1
I am neither a murderer nor a mass-murderer. I am a man of average character, with good qualities and many faults.	3
Yet what is there to "admit"? I carried out my orders. It would be as pointless to blame me for the whole final solution of the Jewish problem as to blame the official in charge of the railroads over which the Jewish transports traveled.	1
Where would we have been if everyone had thought things out in those days? You can do that today in the "new" German army. But with us an order was an order.	1
If I had sabotaged the order of the one-time Fuhrer of the German Reich, Adolf Hitler, I would have been not only a scoundrel but a despicable pig like those who broke their military oath to join the ranks of the anti-Hitler criminals in the conspiracy of July 20, 1944.	1
I would like to stress again, however, that my department never gave a single annihilation order. We were responsible only for deportation.	2
My interest was only in the number of transport trains I had to provide. Whether they were bank directors or mental cases, the people who were loaded on these trains meant nothing to me. It was really none of my business.	2 2
But to sum it all up, I must say that I regret nothing. Adolf Hitler may have been wrong all down the line, but one thing is beyond dispute: the man was able to work his way up from lance corporal in the German army to Fuhrer of a people of almost eighty million.	1
I never met him personally, but his success alone proves to me that I should subordinate myself to this man. He was somehow so supremely capable that the people recognized him. And so with that justification I recognized him joyfully, and I still defend him.	1
I must say truthfully, that if we had killed all the ten million Jews that Himmler's statisticians originally listed in 1933, I would say, "Good, we have destroyed an enemy."	2
But here I do not mean wiping them out entirely. That would not be proper—and we carried on a proper war.	1

Source: From "Moral and Religious Education and the Public Schools" by Lawrence Kohlberg, in *Religion and Public Education* by T. Sizer. Copyright © 1967 by Houghton Mifflin Company.

they have not yet produced statements of their own, the S's tend to prefer the one above to their own level statement.

It appears, then, that patterns of actual usage of stages are dictated by two opposed sequential orders, one of preference and one of ease, with an individual modal stage representing the most preferred stage which he can readily use. It is apparent, then, that the moral stages empirically meet the criterion of sequence and of hierarchical integration discussed in our first section, and that they logically meet it in the sense that each stage represents a logical differentiation and integration of prior concepts as indicated in Table II.2. In some sense, then, one can discuss the stages as representing a hierarchical sequence quite independent of the fact that they correspond to trends of age-development. Table II.3 present[s] statements by Adolf Eichmann, a Nazi leader, which are largely Stage 1 and Stage 2. It can be argued that German adolescents grew up into a Stage 1 and 2 Nazi adult moral ideology in the same sense that it can be argued that Atayal children grow up into a Stage 1 or 2 conception of the dream. In such a case, we would hardly argue that the actual sequence of age-development would fully correspond to the sequence just described.

Preliminary findings from a longitudinal study of American boys speak directly to the issue of the extent to which ontogeny actually follows the logical sequence. These findings are based on 50 boys, half middle class, half working class, studied every three years over a 12-year period. Originally ranging in age from 10 to 16, on terminal study they were 22 to 28. While only the data on development after age 16 has been fully analyzed (Kramer, 1968), the findings fit a picture of ontogenetic change as directed and sequential, or stepwise. The one exception is that at one age period (end of high school to mid-college) 20 per cent of the middle-class boys "regress," or drop in total score. They come up again after college so that none of them are below their high-school level in the late twenties and almost all are above that level. No such temporary "regression" occurs in the non-college or lower-class population. The only cases of "regression" found in the lower-class sample were among six delinquents followed longitudinally. For three of these, reform school and jail had an actual "regressive" effect on morality.

Edward Osborne Wilson (b. 1929)

Edward O. Wilson attended the University of Alabama and Harvard University. He has been a member of the Harvard faculty since 1956 and is presently Professor of Zoology and Director of the Museum of Comparative Zoology at Harvard University. Wilson, a well-known entomologist, has written numerous articles about ants. He is the author of *The Insect Societies* (1971), a work of major importance for the development of environmental and behavioral biology. His *Sociobiology* (1975) immediately became famous and provoked controversy. This massive and scholarly volume extends to the whole animal kingdom, including man, the program begun in *The Social Insects* of organizing the science that aims at discovering and understanding the biological and evolutionary origins of social behavior.

The main views Wilson discusses in our selection come from W. D. Hamilton's "The Genetical Evolution of Social Behavior" I and II (*Journal of Theoretical Biology*, 1964), and Robert Trivers' "The Evolution of Reciprocal Altruism" (*Quarterly Review of Biology*, 1971). Reviews of this book appeared during 1975 in *The New York Review of Books* as well as in most magazines concerned with nature and the biological sciences.

Sociobiology: The New Synthesis

CHAPTER 1 **The Morality of the Gene**

Camus said that the only serious philosophical question is suicide. That is wrong even in the strict sense intended. The biologist, who is concerned with questions of physiology and evolutionary history, realizes that self-knowledge is constrained and shaped by the emotional control centers in the hypothalamus and limbic system of the brain. These centers flood our consciousness with all the emotions—hate, love, guilt, fear, and others—that are consulted by ethical philosophers who wish to intuit the standards of good and evil. What, we are then compelled to ask, made the hypothalamus and limbic system? They evolved by natural selection. That simple biological statement must be pursued to explain ethics and ethical philosophers, if not epistemology and epistemologists, at all depths. Self-existence, or the suicide that terminates it, is not the central question of philosophy. The hypothalamic-limbic complex automatically denies such logical reduction by countering it with feelings of guilt and altruism. In this one way the philosopher's own emotional control centers are wiser than his solipsist consciousness, "knowing" that in evolutionary time the individual organism counts for almost nothing. In a Darwinist sense the organism does not live for itself. Its primary function is not even to reproduce other organisms; it reproduces genes, and it serves as their temporary carrier. Each organism generated by sexual reproduction is a unique, accidental subset of all the genes constituting the species. Natural selection is the process whereby certain genes gain representation in the following generations superior to that of other genes located at the same chromosome positions. When new sex cells are manufactured in each generation, the winning genes are pulled apart and reassembled to manufacture new organisms that, on the average, contain a higher proportion of the same genes. But the individual organism is only their vehicle,

---

part of an elaborate device to preserve and spread them with the least possible biochemical perturbation. Samuel Butler's famous aphorism, that the chicken is only an egg's way of making another egg, has been modernized: the organism is only DNA's way of making more DNA. More to the point, the hypothalamus and limbic system are engineered to perpetuate DNA.

In the process of natural selection, then, any device that can insert a higher proportion of certain genes into subsequent generations will come to characterize the species. One class of such devices promotes prolonged individual survival. Another promotes superior mating performance and care of the resulting offspring. As more complex social behavior by the organism is added to the genes' techniques for replicating themselves, altruism becomes increasingly prevalent and eventually appears in exaggerated forms. This brings us to the central theoretical problem of sociobiology: how can altruism, which by definition reduces personal fitness, possibly evolve by natural selection? The answer is kinship: if the genes causing the altruism are shared by two organisms because of common descent, and if the altruistic act by one organism increases the joint contribution of these genes to the next generation, the propensity to altruism will spread through the gene pool. This occurs even though the altruist makes less of a solitary contribution to the gene pool as the price of its altruistic act.

To his own question, "Does the Absurd dictate death?" Camus replied that the struggle toward the heights is itself enough to fill a man's heart. This arid judgment is probably correct, but it makes little sense except when closely examined in the light of evolutionary theory. The hypothalamic-limbic complex of a highly social species, such as man, "knows," or more precisely it has been programmed to perform as if it knows, that its underlying genes will be proliferated maximally only if it orchestrates behavioral responses that bring into play an efficient mixture of personal survival, reproduction, and altruism. Consequently, the centers of the complex tax the conscious mind with ambivalences whenever the organisms encounter stressful situations. Love joins hate; aggression, fear; expansiveness, withdrawal; and so on; in blends designed not to promote the happiness and survival of the individual, but to favor the maximum transmission of the controlling genes.

The ambivalences stem from counteracting pressures on the units of natural selection. Their genetic consequences will be explored formally later in this book. For the moment suffice it to note that what is good for the individual can be destructive to the family; what preserves the family can be harsh on both the individual and the tribe to which its family belongs; what promotes the tribe can weaken the family and destroy the individual; and so on upward through the permutations of levels of organization. Counteracting selection on these different units will result in certain genes being multiplied and fixed, others lost, and combinations of still others held in static proportions. According to the present theory, some of the genes will produce emotional states that reflect the balance of counteracting selection forces at the different levels.

I have raised a problem in ethical philosophy in order to characterize the essence of sociobiology. Sociobiology is defined as the systematic study of the biological basis of all social behavior. For the present it focuses on animal societies, their population structure, castes, and communication, together with all of the physiology underlying the social adaptations. But the discipline is also concerned with the social behavior of early man and the adaptive features of organization in the more primitive contemporary human societies. Sociology *sensu stricto,* the study of human societies at all levels of complexity, still stands apart from sociobiology because of its largely structuralist and nongenetic approach. It attempts to explain human behavior primarily by empirical description of the outermost phenotypes and by unaided intuition, without reference to evolutionary explanations in the true genetic sense. It is most successful, in the way descriptive taxonomy and ecology have been most successful, when it provides a detailed description of particular phenomena and demonstrates first-order correlations with features of the environment. Taxonomy and ecology, however, have been reshaped entirely during the past forty years by integration into neo-Darwinist evolutionary theory—the "Modern Synthesis," as it is often called—in which each phenomenon is weighted for its adaptive significance and then related to the basic principles of population genetics. It may not be too much to say that sociology and the other social sciences, as well as the humanities, are the last branches of biology waiting to be included in the Modern Synthesis. One of the functions of sociobiology, then, is to reformulate the foundations of the social sciences in a way that draws these subjects into the Modern Synthesis. Whether the social sciences can be truly biologicized in this fashion remains to be seen. . . .

CHAPTER 5   **Group Selection and Altruism**

Reporter: *When you ran Finland onto the map of the world,*
did you feel you were doing it to bring fame to a
nation unknown by others?

Nurmi: *No. I ran for myself, not for Finland.*

Reporter: *Not even in the Olympics?*

Nurmi: *Not even then. Above all, not then. At the Olympics,*
Paavo Nurmi mattered more than ever.

Who does not feel at least a tinge of admiration for Paavo Nurmi, the ultimate individual selectionist? At the opposite extreme, we shared a different form of approval, warmer in tone but uneasily loose in texture, for the Apollo 11 astronauts who left their message on the moon, "We came in peace for all mankind." This chapter is about natural selection at the levels of selection in between the individual and the species. Its pivot will be the question of altruism, the surrender of personal genetic fitness for the enhancement of personal genetic fitness in others.

Group Selection

Selection can be said to operate at the group level, and deserves to be called group selection, when it affects two or more members of a lineage group as a unit. Just above the level of the individual we can delimit various of these lineage groups: a set of sibs, parents, and their offspring; a close-knit tribe of families related by at least the degree of third cousin; and so on. If selection operates on any of the groups as a unit, or operates on an individual in any way that affects the frequency of genes shared by common descent in relatives, the process is referred to as kin selection. At a higher level, an entire breeding population may be the unit, so that populations (that is, demes) possessing different genotypes are extinguished differentially, or disseminate different numbers of colonists, in which case we speak of interdemic (or interpopulation) selection.... The concept of group selection was introduced by Darwin in *The Origin of Species* to account for the evolution of sterile castes in social insects....

Kin Selection

Imagine a network of individuals linked by kinship within a population. These blood relatives cooperate or bestow altruistic favors on one another in a way that increases the average genetic fitness of the members of the network as a whole, even when this behavior reduces the individual fitnesses of certain members of the group. The members may live together or be scattered throughout the population. The essential condition is that they jointly behave in a way that benefits the group as a whole, while remaining in relatively close contact with the remainder of the population. This enhancement of kin-network welfare in the midst of a population is called *kin selection*.

Kin selection can merge into interdemic selection by an appropriate spatial rearrangement. As the kin network settles into one physical location and becomes physically more isolated from the rest of the species, it approaches the status of a true population. A closed society, or one so nearly closed that it exchanges only a small fraction of its members with other societies each generation, is a true Mendelian population. If in addition the members all treat one another without reference to genetic relationship, kin selection and interdemic selection are the same process. If the closed society is small, say with 10 members or less, we can analyze group selection by the theory of kin selection. If it is large, containing an effective breeding size of 100 or more, or if the selection proceeds by the extinction of entire demes of any size, the theory of interdemic selection is probably more appropriate.

The personal actions of one member toward another can be conveniently classified into three categories in a way that makes the analysis of kin selection more feasible. When a person (or animal) increases the fitness of another at the expense of his own fitness, he can be said to have performed an act of *altruism*. Self-sacrifice for the benefit of offspring is altruism in the conventional but not in the strict genetic sense, because individual fitness is measured by the number of surviving offspring. But self-sacrifice on behalf of second cousins is true altruism at both levels; and when directed at total strangers such abnegating behavior is so surprising (that is, "noble") as to demand some kind of theoretical explanation. In contrast, a person who raises his own fitness by lowering that of others is engaged in *selfishness*. While we cannot publicly approve the selfish act we do understand it thoroughly and may even sympathize. Finally, a person who gains nothing or even reduces his own fitness in order to diminish that of another has committed an act of *spite*. The action may be sane, and the perpetrator may seem gratified, but we find it difficult to imagine his rational motivation. We refer to the commitment of a spiteful act as "all too human"—and then wonder what we meant.

The concept of kin selection to explain such behavior was originated by Charles Darwin in *The Origin of Species*. Darwin had encountered in the social insects the "one special difficulty, which at first appeared to me insuperable, and actually fatal to my whole theory." How, he asked, could the worker castes of insect societies have evolved if they are sterile and leave no offspring? This paradox proved truly fatal to Lamarck's theory of evolution by the inheritance of acquired characters, for Darwin was quick to point out that the Lamarckian hypothesis requires characters to be developed by use or disuse of the organs of individual organisms and then to be passed directly to the next generation, an impossibility when the organisms are sterile. To save his own theory, Darwin introduced the idea of natural selection operating at the level of the family rather than of the single organism. In retrospect, his logic seems impeccable. If some of the individuals of the family are sterile and yet important to the welfare of fertile relatives, as in the case of insect colonies, selection at the family level is inevitable. With the entire family serving as the unit of selection, it is the capacity to generate sterile but altruistic relatives that becomes subject to genetic evolution. To quote Darwin, "Thus, a well-flavoured vegetable is cooked, and the individual is destroyed; but the horticulturist sows seeds of the same stock, and confidently expects to get nearly the same variety; breeders of cattle wish the flesh and fat to be well marbled together; the animal has been slaughtered, but the breeder goes with confidence to the same family" (*The Origin of Species*, 1859: 237). Employing his familiar style of argumentation, Darwin noted that intermediate stages found in some living species of social insects connect at least some of the extreme sterile castes, making it possible to trace the route along which they evolved. As he wrote, "With these facts before me, I believe that natural selection, by acting on the fertile parents, could form a species which regularly produce neuters, either all of a large size with one form of jaw, or all of small size with jaws having a widely different structure; or lastly, and this is the climax of our difficulty, one set of workers of one size and structure, and simultaneously another set of workers of a different size and structure" (*The Origin of Species*, 1859: 24). Darwin was speaking here about the soldiers and minor workers of ants.

Family-level selection is of practical concern to plant and animal breeders, and the subject of kin selection was at first pursued from this narrow point of view. One of the principal contributions to theory was provided by Jay L. Lush (1947), a geneticist who wished to devise a prescription for the choice of boars and gilts for use in breeding. It was necessary to give each pig "sib credits" determined by the average merit of its littermates. A quite reliable set of formulas was developed which incorporated the size of the family and the phenotypic correlations between and within families. This research provided a useful background but was not addressed directly to the evolution of social behavior in the manner envisaged by Darwin.

The modern genetic theory of altruism, selfishness, and spite was launched instead by William D. Hamilton in a series of important articles (1964, 1970, 1971a,b, 1972). Hamilton's pivotal concept is *inclusive fitness*: the sum of an individual's own fitness plus the sum of all the effects it causes to the related parts of the fitnesses of all its relatives. When an animal performs an altruistic act toward a brother, for example, the inclusive fitness is the animal's fitness (which has been lowered by performance of the act) plus the increment in fitness enjoyed by that portion of the brother's hereditary constitution that is shared with the altruistic animal. The portion of shared heredity is the fraction of genes held by common descent by the two animals and is measured by the coefficient of relationship, r (see Chapter 4). Thus, in the absence of inbreeding, the animal and its brother have $r = \frac{1}{2}$ of their genes identical by common descent. Hamilton's key result can be stated very simply as follows. A genetically based act of altruism, selfishness, or spite will evolve if the average inclusive fitness of individuals within networks displaying it is greater than the inclusive fitness of individuals in otherwise comparable networks that do not display it.

Consider, for example, a simplified network consisting solely of an individual and his brother (Figure II.1). If the individual is altruistic he will perform some sacrifice for the benefit of the brother. He may surrender needed food or shelter, or defer in the choice of a mate, or place himself between his brother and danger. The important result from a purely evolutionary point of view, is loss of genetic fitness—a reduced mean life span, or fewer offspring, or both—which leads to less representation of the altruist's personal genes in the next generation. But at least half of the brother's genes are identical to those of the altruist by virtue of common descent. Suppose, in the extreme case, that the altruist leaves no offspring. If his altruistic act more than doubles the brother's personal representation in the next generation, it will ipso facto increase the one-half of the genes identical to those in the altruist, and the altruist will actually have gained representation in the next generation. Many of the genes shared by such brothers will be the ones that encode the tendency toward altruistic behavior. The inclusive fitness, in this case determined solely by the brother's contribution, will be great enough to cause the spread of the altruistic genes through the population, and hence the evolution of altruistic behavior.

The model can now be extended to include all relatives affected by the altruism. If only first cousins were benefited ($r = 1/8$), the altruist who leaves no offspring would have to multiply a cousin's fitness eightfold; an uncle ($r = 1/4$) would have to be advanced fourfold; and so on. If combinations of relatives are benefited, the genetic effect of the altruism is simply weighted by the number of relatives of each kind who are affected and their coefficients of relationship. In general, k, the ratio of gain in fitness to loss in fitness, must exceed the reciprocal of the average coefficient of relationship ($\bar{r}$) to the ensemble of relatives:

$$k > \frac{1}{\bar{r}}$$

Thus in the extreme brother-to-brother case, $1/\bar{r} = 2$; and the loss in fitness for the altruist who leaves no offspring was said to be total (that is $= 1.0$). Therefore in order for the shared altruistic genes to increase, k, the gain-to-loss ratio, must exceed 2. In other words, the brother's fitness must be more than doubled.

The evolution of selfishness can be treated by the same model. Intuitively it might seem that selfishness in any degree pays off so long as the result is the increase of one's personal genes in the next gen-

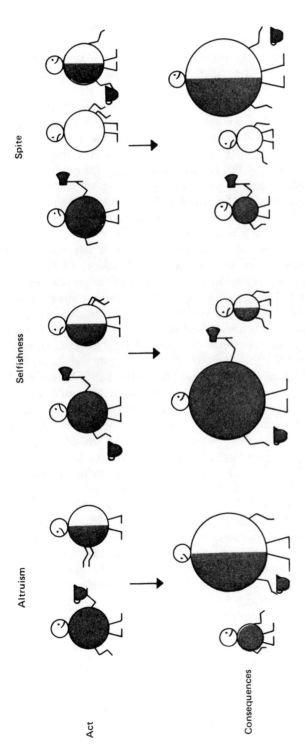

Figure II.1 The Basic Conditions Required for the Evolution of Altruism, Selfishness, and Spite by Means of Kin Selection

The family has been reduced to an individual and his brother, the fraction of genes in the brother shared by common descent ($r = \frac{1}{2}$) is indicated by the shaded half of the body. A requisite of the environment (food, shelter, access to mate, and so on) is indicated by a vessel, and harmful behavior to another by an axe. *Altruism*: the altruist diminishes his own genetic fitness but raises his brother's fitness to the extent that the shared genes are actually increased in the next generation. *Selfishness*: the selfish individual reduces his brother's fitness but enlarges his own to an extent that more than compensates. *Spite*: the spiteful individual lowers the fitness of an unrelated competitor (the unshaded figure) while reducing that of his own or at least not improving it; however, the act increases the fitness of the brother to a degree that more than compensates.

eration. But this is not the case if relatives are being harmed to the extent of losing too many of their genes shared with the selfish individual by common descent. Again, the inclusive fitness must exceed 1, but this time the result of exceeding that threshold is the spread of the selfish genes.

Finally, the evolution of spite is possible if it, too, raises inclusive fitness. The perpetrator must be able to discriminate relatives from nonrelatives, or close relatives from distant ones. If the spiteful behavior causes a relative to prosper to a compensatory degree, the genes favoring spite will increase in the population at large. True spite is a commonplace in human societies, undoubtedly because human beings are keenly aware of their own blood lines and have the intelligence to plot intrigue. Human beings are unique in the degree of their capacity to lie to other members of their own species. They typically do so in a way that deliberately diminishes outsiders while promoting relatives, even at the risk of their own personal welfare (Wallace, 1973). Examples of spite in animals may be rare and difficult to distinguish from purely selfish behavior. This is particularly true in the realm of false communication. As Hamilton drily put it, "By our lofty standards, animals are poor liars." Chimpanzees and gorillas, the brightest of the nonhuman primates, sometimes lie to one another (and to zookeepers) to obtain food or to attract company (Hediger, 1955: 150; van Lawick-Goodall, 1971). The mental capacity exists for spite, but if these animals lie for spiteful reasons this fact has not yet been established. Even the simplest physical techniques of spite are ambiguous in animals. Male bowerbirds sometimes wreck the bowers of the neighbors, an act that appears spiteful at first (Marshall, 1954). But bowerbirds are polygynous, and the probability exists that the destructive bird is able to attract more females to his own bower. Hamilton (1970) has cited cannibalism in the corn ear worm (*Heliothis zea*) as a possible example of spite. The first caterpillar that penetrates an ear of corn eats all subsequent rivals, even though enough food exists to see two or more of the caterpillars through to maturity. Yet even here, as Hamilton concedes, the trait might have evolved as pure selfishness at a time when the *Heliothis* fed on smaller flowerheads or small corn ears of the ancestral type. Many other examples of the killing of conspecifics have been demonstrated in insects, but almost invariably in circumstances where the food supply is limited and the aggressiveness is clearly selfish as opposed to spiteful (Wilson, 1971b).

The Hamilton models are beguiling in part because of their transparency and heuristic value. The coefficient of relationship, r, translates easily into "blood," and the human mind, already sophisticated in the intuitive calculus of blood ties and proportionate altruism, races to apply the concept of inclusive fitness to a reevaluation of its own social impulses. But the Hamilton viewpoint is also unstructured. The conventional parameters of population genetics, allele frequencies, mutation rates, epistasis, migration, group size, and so forth, are mostly omitted from the equations. As a result, Hamilton's mode of reasoning can be only loosely coupled with the remainder of genetic theory, and the number of predictions it can make is unnecessarily limited.

Reciprocal Altruism

The theory of group selection has taken most of the good will out of altruism. When altruism is conceived as the mechanism by which DNA multiplies itself through a network of relatives, spirituality becomes just one more Darwinian enabling device. The theory of natural selection can be extended still further into the complex set of relationships that Robert L. Trivers (1971) has called *reciprocal altruism.* The paradigm offered by Trivers is good samaritan behavior in human beings. A man is drowning, let us say, and another man jumps in to save him, even though the two are not related and may not even have met previously. The reaction is typical of what human beings regard as "pure" altruism. However, upon reflection one can see that the good samaritan has much to gain by his act. Suppose that the drowning man has a one-half chance of drowning if he is not assisted, whereas the rescuer has a one-in-twenty chance of dying. Imagine further that when the rescuer drowns the victim also drowns, but when the rescuer lives the victim is always saved. If such episodes were extremely rare, the Darwinist calculus would predict little or no gain to the fitness of the rescuer for his attempt. But if the drowning man reciprocates at a future time, and the risks of drowning stay the same, it will have benefited both individuals to have played the role of rescuer. Each man will have traded a one-half chance of dying for about a one-tenth chance. A population at large that enters into a series of such moral obligations, that is, reciprocally altruistic acts, will be a population of individuals with generally increased genetic fitness. The trade-off actually enhances personal fitness and is less purely altruistic than acts evolving out of interdemic and kin selection.

In its elementary form the good samaritan model still contains an inconsistency. Why should the rescued individual bother to reciprocate? Why not cheat? The answer is that in an advanced, personalized society, where individuals are identified and the record of their acts is weighed by others, it does not pay to cheat even in the purely Darwinist sense. Selection will discriminate against the individual if cheating has later adverse affects on his life and reproduction that outweigh the momentary advantage gained. Iago stated the essence in *Othello:* "Good name in man and woman, dear my lord, is the immediate jewel of their souls."

Trivers has skillfully related his genetic model to a wide range of the most subtle human behaviors. Aggressively moralistic behavior, for example, keeps would-be cheaters in line—no less than hortatory sermons to the believers. Self-righteousness, gratitude, and sympathy enhance the probability of receiving an altruistic act by virtue of implying reciprocation. The all-important quality of sincerity is a meta-communication about the significance of these messages. The emotion of guilt may be favored in natural selection because it motivates the cheater to compensate for his misdeed and to provide convincing evidence that he does not plan to cheat again. So strong is the impulse to behave altruistically that persons in experimental psychological tests will learn an instrumental conditioned response without advance explanation and when the only reward is to see another person relieved of discomfort (Weiss et al., 1971).

Human behavior abounds with reciprocal altruism consistent with genetic theory, but animal behavior seems to be almost devoid of it. Perhaps the reason is that in animals relationships are not sufficiently enduring, or memories of personal behavior reliable enough, to permit the highly personal contracts associated with the more human forms of reciprocal altruism. Almost the only exceptions I know occur just where one would most expect to find them—in the more intelligent monkeys, such as rhesus macaques and baboons, and in the anthropoid apes. Members of troops are known to form coalitions or cliques and to aid one another reciprocally in disputes with other troop members. Chimpanzees, gibbons, African wild dogs, and wolves also beg food from one another in a reciprocal manner.

Granted a mechanism for sustaining reciprocal altruism, we are still left with the theoretical problem of how the evolution of the behavior gets started. Imagine a population in which a Good Samaritan appears for the first time as a rare mutant. He rescues but is not rescued in turn by any of the nonaltruists who surround him. Thus the genotype has low fitness and is maintained at no more than mutational equilibrium. Boorman and Levitt (1973b) have formally investigated the conditions necessary for the emergence of a genetically mediated cooperation network. They found that for each population size, for each component of fitness added by membership in a network as opposed to the reduced fitness of cooperators outside networks, and for each average number of individuals contacted in the network, there exists a critical frequency of the altruist gene above which the gene will spread explosively through the population and below which it will slowly recede to the mutational equilibrium (Figure II.2). How critical frequencies are attained from scratch remains unknown. Cooperative individuals must play a version of the game of Prisoner's Dilemma (Hamilton, 1971b; Trivers, 1971). If they chance cooperation with a nonaltruist, they lose some fitness and the nonaltruist gains. If they are lucky and contact a fellow cooperator, both gain. The critical gene fre-

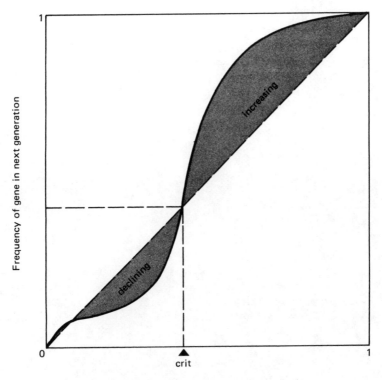

Frequency of gene in next generation

Frequency of gene in generation of selection

Figure II.2 The Condition for the Genetic Fixation of Reciprocal Altruism in a Population

Above a critical frequency defined by the population size and the size and effectiveness of the cooperating network, the altruist gene increases explosively toward fixation. Below the critical frequency the gene recedes slowly toward mutational equilibrium. (Modified from Boorman and Levitt, 1973b.)

quency is simply that in which playing the game pays by virtue of a high enough probability of contacting another cooperator. The machinery for bringing the gene frequency up to the critical value must lie outside the game itself. It could be genetic drift in small populations, which is entirely feasible in semiclosed societies (Chapter 4), or a concomitant of interdemic or kin selection favoring other aspects of altruism displayed by the cooperator genotypes.

Index

Abortion, 51, 73–75
Actions
  basic, 20
  justification of, by rules vs. justi-
    fication of, by consequences,
    14–21
  morality of, relative to circum-
    stances, 48–49
  particular vs. general practice, 23
  relationship to consequences, 18–
    21
Action/consequence components,
  18–19
Action morality and agent morality,
  2
Adeimantus, 33, 40
Agent morality
  and action morality, 2
  and desert, 3–4
  and intention, 3–4
Altruism, 32, 34, 36, 41
  definition of, 36, 39
  genetic basis of, 76–79
  and guilt, 40
  as self-sacrifice, 39
Aristotle, 5–6, 37, 120
  and moral habits, 5
  on the morally good person, 5–6
  The Nicomachean Ethics, 121–166
Atheist and morality, 63–64, 69
Auschwitz, 55
Ayer, Alfred Jules, 10–11, 12, 294
  and emotivism, 10–11
  Language, Truth and Logic, 295–
    305

Benedict, Ruth, 50
Benevolence, 34–35, 36–37
Bible, 66
Book of Mormon, 65
Brainwashing, 75
Buddhism, 66
Butler, Joseph, 33–37, 39–40, 167

on benevolence and self-interest,
  33–35
*Fifteen Sermons Preached at
  Rolls Chapel,* 168–178
and the hedonistic paradox, 36
and Ayn Rand, 34, 39–40
refutation of psychological egoism, 35–36
on self-love vs. particular interests, 35

Capital punishment, 51, 59
Cats, why not obligated to hunt
  mice, 37–38
Christ, 17, 23, 66
Christian ethics, 5, 14, 34, 50
  and altruism, 38–39
Christianity, 66
Confucius, 23
Conscience
  as "internal" sanction, 66–67
  and moral beliefs, 66–67
  as source of moral information,
    64–65
Consequences
  individual vs. collective, 22–23
  short- and long-range, 37
Cultural ethical relativism, 50–51,
  56
Cultural relativism and anthropology, 50–53, 57
Culture
  boundaries of, 52

Definism, 11–12, 25, 63–64, 69, 74
Deontologist, 14–15, 16, 18, 21
  act, 15
  see also Formalism
Descriptive meaning of moral judg-
  ments, 29–30
Divine authority, 68–70
Divine sanctions, 66–67
Dostoevsky, Fyodor Mikhailovich,
  68

411